Anthropology
and the Greeks

International Library of Anthropology

Editor: Adam Kuper, University of Leiden

Arbor Scientiae
Arbor Vitae

A catalogue of other Social Science books published by
Routledge & Kegan Paul will be found at the end of this volume.

Anthropology
and the Greeks

S. C. Humphreys

Departments of Anthropology and History
University College London

Routledge & Kegan Paul

London, Henley and Boston

First published in 1978
by Routledge & Kegan Paul Ltd
39 Store Street,
London WC1E 7DD,
Broadway House,
Newtown Road,
Henley-on-Thames,
Oxon RG9 1EN and
9 Park Street,
Boston, Mass. 02108, USA
Set in 10 on 12 pt Monotype Times by
Kelly & Wright, Bradford-on-Avon, Wiltshire
and printed in Great Britain by
Redwood Burn Ltd,
Trowbridge and Esher

ISBN 0 7100 8785 3

To my parents

Contents

Contents   ix

Acknowledgments

Grateful acknowledgment is made to the following for permission to reprint the articles included in this collection:

The Joint Association of Classical Teachers: 'Classics and anthropology', from *Didaskalos*, 4, 1974, pp. 425–41.

Wesleyan University: 'History, economics, and anthropology: the work of Karl Polanyi' from *History and Theory*, 8, 1969, pp. 165–212; and, 'The work of Louis Gernet', *ibid.*, 10, 1971, pp. 172–96; 'Durkheim in 1972', *ibid.*, 14, 1975, pp. 233–42.

The editors of *La Parola del Passato:* 'Archaeology and the social and economic history of classical Greece', from fasc. CXVI, 1967, pp. 374–400.

Messrs Duckworth & Co.: 'Town and country in ancient Greece', from *Man, Settlement and Urbanism*, ed. P. J. Ucko, R. Tringham, and G. W. Dimbleby, 1972, pp. 763–8; and 'Evolution and history: approaches to the study of structural differentiation', from *The Evolution of Social Systems*, ed. J. Friedman and M. J. Rowlands, 1977.

The Scuola Normale Superiore di Pisa: 'Economy and society in classical Athens', from *Annali*, series II, 39, 1970, pp. 1–26; and 'The social structure of the ancient city', from *Annali*, series III, 4, 1974, pp. 329–67.

The American Academy of Arts and Sciences: ' "Transcendence" and intellectual roles: the ancient Greek case', from *Daedalus*, 104, 2, 1975, pp. 91–118.

Apart from a few small changes made in the interests of clarity, I have not altered any of these articles. A minimum of additional bibliography has been appended in brackets and separate notes.

I am most grateful to Mrs P. Minney for help with the bibliography.

Introduction

Down to the decline of Rome a custom was observed there [at Lake Nemi] which seems to transport us at once from civilisation to savagery. In the sacred grove there grew a certain tree round which at any time of the day, and probably far into the night, a grim figure might be seen to prowl. In his hand he carried a drawn sword, and he kept peering warily about him as if at any instant he expected to be set upon by an enemy. He was a priest and a murderer; and the man for whom he looked was sooner or later to murder him and hold the priesthood in his stead. Such was the rule of the sanctuary. . . . Year in year out, in summer and winter, in fair weather and in foul, he had to keep his lonely watch. . . . His eyes probably acquired that restless watchful look which, among the Esquimaux of Bering Strait, is said to betray infallibly the shedder of blood; for with that people revenge is a sacred duty, and the manslayer carries his life in his hand.

Frazer's *Golden Bough* (1911, pp. 8–9) illustrates admirably the dual attraction which anthropology holds out to the classical scholar, both as a stimulus to the historical imagination and as a theoretical framework for the interpretation of fragmentary data. Frazer fed his imagination eagerly both with the sight of ancient landscapes – his description of Lake Nemi is that of an eye-witness – and with the work of folklorists and ethnographers. But his interpretation of the rules of the priesthood at Lake Nemi was for him the key to a general theory of the evolution of human thought, not merely a footnote to the history of Roman religion; and his whole theory and mode of argument depended on the evolutionist assumptions commonly held by the anthropologists of his day.

I have arranged the essays reprinted in this book to reflect this dual function which I feel anthropology still has for me. The introductory

1

section contains papers on the history of the relation between classics and anthropology, and in particular on the work of Karl Polanyi and Louis Gernet which spans the period between the evolutionist school of the nineteenth and early twentieth centuries and the revived interest in anthropological studies of antiquity after the Second World War. The second section contains some of my earlier attempts to use travel, archaeological data, and ethnographic comparative material as aids in building up a picture of the practical details of economic life in ancient Greece, plus a more recent article on the same theme; while the papers in the final section are more overtly concerned with the problem of relating the surface reality of ancient Greek society as it might have been seen by a contemporary observer to a formal theoretical analysis.

The most important change which has taken place since Frazer's day in the relation between anthropology and classical studies is the change in anthropological theory from evolutionism to comparative functionalism. For L. H. Morgan, Frazer, Jane Harrison, Gilbert Murray, and their contemporaries, evolutionist theory provided a hierarchical scale of civilization on which classical Greece and Rome were clearly ranked as superior to primitive societies even by those who most emphasized the value of comparative data from the life of 'savages' for understanding the earlier history of the ancient world. The classicizing reaction against anthropology which set in after the First World War did not involve a total rejection of evolutionism. It merely shifted the boundary between the unique classical civilizations and the common ground of primitive society further back into prehistory.

Even the anthropologists, in Britain, were slow to realize the full implications of functionalism. While Weber, Durkheim, and their students were developing a comprehensive comparative sociology which included modern industrial societies, historical states and empires, and primitive tribes in a single discipline, in Britain Hobhouse's attempt to develop a general sociology of this kind failed and sociologists continued to concentrate on modern Britain, while Malinowski and Radcliffe-Brown concentrated on the analysis of small-scale primitive societies. It was not until the 1930s that anthropologists trained in the British tradition began to turn their attention to complex modern societies, both African and European. Max Weber's work was scarcely studied until the 1950s. Even today it is often assumed that anthropological work on historical material or industrial societies is best restrcited to the study of small-scale communities.

Nevertheless the argument of the early functionalists that they studied simple societies as simplified models of the functioning of *all* societies implied the abolition of the division of subject-matter between anthropology and sociology. Radcliffe-Brown emphasized that his subject was not anthropology but 'comparative sociology'. From this point of view no society or culture could be privileged as unique, as standing on a plane above the level of anthropological theory or ethnographic comparisons. Radcliffe-Brown had plans to apply his anthropological technique to data from China, in continuation of the work of the Durkheimian Marcel Granet (these plans were to be realized in the work of Maurice Freedman).

The replacement of the evolutionist classification of societies by a general comparative typology implied, as was evident from the work of Durkheim and Simmel onwards, a much more abstract concept of social structure. Durkheim's contrast in *De la division du travail social* (1893) between simple societies composed of segments identical in structure and functions and complex societies made up of interdependent, functionally specialized and structurally differentiated organs – which of course owed much to Spencer and other nineteenth-century organicists – was explicitly designed to span the whole range of social forms. It also stressed the nature of the integration of different groups and institutions within society as the sociologist's major problem. Malinowski and his students found that they needed abstract models to deal with the varied data on the integration and interrelation of different institutions which they brought back from fieldwork even when they were concerned only with simple, small-scale societies.

Consequently the framework within which the ancient historian draws on comparative data from anthropology is now very different from that of evolutionist theory. It is not enough to look for ethnographic analyses of institutions which superficially appear similar to some of those found in the ancient world. Formal similarities of structure can be found between simple and complex societies (Smith, 1956; Douglas, 1970), and the selection of comparative data must be made afresh for each new question asked about the ancient world. In 'Economy and society in classical Athens' I found data on the Tolai of New Britain helpful in considering the intersection in classical Athens of two credit systems, one embedded in a network of reciprocal social relationships and the other limited to specific, isolated transactions and fixed time periods; but it was comparison with fully industrialized modern economies which indicated the important influence on the level of activity of the market in classical Athens of 'wages' for military service and other political duties.

Classicists are still prone to argue that neolithic versions of Greek myths, if we had them, might be amenable to Lévi-Straussian analysis, but written texts are not; that anthropological studies of primitive thought or of 'shame cultures' give insight into archaic Greek culture but that Greek philosophy and Greek tragedy lie outside the province of the anthropologist, or fall inside it only in so far as 'irrational' elements remain in the culture of the classical period; that the emergence of tyrants in the seventh and sixth centuries B.C. belongs to a different class of political events from that depicted in the world of Homer. This view implies not only a far too narrow conception of the scope of modern anthropological theory and research, but also an extremely crude model of primitive or traditional societies as entirely free from innovation, scepticism, and political change. It emphasizes the uniqueness of the Greeks by treating all other societies with which they might be compared as a featureless, homogeneous mass, instead of recognizing that every society and culture contains forms found elsewhere, but in unique combinations. This is the basis for the search in modern anthropology for abstract concepts of form and relationship applicable to all societies; the aim is not to eliminate differences, but to find a precise way of analysing them. Without similarities difference is meaningless.

As the earlier papers in this collection show, I came only slowly to the realization that comparison could only be justified in terms of a comprehensive theory of social structure. I began my research on the Greeks with a problem of technology, the history of merchant ship design and seafaring techniques, and studied the latter partly through 'field' experience sailing round the Aegean in an open, keelless boat which could scarcely make good a course 80 degrees off the wind. This was *la longue durée* at its most static; sailing conditions have changed little in the Aegean since antiquity. The northerly Meltemi which dominates summer sailing has the same characteristics as the 'etesian' winds described in ancient sources; the rocky harbours and channels retain their shape even if the sea level has shifted in places by a few feet; fishermen and caique skippers still navigate often enough without chart or compass. Some are old enough to remember the days of sail, while others had to rely on sail when moving from island to island during the war, to escape German notice.

Such first-hand experience of topography and of the physical conditions of life in the ancient world is valuable. British historians have had a reputation for vigorous topographical exploration in Greece since the last century; timed forced marches over the hills between Athens and Marathon and experimental sprints in hoplite armour are part of the tradition. The wild life of Spartan youths in the bush, in the transition period between adolescence and full military service, takes on a new meaning to those who have seen the miles of *maquis* which stretch between the plain of Lacedaimon and the next cultivable land to the north of it, the plain of Tegea, which Sparta struggled to conquer in the sixth century B.C. Traditional farming techniques used both in ancient times and today are attracting interest from historians; Stella Georgoudis (1974) has recently collected the evidence documenting the practice of transhumance in ancient Greece. Archaeologists are beginning to devote serious study to the reconstruction of the ecological context of the sites they excavate (McDonald and Rapp, 1972; Warren, 1972). Much remains to be done in this field.

Nevertheless, the ethnic composition and social institutions of modern Greece are radically different from those of the ancient world. The peasants I met in Hesiod's part of Boeotia were Albanians, and the grass widows of Ithaca were waiting for the homecoming of the crews of Onassis' tankers. I could learn about the nautical problems of ancient Greek traders by sailing round the Aegean, but it very soon became obvious that the history of Greek merchant shipping could not be written merely as a story of technical progress in shipbuilding and navigation. The decisive factors in the development of merchant shipping were changes in economic institutions rather than nautical technology.

Since I had already been working with archaeological evidence, both in studying trade patterns and in analysing iconographic and archaeological evidence for ship design, I looked first to archaeological data as a source of evidence on social and economic institutions. 'Archaeology and the social and economic history of classical Greece' is a plea for a more historically and sociologically oriented archaeology. Some of the suggestions put forward in this article were influenced by the work of non-classical archaeologists with anthropological training or interests, in the early stages of the 'new archaeology' movement. I have added for this volume some additional bibliographical notes on some of the most important publications in this line of research since 1967; but archaeology in Greece has still scarcely been touched by the new ideas developing in other fields. It is still oriented towards the study of artefacts and excavation sites rather than the study of communities and their culture.

Artefacts and sites do not tell their own story. The archaeological and literary evidence for trade in antiquity posed problems of interpretation which had stimulated argument among ancient historians since Karl Bücher defended his 'primitivist' view of the ancient Greek economy against Eduard Meyer and Beloch in the 1890s. Similar questions about the applicability of modern economic theory and concepts to pre-industrial economies had more recently been raised in economic anthropology by Karl Polanyi, who had also analysed data from the ancient world and had influenced the work of M. I. Finley. It was by this route that I arrived at social anthropology.

Polanyi's advice on historical method paralleled Malinowski's empiricist prescriptions for fieldwork: clear your mind of modernistic or ethnocentric presuppositions, observe native behaviour – in Polanyi's case, the movement of goods and the provision of related services – and repetitive patterns will appear, by means of which institutions can be isolated and subsequently classified in a general comparative typology. There was also a certain presupposition that appropriate values could be deduced from the institutions. The first problem which arises with this framework of analysis when it is used in the study of a single economy rather than as the basis of a general theory, is that almost any economy is bound to contain institutionalized exchange patterns of different types (reciprocal, redistributive, etc.), and therefore the attention shifts from the classification of institutions and societies to the articulation of institutions of different types, with corresponding values, within a single economic system. 'Economy and society in classical Athens' is a preliminary attempt to tackle this problem. It is unsatisfactory because for the most part it fails to penetrate beyond the characterization of specific institutions and values to the underlying structure of the economy as a whole. The article still seems to me sound in its general interpretation of the circulation of money in classical Athens and of the organization of the urban sector of the economy, but it is vitiated throughout by the uncritical application of a modern distinction between 'politics' and 'economics' which prevented me from perceiving the central role of Athenian imperialism in the economic development of the fifth century B.C. I have developed this point in a new article, '*Homo politicus* and *homo economicus*', placed next to 'Economy and society in classical Athens' in this collection because it represents a revision of the views stated in the earlier paper. It now seems to me that the views of Plato and Aristotle on the incompatibility of the traditional economic norms of the agricultural *oikos* with the new norms of the market-place cannot merely be taken at face value as reactions provoked by the growth of the 'commercial sector' of the economy, but have to be interpreted as a response to radical changes in the politico-economic system as a whole. The growth of trade and market activity in Athens received an unprecedented stimulus in the fifth century from the concentration of demand, backed by money, represented both by the Athenian fleet on campaign and by its crews when they came home to the city. The pressure from the *démos* for an active foreign policy in the late fifth and early fourth centuries represented not merely the habitual acquisitiveness of the market dealer, but a valid recognition of the relation between military pay and economic prosperity. This new pattern of circulation of resources through political and non-political channels generated political competition between rich and poor for its control. Plato's assertion that the process of political decision-making was in danger of being subverted by the values of the market subtly transforms the dependence of market activity on political decisions into the suggestion that the assembly was prone to be *psychologically* dominated by the market.

This recent reformulation of my interpretation of the economy of classical Athens coincides to a considerable extent with the neo-Marxist approach most recently argued by D. Lanza and M. Vegetti (1975), in which the key role of tribute and of payment for military and political service in the Athenian economy is fully recognized. In fact, J.-P. Vernant had already pointed out in 1965 that a Marxist analysis of the class struggle in classical Greece had to recognize the complex, tripartite relation between slaves, poor citizens and the rich, and the expression of opposition between the latter two strata through the medium of political institutions. Finley's emphasis on the essential nexus between slavery and the political rights extended to all citizens in the Greek *polis* (see most recently Finley, 1973a) was another indication of the need to transcend the ethnocentrism of the crude Marxist distinction between the 'political' and the 'economic'. Similar considerations have led the neo-Marxist school of Maurice Godelier, in economic anthropology, to develop Polanyi's conception of the pre-industrial economy as embedded in social relationships into a flexible Marxist analysis of primitive societies which recognizes that 'relations of production' may be found in institutions which the anthropologist would *prima facie* classify as belonging to the domain of kinship, religion, etc. (Godelier, 1973).

The problem of the articulation of different modes of production within a single economic system, already mentioned in relation to Polanyi, is prominent also in the work of the Godelier school. However, it is an essential tenet of Marxism for them that this articulation takes the form of a hierarchical structure in which one dominant mode of production exerts a determining influence over the rest, and ultimately over the form of a society in its widest sense. As will be clear from the final paper in this collection, I feel that the question of the different ways in which social institutions can be articulated with and influence each other needs to be approached with a more open mind.

For me, in fact, Polanyi's emphasis on the embedding of the pre-industrial economy in social relationships had different implications. Coming to anthropology as an outsider, I felt that Polanyi's argument indicated that to continue to concentrate on the analysis of economic institutions was not enough: I had to acquire a general grasp of anthropological theory and the analysis of social structures. In a sense, perhaps, I could even say that ontogenesis paralleled phylogenesis: the approach to anthropology by way of Polanyi and other writers on economic anthropology had put me in a position analogous to that of those students of Malinowski who had been well trained in perceiving the multiple interconnections of social institutions, but needed Radcliffe-Brown's work on social structure to provide them with a general framework for their analysis.

Under the influence of Radcliffe-Brown – himself influenced by Durkheim and Simmel – British anthropologists reduced Malinowski's somewhat impressionistic technique of analysing institutions and their functional interconnections to order by developing a set of general formal concepts – social structure, role, corporate group, network, etc. – which provided the tools for a comparative analysis of societies and forms of social relationship. This approach was developed to its fullest extent in kinship theory, and it was for this reason that I turned from the study of Greek economic history to that of kinship in ancient Greece. Despite the elaboration of specialized political institutions in the Greek city-state, the analysis of kinship still provides a general framework for the study of archaic and classical Greek society which includes the criteria and procedures for admission to citizenship, the hereditary transmission of property and, in some cases, religious office, the municipal organization and rituals of villages and city neighbour-hoods, and a considerable proportion of the case material from Athenian lawsuits, besides raising the more elusive problems of assessing the importance of kinship and affinity as a basis for political alliance, and of understanding the significance of the family both to its individual members and as a subject for dramatic representation.

I found two major difficulties in applying the structural-functional approach in its conventional, positivist form to the ancient Greek data, both of which had already been recognized in the critical dis-cussions and reformulations of the structural-functional approach which characterized the social anthropology of the 1950s and 1960s. In the first place, the early functionalist emphasis on the inter-connection of social institutions in a single integrated system – which could be, and indeed was, criticized even as a basis for the analysis of simple societies – was evidently inadequate for the study of societies involved in extensive social change and differentiated into upper and lower strata, urban and rural settlements, dominant and subordinate political units, and a variety of specialized organiza-tional contexts: temple, assembly, gymnasium, market, etc. Different groups and role-sets based on kinship had acquired specialized functions within this complex social system. For example, deme and phratry, both patrilineal clans, controlled recruitment to the citizen body and local religious festivals while the *genos* was primarily concerned with succession to priestly office and, though partly over-lapping in membership with the phratry, had the form of a conical clan with an emphasis on descent as a principle of internal organiza-tion which was lacking in phratry and deme. The concept of a single 'kinship system' required modification to take account both of the discontinuity between these different sets of roles and accompanying norms, and of their different significance in urban and rural contexts or to members of the political elite as against small farmers whose political interests and activities were mainly concentrated at the municipal level (cf. Freedman, 1966). As in the case of Polanyi's classification of economic institutions, the use of an analytical framework derived from comparative theory clarified the structure and functioning of particular institutions in context, but leaves the problem of their articulation unresolved.

Following a line already indicated by Malinowski in *Crime and Custom in Savage Society* (1926), R. Firth, E. Leach, and F. Barth have treated such variation in institutions as affording the individual a field of choice in which to select the behavioural norms most advantageous to him. But in order to understand such choices it is necessary to know how the choosing individual sees and classifies himself and his social surroundings. A method of analysis which places emphasis on the individual's manipulation of alternative social norms must demonstrate that the alternatives are really perceived as such. In fact, however theoretically unsatisfactory and difficult to validate it may be, once we admit some element of choice into social behaviour we are condemned to using the method of *Verstehen* to understand it; we have to try to understand each situation from the actors' points of view and not merely from the external angle of an observer looking at a two-dimensional map. Appeal to the notion of a higher-level set of 'rules for using the rules' does not solve the problem of choice. No amount of elaboration and refinement of our formulation of the rules of behaviour belonging to each culture will enable us to predict unambiguously the outcome of every combination of personalities and pressures.

Lévi-Strauss's dictum (1958, p. 25) that anthropologists study unconscious structures while historians study conscious choices is valid only as a superficial characterization of the main orientation of the two disciplines and experience of their practitioners in the past. Its principal significance today, when sociologists and anthropologists are showing increasing interest in action theory, *Verstehen* and the phenomenological approach in the social sciences, is to remind us that the traditional techniques of interpreting sources, situations and life-histories developed by historians may have something of value to contribute to the other social sciences. Dilthey's formulation of the theory of *Verstehen* was inspired by his work on Schleiermacher's technique of source-interpretation, and by his attempt to understand Schleiermacher's life and ideas (Antoni, 1940).

I myself learnt from working on Polanyi, Gernet, and Durkheim the importance of reading books that they read, trying to become familiar with the intellectual landscape of the social milieu in which they lived, reconstructing as accurately as possible the perspective into which they began to insert their own theories.

The necessity for a sociological analysis of the perspectives of ancient Greek writers was brought home to me by the question invariably raised by anthropologists with whom I discussed my work on Greek kinship, concerning the difficulty of working from a limited range of literary sources representing only the point of view of an elite. My work on the Greek intellectuals was in the first place undertaken as a study of the relation between their place in the society of the Greek city and the image of its structure which they presented. Like James Redfield in his study of Homer (1975), I found it necessary to emphasize the fact that every literary source is an act of communication and not merely the expression of an individual point of view. Historians of literature have long been aware that they must know the norms of each literary genre and the cultural background shared by writer and public in order to be able to assess the choices made by the author being studied. Students of Greek law have developed a sophisticated technique of distinguishing, in the speeches surviving from Attic court cases, the assertions which could easily be controlled by any member of the jury, and therefore must represent actual practice, from those which were more difficult for the hearers to verify and which therefore should be treated with more caution. It is often possible to distinguish with some confidence passages where the orator is deliberately trying to confuse the jurors in the interests of his client. Much of the traditional technique of interpreting ancient literary texts relies on identifying this shared background of common knowledge and culturally shaped expectations common to author and audience, and thence isolating the innovations – for example, significant variations in the narration of a myth – which indicate the particular intentions and preoccupations of the writer in a specific text. Since, however, the texts of archaic and classical Greek culture belong for the most part to a stage of transition between oral and literary communication, it is necessary also to consider the effects on the form in which ideas were presented of the new possibility which writing afforded of addressing an audience stretching as far in space and time as the Greek language could be understood.

This last point indicates, as I have observed in the final study of this volume, 'Evolution and history', another contribution which the historian can make to the comparative study of societies and cultures. Although many societies today are going through processes of modernization, industrialization, spread of literacy, structural differentiation, etc., they do so in an environment which has already predetermined to a large extent the options open to them. The first industrial revolution, the first conversions to Christianity or Islam, the first developments of mathematics or formal logic or scientific historiography can only be studied in the past. Whether we regard anthropology as a natural science concerned with the comparative study of societies and cultures, or as a humanistic discipline which aims at giving its practitioners a deeper insight into their own society and culture by exposing them to radically different institutions and ways of thought, history provides an essential complement: in the first case, because so many forms of social organization and systems of ideas which have existed in the past can no longer be observed today, and in the second case because the lessons that can be learnt from the differences between our society and others need to be complemented by a study of the differences between the past and present state of our own institutions and culture.

To admit that the ancient Greeks occupy, in certain respects, a unique place in human history, and that they stand in a special relation to our own culture and values, does not imply that they are beyond the reach of comparative theory. At the time when Frazer and his critics were arguing over the legitimacy of equating Greeks and 'savages', Durkheim, Simmel, and Weber were already laying the bases of a general comparative theory applicable to the whole range of societies from the simplest to the most complex. Frazer's fundamental mistake – no doubt inevitable in the evolutionist climate of his time – was to confuse inspiration and classification. If Bongo-Bongo rainmaking rites illuminate one aspect of the Greek ritual, that does not imply any general affinity between the Bongo-Bongo and the Greeks. Fruitful interpretations of Greek institutions have been inspired by the Iroquois confederacy (Morgan, 1877), Zulu age regiments (Nilsson, 1912; Jeanmaire, 1913; Ferguson, 1918), the Kwakiutl potlatch (Mauss, 1921), and African *zar* and *bori* spirit possession cults (Jeanmaire, 1951) as well as by many comparisons with more developed societies and more recent history. We do not compare 'societies', we compare ideal types or models of institutions and social forms. Analysis of the logical consistency of the model and assessment of its heuristic value are to a considerable extent independent of the source of the data from which it originated. In constructing a model of the form of the Athenian phratry I used data on the kinship systems of Kurds, Tswana, and Cyrenaican Bedouin. For a study of the *functions* of the phratry a completely different set of comparisons might be more useful.

Walking round the shores of Lake Nemi, running across the plain of Marathon, standing in the palace of Knossos or the *tophet* of Sulcis in Sardinia, living in modern peasant villages or reading ethnographies are all valid ways of providing the stimulus to the imagination which the historian needs. For me, the combination of history and social anthropology has two contradictory implications. On the one hand, it means a conscious recognition that the historian not only uses the technique of *Verstehen* to interpret sources and enter into the perceptions of actors in a foreign culture, but must also recreate imaginatively the material and institutional scenery which the anthropologist in the field can experience directly. On the other hand, it implies the submission of the insights derived from imagination to comparative control and formal expression in ideal types. The tension between experience, whether lived or imagined, and formal analysis is inherent to both history and anthropology.

Part one

Classical studies and anthropology

1 Anthropology and the classics*

The past

Briefly speaking, anthropologists and Classical scholars collaborated or at least regarded each other's work with sympathetic interest from about the middle of the nineteenth century up to the First World War, recoiled in mutual suspicion during the inter-war period, and have been slowly returning to a sympathetic attitude since the Second World War. Elements both of nineteenth-century enthusiasm and of the reaction which followed still influence most classicists' conceptions of Anthropology.

There is an idea that the classicist calls in the anthropologist – like an Anglo-Indian memsahib calling in the native servant – to deal with what Dodds called the 'disagreeably primitive things poking up their heads through the cracks in the fabric of Periclean rationalism'. Anthropologists understandably do not care much for this point of view: they would rather discuss Periclean rationalism itself. Having been forced into the consideration of social change, in the inter-war period, by the changes in the primitive societies they were studying, they are now prepared to tackle any kind of society. This already makes the prospects for the relation between Classics and Anthropology today very different from what they were in the past.

In the nineteenth century the relationship between Classics and Anthropology had its focus in the attempt to reconstruct early stages of Greek and Roman society, and the belief that all societies passed through parallel stages of evolution. At first, in the 1860s, it was the ancient historians who tried to reconstruct primitive society and discover laws of evolution by studying the common elements in early Greek, Roman and Indian institutions in the hope of recovering the social institutions of the Indo-Europeans. When L. H. Morgan wrote his *Ancient Society* (1877) he was still using his knowledge of Greek and Roman society to interpret what he had seen among the Iroquois rather than the reverse. But as information about primitive societies began to flood in, anthropologists developed their own theories about the evolution of social institutions and beliefs, which classicists in turn adopted or adapted in reconstructing early stages of Greek, Roman and Near Eastern history and culture.

Of course difficulties soon appeared. Some Classical scholars found any idea of comparison between ancient civilizations and primitive peoples preposterous and shocking. In broad outlines, however, the history of the relationship between the two disciplines has been conditioned by reactions common to both of them. More serious resistance to partnership between classicists and anthropologists was raised by distrust of the evolutionary schemes proposed by anthropologists (which were rapidly becoming too many for credibility) and of the quality of the evidence and arguments put forward to support them; and above all by the inability of theories of unilinear evolution to solve historical problems in individual cultures. By the late nineteenth century an ancient historian trained to the Mommsen standard in analysing social institutions and political systems was, judged by rigour of analysis and argument, a far better social scientist than any contemporary anthropologist. After all, this was the school which produced Max Weber. Eduard Meyer – a product of the Mommsen era if not of the Mommsen school – had no difficulty in producing a masterly survey and criticism of current anthropological theory as the first volume of the second edition of the *Geschichte des Altertums* in 1907, nor in setting the study of kinship in early Greek society for the first time on a firm footing.

Above all, however, new data were coming in which required historical as well as evolutionary classification. For the classicists Schliemann's excavations at Troy and Mycenae, and then Evans's discovery of Minoan Crete, meant a shift of interest from the study of myths as evidence for primitive institutions or beliefs to the attempt to extract from them genuine folk memories of historical events. The exploration of Africa, Australia and the Pacific faced anthropologists with comparable problems in classifying cultures and trying to reconstruct their historical contacts and migrations.

Consequently there was a return to concentration on individual cultures, both in Classics and in Anthropology, which fitted in with the general current of historicism at the turn of the century. In British Anthropology this reaction led to the tradition of intensive fieldwork in a single community inaugurated by Malinowski during the First World War, and to an almost complete cessation of comparative studies. The new models of Comparative Sociology developed by Max Weber and Durkheim did not become fully effective until the 1940s even in Anthropology.

Nevertheless Weber, Durkheim and Malinowski had firmly committed Sociology and Anthropology to studying and conceptualizing social systems as wholes in which institutions and ideas – social structure and values – were integrally linked. It was at this point that Classics and the social sciences parted company. In Classics – and perhaps in historical studies generally – the trend of the inter-war period was towards increased specialization. Paradoxically the *Annales* school in France, by setting up an opposition between political history and socio-economic history, may well have encouraged this trend. In Classical Studies politics, economics, law, religion, literature and philosophy have been treated as separate subjects. One of the results of this fragmentation was that such interchanges of ideas between Classics and the social sciences as still occurred in the inter-war period were of a piecemeal and eclectic kind. Nineteenth-century evolutionary theory was still accepted, if uneasily, in discussions of the earliest stages of Greek kinship and religion, while the influence of William James or Freud became prominent in the treatment of religion in later periods. Scholars who insisted on the uniqueness of Greek culture did not find it inconsistent to accept the application of modern economic theory to Greek economic history. The Roman *gens* somehow had to stretch from a beginning *à la* Fustel de Coulanges to an end *à la* Namier – with a lot of unasked questions in between.

It is of course on the point of the dangers of modern economic theory that Anthropology, through the work of M. I. Finley, has made its greatest impact on Classical Studies since the war. I suspect it may be generally true that when historians avoid comparative studies they fall most easily into the trap of assimilating the society they study to the only other society they know – that in which they live. Modernistic comparisons are noticeable in the inter-war period not only in economic history but also in expressions of sympathy for the Hellenistic world (bourgeois, cosmopolitan, bureaucratic, something of an anti-climax, yet precariously preserving its Greek values), and in the treatment of religion: no longer seen as a phenomenon ubiquitous in primitive society and gradually losing importance in the course of social evolution, religion came to be treated almost as a psychological constant – man's reaction to the inevitable uncertainties and mysteries of life and death. The focus of research shifted from the origins of rituals and myths to the cults and creeds of the Hellenistic world and the Roman empire. William James's *Varieties of Religious Experience* (1902) signposted the way, with Freud in the background. What Gilbert Murray called a 'failure of nerve' might happen in any society – ancient or modern.

I do not wish to denigrate the work produced on ancient religion in these years. The questions asked were certainly more profound than those of the evolutionists, and the responses produced by scholars of the quality of Wilamowitz, Murray, A. D. Nock, Festugière, Latte and Nilsson provide material for a very important chapter in the history of Classics in European culture. But I do not think that they have bequeathed to us a method for studying ancient religious history. In the case of Greek religion at least, the response was intuitive and predominantly aesthetic, rather than historical. And the individualistic, psychological approach to religion is by nature ill-equipped to deal with differences between societies and periods. This criticism applies also to the treatment of religion by anthropologists in the inter-war years, which shows the same concentration on the function of religion for the individual believer: for example, in Malinowski's treatment of Trobriand magic as a way of reducing anxiety, or Evans-Pritchard's demonstration of the coherence of Zande witchcraft beliefs as a way of explaining misfortune.

The approach is attractive because it is egalitarian: it puts all religious beliefs on the same footing, instead of separating 'primitive thought' from 'higher religions'. But it carries the danger of treating all religions as the same and ignoring marked differences in organization, scope of activity and articulation with other institutional spheres.

Dodds's *The Greeks and the Irrational* (1951) still belongs in my opinion to this inter-war trend. The fact that Dodds was making the Greeks irrational while Evans-Pritchard was making the Zande rational does not seem in this context to make a crucial difference. The strength of Dodds's book, it seems to me now, is in the determination to think Greek culture in its own terms. The use of comparative material made an impression at the time of publication but will not in the long run, I think, be judged one of the most effective aspects of the book. The anthropological theory was drawn from a school – the American 'Culture and Personality' school of Ruth Benedict and Margaret Mead – which was based on shaky psychological foundations, and furthermore attributed a crucial role to the use of data on child-training which simply were not available for ancient Greece. They were weak in the analysis of social structure and could not provide the analytic tools needed for a re-assessment of the structure of archaic Greek society. Perhaps I have a partisan viewpoint, but I think the British Social Anthropology developed in Oxford by Radcliffe-Brown and Evans-Pritchard would have been more useful. An exchange of ideas between Evans-Pritchard and Dodds on the subject of rationality in religion would certainly have been worth hearing.

The present and the future

In the first place, the relation between Classics and Anthropology must be a relation of active debate. It is difficult if not impossible to gain an understanding of the methods and critical standards in argument of another discipline without personal contact and discussion. Up to the First World War both classicists and anthropologists took it for granted that their relationship should be one of exchange of ideas and collaboration in developing theory; we have to try to re-create this situation.

On the other hand the aims of the relationship are now quite different. Anthropologists are not likely to offer us help with filling in the blanks in our knowledge of Bronze Age kinship or religion. But they *can* offer a framework within which we can try to put together fragments of Greek culture and society studied in isolation, into a coherent whole. And this does seem to be a crucial need at present for Classical Studies generally. The fact is that at present Classics and ancient history (and archaeology) are taught in separate lectures if not separate departments – with results which we all find disquieting. Classics students are often bored by the ancient history they are taught; and history students, presumably, learn little or nothing of Greek or Latin literature beyond the historians. To say that each is necessary as 'background' for the other is surely not a satisfactory basis for closer collaboration. Should we not rather be saying that Greek and Latin literature were produced by historical societies with changing structures, which exercised constraints over

creative thinkers in ways we must try to understand; and that Greek
and Roman history is known to us very largely through the works of
Greek and Roman historians, which are literary products following
traditional thought-patterns and rules of genre which the student of
ancient history must take into account? It is equally important to
know how Sophocles experienced Athenian society and how
Thucydides experienced prose.

These questions belong to the sociology of knowledge: still at
present a relatively little-explored field in which most work is tentative and hypothetical. It may therefore seem that I am claiming too
much for anthropology in suggesting that it could be relevant here.
After all, one can find in work by Classical scholars on particular
genres and individual authors answers to the questions I have
suggested: for example, in Momigliano's work on ancient historiography, or Bernard Knox on Sophocles (*The Heroic Temper*, 1964),
or Jacqueline de Romilly's *Histoire et raison chez Thucydide* (1956).
But I think if we are ever to try to link the teaching of Ancient
History and Classics *to undergraduates* along the sort of lines I have
suggested, it will be very difficult to put it across consistently and
comprehensibly unless the assumptions about the relation between
society and literature on which the linkage is based are made explicit.
Otherwise both teachers and students will depend entirely on the
hazards and fashions of research – the availability of ready-made
books written in a way which happens to coincide with the needs of
the course. Of course we all do depend on that anyway to a great
extent. But surely the function of secondary literature is to help the
student to look at the ancient evidence with sharper perceptions,
and to distinguish rational methods of interpretation from arbitrary
conjectures. And that means discussing method.

Historians and philologists share a habit of leaving their assumptions about psychology, culture and social relationships unstated –
and even, for the most part, consider this a positive virtue. This, I
would suggest, is the essential point of difference between the arts
and the social sciences. Social scientists are committed to making
their assumptions explicit and trying to prove the validity of their
interpretations of particular cases – either by constructing a rigorous
chain of argument or by producing empirical evidence that the
interpretation can be generalized (usually, in fact, by a combination
of the two methods). What I want to do in the rest of this paper is
to give three examples of ways in which Classical scholars with a

training in one or other of the social sciences have been trying to introduce new standards of rigour in argument into Classical Studies. The first is the effort to tighten up our reasoning about numbers and economic/ecological data which is Keith Hopkins's speciality. The pioneer work in this field was the research on ancient population carried out from the 1880s onwards by the German historian K. J. Beloch. The second is concerned with our reasoning about institutions, is practised by Finley and, I hope I can say, by myself, and goes back through Max Weber to Mommsen. The third is the structuralist analysis of myth and ritual developed by Jean-Pierre Vernant and his school in Paris, which derives ultimately from the structuralist linguistics of de Saussure, through the anthropology of Claude Lévi-Strauss.

Three examples of the use of social science methods in classics

1 *Economic—ecological*

Hopkins's work is concerned with the logic of numbers. It is obvious enough, I imagine, that all too often we read ancient texts without stopping to work out the implications of the figures – to ask how many people a farm of a given size could feed, or what sort of magnitudes the Attic tribute figures represent. What seems to me particularly important, and new, about Hopkins's work is that he uses comparative data (on life expectations, crop yields, etc.) not merely to criticize or place in context individual figures, but to establish limits of variation within whole processes; and he builds these models together into an interlocking whole in such a way that it becomes possible to calculate the implications of making a guess of one size rather than another even where we have no secure data.

The use of comparative figures drawn from modern societies, even 'underdeveloped' ones, in different parts of the world can of course only indicate approximately the possible range of figures acceptable for ancient conditions. Another type of research being developed now by archaeologists is the intensive study of the ecology and production patterns of specific Mediterranean areas in the hope of being able approximately to reconstruct ancient conditions. Some work of this kind was done by Peter Warren's team excavating Myrtos in south-east Crete, and more by the University of Minnesota's Messenia project under W. McDonald and G. Rapp; Michael

Jameson of the University of Pennsylvania is currently doing a similar
study in the Argolid (Jameson *et al.*, 1976). The difficulties of reconstructing ancient conditions are of course formidable, but I
think it is equally obvious that a great deal will be learnt from making
the attempt. Social anthropologists as well as geographers, geologists
and biologists are already collaborating in this type of research.

2 *Institutions*

It is only for the sake of brevity that I have presented the two above
approaches as if they could be carried on without consideration of
the specific institutions and culture of each period; of course this is
presupposed. When we turn from the logical implications of numbers
to the logic of institutions, cultural categories cannot be left out of
consideration. Mommsen's *Staatsrecht*, read in the context of current
work in Anthropology, seems astonishingly modern because it
combines a structural-functional analysis of the Roman state with
an attempt to delineate the categories used by the Romans in thinking
about government.

The best work on ancient institutions up till now has come from
those who, like Mommsen, took their social science training from
law. This is still the case with Moses Finley. In Britain, however,
though lawyers played a major role in the development of Social
Anthropology in the nineteenth century, law has ceased to be regarded as a general training for public life and has become one of
the most strictly vocational forms of education. This is, I think, a
grave loss for Classical Studies, and something about which classicists
should take serious thought. In the present position, however, there
is little doubt that in this country an ancient historian who wants a
training in analysing social institutions will get more from Anthropology or Sociology than from Law.

Two examples from Finley's analysis of Sparta (Finley, 1968c)
will make clearer what I mean by the logic of institutions. Finley
put his finger on two contradictions in the Spartan social system
which were constant sources of tension. One was that despite the
ideal model of equal land-holdings there was apparently no regular
mechanism for keeping land-holdings equal. *Klēroi* seem to have
been transmitted by the normal Greek patterns: equal inheritance
rights for all sons, marriage of heiresses to near kin and, presumably,
adoption. Consequently sons of prolific families were liable to find

themselves in difficulties. The second contradiction stemmed from the combination of egalitarianism and authoritarianism in the same social system. A society which trains its members to unquestioning obedience must see that in every situation there is someone for them to obey – a leader whose authority rests on superiority and experience, not the chance of the lot. Sparta did not train all her citizens to be leaders and consequently did not in practice make them all equals.

This second point shows how closely interwoven the cultural and structural elements may be in the 'logic of institutions'. This point is central to all Finley's work: for example in his demonstration that before asking questions about the implications of slavery in ancient society it is necessary to see just how different ancient societies divided up the continuum running from freedom to the chain-gang; or his analysis of the barrier separating land transactions from money transactions in Classical Athens (see now Finley, 1973a).

Studies which I would regard as concerned with the logic of institutions cover a wide range. On the one hand there are the institutional correlates of structurally well-defined values such as the Spartan emphasis on obedience. Again one can study, as Hans-Julius Wolff (1944) has, the relations of logically linked jural concepts such as marriage, legitimacy and citizenship. Marriage and legitimacy are definitionally-linked concepts applicable to almost all societies: the fact that in the Greek *polis* both tended to be linked also to the concept of citizenship caused inconsistencies, and eventually changes in the institution of marriage, when non-citizens began to form a substantial element in city populations. Or again one may be concerned with the operational requirements of institutions. I found, for example, in studying the *genos* in archaic Greece that its form varied quite regularly with changes in the rules for appointment to office: it became clear that the noble Eupatrid *genē* in Attica must have constituted themselves as closed corporate groups when the Eupatrid monopoly of office and annual archonships were introduced, most probably in the seventh century B.C. No other mechanism was available for establishing whether a candidate for office was of Eupatrid descent or not, and such a mechanism was absolutely requisite for the working of the monopoly.

One final example, just to indicate that in connecting this approach with Mommsen I do not mean to recommend legal formalism. In the discussions of the Demotionidai inscriptions considerable weight has been given to the formalist argument that a candidate whose application for phratry membership was rejected by the phratry could not have appealed *to* the phratry – 'appealing from phratry in assembly to phratry in court'. What seems not to have been considered is the procedure in phratry votes, which is described in [Demosthenes] XLIII. Votes on admission to the phratry took place on the third day of the *Apatouria*, along with a considerable programme of other festivities (vividly represented in the second half of Aristophanes' *Peace*), and the vote was taken while the sacrifice for the boy's initiation (*koureion*) was on the altar. It was part of a religious ritual in which there was no time or place for argument, the calling of witnesses or any other regular legal procedure. Other candidates were queueing up with their sheep – those already passed were beginning to roast theirs – younger brothers were running around reciting poetry – and so on. There was every reason for the phratry to sit again later on as a court and reconsider its verdict when the rejected applicant and the phratry's own spokesmen had had time to prepare their case, and the *phratēres* had time to listen.

Implicit in all the approaches I am discussing is the necessity of thinking in the language and categories of the society being studied and making every effort to see each institution as an ongoing process of co-operation and conflict between live people in specific surroundings – to get as close as possible to the position of the Anthropological observer in the field. There is also a clear emphasis on the difficulties of understanding another culture, which again suggests a parallel between the Classical scholar and the anthropologist. We try to see the Greeks as 'desperately foreign' as a way of avoiding the pitfalls of over-familiarity (Finley, 1968a). This attitude is most obviously necessary in dealing with myth, rituals and symbolic thought in general.

3 *Myths, rituals and symbolic thought*

The work in this field being done now by J.-P. Vernant, P. Vidal-Naquet, M. Detienne and their students is not easy to summarize. They differ from each other to some extent in background and interests and are still actively engaged in the attempt to define their aims and methods both in relation to each other and in relation to alternative approaches to myth and religion in Classics and in

Anthropology. Vernant has a particular interest in the comparison and history of psychological categories derived from the 'Historical Psychology' of I. Meyerson: recently he contributed to Meyerson's 'Festschrift' a brilliant article on the applicability of the concept of the will to Greek tragedy (Vernant, 1972). Detienne is actively involved in discussion with anthropologists about Lévi-Strauss's structural analysis of myth. Vidal-Naquet seems to be more concerned with the problems of applying structuralist analysis to history. What follows is *my* assessment of the significance of their work, which does not necessarily coincide with *theirs*.

In my view the most important aspect of their approach is the idea that the aim of the analysis of myth and ritual is not to produce some kind of 'explanation' of each rite or myth, but to reconstruct a mental map of the concepts and symbols used in the whole body of Greek myth and ritual which represents the patterns of association and opposition which recur in the material, and does not depend on any advance preconceptions about the 'meaning' of symbols.

As I said, the method derives from the structuralist linguistics of de Saussure. There is doubt and disagreement about the validity of the analogy in detail which I have no time to discuss here; I do not think this disagreement affects the importance of the parallel in directing attention away from the 'message' of a single speech-act or myth to the rules of the language or sign system taken as a whole.

This change of orientation has been badly needed in studies of Greek myth and religion, which by concentrating on the search for 'origins' have fragmented the material into strata or regional divisions – 'Mediterranean', 'oriental' and Indo-European gods, Thessalian and Achaean myths – while neglecting the articulations which made the pantheon and the corpus of myths, syncretistic as it undoubtedly was, a coherent part of a culture with a high degree of integration.

Objections have been made to the attempt to apply structuralist methods of analysis to Greek myth, on the grounds that we know Greek myths only through written texts in genres which cannot be put on a par with the myths of primitive societies. This objection is premature. In fact the structural analysis of myth includes two separate operations: first, the analysis of patterns of association and opposition found in myth *and in the culture to which the myth belongs*, and, second, the analysis of the combinations and transformations of these patterns in a related group of myths. The second operation *may* be applicable only to myth, or only to myths from 'primitive' societies, but the former should be applicable to any culture; and in fact the Vernant school have shown that the method enables them to support their new insights into Greek culture with a wide range of evidence. Vidal-Naquet's study of the myth of the 'Black Hunter' (Vidal-Naquet, 1968a) drew on ritual, treatises on hunting, red-figure vases and Sophocles' *Philoctetes*; the study of *mētis* carried out by Vernant and Detienne ranged from Homer and Archilochus through Aristotle to Oppian (Detienne and Vernant, 1974). Dogmatic statements about the discontinuity between myth and tragedy, myth and history or myth and philosophy are surely premature. They rest mainly (a) on the ethnocentric belief that tragedy, history and philosophy are fundamentally different from 'primitive thought' and (b) on an equally ethnocentric artificial category, 'myth', which needs to be analysed into a bundle of characteristics which all recur in other forms of thought and communication, though not in the same combination. Myths have the same self-contained quality, combined with an implicit appeal to the audience's shared cultural experience, which is found in poetry and fiction; on the other hand they often have the immediately comprehensible structure and the promise of explaining fundamental puzzles, offered by modern ideologies.

It may seem that if no *a priori* limit can be set to the field within which associations of ideas are to be traced, and if the research aims strictly to discover patterns of combination and opposition, without considering 'meaning', it could have neither a beginning nor an end. Certainly it is inherent in this type of research that it is cumulative; each new study will add something to those which have gone before, and in so doing may reveal deficiencies not previously noticed. Much of the Vernant school's earliest work was concerned with the ambiguous type of cleverness which the Greeks called *mētis* and with the opposition between nature and culture – and both of these themes seem to owe a good deal to Lévi-Strauss.[1] More recently, however, the choice of focus seems to have been determined more by estimates of what was central in Greek life and thought – with studies of sacrifice, marriage, the place of man between gods and beasts, slavery – and there has been an emphasis on the necessity of studying the Greek pantheon as a system instead of taking individual deities in isolation. Laurence Demoule-Lyotard, for example, published an article in *Annales* (1971) studying the relations between Hermes, Pan, Nymphs, Dionysus, Satyrs, Priapus and Demeter in dedicatory epigrams in the *Anthology;* the distribution of different types of offering between them, and the cases of joint dedication to two or more divinities. There is a vast amount of work of this kind to be done; and if the study of Greek religion is ever to be freed from embarrassed murmurs about fertility cults, oriental influences and animism, this is surely the way to set about it. Detienne has already tackled a notorious Frazerian stamping-ground in his study of the cult of Adonis (Detienne, 1972). Despite all the problems of method and theory which remain to be solved, therefore, I regard this work as an extremely important new departure which has already proved capable of generating research and has the major virtues of being clear in its main methodological outline and oriented towards seeing what is in the texts rather than imposing on them theories derived from other cultures, primitive or modern.

Conclusion

Behind all three approaches I have discussed – study of the logic of numbers, of institutions and of symbols – lies the notion of *system*, in the sense that all of them require the researcher to start with the assumption that the datum he is considering can only be defined and understood in terms of the relationships which link it to other data. These may vary from close interdependence to much looser forms of association – and the notion of system boundaries is very problematic. But the notion of system does point to two aspects of modern Anthropology which I believe will determine the character of any collaboration established with Classical Studies. The first is that comparison in anthropology is no longer concerned with substantive data – customs and symbols – but with forms of relationship. This makes Anthropology a much more abstract discipline than it was in the nineteenth century, and it means that joint degree courses will contain a substantial theoretical component. This combination of theoretical work and analysis of substantive data seems to me a very good form for an undergraduate course. (After all, I was brought up on Oxford Greats, if the comparison is not considered blasphemous. In fact Anthropology has one advantage not offered by Greats, which is that the student is actually required to apply the theory to the substantive data.) Furthermore – this is the final point I want to

bring out in connection with the notion of system – an anthropological approach implies a constant search for connections between
different aspects of social life and culture, which means that the
traditional boundaries between subject specialities in Classical
Studies will constantly be overridden or called into question.

This is – I hope – the main reason why the idea of a closer relationship with Anthropology is becoming attractive to classicists today.
It is certainly the reason why the combination attracts students. But
it will be very difficult to transform teaching arrangements to achieve
this more holistic approach. It means not merely producing one
hybrid like myself to teach a link course, but combined efforts by
whole departments to change courses and syllabuses. This is one
challenge which University Classics departments have to face if they
wish to continue to attract sufficient numbers of students. The other
challenge which is becoming evident is a very encouraging phenomenon: the number of students who want to start Greek or Latin
at the University.

2 History, economics and anthropology: the work of Karl Polanyi

I

Historians in their consideration of theory have to concern themselves not only with 'theories of history,' but also with the theory of the other social sciences. Social scientists perhaps hope that one day they may be able to announce that *dum Romae consulitur, Saguntum expugnatum est*. This article is in the nature of a 'report from Saguntum.'

Economics, being the most 'scientific' of the social sciences, the most ready to formulate laws, is particularly apt to provoke conflict. The present debate over the 'new economic history,' with its emphasis on the use of models and of econometric techniques, is an example. Those who accuse 'Cliometrics' of dehumanizing history are in fact asking whether economic laws are valid for all periods and types of society. The new economic historians claim, with some justice, that they have not introduced economic laws and methods of inference into history, but only questioned some hypotheses which already implicitly relied on them. But their methods in any case have brought into prominence the question of the range of the deductions from economic theory possible at any point in time, and the question whether economic theory becomes less valid as we move further from the modern economy.[1]

Historians of economic development are disturbed not only by the prospect of having their theories falsified or their problems solved by economists, but also by invitations to take up the ancient position of the historian as a practical adviser. Here their position comes particularly close to that of the economic anthropologist.[2] Anthropologists are increasingly involved in the study of economic development and social change, and this has produced both murmurs of conflict between 'pure' and 'applied' anthropology, and a heated debate on the relevance of modern economic theory for the analysis

31

of primitive or peasant economies. This debate would in any case be of interest to historians, but it is particularly relevant because it arose out of the work of an economic historian, Karl Polanyi, who was concerned with past civilizations even more than with primitive existing societies.

Polanyi's thesis, briefly stated, was that economic theory applies only to the modern market economy and cannot serve the needs of the economic anthropologists or the historian of pre-market civilizations. Nineteenth-century Europe 'disembedded' the economy from the social structure, freed economic motives from social control and set in motion a process by which economic considerations came to dominate society. 'Once the economic system is organized in separate institutions, based on specific motives and conferring a special status, society must be shaped in such a manner as to allow that system to function according to its own laws' (Polanyi, 1944, pp. 63-4). To understand earlier or less developed societies, in which economic relations are still 'embedded' in the social system (or in Mauss's terminology, economic transactions cannot be separated from the 'faits sociaux totaux' in which they are incorporated),[3] we need a new theory of comparative economics. In non-market societies the economy cannot be distinguished by reference to an interrelated flow of rational calculations. Instead, the historian or anthropologist must start from the material objects which serve to satisfy wants, and follow their movements to see what operational patterns and groupings emerge.[4] Four such patterns are suggested by Polanyi: reciprocity, or 'movements between correlative points of symmetrical groupings in society'; redistribution, or 'movements towards an allocative center and out of it again'; exchange, or 'vice-versa movements . . . under a market system'; and householding, the pattern of peasant subsistence agriculture.[5]

Although the essence of these views had been presented by Polanyi in *The Great Transformation* (1944), they did not reach anthropologists and ancient historians until the late 1950s, when the collective volume *Trade and Market in the Early Empires* was published (Polanyi, 1957a), and other researches inspired or influenced by Polanyi began to appear. By this time Polanyi was seventy and neither his disciples nor his critics have made much attempt to enquire into the background of his thought or the formative influences of his youth. The result has sometimes been that what was original in his thought has been underrated, while what was part of a common culture has been separated from its context and taken for perversity.

1886–1933: Hungary and Austria

Economic anthropologists would do well to remember that Polanyi was born only two years after Malinowski. He grew up in the radical bourgeois society of Budapest – an intellectual Jewish community cut off from political power, but expecting change. Universal suffrage had been introduced in Austria in 1907, and the political and economic dominance of the Magyar landowning aristocracy was seen as an anachronism which could not last. Preparation for the new order took the form of theoretical discussion rather than political action.[6] Formal education was provided by the Law faculty in the universities, which included political economy and constitutional history in its syllabus, while outside the curriculum Marxism and sociology were major interests.[7] Karl Mannheim (who came from the same background as Polanyi), discussing the influence of Marxism on German sociology in this period, has made some observations which seem relevant to the position of sociology as well as Marxism as non-academic subjects in Hungary.

> Marxian theory, like many other social theories, counted only as an 'opposition theory,' i.e., academicians did not concern themselves with this branch of knowledge. This had the advantage that many urgent problems of everyday life and of political tensions were given a sociological interpretation in this non-academic discipline; but it had the disadvantage that those theories were abused for propaganda purposes, and, since they were handled by laymen, an element of dilettantism inevitably crept into them.[8]

Interest in sociology was not solely inspired by Marxism. The economic 'take-off' which Marx had observed in England came later on the Continent, and thus problems of economic growth, in which the social consequences of industrialization predominated in Germany and the existence of large 'underdeveloped' agricultural areas in Eastern Europe, gave sociology at this time a position not unlike that of anthropology in the general culture of the intelligentsia in America, France, and England today. As the current interest in anthropology reflects Western society's attempt to come to a new

understanding with Africa and Asia, so sociology (with psychology)
served as a focus and common ground of discussion for those who
struggled to understand the crisis of European society between the
two world wars. 'It is precisely in the field of sociology that the
spiritual and cultural forces of post-war Germany sought to shape
themselves' (Mannheim, *loc. cit.*).

Sociologists' interest in Marxian theory had initially been concerned with the validity of the materialist analysis of capitalism, with
the empirical study of social classes, and with the development from
the theory of classes of the sociology of knowledge.[9] But the development of world-wide economic crisis and the example of a new type
of economy in Russia led to increased interest in Marx's analysis of
the weaknesses of the capitalist system, and in the possibility of a
socialist alternative. It was this which was to be the mainspring of
Polanyi's work on comparative economics. He contributed an article
on socialist accounting to the *Archiv für Sozialwissenschaft* in
1922,[10] in which he already voiced his belief in the social and moral
superiority of the centrally planned socialist economy, guided by
'social demand' rather than by the demands of individual consumers.
From 1924 to 1933 he worked for the Viennese weekly *Österreichische Volkswirt* as a leader-writer and commentator on international (especially English) politics and finance. The effect of these
years of closely following the spread of economic crisis and the rise
of Fascism can clearly be seen in *The Great Transformation*. But that
his economic interests were combined with a more general interest
in sociology, important for his later development, can be seen in
pieces such as 'Lancashire als Menschheitsfrage,'[11] an analysis of the
social and economic reasons for the superior efficiency of Japanese
cotton production; 'Wirtschaft v. Demokratie,'[12] a discussion of
the growing tendency for the political choice between right and left
to be seen in economic terms; or 'England für Budgetwahrheit,'
from which I quote a passage which gives a good example of Polanyi's
sociological bent:

Die parteipolitische Dramatisierung der Budgetdebatte dient in
England einem geistig-moralischen Zweck von höchster volks-
bildnerische Bedeutung. Was dem Unverständs als Schlagwort-
politik dünken mag, ist in Wahrheit ein Kampf um sachlich
gebundene Symbole, an denen sich das Verantwortungs-
bewusstsein eines ganzen Volkes schult. Die Einschätzung des

vernünftigerweise zu erwartenden Ueberschusses wird zum Massstab der Vorsicht und des Ernstes, mit der sich die Bevölkerung ihren Zukunftsaufgaben widmet, die Zustimmung oder die Ablehnung der vollen Arbeitslosenunterstützung wird zum Prüfstein der sozialen Gesinnung der Regierung. . . .[13]

Sir Karl Popper, in *The Open Society and its Enemies*, mentions a discussion on the methods of the social sciences with Polanyi during this period which is of some interest.

The theory that while the physical sciences are based on a methodological nominalism, the social sciences must adopt essentialist ('realistic') methods, has been made clear to me by K. Polanyi (in 1925); he pointed out, at that time, that a reform of the methodology of the social sciences might conceivably be achieved by abandoning this theory.

Popper adds: 'The *nominalist* attitude in sociology can be developed, I think, only as a technological theory of social *institutions*.'[14] (Methodological nominalism 'instead of aiming at finding out what a thing really is, and at defining its true nature [which is the aim of essentialism] . . . aims at describing how a thing behaves, and especially, whether there are any regularities in its behaviour.'[15] This record throws an interesting light on preoccupations which Polanyi came to express much later in *Trade and Market*. His concern there with the problem of defining 'the economy' is indeed a typically essentialist one; but his decision to concentrate on institutions and the operational analysis of patterns of economic behavior in 'applying the substantive approach . . . to a classification of empirical economies and . . . trade, money and market institutions'[16] is nominalist.

Process and institutions together form the economy. Some students stress the material resources and equipment – the ecology and technology – which make up the process; others, like myself, prefer to point to the institutions through which the economy is organized. Again, in inquiring into the institutions one can choose between values and motives on the one hand and physical operations on the other, either of which can be regarded as linking the social relations with the process. Perhaps because I happen to be more familiar with the institutional and operational aspects of man's livelihood, I prefer to deal with the economy primarily as a matter of organization, and to define organization in terms of the operations characteristic of the working of the institutions. . . .[17]

The distrust of theories about motives expressed here can again be linked with early discussions with Popper stressing that sociology must study institutions and not 'human nature'; 'social institutions . . . must have existed prior to what some people are pleased to call "human nature" and to human psychology.'[18]

Polanyi's thought is also clearly related to the main movement of this period in sociology, the exploration of the sociology of knowledge. His assertion that economic theory is valid only for the analysis of the society which produced it belongs, in this context, with Lukács's 'Der Funktionswechsel des historischen Materialismus' (Lukács, 1923, pp. 229–60), Eduard Heimann's article 'Sociological Preoccupations of Economic Theory' (Heimann, 1934), Adolf Löwe's lectures at the London School of Economics on *Economics and Sociology*, published the following year,[19] and Talcott Parsons's discussion of 'The Motivations of Economic Activities,' which appeared in 1940.[20] Pointless controversy has been generated by the treatment of Polanyi's views as an attack on the development economics of the 1960s, when they really belong to this totally different line of thought.

1933–47: England

Although *The Great Transformation* draws extensively on historical material collected in England, the effect of Polanyi's stay there and of English contacts on his thought is difficult to assess. He spent part of the period lecturing in the United States, and *The Great Transformation* was written at Bennington College, first published in New York (1944), and had a much greater success in America than in England. Yet he says in his introduction that the main thesis of the book was developed while lecturing for the W.E.A. in England in 1939–40; so the influence of the new English historical material (which might seem now of minor importance, since it played no part in the later development of his work) in the genesis of his theories should not be underrated. Polanyi had already been concerned with workers' education as part of the activities of the Galilei Circle in

Budapest; his admiration for English socialism, as well as his evident gift for teaching, must have made his lectures to English workers on the history of socialism in England a stimulating experience for him, as well as for his hearers.[21] And the political and economic preoccupations of his Austrian years were of course equally relevant in England. Concern with tracing the causes of Fascism was naturally especially prominent among refugee thinkers who were frequently asked for accounts of its development and felt it one of their main tasks to give the English public a clearer idea of what they were fighting against; and the main theme of *The Great Transformation*, the need for a planned socialist economy and the rejection of the argument that only a free market system could preserve liberal values, was an equally central topic of discussion.[22]

Polanyi's advocacy of economic planning as the cure for the ills of society was criticized by a reviewer for its impracticality,[23] and this again was characteristic of the period in which it was written. The economic crises of the pre-war period, the shock of the rise of Fascism and the Second World War, and the feeling that the war years represented an interlude of temporary expedients in government which when peace came would give way to an extensive reform and reconstruction of society, produced a strongly Utopian current of thought in all but the most steadfast minds; a Utopianism which took the form of visions of a morally regenerated society rather than concrete proposals for changes in the social system.[24] This concern with moral and religious issues can clearly be seen in the group of socialists and communists with whom Polanyi collaborated in writing *Christianity and the Social Revolution* (Polanyi, Lewis, and Kitchin, 1935) shortly after his arrival in England.

The combination of a defense of socialist economics with an explanation of the causes of Fascism and a history of the rise and fall of laissez-faire capitalism is a remarkably ambitious program, but characteristic of the preoccupations of the time. What is more surprising is that *The Great Transformation* should also have included a discussion of primitive economics containing suggestions for new lines of research which were still able to stimulate anthropologists many years later.

Despite the importance of Malinowski as a source for Polanyi's account of primitive trade, and his admiration for the work of Radcliffe-Brown (Polanyi's stress on the integration of primitive society, and disregard of the existence of competition and conflict, resembles the approach of the structural-functional school of British anthropology), this development of Polanyi's thought seems more closely related to the tradition of Bücher, Tönnies, Max Weber, Sombart, and, more immediately, Thurnwald, than to any contacts made in England.[25] In fact the strength of his approach was its methodological originality and wide range of comparisons in a period when anthropology and to some extent sociology, too, were dominated by concern with fieldwork, and the establishment of both subjects in the universities had narrowed the cultural background of their recruits, who no longer had the prior training in handling historical material which had formed the foundation for the comparative studies of men like Weber and Mauss.

Polanyi's interest in anthropological material was of course part of his Utopian outlook; the influence of primitivism and romanticism has often been strong in economic history, and this period would make an interesting study. The apparent failure of economists to control the crises of the inter-war years shook faith in economic theory and opened the field to eclectic searches in comparative economics for new doctrines.[26] The classical scholar Bernhard Laum,[27] for instance, moved from a study of the religious aspects of the economy in ancient Greece to an historical justification of the Nazi 'closed economy' (*Geschlossene Wirtschaft*, 1933) and a chair in economic history. The preface to Laum's later *Schenkende Wirtschaft* (1960), in which he recalls the impression made on him by the wholesale dumping and destruction of food in the 1930s, is a useful reminder that these irrational attempts to discover solutions to the economic crisis in the remote past corresponded to a situation in which the policy laid down by economic theory produced results which seemed to be in glaring contradiction with social rationality.

1947–64: America

Polanyi too became a professor of economic history, at Columbia University, in 1947. Here the contradiction between his socialism and his primitivism, which had made *The Great Transformation* a failure as a contribution to socialist economics, was resolved by a separation of the two. In economic history he turned soon from the history of capitalism to developing his ideas on 'the place occupied by economic life in society' through the study of non-market societies.[28] His concern with the problems of socialist economics reemerged only in his last years in his connection with the review *Co-Existence*, lectures in Hungary and Italy, and his influence on Paul Medow's work on the humanistic aspects of economic planning.[29]

Between 1943–4 and 1947–8, therefore, there seems to have been a distinct shift in Polanyi's balance of interests. The discussion of pre-market economies is the least developed section of the argument in *The Great Transformation*, and the one which attracted least attention from R. M. MacIver in his introduction to the book, from reviewers, and in the extensive and enthusiastic discussion of Allen M. Sievers (*Has Market Capitalism Collapsed? A Criticism of Karl Polanyi's New Economics*).[30] Yet by 1948 Polanyi had already formulated the program of research into the origin of economic institutions (later 'the economic aspects of institutional growth') which he worked on with a team of collaborators until the publication of *Trade and Market* in 1957.[31]

The change reflects the move to a country where anthropology had a much more important position than it had in pre-war Austria or wartime England; but it also reflects the move from a political world to an academic one.[32] The relevance of Polanyi's economic anthropology to the problems of linking underdeveloped areas to the market system has been discussed by his follower George Dalton,[33] but Polanyi himself did not in his publications of the American period develop the implications of his theories for America's post-war problems. In *Trade and Market* only one chapter, that on the Berbers of the Moroccan highlands, is devoted to a modern society; the rest of the material is drawn from ancient Mesopotamia and Greece, the Aztec and Maya civilizations, eighteenth-century Dahomey, and pre-imperial India.

Polanyi's own work was concentrated on Mesopotamia, Greece, and Dahomey. He contributed chapters on Mesopotamia and Greece, as well as theoretical discussions, to *Trade and Market*. In the Oriental Institute symposium *City Invincible* (Kraeling and Adams, 1960) he discussed Bronze-age methods of accounting in Mycenae and Alalakh (Syria), and Greek markets,[34] and he developed his ideas on the 'port of trade' in an article 'Ports of Trade in Early Societies' in the *Journal of Economic History* in 1963. He also analyzed material on the history of Dahomey which he had been collecting from 1949 in the posthumously published *Dahomey and the Slave Trade* (Polanyi, 1966).[35] Further discussions of his theoretical standpoint also appear in this work, as well as in the article 'Anthropology and Economic Theory' and in the paper 'The Semantics of Money Uses.'[36]

Before discussing systematically the different lines along which Polanyi's researches developed in his American years and assessing the value of his work and the validity of the criticisms brought against it, it may be useful to give a brief survey of related work carried on under Polanyi's influence, and of the main lines of the controversies he and his followers have aroused.

Polanyi's most enthusiastic disciples are George Dalton and Paul Bohannan. Dalton wrote his Ph.D. thesis on 'Robert Owen and Karl Polanyi as Socio-Economic Critics and Reformers of Industrial Capitalism,' and has expounded Polanyi's theoretical position in a number of articles; he contributed to the debate on the concept of surplus, and has followed Polanyi's lead in research on markets and primitive money.[37] Dalton and Bohannan jointly edited a volume, *Markets in Africa* (1962), which many would regard as the most important product of the Polanyi school.

Bohannan, following the lead of his Oxford teacher Franz Steiner, had been working independently on lines similar to Polanyi's in his study of exchange among the Tiv of central Nigeria.[38] Polanyi's influence is acknowledged in his 1959 article, 'The Impact of Money on an African Subsistence Economy.'[39] He is largely responsible for developing the important conception of independent 'spheres of exchange' in primitive economies: goods with high prestige value (e.g. cattle, slaves) move in a separate sphere of circulation and are not exchanged, except in emergency conditions, for commodities from a sphere with low prestige value, such as food. Although closely associated with both Polanyi and Dalton, he has not taken part in the controversy over Polanyi's views on the irrelevance of economic theory to economic anthropology, which was largely aroused by Dalton's articles in the *American Anthropologist*.

Marshall D. Sahlins, who was at Columbia University during Polanyi's time there, has not associated himself so closely with Polanyi's theoretical position, but has gone further than any other anthropologist in attempting to use and develop Polanyi's typology of economic patterns of organization. His use of the concepts of reciprocity and redistribution in the articles 'On the Sociology of Primitive Exchange' and 'Exchange-Value and the Diplomacy of

Primitive Trade'[40] will be more fully discussed below. Other anthropologists in the United States who have shown interest in parts of
Polanyi's work are Manning Nash and Cyril S. Belshaw.[41] Reactions
from anthropologists in Britain are now conveniently collected in
Themes in Economic Anthropology (Firth, 1967). Polanyi's institutional and operational approach is on the whole found congenial,
but British anthropologists feel that they are, and should be, drawing
nearer to economists in their interests and methods. In France,
Polanyi's views have been extensively discussed by Maurice Godelier,
Rationalité et irrationalité en économie (1966),[42] and have influenced
the work of Claude Meillassoux on African markets and on the
relation of primitive economies to social structure.[43] Discussions of
economic anthropology in France are complicated by the desire to
conform to structuralist method and Marxist theory, without clear
guidance from either Lévi-Strauss or Marx.

Among sociologists, Neil J. Smelser discussed Polanyi's theories
in an important review of *Trade and Market*,[44] and the modified
version of Polanyi's typology of institutions which he put forward
(reciprocity, redistribution, mobilization, market) was used by S. N.
Eisenstadt in *The Political Systems of Empires* (1963), and by Manning Nash, 'The Organization of Economic Life' (Nash, 1964).
Wilbert E. Moore and Bert F. Hoselitz have also been influenced to
some extent by Polanyi in their work on economic sociology.[45]
Polanyi's emphasis on the limitations of economic theory for the
analysis of the economy in its social context, which has so disturbed
anthropologists, is not considered either novel or controversial by
sociologists. The criticism of Parsons's and Smelser's *Economy and
Society* (1956) for interpreting all relations between parts of the
social system in economic terms (input and output, etc.), put forward
in *Trade and Market*, has not provoked any comment; this is perhaps
a pity, since the role of economic analogies in social theory, in
particular the extensive use of the concept of 'equilibrium,' needs
critical examination.

Trade and Market attracted attention from students of Indian
history through Walter C. Neale's chapter 'Reciprocity and Redistribution in the Indian Village.' Neale continued his study of the
non-market character of the economy in pre-imperial India in
Economic Change in Rural India (1962). The 'port of trade' has been
discussed in relation to Indian material by Anthony Leeds, who
took part in Polanyi's Columbia research project: and Indian

markets, again with reference to the Polanyi school, by D. P. Sinha.[46]

Polanyi's impact on the study of the economic history of the ancient world will probably, in the long term, turn out to be more significant than his influence in economic anthropology. Harry W. Pearson has given a clear account in *Trade and Market* of the stalemate reached in the long-standing debate between 'modernists' and 'primitivists' over the character of the economic system of the classical world.[47] The imprecision of the terms in which the argument was conducted is well illustrated by Rostovtzeff's much quoted pronouncement that 'by the Hellenistic period the economy of the ancient world was only quantitatively, not qualitatively different from that of modern times.'[48] In such an atmosphere Polanyi's suggestion that the question to be asked was not 'What type of economy?' but 'What kind of institutions, and how did they work?' brought a real breath of new life.

Polanyi's ideas have been transmitted through two ancient historians who took part in the Columbia research project, Moses Finley in Greek history and A. L. Oppenheim in Assyriology. Both were critical in their reception of Polanyi's interpretations: Finley declined to contribute to *Trade and Market*, and Oppenheim's chapter presents a rather different view of Mesopotamian society from Polanyi's. Nevertheless, the impact of Polanyi's ideas can clearly be seen in their work and, through their influence, in current orientations in the study of ancient economic history. Without their personal contact with Polanyi and interest in his views, it is likely that *Trade and Market* would have passed almost unnoticed by ancient historians.[49]

Finley has been even more insistent than Polanyi on the nonmarket features of the Greek economy. Whereas Polanyi concentrated on the difference between Greek markets and modern ones, Finley stresses the minor importance of markets in the total pattern of production and economic transactions. Before joining Polanyi's Columbia research group he had already demonstrated by an analysis of mortgage documents that land in classical Athens, though freely alienable, belonged to a 'prestige sphere' and not to the sphere of profit-making transactions in the market, and he has for many years studied the social, psychological, and economic implications of slavery; both these lines of research emphasize for the ancient world the distinction which Polanyi made in his survey of European economic history in *The Great Transformation*, and which was more clearly formulated later by Bohannan and Dalton in *Markets in Africa*, between the market for commodities and the market for the main factors of production, land and labour.[50] In closer association with the ideas of Polanyi, Finley has also developed the theme of reciprocity in the early economy of Greece in his study of Homeric society, *The World of Odysseus* (1954),[51] and has polemicized vigorously against the mistaken application of modern economic theory to ancient conditions.[52] Recently he has named administered trade, the 'port of trade,' and market regulations in a list of suggestions for research put forward at the second international conference on economic history in 1962. Students under his supervision have worked on the economics of public building in Greece, and on economic relations between Greece and Egypt and the organization of Naucratis as a 'port of trade.'[53]

Polanyi's main effect on Oppenheim and other orientalists, on the contrary, has been to stimulate new research governed by the attempt to prove him wrong. He claimed to have discovered, apart from the generally 'redistributive' nature of the economy (which was nothing new), a total absence of markets, and evidence for exchange at set equivalencies and for administered, risk-free, long-distance trade conducted by royal officials (the *tamkāru*) at prices fixed by treaty. Oppenheim's general approach to his subject agrees with Polanyi's – he sees it as the task of the orientalist to draw on anthropology for new methods of interpretation and safeguards against the misuse of modern concepts. But he seems to feel, in common with other orientalists,[54] that although Polanyi's criticisms of the uncritical assumptions of the existence of market conditions were justified, he exaggerated the role of redistribution and of the palace and temple in the economic organization of ancient Mesopotamia. Oppenheim in *Trade and Market* denied that any period or area attested in cuneiform documents could be fully or adequately characterized as redistributive: 'the entire development of Mesopotamian economy is marked by continuous shifts in emphasis which bring now one and now another form of economic integration to the foreground without the others completely disappearing at any time' (Oppenheim, 1957, p. 29). In reaction against Polanyi's overemphasis on the palace system, the best documented and most comprehensible aspect of the Mesopotamian economy, Oppenheim has tended to concentrate his own researches on the non-redistributive elements in the economic life of cities, and on the private activities of merchants as opposed to the 'administered trade' emphasized by Polanyi.[55] A few references to market prices have been pointed out,[56] but the question of markets has not been fully discussed; and there has been no serious discussion of Polanyi's theories on the economic and political characteristics of the 'port of trade.' The results of the research of R. G. Sweet on 'Moneys and Money Uses in the Old Babylonian Period,' a study under Polanyi's influence, supervised by Oppenheim,[57] have not yet appeared. Polanyi's influence in this field could perhaps fairly be summed up by saying that although he may have generalized too hastily, he has made orientalists look at their material with a sharper eye for the details of institutional and operational problems and with fewer preconceived ideas.

I shall only indicate briefly here the main directions of criticism and opposition to Polanyi's views, which will be discussed more fully in the second part of this paper. Dispute has mainly centered round the question of the applicability of modern economic theory to non-market economies.[58] I hope that the biographical details given above may help to suggest that if Polanyi's opinions on this subject are seen in their historical context, they do not appear so perverse as some participants in the controversy have thought them. A more interesting discussion, which is still in its early stages, is arising from the divergence between Polanyi's approach to primitive economics and Marxist theory (cf. below, pp. 63f.). Starting from the attack in *Trade and Market* on the notions of 'scarcity' and 'economic surplus' as existing independently of cultural definition, this debate is now widening to include the general orientation of Polanyi's economic analysis, based on patterns of allocation instead of relations of production. The idea was not new that in societies with primitive techniques of production, and limited facilities for transport, exchange, and storage, disbursal of wealth may be more significant than accumulation, and economic competition may be directed to control over persons rather than over land, capital, and equipment;[59] but Polanyi has gone further than any of his predecessors toward developing a theory of comparative economics, and in particular the relation of economic institutions to social structure, centered on allocation. In so doing, he presented the question of the relevance of Marxist theory to primitive economic systems in a sharper form.

In general, the reaction to Polanyi's work has been to follow up his initiative in research into specific institutions – markets, money, and so forth – with little criticism of his own views on these topics, and to attack his general theoretical position often in a rather superficial manner, without touching the fundamental questions of the method needed for the comparative study of economic institutions in their social context. Little can be said about the latter here. But even in his discussion of individual forms of economic organization, such as the market or the port of trade, Polanyi raised wide issues which are worth more examination than they have so far received. In the second part of this article I shall discuss Polanyi's ideas in three groups: (1) the use in non-market economies of forms of economic organization typically associated with the modern market system, (2) economic theory, especially the concepts of surplus and scarcity, and (3) Polanyi's four categories of institutional patterning of the economy: reciprocity, redistribution, householding, and (market) exchange.

II

1 *Money, markets, and trade*

It was an important part of Polanyi's campaign against the misapplication of modern economic theory to show that the presence of money, markets, or other economic institutions with the function of regulating trade or organizing complex movements of goods, could find a place in non-market economies as well as in a market system of the modern type.[60]

Money and accounting devices. Polanyi discussed money in his article 'The Semantics of Money Uses' (1957b) and in the final chapter of *Dahomey and the Slave Trade.* The former article remained almost entirely unknown until the publication of his *Essays* (Polanyi, 1968). In it Polanyi argued that the three uses of money – as a medium of exchange, as a standard of value, and as a means of payment – are not necessarily interconnected. They may arise independently, and different currencies may be used for the different purposes. In particular it is a grave mistake, a misunderstanding arising from the modern experience and theory of money, to assume that the exchange use of money is historically prior to its other uses. This point has been made independently by others;[61] but Polanyi further insisted

that it is possible not only for money to be introduced in societies
where it has no exchange use, or an exchange use only within a
limited sphere,[62] but also for currencies and accounting devices of a
considerable elaboration to develop, without implying any tendency
in the societies concerned to move toward a market economy of the
modern type. This had indeed happened in the 'redistributive
economies of ancient Mesopotamia and the kingdom of Dahomey.
In his article for the symposium *City Invincible* Polanyi argued that
in the ancient Near East barley was used in payments, and silver as a
money of account, without either developing into an exchange
currency;[63] and he drew attention to the method of 'staple accounting' at Mycenae, by which taxes were assessed in units of staple goods
(corn, wool, oil, etc.) levied on a set measure of land, without the
need for a common money of account. In *Dahomey and the Slave
Trade* he asserted that the cowrie currency of Dahomey, with its
elaborate series of strings of shells forming different 'denominations,'
was the creation of the state. The formation of the currency system
and the setting of fixed equivalencies went together, and both were
closely connected with the organization of tax collection and of
payments (rations) to soldiers and other state employees.

Cowrie money in Dahomey was also obligatory in the local food
markets, and legend ascribed the creation of both money and markets
to the same king. 'Exchange [as a use of money] develops not from
random barter acts of individuals but in connection with organized
external trade and internal markets' (Polanyi, 1968, p. 195; 1957b).
A thorough analysis of the role of the state in the development of
money and markets in Dahomey would require a detailed comparison with the economic institutions of other West African societies.
Polanyi's treatment is impressionistic, but his insights are worth
pursuing. The institutional history of cowrie money and the relation
between markets, money uses, and the economic functions of the
state all need further research. (One may note in comparison that in
medieval Europe the right to hold markets and to coin money were
often granted together.)

Markets. Given Polanyi's deep-rooted opposition to the old idea
that man has 'an innate tendency to truck, barter and exchange one
thing for another,' the existence of markets in comparatively
primitive economies was bound to be a problem to him. In *The
Great Transformation* he was more concerned with showing that
local markets were unimportant in the rise of capitalism than with

the working of the primitive market as such; he dismissed markets in pre-industrial societies as subsidiary features of the economy, isolated from each other and hemmed in by tabus and restrictions, so that their influence could not spread. Following Bücher and Thurnwald he classified the ancient Greek economy as a house-holding system, although he sketched the idea, developed further in *Trade and Market*, that Aristotle's distinction between *oikonomia* and *chrēmatistikē* (production for use and production for gain) was a recognition of the contrast between the embedded economy and the disembedded market system, and he had some hesitation about the importance of markets and trade in the classical world – Aristotle

> failed to see how impracticable it was to ignore the existence of markets at a time when Greek economy had made itself dependent upon wholesale trading and loaned capital. For this was the century when Delos and Rhodes were developing into emporia of freight-insurance, sea-loans, and giro-banking, compared with which the Western Europe of a thousand years later was the very picture of primitivity.[64]

There is clearly a problem here, which could not be resolved merely by remarking that 'the Greco–Roman period . . . was characterised by the grand scale on which redistribution of grain was practised by the Roman administration in an otherwise householding economy.'

Markets are discussed in *Trade and Market* in Francisco Benet's chapter 'Explosive Markets: the Berber Highlands'[65] as well as in Polanyi's 'Aristotle Discovers the Economy.' The markets of the highland Berber of the Atlas were price-making markets, but rigidly limited in their sphere of influence. All but the smallest debts had to be settled by the close of the day's trading, and the groups who met under the protection of the 'peace of the market' were frequently at feud, and had little contact outside these meetings. Economic relations within the group (village or canton) were based on re-ciprocity.[66] As an institution serving predominantly to integrate exchange between members of different groups, this type of market has some features in common with the port of trade, to which we shall return later. Benet's account emphasizes the contradiction between reciprocity and market exchange, which is resolved by strict separation of the physical locations – village and market – in which the two patterns of behavior are applicable. If this were not the case 'these contraries would come to a head-on collision.' This point

again is significant for Polanyi's view of the port of trade as a mechanism for limiting contact between incompatible economic systems.
Benet also brings out the 'disembedded' nature of transactions in
the market: 'markets are here external places for exchanges between
individuals who are shedding the corporate personality of which
they were a part within township and village' (Benet, 1957, pp.
212–13).

Both these themes recur in Polanyi's discussion of classical Athens
in *Trade and Market*. The contradiction between reciprocity and
market exchange is reflected in Aristotle's contrast between natural
and unnatural exchange. Natural exchange is an arrangement for
sharing (*metadosis*) between producers, while the activity of the professional trade or shopkeeper, who does not produce, is unnatural.
His way of life, being directed to the acquisition of wealth (*chrēmatistikē*) instead of the satisfaction of concrete household needs and
the maintenance of neighborly relations, foreshadows the disembedding of the economy.[67] In Polanyi's view this tendency toward
the disembedding of the economy was not fully realized in classical
Greece because there were few markets outside large towns, overseas
trade and market were kept separate, trade prices were regulated by
treaty, and market prices were set by authority or at least stabilized
by pressure to adhere to the norm of the 'just price.'[68] However, in
Aristotle's time there was a significant increase in attempts to make
profits on price fluctuations.

The sharp eye of the theoretician had discerned the links between
the petty tricks of the huckster in the *agora* and novel kinds of
trading profits that were the talk of the day. But the gadget that
established their kinship – the supply-demand-price mechanism –
escaped Aristotle. The distribution of food in the market allowed
as yet scant room to the play of that mechanism; and long-distance
trade was directed not by individual competition but by institutional factors. Nor were either local markets or long-distance
trade conspicuous for the fluctuation of prices. Not before the
third century B.C. was the working of a supply-demand-price
mechanism in international trade noticeable. This happened in
regard to grain, and later, to slaves, in the open port of Delos. The
Athenian *agora* preceded, therefore, by some two centuries the
setting up of a market in the Aegean which could be said to embody
a market mechanism. Aristotle, writing in the second half of this

period, recognized the early instances of gain made on price differentials for the symptomatic development in the organisation of trade which they actually were.[69]

Polanyi did not discuss the question of restrictions surrounding the market in this section of *Trade and Market*, but he made it the focal point of his treatment of classical Athens in *City Invincible*, where he argued that the Greek *agora* was not 'the germ of an institution capable of linking up with similar entities to form a market system of limitless scope,' but was strictly limited by the laws of the city it served and the refusal of the Greek cities to relax their discrimination between citizen and non-citizen. But in the discussion which followed, J. A. O. Larsen showed that Polanyi's view of the control exercised over the market was greatly exaggerated; foreigners were not barred from selling in the Athenian *agora*, and there is little evidence of price control.[70]

Although Polanyi's emphasis on price control was important in pointing out a topic which had hardly been touched by research, he was probably wrong in regarding fixed prices as a major difference between primitive and modern markets. His claim that where prices are fixed exchange is integrated by the price-fixing authority and not by the market mechanism seems to hint at an analogy between the fixed prices in primitive markets and the planned economy of the modern socialist state[71]; but this analogy cannot be maintained. The major distinction between the modern economy (capitalist or socialist) and that of earlier or less developed societies is that exchange prices in the latter, whether fixed or bargained, have little connection with production decisions. Polanyi himself made a 'modernist' error in supposing that the process by which prices are decided is in all markets, and in all societies, related to the integration of 'the economy' as a whole. Bohannan and Dalton showed in their introduction to *Markets in Africa* (1962) that the main distinction between the peripheral markets of the primitive economy and the modern market system is that prices in peripheral markets have little or no feedback effect on production decisions. The peripheral market is isolated from other markets by poor communications, and insulated from affecting production decisions by an agricultural context in which the bulk of the harvest is consumed by the producer, by reluctance to depart from traditional patterns of production and by the fact that land and labor are not transacted in the market.

Limited storage facilities as well as transport difficulties restrict the trader's opportunities of profiting from price fluctuations.[72] Whether prices in peripheral markets are fixed by authority, held level by just price norms, or freely bargained does not in such conditions much affect their inefficacy in altering the flow of supply.

Polanyi, however, held also that fixed prices were essentially different from bargained ones in that the latter involve an inescapable element of antagonism.

> No community intent on protecting the fount of solidarity between its members can allow latent hostility to develop around a matter as vital to animal existence, and, therefore, capable of arousing as tense anxieties as food. Hence the universal banning of transactions of a gainful nature in regard to food and foodstuffs in primitive and archaic society. The very widely spread ban on higgling-haggling over victuals automatically removes price-making markets from the realm of early institutions.[73]

This is a question which would deserve more research, and suggests that the work which has recently been done on primitive and peasant markets by social anthropologists[74] might usefully be supplemented by a more psychological or cultural-anthropological study of attitudes toward market transactions and of the relation of haggling to other competitive or agonistic culture traits.[75] Considerable progress has been made in the last few years in studying markets, but much work remains to be done on fixed prices, just price norms, sellers' price-setting decisions in price-making peripheral markets, devices for control in situations of scarcity,[76] and the like. The antithesis between 'fixed prices' and haggling is in any case illegitimate, since it ignores the common case in which the seller sets a price in accordance with his assessment of the conditions in the market, but does not bargain individually with customers. A full discussion of the subject should take into account prices for services as well as for goods sold in the market; indeed selling in the market may in many societies be regarded more as the provision of a service than as an entrepreneurial activity.[77] This is an obvious case for asking whether modern economic categories are applicable to all cultures.

If we leave aside for the moment the monopolistic price-fixing of what Polanyi called 'administered trade,' and consider only internal markets, we find that fixed prices may be fixed either by group action among sellers or by the market authority in consultation with sellers. They may be fixed either absolutely or relatively; in classical Athens the price of flour and of bread was fixed by law in relation to that of corn, but the latter was not fixed.[78] The fixed prices of West African markets are fixed by the associations of sellers of each article at each market; the fixing has no apparent connection with keeping prices stable in the long run, but only ensures that sellers do not undercut each other.[79] In T'ang China prices were fixed by market officials, in consultation with traders' associations, for ten-day periods; detailed lists of prices for high, medium, and low qualities of each article were published. These prices formed the basis for legal assessments of damages, rates at which the government purchased goods, tax equivalencies, etc., as well as introducing order into the market. (Chinese mandarins shared Polanyi's low opinion of markets.) The government would on occasion throw some of its own stocks of grain or other goods on to the market to bring prices down – which shows that market prices, although 'fixed,' were regarded as indicating the state of supply, and that there was no question of regulating production by fixing prices in the market.[80] The Athenian state had no stocks of its own for such an operation; but if the price of corn rose too steeply, a relief fund would be opened and the money subscribed would be used to purchase corn at the current market price and resell it at the 'normal' price.[81]

Thus although the Chinese material reveals a feeling that markets are disorderly places which must be strictly policed and will be more orderly if bargaining is eliminated, and the West African situation perhaps reflects the *sellers'* fear of getting the worst of it in haggling,[82] fear of aggressive and anti-social behavior is clearly not the only factor involved in price-fixing. Long-term fixing seems to be unusual, although in South Dahomey the women's 'rings' are counterbalanced by a male association which has to give formal consent before any major change can be made in the amount of goods sold for a particular price.[83] These changes are regularly made with the seasons, and it is significant that price alterations are expressed as changes in volume rather than changes in price. There is ample evidence that minor price fluctuations in peripheral markets often take this form. Extension of credit is another way of introducing more flexibility into transactions at a 'fixed' price; both quantity variation and credit are important ways of favoring regular customers and fulfilling 'reciprocal' obligations while still nominally adhering to the market principle of the same terms for all comers.[84]

Social sanctions in enforcing the 'just price' are probably more important than formal price-fixing in stabilizing prices. Like the fixed price, the just price is a market price – the normal market price for the place and the season, *secundum forum commune* as the medieval theologians said – the price which gives the trader a fair return on his costs but protects the customer from fraud, greed, or monopoly.[85] In markets where higher prices will not call forth increases in supply, some mechanism to prevent traders exploiting situations of scarcity or monopoly is essential. It was not an increase in profit-making on differences in price between different markets which worried Aristotle, but the exploitation of scarcity. In the Athenian case cited above, the merchants' prices need not be regarded as unjust (though accusations of infringing market regulations were likely to be frequent in times of corn shortage), but the high prices are contrasted with the *normal* price;[86] popular pressure forces the state to take action, but not against the trader, who still receives his full price. Nevertheless, the fact that sanctions can be exercised against sellers who charge an 'unjust' price puts pressure on them to keep prices level as far as they can. But with the just price the emphasis is not on the hostility aroused in bargaining, but on preventing the exploiting of the customer by the seller. The conception of the just price is closely linked with the publicity, supervision, standard weights and measures, and administration of justice provided by the market. The just price does not vary with the status and relationship of buyer and seller, and the same is true of the law of the market, where the market has its own machinery for settling disputes.[87] Thus, although the just price may be seen as society's reaction against allowing free play to the forces of the market, or at least to the acquisitive motives of the trader, it can also be seen as an important step on the path from *Gemeinschaft* to *Gesellschaft*. It seems possible that the medieval serf or Greek freedman would have regarded bargaining in the market as a welcome liberation from the disabilities of his status rather than a threat to social harmony.

A further line of research into methods and effects of price control might lead one to enquire how far set equivalencies in societies without markets (in reciprocal exchange, ceremonial payments, etc.) are associated either with flexibility in the length of time allowed before the return payment must be made, or with exchanges and payments which only take place at certain seasons of the year.[88] Is a fluctuating price system a more efficient way of organizing all-the-year-round exchange? Following Polanyi's lead in his paper 'The Semantics of Money Uses,' one must also distinguish carefully between price-fixing in exchange and in *payments* (fines, religious dues, taxes, etc.). The question of treaty prices in 'administered trade' also needs further enquiry. Little evidence so far has been collected about treaty prices and the procedure for setting and adjusting them, and one would like to know how far the rulers who set the prices also controlled production or supply of the goods concerned. This problem, however, like that of the legal and religious restrictions surrounding the market, and of the separation of market transactions from reciprocal or other contexts, requires that the port of trade as well as the market should be brought into the discussion.

Ports of trade. The port of trade is Polanyi's name for a settlement which acts as a control point in trade between two cultures with differently patterned economic institutions – typically, between a market and a non-market economy, or rather between a non-market society and professional traders, who may belong to the market pattern even if the society from which they come, as a whole, does not.[89] The port of trade may be independent of both societies involved in the exchange, as in the case of the Phoenician ports of antiquity which, Polanyi argues, were not incorporated into the empires of the great powers of the hinterland because they recognized the 'cultural perils' of too close a contact with trade (Polanyi, 1957a, p. 60); it may be controlled by the trading power, as in the case of the Assyrian trading colonies in Asia Minor in the second millennium B.C., some of the Aztec ports of trade, and many European colonies later;[90] or it may be controlled by the land power, as in the relation between Dahomey and Whydah discussed by Rosemary Arnold in *Trade and Market* and by Polanyi in *Dahomey and the Slave Trade*, or between the Indian ports and inland capitals described by Leeds.[91] The last type was the one which most interested Polanyi. He saw the port of trade controlled by a non-market power as a device which shielded the controlling state from influences which would otherwise have disrupted its economy and society.

Trade was here treaty-based, administered, as a rule, by special organs of the native authorities, competition was excluded, prices were arranged over long terms. Ports of trade usually developed in politically weak spots, such as small kingdoms near the coast, or chieftains' confederacies, since, under archaic conditions, strangers shunned territories that were incorporated in military empires. To the hinterland empires the 'ports' served as a 'bread basket,' that is, a source of supply. Even powerful rulers were wary of laying their hands on the 'port' lest foreign traders and strangers shy off and trade suddenly dry up. Independent trade areas of this kind, harboring numbers of warehouses, storing the goods of distant peoples, while the local population of the area itself did not engage in trading expeditions, have been found to exist in widely different parts of the globe.[92]

The port of trade offers military security to the inland power; civil protection to the foreign trader; facilities of anchorage, debarkation and storage; the benefit of judicial authorities; agreement on the goods to be traded.[93]

The essential features of the port of trade are that it stands as a 'buffer,' both politically and economically, between the trader and the hinterland whose products he wishes to buy; that trade is strictly supervised and confined to official channels (traders' movements are also frequently supervised and restricted); and that in consequence local market exchange and the long-distance trade are kept completely separate.

Polanyi here has certainly pointed to some important features of 'archaic' trade, but his explanation of them is not entirely convincing. Robert B. Revere's discussion in *Trade and Market* of the port of trade as a no-man's-land or buffer state,[94] though it started from a suggestion by Polanyi that he should study 'Archaic Thalassophobia,' fails to take into account two obvious features of Bronze-age civilization in the Mediterranean: that sea-power was of no military importance,[95] and conversely that a fortified coastal city was almost impregnable. It was difficult to take a fortified city except by siege, and a coastal city could not be cut off from all sources of supply;[96] and since coastal cities were of little strategic importance to great land powers like the Assyrians or the Hittites, there was no pressing need to subdue them. Tribute from coastal cities was of course welcome, and could often be exacted by threats of force, but the fruits of trade were still of minor importance compared with grain and manpower. Where ports of trade were controlled by the inland power, they remained peripheral because trade was peripheral; the inland capital continued to be the central focus of political and military preoccupations and power.

It seems doubtful, therefore, whether neutrality or distance from the main centers of power is an essential aspect of the economic functioning of the port of trade. It is true, however, that even if not strictly neutral, it has an administration of its own which differs in some respects from that of the hinterland. In this it resembles many markets and especially fairs, which share features both with the market and with the port of trade.[97] Revere suggests that the port of trade originated in the neutral meeting place where silent trade or simple forms of barter were carried on; it used to be commonly assumed that markets, too, began as neutral meeting places outside city walls, and sometimes even on frontiers.[98] This need not be true of all markets,[99] but it is undoubtedly true of many; and in studying restrictions, tabus, and special legal institutions associated with markets it is essential to distinguish inter-state markets from those which predominantly serve only a single community. Polanyi's insistence on the restrictions surrounding markets and ports of trade was a valuable insight, but many aspects of the problem have to be studied before we can see how far these restrictions reflect a fear of, or instinctive reaction against, the beginnings of a disembedded economy.

In the first place, inter-state markets and ports of trade are areas where men from different communities meet. This is likely to create tensions (cf. the Berber markets described in *Trade and Market*), and it obviously creates legal problems. A judicial authority which all will accept, and which will settle disputes on the spot, is a necessity. In the port of trade, restriction on foreigners' movements may be required to prevent them from outraging local custom, from being mobbed,[100] or from acting as spies. Since the port or market authority is responsible for disputes arising from traders' transactions, it may, not unreasonably, require them to make these in an approved place and form.[101] A further reason for supervision is that taxes and dues are commonly collected in markets and on long-distance trade. None of these factors – and together they account for many features of the market and port of trade – is connected with the question of the effects on local economic institutions of allowing unrestrained movement to traders and their goods.

I have discussed the port of trade and the market together because, although Polanyi stresses their separation, he applies to both the same argument that these specialized institutions devoted to exchange are not necessarily to be understood as features or harbingers of a modern market economy, but may be surrounded by restrictions which insulate the institutions of a non-market economy from their influence. In the case of the markets, recent studies of peasant economies suggest that restrictions surrounding markets are not an important cause of their failure to expand; the determining factors are transport and communications, and opportunities for wage labor and cash cropping. The feeling of conflict between reciprocal obligations and market trade can be mitigated by compromise.

The port of trade, as a mechanism for transferring goods from one system to another, has positive qualities as well as the more negative function of limiting contacts. It is typically associated with re-distributive systems, and typically involves the collection of commodities which lend themselves to political control (corn, slaves, precious metals), and the distribution of luxury goods to a limited privileged class. Political power is more effective in collecting these goods than market institutions would be. Most of the corn trade in the ancient world was based on the collection of corn as tax or tribute;[102] ancient markets were incapable of the task of attracting corn from the peasant in sufficient quantity to supply the great cities. Polanyi tends to present the port of trade as a restriction on the trader's activities, but it was equally a means of overcoming the formidable difficulties he would have faced had he tried to deal directly with producers.

The separation of trade and markets requires more detailed consideration than Polanyi gave it. His point that a lively trade could be carried on in a place which had no markets, and that where both existed they might be kept entirely separated, was an important warning against misunderstanding early economic institutions, but a distinction must be made between keeping the trader out of the local market, as a foreigner who can only be dealt with by skilled specialists or who needs protection, and keeping his goods out of the market because they belong to a prestige sphere.[103]

There is also a danger in Polanyi's discussions of 'administered trade' and of the role of 'officials' in a redistributive economy, that anachronistic concepts drawn from modern bureaucratic systems may be taking the place of those earlier borrowed from the modern market economy. We badly need a study of the Mesopotamian concept of an 'official' and the behavior expected from him; but it seems unlikely that the *tamkarum* or other 'officials' in Kultepe-Kanis, the Assyrian trading settlement in Cappadocia, could have been expected to act solely as 'officials' in the sense in which the term is understood in the modern developed bureaucracy. Their position would require them to enter into contact with local rulers or those who controlled the commodities with which trade was concerned; these contacts would inevitably have some of the characteristics of a 'total' social relationship, which would surely include transfers of material goods. The idea that the *tamkarum* must be *either* an official *or* a private entrepreneur seems to me anachronistic.

In introducing the concept of the port of trade, Polanyi pointed to an institutional complex of great interest, not only for economic history but for the study of culture contacts in general.[104] His own account of the system of 'sortings' and the 'ounce trade' devised by European traders at Whydah to reconcile their own monetized, profit-making trade with the different requirements of Dahomean trade in staples bartered at traditional rates[105] is a fascinating discovery and a model for future studies of early economic culture contacts – a neglected field. As with many of his ideas, his presentation of the port of trade is built up impressionistically from an assortment of significant features whose associations and inter-relations need further study. His definitions are not to be treated as final, but as starting points for further research. Like all those who cover a wide range of materials in comparative studies, his assertions are frequently inadequately supported if not demonstrably wrong – I have indicated some of the points which I find questionable – but the problems he raises are not trivial.

2 *Economic theory*

The part of Polanyi's theory which has attracted most criticism is his contention that modern economic theory cannot be used to analyze the working of primitive economies, and, closely related to this, the argument that 'economy' has two meanings, the formal and the substantive meaning, which only coincide in the modern market economy. Hence the comparative study of economic systems must start from the substantive meaning of 'economy' and not from the formal meaning. In the substantive sense, according to Polanyi, the economy is

an instituted process of interaction between man and his environment which results in a continuous supply of want-satisfying material means. Want-satisfaction is 'material' if it involves the use of material means to satisfy ends; in the case of a definite type of physiological wants, such as food or shelter, this includes the use of so-called services only.

The formal definition of the economy is 'the allocation of scarce means to alternative ends.'[106] Polanyi's distinction is closely related to Max Weber's distinctions between 'economic action' and 'rational economic action,' and between substantive and formal rationality.[107]

The disagreement between Polanyi and his critics on both these points is mainly one of emphasis. Polanyi emphasized the dangers of unconscious misapplication of modern economic concepts to primitive and archaic societies, and was interested in the study of the institutions which serve in non-market economies to produce the 'continuous supply of want-satisfying material means.' Raymond Firth, who is generally held up as the champion of the opposite view,[108] emphasizes the danger that anthropologists may miss significant facts, or fail to ask questions, which familiarity with economic theory might have brought to their attention, and he is interested in the study of processes of choice and decision-making in primitive economies. The two approaches have been profitably combined in recent studies of peasant markets. Increasing interest in social factors among economists and increasing sophistication in handling economic concepts among anthropologists are likely to make Polanyi's warnings seem less and less relevant.[109] Nevertheless there remains a marked divergence of method between Firth and Polanyi in that Firth attaches a positive value to the use of concepts drawn from economic theory in anthropology – he recently edited a volume entitled *Capital, Saving and Credit in Peasant Societies*[110] – whereas Polanyi, I think, would have regarded the use of such terms both metaphorical and dangerous. Firth, naturally, is aware of the dangers; but the question whether such terms, applied to a primitive or peasant society, have the same meaning as they do in the context of the modern economy, or function only as illuminating metaphors, is a difficult one. I shall return to it later.[111]

It is perhaps worth noting that Polanyi's 'essentialist' problem of definitions is not confined to economics. There are comparable difficulties in comparing 'embedded' and 'disembedded' art,[112] and a debate more closely connected with our present concerns exists in the study of primitive law, where Max Gluckman has recently

attacked Bohannan's Polanyist emphasis on the dangers of transferring concepts from Roman law to other societies.[113] Gluckman's
response to Bohannan's relativism, if I understand him rightly, is to
maintain that different legal systems can be compared with the help
of basic categories such as 'obligations,' 'rights,' and 'procedure for
settling disputes'; these would seem to correspond to Polanyi's
demand for a series of substantive categories to be used in
comparative economics.

Another particularly controversial part of Polanyi's theory was
his protest against the use of the concepts 'scarcity' and 'surplus' in
comparative economics.[114] In the case of scarcity, this argument was
bound up with his distinction between the formal and substantive
meanings of 'economy,' scarcity being an essential element in the
formal definition of the economy as 'the allocation of scarce means
among alternative ends.' Smelser, whose review of *Trade and Market*
was the most important critique of Polanyi's ideas,[115] seems to favor
the idea of a substantive definition of the economy, but maintained
that scarcity must be included in it: 'Mastery over scarce means is one
of the necessary ingredients in defining the economy in a way which
can be compared from society to society.' Since in Parsonian theory
any social system has the function of achieving a balanced allocation
of means among alternative ends,[116] a substantive specification of the
type of means concerned is essential to distinguish the economy from
other sub-systems of society. But the definition of the economy must
also identify it as the 'adaptive' sub-system of society, and this
appears to be Smelser's reason for retaining 'scarcity' in his definition.

Insofar as the adaptive function consists in 'readying resources for
use in directed behaviour' (Smelser, 1959b), i.e. in the organization
of production, it is presumably covered by Polanyi's definition of the
economy as 'an instituted process of interaction between man and
his environment which results in a continuous supply of want-
satisfying material means.' But the term 'adaptive' perhaps suggests
also that the economy is the most flexible sub-system of society in its
response to changing requirements or minor disturbances in
equilibrium – this sensitivity of response being, perhaps, produced
by the breaking down of the process of goal-attainment into a
multiple series of small-scale choice situations. Polanyi would
probably have argued that this was true of the modern market
economy, but not necessarily of other types of economic organization. But it is worth enquiring whether even in more rigid and

traditional societies the economy does not still offer relatively more
flexibility and more choice situations than other parts of the social
system, and therefore serve both as an area of potential instability
and as a locus for compensatory movements in reaction to disturbances in equilibrium in other parts of the social system. Such specula-
tions were, however, outside Polanyi's field of interest, because he
wanted to proceed from a substantive definition of the economy to
an *empirical* study of the place of the economy in society, without
any theoretical presuppositions about the function of the economy.
It may therefore be a mistake to judge his substantive definition
of the economy as an attempt at a complete and exhaustive
definition.

Smelser hints at another criticism of Polanyi's rejection of 'scarcity'
in saying that 'the institutionalization of attitudes and behaviour is
not an alternative to scarcity, but one of the components in its
determination,' but he does not pursue the subject. What is most
obviously missing from Polanyi's substantive definition of the
economy is surely the notion of *value*.[117] Mauss, in discussing the
problem of defining the economy, suggested that

> Les phénomènes économiques se définissent dans une certaine
> mesure par la présence de la notion de valeur, comme les
> phénomènes ésthetiques se signalent par la présence de la notion
> du beau, les phénomènes moraux par la présence de la notion du
> bien moral.[118]

This emphasis on the notion of valuation is particularly important
for the primitive economy, where the allocation of goods is so closely
bound up with rights, obligations, compensation, rank, and
prestige.[119]

Lévi-Strauss has suggested that economic systems, like kinship
systems, can be regarded as a kind of language; Talcott Parsons, in
Societies: Evolutionary and Comparative Perspectives (1966), speaks
of 'symbolic codes' which regulate social communication. Though
Parsons emphasizes that 'valued objects' (valuation) and 'values'
must not be confused,[120] an attempt at a more detailed analysis than
he gives in this book would require a closer comparison of the
functioning of symbolic codes in the different sub-systems of society,
leading, in the case of the economy, to the question of the relation
of the hierarchy of valued objects to values, on the one hand, and
to environmental conditions on the other hand.

Polanyi's failure to discuss value may be connected with his reluctance to recognize the existence of economic competition in primitive societies. The positive side of his views on 'scarcity' was his emphasis on the need to study empirically the reactions of different societies to scarcity situations such as crop failure, and their institutionalized means of adapting to fluctuations in supply.[121] In reaction against the conception of primitive man as 'economically irrational,' anthropologists are now inclined to argue that the apparently wasteful displays or destruction of wealth in some primitive societies (the piles of rotting yams which so impressed Malinowski in the Trobriand Islands) may after all fulfill an important economic function in encouraging more intensive production, and so insuring against a poor harvest. But there are few studies of adaptation to scarcity; few anthropologists spend long enough in the field to be sure of having first-hand experience of both lean and fat years, and non-economic interests are likely to create a stronger emphasis on periods of prosperity and feasting.[122]

A different use of the concept of scarcity has been made by George M. Foster, who has attempted in a paper 'The Peasant Society and the Idea of Limited Good'[123] to derive some features of the *Wirtschaftsethik* of peasant societies from chronic shortage of land and the uncertainties of traditional subsistence agriculture. Although Foster does not refer to Polanyi, his theory might be seen as an example of 'scarcity as a generally acted upon *cultural definition of situations*'[124] arising from the limited supply of a particular resource, land, rather than from the assessment of all resources in terms of money, and so, perhaps, as an example of an intermediate stage in the convergence of the formal and substantive meanings of scarcity.

Pearson's chapter 'The Economy Has No Surplus: Critique of a Theory of Development' in *Trade and Market*, attacking the concept of surplus, closely parallels Terence K. Hopkins's treatment of scarcity in the same volume (H. Pearson, 1957a; T. K. Hopkins, 1957). The blanket use of 'surplus' to cover all goods produced above the bare subsistence requirements of the producing society obscures the way to analysis or comparison. 'There are always and everywhere potential surpluses available. What counts is the institutional means for bringing them to life.'[125] Structural change cannot be adequately explained by pointing to increases in production. The 'theory of development' criticized is the Marxist one, best known in the writings of Gordon Childe, which sees social evolution, especially in the prehistoric period, as a series of 'revolutions' set off by improvements in production techniques. Similar objections to materialist explanations of social change have been made recently by others in a variety of contexts. The critics of Wittfogel's elaboration of the 'surplus' theory in his work on 'Oriental despotism' have shown that extensive canal works do not accompany the *rise* of 'hydraulic civilizations'; much irrigation is organized at a local level, not by central bureaucratic control, and the operations of largest scale tend to be connected with the supply of water to cities rather than with opening up new areas for agriculture.[126] Modern economic historians are saying that the importance of technical innovations in the Industrial Revolution has been overstressed, and that more attention must be given to changes in economic organization.[127] Parsons, discussing the differences between primitive and 'intermediate' societies, focuses on the development of political institutions capable of more effective mobilization of resources, rather than on technical development and increased productivity.[128] In the study of underdeveloped countries, too, it is realized that levels of saving and investment depend on economic institutions as much as on levels of production.

Even Polanyi's critics accept that increases in production and institutional arrangements for the recognition and use of surpluses must be empirically studied.[129] They hold, however, that environment and technology, especially through their effects on population density, play an extremely important part in the evolution of human societies, and therefore that the empirical study of surpluses should be one of the main concerns of economic anthropology. Concentration on the term 'surplus' has unfortunately tended to obscure the real difference between these critics and the Polanyi school, which is about the relative importance of methods of production and efficiency in exploiting the environment and of procedures of allocation, in the study of economic anthropology.[130] In the interests both of comparative economics and of the study of change, a swing back to interest in production among economic anthropologists is probably needed. The differentiation of social anthropology as a specialized discipline has meant that the institutional aspects of economic anthropology have been overemphasized, and this tendency has been reinforced by ambivalent attitudes toward the interest of economists in 'development potential' and dislike of passing judgment on the productive efficiency of primitive societies[131] – echoes of the defense of the 'economic rationality of primitive man.'

3 *Reciprocity, redistribution, householding, and market exchange*

Polanyi's typology of economic institutions is not, as has been claimed by Smelser, only a typology of exchange systems. It is certainly applicable to the organization of labor, as Polanyi showed more clearly in his last work, *Dahomey and the Slave Trade*: reciprocal labor patterns are common in primitive societies, corvée labor can be classed as redistributive, and slavery belongs to the householding pattern. (It is more difficult to associate different patterns of land tenure with Polanyi's categories, and he did not deal with this problem.) Polanyi seems to have regarded exchange of goods as the primary pattern, and allocation of resources as secondary. This is surely where he made his radical break with Marxist theory; in comparison, the attacks on 'scarcity' and 'surplus' are of minor importance. The central point is that social relationships, expressed in and sustained by transfers of material goods, come before *Produktionsverhältnisse*.

Claude Meillassoux, attempting to reconcile Polanyi's approach with Marxism, has defended the central position of allocation in his system by arguing that in primitive societies where tools are simple and land is not a scarce resource control has to be exercised directly, through personal relationships, and not via control of the means of production. Such a society, he seems to suggest, could also exhibit a form of class conflict, between old and young. This view has been sharply attacked from the point of view of orthodox Marxism,[132] but finds parallels in some non-Marxist work on economic anthropology.[133] Further discussion of the relation between patterns of allocation and the organization of production is clearly needed.

Polanyi, however, would hardly have approved of Meillassoux's enterprise, for two reasons. One is that his own work was based on the political conviction that the function of the economy should be to strengthen social relationships and eliminate conflict by an allocation of wealth conforming to the values of each society. The subordination of economic organization to social ends, which for Marx existed only in primitive communism and the communist Utopia of the future, was for Polanyi a feature of all societies except that dominated by the modern market system. Consequently (the second reason), he did not consider the theories of Marx relevant for the analysis of non-market economies. He agreed with Marx's indictment of capitalism and cited the 'Economic-Philosophical

Manuscripts of 1844' as evidence that 'The essential philosophy of Marx centred on the totality of society and the non-economic nature of man,' but held that as economic historians Marx and his followers had made the common mistake of interpreting other ages by the light of the economic and social organization of their own times.

> Given a definite structure of society, the class theory works; but what if that structure itself undergoes change?... Though human society is naturally conditioned by economic factors, the motives of human individuals are only exceptionally determined by the needs of material want-satisfaction. That nineteenth-century society was organized on the assumption that such a motivation could be made universal was a peculiarity of the age. It was therefore appropriate to allow a comparatively wide scope to the play of economic motives when analysing that society. But we must guard against prejudging the issue, which is precisely to what extent such an unusual motivation could be made effective.[134]

Marx had not even produced a theory of socialist economics,[135] much less a guide to the understanding of the place of the economy in primitive societies.

Leaving aside the question of the basis of Polanyi's classification, what of the choice of categories? Three types only were proposed in *Trade and Market*, Polanyi's best-known work: reciprocity, redistribution, and (market) exchange; but in *The Great Transformation* these had been accompanied by a fourth category, householding, and Polanyi returned to this again in *Dahomey and the Slave Trade*. At the time of *Trade and Market*, Polanyi apparently excluded householding on the grounds that 'as it always applies to a group smaller than society, it does not encompass all the systems of relationship found there.'[136] Householding in any case is a vague term defined mainly by the absence of the inter-group relations which interested Polanyi; the peasant subsistence smallholdings and manorial estates linked under this heading by Karl Bücher,[137] from whom Polanyi took over the concept, resemble each other mainly in being self-sufficient; and the manor at least could be seen as a redistributive system. Polanyi probably took up the concept again in *Dahomey and the Slave Trade* because for the first time he was trying to give a full description of one society's economic institutions, instead of selecting different patterns for study in different societies, and found that reciprocity, redistribution, and markets did not account for every aspect of the economy in Dahomey. The system of land inheritance and Dahomean ancestor worship 'merge the habitational unit or compound and the kinship unit into an unbreakable social entity,'[138] which has the economic functions of distributing land and mobilizing wealth for religious ceremonies.

Householding remains anomalous among Polanyi's categories because it represents the economic aspect of the basic social unit, whereas the other three categories all refer to the organization of economic relations *between* units. Reciprocal prestations of food and other gifts, labor, or hospitality occur typically between affinal groups, or between neighbors. Market exchange makes transactions possible between individuals irrespective of their social relationship. Redistribution requires central collection and allocation by a higher authority, but can be seen as satisfying the basic unit's need for services and goods which it cannot produce alone by providing an institutionalized channel for the pooling of resources.

Smelser in his review of *Trade and Market* proposed to divide the category of redistribution into two: systems in which central collection is genuinely followed by redistribution, as in the division of the harvest among different castes in the Indian village,[139] and those in which collection serves to mobilize resources for the enterprises of the ruling group – pyramid-building, for example. But the two functions are frequently carried out by the same organization, and justified in the same way as serving collective interests; the distinction between immediate material distribution and the deferred or less measurable benefits of the ruler's activities as priest or warleader does not seem sharp enough to warrant classing 'mobilization' as a separate category.

Smelser's reason for this modification is betrayed by his further suggestion that his four categories (reciprocity, redistribution, mobilization, and market exchange)[140] correspond to the four functional sub-systems of society in Parsonian theory. Reciprocity corresponds to the function of latent pattern-maintenance and tension-management; redistribution to the allocation of rewards and facilities according to the integrative requirements of society; mobilization to goal-attainment; market exchange to adaptation. Each type of exchange is embedded in a different social structure. Reciprocity is embedded in the structure of the segmental units (families, neighborhoods, clans, etc.) between which reciprocal prestations occur; redistribution in the system of social stratification which determines dues and rewards; mobilization in the system of political authority; market exchange in the market mechanism and the system of specifically economic roles and institutions associated with it. In most societies all four types of exchange can be identified, but their relative importance depends on 'the value-system of the society in question, the level of differentiation of its social structure, and the complexity of the demands of its internal and external situation.' Further study, he suggests, should be devoted to clarifying the relation of economic institutions to social structure along these lines.

A different approach is adopted by Marshall Sahlins,[141] who has attempted to build up a model of the sociology of primitive exchange based on the two concepts of reciprocity and redistribution, representing 'horizontal' and 'vertical' exchange patterns. Householding is regarded as a small-scale redistributive system; reciprocal transactions are graded from 'generalized reciprocity' or pure altruism through 'balanced reciprocity,' in which giver or seller receives a fair return, to 'negative reciprocity,' in which each party tries to maximize his own advantage. Haggling, barter, gambling, chicanery, and theft are examples of 'negative reciprocity.' The position of an exchange on this scale is conditioned by the 'span of social distance' between those who exchange. Social distance may be simply the degree of closeness of kinship or neighborhood, or may be affected also by differences in rank or wealth. The reciprocal relationships of the powerful and the rich have a wider radius than those of the poor or insignificant. There may be a sharp distinction in type between in-group exchanges and those with outsiders, or the latter may be assimilated to in-group patterns by the formation of trade-friendships or partnerships, relations of blood-brotherhood, and so on. Again, different modes of exchange may be prescribed for different classes of goods.[142] The patterning of exchange may be influenced by a general tendency to individualism or to cooperation in the moral attitudes of the community.[143] The mode of exchange will also be influenced by the social structure. Sahlins suggests that 'balanced reciprocity' is likely to be found in segmented societies consisting of autonomous settlements only loosely linked by kinship and clan organization, and that it is particularly in such societies also that primitive money is likely to be found. These societies have connections too wide and tenuous for exchange to be structured entirely by 'generalized reciprocity,' and do not have a sufficiently strong central power for a redistributive system.

Although both Sahlins's and Smelser's articles contain many suggestions which could form the basis for further empirical research,[144] they both discuss Polanyi's classification mainly from a formal point of view, and modify it in order to produce a neater formal model. It was natural that attempts should be made to link Polanyi's economic patterns to types of social structure, but many problems remain, especially in analyzing the interrelations of different patterns within a single society. There was a certain ambiguity in the way in which the scheme was presented in *Trade and Market*. Although it was made clear there that Polanyi's categories referred to institutional patterns which might coexist in a single economic system,[145] the societies discussed were presented as dominated by one type of economic organization. Where two patterns existed in a single society, stress was laid on their incompatibility, as in the case of reciprocity and market exchange among the Berbers, or redistribution and European market trade in Dahomey.

Polanyi hoped that his research would form the basis of a 'new science of comparative economics,' but these attempts at developing it seem perhaps a little premature. It might be wiser to continue with Polanyi's empirical and operational approach, testing the usefulness of his categories in historical and anthropological studies and seeing what problems arise in trying to apply them, before attempting to use them as a basis for more ambitious theoretical constructions. His categories should be regarded as sketches of some areas in a largely unexplored territory rather than as coordinates in a diagram.

In *Dahomey and the Slave Trade* Polanyi for the first time applied his typology to the analysis of a single society's economic system in all its aspects. As has been said, this led him to modify his classification by reintroducing householding as a category, and even this did not enable him to give a very satisfactory account of land tenure or inheritance. The main weakness of his account, however, is that the reciprocal, redistributive, householding, and market sections of the economy are described in separate chapters, with little attempt to explain their interrelations. We are not told how the individual reconciles his various economic commitments, nor how the general value-system maintains the separation of different institutional patterns and the attitudes appropriate to each. This is partly the fault of the sources;[146] but Polanyi does not discuss the implications of,

for instance, the apparent tendency to present the redistributive
system as an all-inclusive higher level household, or of the fact that
the market-women's goods were not grown on family land but
bought from large plantation-type farms, which must have facilitated
the separation of householding and market spheres.

Smelser was justified in criticizing Polanyi's 'radical institutionalism'; the analysis of institutions alone will reveal little, if they are not
related to environmental conditions on the one side, and to values
and *Wirtschaftsethik* on the other. But institutions may still make a
good starting point for the study of values. In my own subject, the
economy of ancient Greece, an approach through Polanyi's categories, though certainly not the only one to be pursued and not
capable of answering all our questions, seems to me to have produced
some interesting results.

Although many details in the interpretation of the Mycenaean
Linear B tablets are still obscure,[147] they show at least that the
economy of the more advanced areas of Greece in the Bronze Age
was dominated by a redistributive system of the kind known from
the palace archives of the ancient Near East. Taxes in grain, wool, oil,
and wine accumulated in the palace store-rooms; land tenures were
minutely recorded, status distinctions formalized, trade relations
with distant regions stimulated, and a high level of craft specialization achieved through the centralization of wealth and administrative
capacities of the palace system.

This system in Greece did not survive the upheavals of the end of
the Bronze Age. In the Near Eastern civilizations the old structure
survived the crisis, but in Greece cities and palaces were destroyed,
trade and other regular communications broke down, writing was
forgotten; the startling impoverishment of material culture revealed
in the archaeological record was accompanied by extensive depopulation and a major breakdown of the religious, political, and
economic institutions which had centered on the palace.[148] One of
the most important aspects of the discovery of the Mycenaean
civilization for the ancient historian is that the development of the
Greek polis appears no longer, or at least not only, as a product of
Indo-European tribal organization, but as a social system growing
out of the ruins of an 'Oriental despotism.'

Whether the society portrayed by Homer should be regarded as an
attempt to refashion the Mycenaean kingdom on a small scale or as
a segment cut loose from it is not clear. Redistributive institutions, in

any case, survived, but no longer form a bureaucratically organized system. The chief must justify his wealth by generosity; beggars and strangers come to his house for entertainment, he provides for feasts and sacrifices, and leads in expeditions abroad to raid, trade, or exchange gifts with other princes. It is he who provides for the few specialists who remain in the Greek world – the expert shipwrights, poets, and doctors who travel from one patron to another.

The main emphasis in the Homeric poems, however, is on reciprocal gift-exchange between these leaders. Hospitality and generosity to equals is far more important than relations with inferiors. (Similarly, Hesiod stresses the necessity for the peasant to be generous in his dealings with his neighbor, but prefers to keep clear of the 'gift-devouring *basileis*.'[149] The poor man, it seems, now only approaches the rich with gifts out of fear or desire for favor – he has no regular obligation to pay dues, he is predominantly a 'householder.') But the stress on generosity in the gift-giving system of the rich includes the obligation to give to those who cannot make returns; reciprocity and redistribution are linked in the system of values. Both patterns no doubt were inherited from the Mycenaean age, but the *basileus* now has to rely mainly on his own resources and exertions for the wealth needed to live up to his ideals, and the gift-exchange and displays of wealth which were part of the courtly pattern take on a competitive edge in an age of more fluid status distinctions and a struggle for power and prestige among a class of equals.

By a process which we are not yet able to trace clearly, the competition for power and prestige among the Greek nobility, from about the seventh century onward, moved away from the display of wealth at home and attraction of a personal following to displays of munificence in the city center and contests for political office and political support independent of personal ties. In view of this increasing differentiation of the political structure, and the structural differentiation of the economy which will be discussed below, it is interesting to see that Athens relied on the redistributive ethic to supplement her taxation system. Distribution to dependants was replaced by gifts made to the people as a whole, and the transaction was depersonalized on both sides – not only was no individual recipient put in an inferior position, but the givers were shorn of much of the prestige of giving: the class who had once set up fine buildings under their own names and commanded their own warships in battle[150] were restricted to the limited possibilities of display in the upkeep of a state trireme or paying for a dramatic performance whose success was credited to the playwright rather than to the *choregos*. Yet the speeches from the fourth-century lawsuits reveal the constant pressure on the rich to justify the possession of their wealth by undertaking more of these liturgies than the minimum prescribed, and spending more generously on them than was strictly necessary.

The kinship system, so far as can be seen, did not have important economic functions. The rules of inheritance were naturally important in the transmission of land, and clans had religious functions which provided occasions for sacrifices and feasting, but the reciprocal prestations of gifts between relatives familiar from primitive societies seem to have no counterpart in ancient Greece. Hesiod is concerned with relations among neighbors; there is no suggestion in the *Works and Days* that kinship groups play an important part in the life of rural Boeotia.[151] Nor do kinship ties play much part in the relationships of the Homeric nobility; they are replaced by the elaborate linkages of guest-friendships, often themselves inherited from one generation to another.

The peasant householder therefore had few occasions to exchange with others. If his neighbor asks for a loan he must be generous, lest he need one himself later, but he should try to be independent of such aid. If he exhausts his neighbors' goodwill, no one will help him; if he turns to the rich for aid or protection, he may risk losing the land which is the mark of his free status in the community. His main economic aim is to support his family with as few dealings with others as possible. The few village craftsmen make little difference to this pattern; probably they barter their products at fixed equivalencies.

But overseas trade between Greece and the Near East, which had almost entirely ceased during the 'Dark Age,' had been resumed by the ninth century, and the trader was the first 'market' element in the Greek economy. Long-distance traders, as opposed to the few peasants who ventured to ship a cargo to the nearest town, were probably landless men, detached from their own community, often no doubt combining piracy with trade. It has been observed that all Homer's traders are non-Greeks; this does not reflect the actual situation in the eighth century, but was an idealized solution, which persisted for centuries (Athenians in the fourth century still tended to speak as if all traders were non-citizens), to the contradiction felt between the behavior of the trader and the *Wirtschaftsethik* of the community. It was recognized that the trader felt no obligation to be generous in selling his wares, and that his transactions were not embedded in any social relationship; even if he was not a foreigner, dealings with him were conducted as if he was not a member of the community. This solution of the contradiction between the ethics of reciprocity and of market dealing was facilitated and for a considerable time limited in its effects by the fact that the rich regarded the trader as an inferior creature and the peasant had little to do with him; but it had the consequence that as trade increased there was an increasing tendency to the differentiation of 'economic' situations, roles, norms of behavior, and motives.[152] When the Peloponnesian War forced the peasants of Attica to take refuge inside the city, the market grew rapidly in importance, and with it came the extension of the 'market mentality.' The uprooted peasant had few opportunities for wage labor even if he had been willing to compete with non-citizens and slaves; his needs were at least partly met by the pay he received as soldier, rower, or juror, and if he needed more money his easiest course was to turn petty trader – the Sausage-Seller of Aristophanes' *Knights*. Cut off from the restraints of his old local community, he would adopt the ethic of the market; and as he no longer produced for his own subsistence, but relied on a cash income, he would tend to extend his 'economic' attitude to all questions where money was concerned. Political conflicts between rich and poor sharpened; the rich tended to blame the greed and irresponsibility of the *dēmos* for mistakes in policy, and became less willing to contribute financially. In the fourth century there were men who sold land to make their wealth 'invisible' to the eye of the informer and so avoid taxation. Demosthenes complains that politicians are making money out of their position in office, and that they are more interested in ostentatious houses for themselves than in the adornment and prosperity of the city.[153] Wealth and the traditional status hierarchy were becoming increasingly separated; some of the richest men in Athens at this time had begun their careers in banking or trade as slaves. One of the most significant instances of the structural differentiation of the economy was the development of a separate legal category of commercial suits in which not only foreigners but even slaves, who normally had no legal capacity, could appear.[154]

Thus, what disturbed the philosophers of the fourth century was not, as Polanyi thought, an increase in profit-making on price differentials, but the disembedding or structural differentiation of the economy, leading to the application of 'economic' criteria and standards of behavior in a wide range of situations recognized as economic above all by the fact that money was involved; the old civic virtues of generosity and self-sufficiency were being replaced by the market attitudes of the trader.[155]

The value of Polanyi's categories here is that they provide a rough-and-ready classification of economic institutions and the different values maintaining them, and indicate the areas in which contradictions and conflict are to be looked for. The use of Parsons's theory of structural differentiation instead of Polanyi's crude contrast between embedded and disembedded economic systems gives the outlines of a dynamic analysis.[156] But from this a new question arises. Would a decrease in the importance of market institutions in a society which had reached this level of differentiation produce a revival of the attitudes whose loss Aristotle and Polanyi deplored? In the Roman Empire the state increasingly had to take over the functions of the market system in order to ensure an adequate supply and distribution of food to the city population. This change *was* accompanied by an increase in private redistribution (which had always been more important in Rome than in classical Greece).[157] The process of bureaucratization of the economy and the rise under the influence of Christianity of new attitudes to economic matters has never really been studied. Although Polanyi never faced the difficulties of applying his theories to the history of economic institutions and attitudes in Europe between the fourth century B.C. and the beginning of market capitalism, it is not impossible that they may have something to contribute here as well as in the study of primitive and archaic societies.

If Polanyi exaggerated the contrast between primitive *Gemeinschaft* and modern *Gesellschaft* and so failed to deal with intermediate forms, some of his critics have erred in the opposite direction. They find no difficulty in comparing the 'extensive credit facilities' of primitive society with those of the modern economy. Yet there is an immense gulf between the personal economic relationships of a small community and the impersonal modern transactions resting on legal institutions which have taken centuries to develop. At the present time, when culture contact and development programs bridge the gap in a short period, it is perhaps especially tempting to look at the similarities between 'custom and contract' rather than at the differences. But the history of the long and tortuous process of evolution needed to produce contractual forms of such apparently simple operations as sale, loan, and credit[158] must not be forgotten. The main danger in the separation of anthropological from historical comparative studies seems to be that the study of social change is split into two separate departments; historians, until very recently, have concentrated on evolution and ignored acculturation,[159] while anthropologists study the changes in primitive societies produced by contact with the ideas and economic institutions of 'developed' countries, and lose sight of the questions about the origins of institutions which originally stimulated the growth of anthropology.

Additional note

A valuable further analysis of Polanyi's career and background may now be found in Salsano, 1974; see also Lichtheim, 1970. Polanyi's theories and their relevance to economic history and economic anthropology are discussed in Godelier, 1974; Garlan, 1973; and Vallensi *et al.*, 1974. Two further papers by Polanyi have been posthumously published (Polanyi, 1971a, 1971b). Dalton's essays in economic anthropology are collected in Dalton, 1971c.

Recent developments in economic anthropology are well represented in Firth, 1972; Sahlins, 1972; Godelier, 1973; and H. Schneider, 1974. Sahlins (1972) makes an important contribution to the development of Polanyi's work on 'householding' and reciprocity as modes of economic integration. There has been a general tendency, however, to criticize Polanyi's typology as too formalistic. Patterns of allocation formally classed as 'redistributive' can play very different roles in different social units and systems. The most conspicuous use of Polanyi's theories in recent years has been the adoption of his conception of the 'embeddedness' of the economy in pre-industrial societies by neo-Marxist anthropologists in France and elsewhere (see Godelier, 1973; also English discussions in two new periodicals, *Economy and Society*, Routledge & Kegan Paul, London, 1972 ff., and *Critique of Anthropology*, 21 Dunollie Road, London N.W.5, 1974 ff.). They draw the conclusion that any set of relationships which would be characterized in functionalist anthropology as forming the kinship system, religious system or political system of a society may function also as relations of production; this set of relationships will constitute the dominant institutional structure of the society, and the determining role 'in the last instance' of economic factors can only be demonstrated through showing by diachronic analysis that changes in the location of relations of production correlate with changes in the hierarchy of institutional structures in the society. So far the fruitfulness of this formulation has been demonstrated mainly in permitting the assimilation into Marxist theory of the achievements of synchronic structural-functional analysis in the style of Durkheim and Radcliffe-Brown. Whether it can also provide a basis for introducing the dynamics of Marx's diachronic analyses into social anthropology remains to be seen.

In ancient history, Finley (1970) is particularly close to Polanyi's concerns. His general survey (1973a) is more Weberian in style, concerned with the stratification and structure of ancient society and the effects of status on economic behavior; the 'embeddedness' of the economy leads to emphasis on the analysis of values rather than to the study of the correspondence between social relationships and forms of exchange which fascinated Polanyi, and which is now being developed by the school of Godelier. Marxist critics among ancient historians have not been slow to react against Finley's rejection of the Marxist concept of class in favor of a more complex Weberian analysis of stratification (*Marxism and the Classics*, 1975), and against his 'implicit anti-economism' (Di Benedetto, 1975). They are certainly right to point out his inadequate treatment of differences and conflicts between the values and interests of different groups (which cannot be regarded as a necessary consequence of his choice of analytical framework). But the real question, it seems to me, is whether the argument is still to be posed in terms of the relative primacy of political *or* of economic factors. J.-P. Vernant argued already in 1965, along lines similar to the approach developed by Godelier, that in ancient Greece (and Rome) politico-jural status and political roles played a dominant part in determining the distribution of production factors and goods (Vernant, 1965b). The implication of Polanyi's concept of 'embeddedness' is that we need to escape altogether from the opposition of 'political' and 'economic', and develop a new substantive analysis of production and distribution in the ancient world which does not separate war, jurors' pay, and tribute from trade, agriculture, and markets. Finley states early in his book that the main sources of upper-class wealth were political, yet his discussion of 'the State and the economy' scarcely goes beyond Hasebroek's demonstration (1928) that ancient states had no 'economic policy' in either the mercantilist or the modern sense. The extremely important part played by the State in the distribution and circulation of money, goods, and even land (conquest, colonization, confiscation) is hardly mentioned. See below, chapter 7, for further discussion of these points.

3   The work of Louis Gernet

Gernet is of interest because he was both a classical scholar and a sociologist trained in the school of Émile Durkheim. He provides a link between the work of anthropologists of the late nineteenth century who turned naturally to the classical world for material – stimulating, in their turn, Jane Harrison and the early Cornford, already influenced by Durkheim – and a modern generation of classical scholars who are again turning to anthropology. Since Lévi-Strauss's work on myth is becoming one of the main foci of this interest,[1] a particularly interesting aspect of Gernet's work is the evidence it provides for the relations between linguistics and sociology in the Durkheim school.

Gernet was born in 1882 and died in 1962.[2] He took the 'agrégation de grammaire' at the École Normale at a time when Paris was a leading center for the study of comparative philology and, in particular, of the relation between language and society. Meillet was teaching at the École des Hautes Études; Bréal was giving his last lectures at the Collège de France. Meillet wrote for the *Année sociologique*, and the Durkheim school in general was keenly interested in the study of language, both because of its central importance as a social phenomenon and because 'positive' research in the social sciences had achieved its greatest successes in linguistics. Mauss was a remarkable linguist; André Durkheim had been studying under Meillet before his early death in the First World War; Bianconi, another of those lost in the war, had been working on Bantu languages and categories of thought, perhaps in response to a suggestion from Meillet; Meillet's pupil Maurice Cahen worked with Henri Hubert and Mauss.

From 1907 to 1910 Gernet was one of the small group of young scholars engaged in research at the Foundation Thiers (directed by Durkheim's teacher Émile Boutroux). In the year immediately junior to Gernet was Marcel Granet, who applied Durkheimian sociology to the study of ancient China as Gernet did for Greece. Two years below him were Marc Bloch and another Durkheimian, Georges Davy. During this period Gernet took a degree in law, published the memoir on the corn-supply of classical Athens which he had written at the École Normale (which earned him an approving notice from Simiand in the *Année sociologique*)[3] and worked on his two theses: the minor one a translation and commentary of book IX (criminal law) of Plato's *Laws* (1917a), and the other the *Recherches sur le développement de la pensée juridique et morale en Grèce* (1917b). Penal law was a subject in which Durkheim was deeply interested; another work of the school, Paul Fauconnet's *La Responsabilité* (1920), lies close to some of the problems treated by Gernet in *La Pensée juridique*.[4] Davy was working, in consultation with Mauss, on a related subject, the origins of contract: his *La Foi jurée* (1922) and Mauss's 'Essai sur le don' (1925a) were closely linked and go back to this period.[5] Gernet gave a paper to the Association des Études Grecques in 1911 on *engyē* (betrothal and suretyship) which was clearly related to their work; it appeared in expanded form in the *Revue des études grecques* in 1917 as 'Hypothèses sur le contrat primitif en Grèce.'[6] And while Gernet was studying *hybris* and related notions for *La Pensée juridique*, another Durkheimian and friend, Maxime David, was doing the same for *aidōs* and *timē*.[7]

Indeed, Gernet had already been connected with the Durkheim school for some years. Between 1903 and 1906 he contributed reviews of works on economics and socialism to the *Notes critiques* edited by the economist François Simiand. His first reviews for the *Année sociologique* appear in the volume for 1906–1909. From about 1905 he had been a member of a socialist study group formed under the influence of Lucien Herr, the librarian of the École Normale and friend of Jaurès, and which included a number of Durkheimians: Mauss, Simiand, Halbwachs, Granet, Robert Hertz, Henri Lévy-Bruhl, and several more.[8]

They were at this time a very close-knit group of personal friends, united in intellectual collaboration, political convictions, reverence for Durkheim, and the excitement of applying new ideas in concert to a wide variety of subjects. Apart from formal co-authorship – particularly noticeable in the case of Mauss, who wrote several works in collaboration with others and whose thought is often difficult to separate from that of Durkheim – the same motifs crop up again and again even in independent studies. Some examples have already been given, and more can easily be added. The problem of the religious origins of economic value, mentioned in a footnote in *Les Formes élémentaires de la vie religieuse* (Durkheim, 1912), was taken up by Mauss, Célestin Bouglé, and – in 1948 – Gernet. Robert Hertz's work on the preeminence of the right hand was complemented by Granet's study of right and left in China. Mauss's ideas on gift-exchange were applied by René Maunier to the study of a Berber society in North Africa. The suggestions for the study of collective representations of time sketched by Durkheim and Mauss in 'De quelques formes primitives de la classification' were developed in the religious sphere by Henri Hubert and in the sphere of law by Gernet (in 1956).[9] And one could go on.

Gernet's early reviews for the *Année sociologique* show clearly his consciousness of belonging to a school and a consequent tendency to treat non-Durkheimian studies of ancient Greece – with the exception of those of Glotz[10] – with a certain amount of intolerance. He found much current work vague, rhetorical, scholastic, and lacking in comprehension of 'les réalités sociales' – not without justification, when A. Croiset could attempt to explain Greek democracy in terms of a national 'aptitude aux idées générales.'[11] His arrogance, however, was not merely that of a young man with a new fad. Sociology, he says in one of these early reviews, requires a 'précision minutieuse et sévère.'[12] It was a discipline in the strict sense of the word, not merely a matter of learning a new jargon.

In 1911 Gernet went to teach at La Flèche, near Tours; about 1917 he went to the University of Algiers, where he remained until after the Second World War. It was not until 1948, when he was sixty-six, that he began to teach in Paris, at the 6ᵉ Section of the École Pratique des Hautes Études, under the rubric of 'sociologie juridique,' with his friend Henri Lévy-Bruhl. (At this time he also took over the position of general secretary and chief editor of the *Année sociologique*, a post he retained until the end of his life.) For thirty years, then, from 1917 to 1947, he worked in comparative isolation – the more so in that the Durkheim school lost a good deal of its vitality and coherence after the death of Durkheim and so many others in the First World War. Only two issues of the *Année sociologique* were produced in the 1920s (one incomplete); in the 1930s it was split into five sections, each dealing with a different branch of the subject. This division into small cliques did not favor the maintenance of a coherent point of view or of old ties, nor the attraction of new recruits. Gernet did not write for it during this period. Mauss produced little in the 1930s; the most active in the *Année sociologique* among the old Durkheimians at this time seems to have been Maurice Halbwachs, who had little sympathy for the evolutionary and comparative aspects of the school's work.

The élan had passed to the historians, to Henri Berr and the *Annales* group. Gernet wrote a volume on Greek religion for Berr's 'Évolution de l'humanité' series in 1932,[13] and he reviewed for *Annales*, but he was too convinced a sociologist to sympathize with Febvre in his program of asserting the rights of history against sociology.[14]

Nor does Gernet seem to have been closely involved in the anthropological work which was being done in North Africa while he was in Algiers, perhaps partly because the anthropologists there were beginning at this time to turn away from the search for the 'primitive' toward the study of colonialism and social change.[15] Gernet may, however, have had some influence on Jacques Berque, who studied Greek with him and produced a book on North African contracts in 1936 as the fruits of his first fieldwork.[16]

The combination of classical studies and anthropology was no longer favored either by anthropologists or by Hellenists. In anthropology the functionalist reaction against evolutionism almost entirely eliminated historical interests.[17] In Greek studies the dominant figure was Wilamowitz, who had withdrawn from many of the fields opened up by Usener. Gernet himself concisely characterized Wilamowitz's attitude in a review of *Der Glaube der Hellenen* in 1934:[18]

> Dans un livre où le cadre est pourtant celui d'un développement historique, on est assez déconcerté de voir conseiller au lecteur, s'il est un peu pressé, de sauter tout simplement le chapitre sur 'les Dieux préhelléniques'; et, à plusieurs reprises, Wilamowitz trahit le désir impatient de sortir d'un passé un peu trop nébuleux et peut-être un peu trop barbare. Par ailleurs, son hostilité persistante à tout emploi de la méthode comparative ne s'explique pas seulement par une attitude critique; elle a quelque chose de sentimental: on y sent une défiance qui procède d'une antipathie.

In England, the enthusiasm of Jane Harrison and the young Cornford for Durkheimian sociology was replaced by caution. Gilbert Murray, although Jane Harrison influenced his early work and he continued to

accept the importance of the influence of society on thought and literature, shared Wilamowitz's antipathy to the primitive. Reactions in
France were perhaps milder, but Gernet's wholehearted commitment
to sociology was not in his favor. Jeanmaire, though he achieved a
teaching position in Paris, was a marginal figure for the same reason.[19]

Thus Gernet's failure to achieve recognition was largely due to
changes in the intellectual – and, to some extent, political and
religious – climate of opinion in France after the First World War.
One may add that in personality he combined an uncompromising
adherence to his original political and intellectual commitment with
extreme shyness and lack of self-assertion. Even when he returned to
Paris after 1947, he had few pupils. Although he was widely recognized as an authority on Greek law, and as an excellent editor of texts
in this field, he attracted little attention as an interpreter of Greek
society.[20] Some of his colleagues' descriptions of Gernet as he was in
this period – his beard, his ties, his hat – suggest that he was seen as
a sort of Rip van Winkle, a figure from a past age; and his sociological interests were perhaps seen in the same light. The attention
his sociological work is now receiving – symbolized by the unusual
commemoration ceremony at the Collège de France four years after
his death[21] and the posthumous publication of the collection of articles
entitled *Anthropologie de la Grèce antique* (Gernet, 1968) – reflects a
change in intellectual climate which, regrettably, came too late for
him, though one of the main influences in this change has been the
work of his pupil Jean-Pierre Vernant.[22]

Before discussing Gernet's methods it may be useful to make the
attempt to summarize his conception of the chronological development of early Greek society. It is not easy to do so, and Gernet might
well have repudiated an attempt to interpret his work in evolutionary
terms. He developed his ideas mainly in separate articles, and concentrated on analyzing patterns of rites and 'representations' rather
than situating them precisely in a chronological framework; and he
had a sophisticated awareness of the methodological objections to
the search for 'survivals.' But with the help of the first four chapters,
'La Formation du système de l'époque classique,' of *Le Génie grec
dans la religion* (1932a), an outline can be traced of some interest
for the history of the development of Durkheim's ideas by his pupils.

The earliest institutions which Gernet thought he could identify
in his Greek material were the peasant festivals discussed in the article

'Frairies antiques'[23] and in the chapter 'Fêtes de paysans' in *Le Génie grec dans la religion*. He deduced their primitive character from the lack of differentiation of roles (no priests, no kings nor chiefs), segmentary character of the social groups concerned, rural milieu and association of natural phenomena with religion (springs, lakes, mountain peaks, conspicuous rocks), and the seasonal rhythm of the religious calendar (the season of festivals is winter, when agricultural work is slack and store-rooms are full). Though Gernet never suggested that traces of totemism could be found in Greece,[24] his conception of this earliest stratum in Greek institutions clearly bears a strong relation to Durkheim's *Les Formes élémentaires de la vie religieuse* (1912). Very similar theories about early Chinese festivals had been put forward by Marcel Granet.[25] The conservatism of peasant society and the permanence of the natural landmarks with which such festivals were associated explained their survival: Gernet believed that the 'frairies' belonged to a Mediterranean, pre-Indo-European institutional stratum. These festivals were reunions of segmentary, identically based groups corresponding to the later deme (village) or phratry,[26] which met together to exchange food, gifts, and women, to worship the dead, and to insure fertility for the fields; they were characterized by hospitality to strangers and emphasis on generosity and reciprocity. The influence of Mauss's 'Essai sur le don' is obvious here; but Gernet made a distinction between these contributions to a common festival and the potlatch which, he thought, implied chiefship and would thus in Greece belong to the Indo-European stratum.[27] It is worth noting here also the assertion of a Durkheimian point of view on the question of ancestor-worship, in implicit opposition to Fustel de Coulanges: the worship of the dead is originally a collective activity associated with the widening, and intensification, of social relationships in religious ceremonies which unite a number of small groups; the development of family ancestor-cults comes later.[28]

The next stage Gernet shows us is the development of secret societies with a hierarchic organization of initiation-grades: the 'confréries' of dancers associated in Greek legend with metal-working (Dactyls, Telchines, Corybantes), with the mystery-cults, and with the use of animal masks, as in the bear-dances of Artemis Brauroneia and a number of legends of 'wolf-men' which he studied in 'Dolon le loup' (1936a).[29] A third, still prehistoric level of development would be the divine kingship remembered in legends such as that of the

Golden Lamb of the Pelopidae, the Golden Fleece, or the contest
between Minos and Theseus, and in the figure of the magician-king,
controller of winds and weather (Aeacus, Salmoneus).[30]

For Marcel Detienne, one of the younger heirs of the Gernet
tradition, the 'magician-king' is the Mycenaean *wanax*. Gernet,
writing mainly before the decipherment of the Mycenaean Linear B
tablets, does not attempt to relate this element in myth to an historical
stage of Greek society. The earliest historical Greek social organization for him is that of the aristocratic *genē* (lineages), which had
taken over many of the old cults from divine kings or secret societies
and formed a 'feudal' society of warriors supported by peasant
farmers who had no part in war or voice in local affairs.[31] Homer
represents this aristocratic society's idealized view of its own past:
the Ionian migration, separating the Greeks of Asia Minor from the
old landmarks and heroes' tombs, marks a turning point in the
evolution of the hero from chthonic power to epic 'Held.' Behind
the transformation of myth into poetry lies a physical cutting of
roots.[32]

In this world of the nobles, as it can be reconstructed from Homer,
Hesiod, and later evidence, we begin to see more clearly. The noble
genē (the *genos* organization is confined to the aristocracy) monopo-
lize cults:[33] they fight and breed horses; they compete in games; they
'lay down the law' (*themistes*); they display their wealth at funerals
and weddings.[34] At an early stage the kin groups are flexible units,
ready to admit new members by adoption to increase their strength.
But later their boundaries begin to harden. They appropriate
peasant land (' "Horoi" hypothécaires', Gernet, 1955b), and the
preservation and transmission of estates becomes a more pressing
concern; endogamy increases and adoption is discouraged. A smaller
unit, the *oikos* ('house'), comes to the fore, using testamentary
adoption (a new form) as a means of preserving the line in the
absence of heirs.[35]

The increasing ambitions of the nobles provoke a counter-current
of opposition from below. The worship of Dionysus, though it may
have been influenced by Asiatic cults, is a revivalistic transformation
of the old peasant religion in the form of a collective experience of
trance and ecstasy open to all: a development from totemic 'participation' to orgiastic 'possession.'[36] Archaic Greek society is a
society conscious of *anomie*: already present in Hesiod, this consciousness is expressed still more clearly by Solon and Theognis.[37]

'Wise men' are called in to diagnose and expurge pollutions and heal dissension – shamans, diviners, lawgivers. Greek philosophy has its origins in a tradition of shamanism and divination; Greek law owes its formulation at least in part to a religious obsession with pollution arising from this consciousness of *anomie*.[38]

The rise of the Greek state is thus seen as a positive reaction of the collective consciousness to social crisis, which finds its expression above all in law. Gernet saw three sources for Greek penal law: the ritual means of treating pollution and acts of desecration developed in the religious sphere, the self-help procedures of kin groups, and the formalized procedures of 'Volksjustiz' accepted by the local community.[39] The origins of judgment, and of the conception of offenses as injury to the community as a whole, and not only to the victim and his kin, again derived from a combination of religious, aristocratic, and popular sources: the disciplinary powers and clear consciousness of *eukosmia* and *akosmia* (order and disorder) associated with religious festivals, the decision (*krisis*) of a king or judge under oath, the validation by the audience at aristocratic games of victory and the award of prizes, the acknowledgment by neighborhood witnesses, assembly, or magistrate of the justification of self-help procedures.[40]

The moral ethos of the Greek city is an aristocratic one: *isonomia* (equal rights), *agon*, the free exercise of reason (*gnomē*) in *krisis*, are aristocratic concepts.[41] But they are concepts which lend themselves to extension; the circle of spectators at the games will become the popular jury. In war, in politics, in law, the aristocracy had once conceived itself as the whole of society, and as a society of equals, and this conception was maintained as the group to which it applied was extended. In subduing and controlling the excesses of the aristocratic 'dynasties,' the city found confidence in its own powers: in assigning their place to the different elements within it, it became conscious of its composition; in the creation of a system of written law, it developed its conception of justice and specified the conduct it would not tolerate.[42]

In Gernet's work, the search for 'survivals' of the primitive and the bizarre in ancient Greece practiced by the anthropological school of Frazer, Lang, and Jevons matured into an analysis of the component traditions incorporated and transformed in the institutions of the Greek city: of the cadres of transmission, and of the process of transformation from the concrete patterns of mythical images, rites, and statuses to the abstract exercise of 'positive' reasoning. Gernet's work does not show a strong line of chronological development; he was preoccupied throughout his life with the problems suggested by his early Durkheimian training. But one can perhaps trace a shift in emphasis between the early papers like 'Frairies antiques' (1928), 'Fostérage et légende' (1932b), and 'Dolon le loup' (1936a), in which he is still reaching far back into the Greek past, and those of the postwar period, where the stress is on the immediate antecedents of the institutions of the city, the process of transformation, and the problems of interpreting classical Greek memories of an earlier stage of society. The use of comparative material and the search for 'origins' were discouraged by the prevailing trend both in classical studies and in anthropology.[43] In his introduction to the *Études sociologiques sur la Chine* of his friend Marcel Granet, Gernet remarked that, though he might be considered one of the leading sociologists of his time, Granet

> ne s'est jamais occupé que de sinologie. On ne trouvera pas, dans ce qu'il a écrit, de considerations abstraites: ce sont toujours des réalités indigènes qu'il analyse. Très peu d'un vocabulaire qui pourrait passer pour spécifique: je crois qu'il l'évitait. Peu de comparatisme: il s'interdit même parfois la comparaison; et lorsqu'il y recourt, assez discrètement, la matière lui est généralement offerte par des sociétés en accointance avec celle qu'il étudie pour elle-même. (Gernet, 1953b, p. v)

Yet Granet had drawn as much inspiration from the work of Durkheim and Mauss in his youth as had Gernet. Granet, too, encountered suspicion from his more strictly philological colleagues.[44] The reaction Gernet noted in Granet's work appears also in his own. But this shift in emphasis is not only the result of negative pressure from the general trend of opinion. It can also be linked to Gernet's interest in the methods of philology and linguistics, and to changes in this field. A criticism of Georges Dumézil made by Gernet in 1955[45] is relevant here. Dumézil claimed, Gernet said, to be modeling his study of Indo-European myth and ritual on the methods of comparative philology; but the reconstruction of *Ursprachen* or, in Dumézil's case, 'primary complexes' common to all Indo-Europeans, is no longer the main concern of comparative philologists. They are now more interested in studying the transformations of the original language through contact with different linguistic sub-strata, and in response to different milieux and social systems.

This change in comparative philosophy began in Gernet's youth. His first major work, the *Recherches sur le développement de la pensée juridique et morale en Grèce* (1917b), is subtitled 'Étude sémantique,' and was one of the earliest ventures in what we should now call structural semantics.[46] The 'collective representations' attached to the terms he was studying (such as *dikē, adikia,* and *hybris*) are revealed not only by the meaning and use of each term in different periods, but also by the syntactical constructions in which they occur, by the coinage of new words from the same roots, and by the relations of association or contrast between terms: the whole semantic field has to be studied.[47] Gernet had already used this technique in an article of 1909,[48] showing that the Greek word for murderer, *authentēs*, was originally always used with the designation, in the dative case, of the man whose duty it was to exact vengeance. The slayer was not a murderer *tout court*, that is, an offender against society, but a murderer in relation to the kin of his victim. The construction corresponded to the procedure in Athenian law, where prosecution for murder had to be initiated by a kinsman of the deceased. In *La Pensée juridique*, he studied the shifts in the semantic field produced by the coinage of new words: *dysnomia* was created in antithesis to *eunomia* (which in Homer had been contrasted with *hybris*), *adikein* and *adikēma* were added to *adikia* as the notion of 'offense' gained in precision with the development of penal law. *Hybris*, losing its old meanings to *dysnomia* and *adikēma*, was drawn into a new ambit of meditation on the 'offender' and his psychology. Words, 'representations,' and institutions interact in an ever-moving system.

Methodologically, *La Pensée juridique* is a remarkable book, still relevant today in view of the current interest of anthropologists in the use of linguistic materials and techniques.[49] A similar study was produced at the same period by Meillet's pupil Maurice Cahen (1921).[50] Cahen set out to apply the methods of the *Wörter und Sachen* school to social institutions rather than material objects: in *La Libation* he studied early Scandinavian institutions of feasting and gift-exchange similar to those studied by Mauss in the 'Essai sur le don' and by Gernet in 'Frairies antiques.'[51] Both Cahen and Gernet explicitly set themselves in opposition to an older method of semantic research which sought to find through etymology the 'basic' meaning

of a word, and 'derive' from this its other usages. Both stressed that
the 'original meaning' of a word must be attached to a precise
institutional context: 'les mots qui véhiculent des notions morales
sont d'abord attachés à la représentation concrète des activités
sociales, et notamment des gestes obligatoires.'[52] This original meaning was only the point of departure for a process whose detailed
course depended on a series of historically situated choices between
linguistic, conceptual, and institutional alternatives. Both Gernet and
Cahen referred to Meillet's article 'Comment les mots changent de
sens,'[53] and stressed that the study of semantic change could not
be separated from that of the change of institutions.

What Gernet emphasized more clearly than Cahen was the need
to study words, 'representations,' and institutions as a *system*. It
seems to have been Mauss who particularly stressed, in the Durkheim
school, this aspect of social phenomena.[54] Difficult as it is to separate
Mauss's thought from that of Durkheim, one can, I think, say that
in general Durkheim was more interested in the epistemological
problems of sociology and Mauss in the concrete details of method.[55]
In an article on 'Divisions et proportions des divisions de la sociologie' in the second series of the *Année sociologique*, Mauss developed the idea (already suggested in Durkheim, 1896) of a 'horizontal'
classification of sociological phenomena, cutting across the usual
'vertical' division by subject matter (sociology of religion, law,
economics, and so forth), based on three levels: 'morphologie
sociale,' 'physiologie des pratiques,' and 'physiologie des représentations.'[56] The biological analogy was difficult to maintain in practice,
but it is worth noting Mauss's idea of furnishing 'a sort of arithmetical proof that one has been complete' in studying a social
phenomenon, by tracing at each level the morphological groupings,
actions, and ideas associated with it.

> Séries de faits sociaux qui apparaissent comme purement
> rationelles, idéales, spéculatives, imaginatives ou sentimentales et
> ineffables, telles la musique ou la poésie et la science, sont pleines
> d'actes, d'activités, d'actions, d'impressions sur les sens, sur la
> respiration, sur les muscles, ou de pratiques et de techniques.
> (Mauss, 1927a, p. 150)

And a morphological grouping may affect a whole range of
'physiological' phenomena, as Mauss and Beuchat showed in their
'Essai sur les variations saisonnières des sociétés eskimos':[57] 'à ces

deux formes de groupement [winter and summer camps] corre-
spondent deux systèmes juridiques, deux morales, deux sortes
d'économie domestique, et de vie religieuse.' Granet found an ideal
field for the application of this method in ancient Chinese society,
where the opposition between Yin and Yang is played out at every
level from philosophical theory to the details of etiquette, cooking,
and the orientation of buildings.

Gernet's most striking application of this method is his article
'Les Origines de la philosophie' (1945). (I quote at some length in
order to give an idea of the highly individual style in which Gernet
builds up an argument, working, as Vernant has said, 'en pointillé.')
He approaches the question of the origins of philosophy not in terms
of ideas, but of 'collective representations' of a role – 'l'idée que le
philosophe se fait de lui-même et qu'à l'occasion on s'en fait autour
de lui.'

> Que le philosophe se présente comme un personnage singulier (et
> supérieur) . . . c'est bien une réalité, c'est-à-dire une croyance
> assurée de la part des intéressés et quelque chose aussi que confirme
> l'acceptation ou l'hostilité du milieu social. Cette singularité
> voulue se prolongera très tard: les adeptes des philosophies post-
> aristotéliennes (qui sont un équivalent de religion privée) se doivent
> de ne pas rassembler à tout le monde. Quant aux plus anciens
> philosophes, il n'est que de penser à un Empédocle ou à un
> Héraclite, aux allures fastueuses de l'un, à l'isolement farouche de
> l'autre, et de se référer en général à la littérature anecdotique,
> pour se rendre compte qu'ils ont dû rechercher un style de vie bien
> personnel.

The images the early philosophers used in presenting themselves,
related to their 'semantic field,' reveal some of the antecedents of the
'representation' of the philosopher. Parmenides' account of his
voyage in the chariot of the Daughters of the Sun to the Gates of
Night and Day and his revelation of the paths of Truth and Opinion
draw on traditional images from Greek mysticism:

> Il y a chez Parménide une représentation qui est utilisée à deux
> fins dans ce seul prélude, c'est celle de la Voie; on la retrouve
> ailleurs, non moins obsédante: elle a dû avoir un correspondant
> réel dans les mystères. Elle est multiple . . . chemin qui mène à la
> béatitude, chemin qui mène à la révélation, 'chemin de vie,'

'chemin de recherche.' Une pensée discursive voudrait ici distinguer, analyser. Mais une analyse risquerait de fausser. L'image, qui est par excellence une image de mystère, se rapporte en principe au sort bienheureux qui peut suivre la mort terrestre: elle se rapporte aussi à l'initiation qui assure de ce privilège et qui, dans le symbolisme des mystères, est présentée et sentie comme une mort suivie de résurrection. Non moins spontanément, elle fait penser à la règle de vie qui, dans les confréries du genre orphique et pythagoricien, est une condition et une garantie de salut. Mais aussi bien, chez l'élu solitaire assuré de sa vérité à lui, l'idée de révélation, associée à l'idée du 'chemin de recherche,' est en train de devenir celle d'une connaissance qui est déjà, proprement, connaissance philosophique: c'est le cas de Parménide.

Through ideas of divine revelation, of the voyage of the soul in search of knowledge, of metempsychosis, a new conception of the soul was developing. But this, too, had its correspondence with the level of 'physiologie des pratiques':

Le Phédon rappelle une 'tradition antique' selon laquelle la purification consiste a 'rassembler l'âme,' à la 'ramasser sur elle-même de tous les points du corps' pour la saisir dans son être absolu et pour la libérer de la fatalité des morts successives. Cette conception, on a pu la mettre en rapport avec une théorie orphique, elle-même issue de très vieilles idées et suivant laquelle l'âme est 'dispersée' dans le corps où elle a été apportée par les vents: dans la pénsee des sectes, elle avait un sens très concret. Mais très concrète aussi est celle des *exercises* auxquels elle correspond et que notre mot ascétisme rappelle dans son étymologie: si, à propos de Pythagore, nous traduisons vaille que vaille 'tendre les forces de son *esprit*,' le texte donne le vieux terme de *prapides* qui signifie proprement le diaphragme. Pour partielles qu'elles soient, ces indications ne laissent pas d'être convergentes. La notion de l'âme que le platonisme a finalement recueille avait jadis été associée à quelque chose comme une discipline de *shamane*.[58]

It was Mauss who had pointed out the sociological interest of 'Les Techniques du corps,'[59] and it was Mauss's 'arithmetical proof of completeness,' together with the extension of the 'semantic field' technique to actions and 'representations,' which gave Gernet the framework for the 'précision minutieuse et sevère' which he had set as his standard.

Mauss was principally interested in transpositions and correspond-ences between social phenomena of different types in the same temporal plane: for Gernet, dealing with several centuries of Greek history, persistence and transformations through time were essential problems. He believed he had found, in myth, evidence of early Greek institutions; how was the persistence of these memories of past behavior patterns to be explained? Could the use of the tech-nique of recognizing 'survivals' of early institutions be justified in a structural-functional type of analysis which emphasized the systemic nature of culture patterns? Gernet seldom refers explicitly to these problems, and he tends to avoid technical terms: 'survivance' and 'mémoire collective' are rarely used. He preferred a vaguer and more impressionistic vocabulary, ranging from 'tradition' and 'souvenir' to 'héritage,' 'arrière-plan,' 'résonance,' and 'hantise.' This is typical of Gernet, who always refuses to push his technique of analysis to the point at which an explicit confrontation of methodological difficulties would be unavoidable. Francis Cornford, a more aggressive con-temporary who employed a more superficial knowledge of Durkheim in working on the evolution from religion of Greek science and philosophy, had already explicitly stated the problem in a paper of 1921 on 'The Unconscious Element in Literature and Philosophy.' He thought Jung had provided the solution. Later he seems to have abandoned this idea and settled for a preservation of mythical images in the 'poetic tradition.' His later research was increasingly concerned with the detailed analysis of texts and the history of individual themes; but it would be a pity if he were to be remembered for this alone.[60]

If Gernet did not face the problem of 'survivals' explicitly,[61] he never abandoned it. The theme recurs constantly in his work. In law, at least, this type of research was traditional: the tendency to con-servatism in legal institutions remained a fundamental presupposi-tion.[62] It is interesting to note that Marc Bloch, in an important review of Halbwachs's *Les Cadres sociaux de la mémoire* (Halbwachs, 1925), reproached Halbwachs for paying insufficient attention to the transmission of 'collective memory,' and for failing to recognize the importance of the history of law for his subject.[63] Since Maine, an evolutionary trend from the concrete and qualitative to the abstract and quantitative, from 'status' to 'contract,' had been generally accepted. The evolution of law played a central part in Durkheim's analysis of the transformation from mechanical to organic solidarity.[64] Processes of innovation, such as the use of legal fictions, had been studied: Tarde had drawn analogies with the processes of linguistic change.[65] But Gernet's detailed study, in 'Droit et prédroit en Grèce ancienne' (1951b), of the process by which pre-legal rites and constraints were transformed into the 'symbolisme réfléchi' of archaic procedure, and then into a more abstract formulation, was something new. Mauss had reminded lawyers that 'les choses du droit comme les choses du mythe doivent être prises dans l'ensemble, dans les tissus dont elles font partie et non pas abstraitement.'[66] Law had to be studied as a system of representations, or, as Gernet said, a language.[67]

The metaphor is common in the work of the *Année sociologique* school. Mauss had spoken of the 'langage par geste' of ritual; Granet had written on 'Le Langage de la douleur d'après le rituel funéraire de la Chine' (1922b).[68] In 'La Notion mythique de la valeur' (1948a), Gernet touched briefly (and in a characteristic tone) on the problems of using myths for an analysis of Greek 'representations' of value:

> Il n'y a pas de 'méthode' pour l'analyser. Il faut lire des histoires, simplement. Mais des histoires supposent ou suggèrent certaines attitudes humaines: il convient d'y avoir égard si on veut lire comme il faut. Et une histoire en entraine une autre: il y a des similitudes qu'il est bon de ne pas laisser échapper *a priori* par phobie du rapprochement arbitraire. Au fond, on ne demande qu'une permission, qui est d'admettre qu'une mythologie est une espèce de langage. On sait comment les 'signifiants' fonctionnent dans une langue: en s'inspirant quelque peu de la leçon des linguistes, on dira que nous avons à tenir compte, d'une part, des connexions qui existent entre les éléments ou les moments d'une même histoire (et qu'on peut présumer parfois d'autant plus profondes que la raison d'être n'apparaît pas du premier coup et semble même parfois échapper aux conteurs); d'autre part, des associations en vertu desquelles un épisode, un motif ou une image évoquent une série similaire. Connexions et associations aident à comprendre – dans un certain sens du mot. Mais il ne faut pas être pressé.[69]

articles on Bouglé, Davy, Granet, Halbwachs, and Simiand. E. E. Evans-Pritchard's introduction to Hertz, 1960 is helpful; see also Fauconnet, 1927 and Lukes, 1972. Honigsheim, 1960 lacks discrimination.

On linguistics and the Durkheim school: Mauss, 1925b; 1927b, pp. 4–5; 1937; 1907; Meillet, 1930; Febvre, 1913; Sommerfelt, 1938. On religion and economic value: Durkheim, 1912, p. 598 (anticipated in Durkheim, 1899); Mauss, 1914; 1966, p. 266 (1925a); Bouglé, 1922; Gernet, 1948a. On the right and left hand: Hertz, 1909; Granet, 1933; 1934, pp. 297–307. On gift exchange: Maunier, 1927; cf. Gernet, 1928. On time: Hubert, 1909; Gernet, 1956a.

The *Annales sociologiques* appeared as follows: series A, general sociology: 1–4, 1934, 1936, 1938, 1941; series B, sociology of religion: 1–3, 1939 = Granet, *Catégories matrimoniales* (Granet, 1939), 4, 1940; series C, sociology of law: 1–3, 1935, 1937, 1938; series D, economic sociology: 1–4, 1934, 1937, 1938, 1940; series E, social morphology, technology, aesthetics: 1–3, 1935, 1937, 1942. See also Mauss, 1933. Halbwachs was the general secretary. His main interests were social morphology and demography, the use of statistics to demonstrate 'social facts' as developed by Durkheim in his work on suicide (Durkheim, 1897; Halbwachs, 1930), and the exploration of the borderland between sociology and psychology, especially in the study of 'class psychology' and of memory. This was an original selection from the Durkheimian inheritance which brought him closer than his colleagues to other sociological schools – the group of Park and Burgess in Chicago (where he spent a year in 1930), and the Le Play tradition (cf. especially Halbwachs, 1913 and 1933; both works are closely related to the interests of Simiand). See Friedmann, 1946.

The evolutionary sequence traceable in Gernet's work is more explicitly used in Moret and Davy, 1923 and in the work of Marcel Granet, especially Granet, 1926 (dedicated to Mauss; pp. 602–19, series totemism-confreries-potlatch-city); cf. the discussion of this work in Halbwachs, 1926. Gernet also shared with Granet the method of recovering from the analysis of myth and ritual a number of 'milieux documentaires' (Granet, 1926, p. 49) as a basis for the history of institutions (cf. discussion in the introduction to Granet, 1926, and in Granet, 1929, pp. 156–60). Gernet and Granet were friends; the latter was bolder both in historical construction and in the explicit discussion of questions of method.

The connection between Granet's *Catégories matrimoniales* (1939) and Lévi-Strauss's *Les Structures élémentaires* (1949) is well known, but the even more striking parallels between Granet's analyses of Chinese thought and Lévi-Strauss's work on myth and classification systems have been less noticed. The Chinese appear to occupy in this field the privileged position of indigenous structuralist theorists attributed by Lévi-Strauss to the Australian aborigines in the analysis of kinship systems (Lévi-Strauss, 1958, p. 309). Cf. Mills, 1940, and Gernet's remarks on the influence of Granet on G. Dumézil (Gernet, 1954b).

The evolutionary schema discussed above also appears, more surprisingly, in Cornford, 1912, pp. 92–6, and Jane Harrison, 1912 (especially pp. 45 f., 127), accompanied by a thoroughly Durkheimian theory of the evolution of religion which they appear to have worked out independently (perhaps with the help of the lectures by Radcliffe-Brown which Jane Harrison attended in Cambridge in 1909; Harrison, 1912, p. 125) from Durkheim's 'Sociologie religieuse et théorie de la connaissance' (Durkheim, 1909; an early draft of the first chapter of Durkheim, 1912). See also Harrison, 1921, pp. 6–26. Cornford's enthusiastic application of Durkheim's theories on primitive classification and the religious origins of philosophy to the early Greek philosophers (Cornford, 1912) was disconcerting even to the *Année sociologique* school (see David, 1913a, and the similarly dubious reception of Harrison, 1912; David, 1913b). It is not easy to see from his unfinished last work, *Principium Sapientiae* (Cornford, 1952), what were his later views on the relation between archaic Greek society and the thought of the first philosophers. Note, however, the emphasis on elaboration and criticism of the mythical tradition in poetry as an intermediate stage between 'religion' and 'philosophy' (e.g. 1952, p. 144) and see Murray, 1943. A closer association between philosophy and social structure is maintained by Vernant, 1962. (See also below, chapter 9.)

Appendix II   Durkheim in 1972

The independent decision of three young scholars to re-study Durkheim's life and work reflects clearly the currently felt need to re-examine the problems, methods, and assumptions of the founder generation of academic sociologists as a means of criticizing and clarifying present orientations in the subject (Lukes, 1972; Wallwork,

1972; La Capra, 1972). Though Marx and Weber are perhaps receiving even more attention, several reasons make Durkheim a particularly appropriate focus for this process of reappraisal. His influence in sociology and social anthropology spread rapidly and has been extraordinarily pervasive; even Max Weber, though since 1950 increasingly taking Durkheim's place as the leading 'classic' in the sociological corpus, has to some extent been seen through Durkheimian spectacles. Despite Talcott Parsons's attempt to use Weber's action theory as a bridge between sociology and psychology (not a very successful idea), sociology has essentially followed the positivistic line of Durkheim; it is only in the last few years, with the rise of new approaches based on the work of Alfred Schutz and G. H. Mead, that attempts to follow up Weber's emphasis on the meaning of action for the individual have begun to attract general attention. And the especial popularity of *The Protestant Ethic and the Spirit of Capitalism* (Weber, 1904–5) among Weber's works is partly due to the ease with which its thesis can be translated into Durkheimian terms.

Furthermore, Durkheim comes directly under attack as a result of the reaction in current sociology against functionalist studies of integration and the influence of shared values, in favor of emphasis on contradictions and conflicts. At the same time, however, French structuralism has brought Durkheimian ideas into new prominence; even Marxism, in France, is appearing in Durkheimian clothing, in the work of Althusser and Godelier. There is tension between appreciation of the abstract, relational approach to social phenomena, of which Durkheim was one of the pioneers in his work on social structure in the *Division of Labor in Society* (1893) and on the sociology of knowledge in *Primitive Classification* (Durkheim and Mauss, 1903), and the realization that it directs attention away from the claims and problems of substantive social units with which a politically-oriented sociology must concern itself.

Durkheim's importance for the understanding of French culture is not confined to structuralism. The *Annales* school of historians, too, despite some polemic over disciplinary boundaries, owed much to him both in their positivist emphasis on the use of statistics and in their concern with 'collective representations'; Durkheim is one of the pivots of the transformation of German *Kulturgeschichte* into French sociological history.

To reassess the work of a figure still central to the discipline, in a period of transition and uncertainty, is not an easy task. It is noticeable that whereas Robert Bellah, in his introduction to the new Heritage of Sociology volume *Émile Durkheim on Morality and Society* (Bellah, 1973), knows clearly what Durkheim means to him as a sociologist of religion, the three younger writers – none of whom is a practicing grassroots sociologist – are much less certain in their perspective. Too personal an approach may, of course, lead to distortions; but Bellah's sympathy for Durkheim's conception of the place of religion in society gives him a real insight into Durkheim's position as 'high priest and theologian of the civil religion of the Third Republic' and the strong personal moral commitment which underlay all his work. Bellah rightly points out that in his inaugural lecture at Bordeaux in 1887 (Durkheim, 1888), Durkheim already included collective representations among the social facts which sociology should study (the influence of German *Kulturgeschichte* and of Savigny's conception of the relation between law and culture should be examined here). In a sense, perhaps, Durkheim did not become more idealist in his later work, but less positivist; although ostensibly remaining committed to positivism, his work on religion derives much of its value from its imaginative insights into the social experience of participants in ritual – while at the same time remaining firmly anchored to Durkheim's earlier interest in social structure. Bellah's introduction perhaps gives too little attention to the formal aspects of Durkheim's work which led on to structuralism. But it is a perceptive and well-judged portrait.

Lukes's work (1972) is likely to stand for some time as the definitive *explication de texte* for Durkheim, as well as providing invaluable tools of reference in a complete bibliography of Durkheim's writings and a carefully researched list of his lecture programs. As an *explication de texte* it has the virtues and the defects of its genre. Durkheim's work is excellently annotated, in the sense that we are always given enough background information to understand the text, and references leading to more detailed studies. Lukes discusses the whole corpus of Durkheim's writings instead of concentrating, as most do, on the best-known works, and so is able to make full use of Durkheim's generous provision of commentaries on himself; the chapter on Durkheim's *Pragmatism and Sociology* (1914) and its relation to *Primitive Classification* (1903) and *The Elementary Forms of the*

Religious Life (1912) is particularly valuable. At the same time Lukes provides a critical analysis and evaluation of Durkheim's arguments and key concepts, pointing out their internal weaknesses. There are, however, aspects of intellectual biography which this text-based approach inevitably misses. We do not really get a clear idea of the world in which Durkheim grew up and took his own intellectual bearings, nor of his impact on French society and culture as a public figure, reviewer, and teacher. Lukes gives a lively account, it is true, of the resentments aroused by Durkheim's pontifical airs; but his decision to say little about the work of the other members of the *Année sociologique* school, understandable as it is in view of the size of the task, enables him to avoid coming to grips with the phenomenon of Durkheim's intense faith in the science he had created and capacity to inspire the same faith in others.

Pointing out the internal weaknesses in Durkheim's arguments is rather too easy a game. Certainly he was a contradictory performer: a programmatic empiricist who constantly lapsed into mystical dogmatism, a keenly polemical arguer who failed to see the gaps between his own insights and the arguments he used to support them. The real question to be asked concerns the validity and vitality of his insights rather than his arguments. And here the work of two generations of sociologists and social anthropologists in developing and testing Durkheim's ideas must be taken into account. A critical analysis of Durkheim's distinction between the normal and the pathological in society is not an adequate basis for an assessment of the strengths and weaknesses of functionalism.

The high degree of integration in the work of the *Année sociologique* school, besides being – especially considering the brilliance and originality of Mauss, Halbwachs, Granet and even lesser-known members of the school – an extraordinary phenomenon in itself, also makes the whole corpus very valuable as a commentary on Durkheim and as a guide to the content of his teaching. (The separate but closely related position of Lucien Lévy-Bruhl also requires study.) Even a rapid survey would have indicated the perspectives opened and those concealed by Durkheim's approach. His focus on the relation between structure and integration – mechanical solidarity based on similarity in homogeneous structures, organic solidarity based on complementarity in complex ones – soon led Mauss (and Radcliffe-Brown) to criticize his initial simplistic formulation and stress the role of exchange in simple societies. The school as a whole remained

weak in analyzing the articulation of different types of organization
in complex societies, tending to treat them as evolutionary strata,
but Mauss at least was aware of this problem too (Mauss, 1932).
The fertility of Durkheim's approach for the analysis of ritual
scarcely needs illustration. On the other hand, the failure of the
school to produce any work on political institutions (except in the
field of law) shows up strikingly his weakness here. In economics,
Halbwachs's treatment of social class and the work of Simiand show
both the strengths and the limitations of the Durkheimian stress on
collective representations; the advances in social psychology are
often made at the expense of a grasp of the essential structural
factors. It would be interesting, from this point of view, to contrast
Simiand's treatment of the role of money and consumer attitudes to
it in the dynamics of economic cycles with that of Keynes.

Wallwork's book (1972) is, like that of Lukes, text-focused, but has
an original perspective; the recent interest of moral philosophers in
'institutional facts' and the 'is–ought' problem, favoring a more
naturalistic, empiricist approach to ethics, has stimulated Wallwork
to re-study Durkheim's contribution to moral philosophy. This
orientation admittedly at times puts Wallwork at cross-purposes with
his author. The aim of the modern moral philosophers with whom
he sympathizes, to reach through cross-cultural studies universally
applicable precepts for an individual-based ethics, is hardly one with
which Durkheim would have sympathized. Although he has a useful
chapter on 'moral communities' (the family, professional groups, the
state; the school should have been included here), Wallwork does
not allow sufficient weight on the whole to the structural emphasis in
Durkheim's moral theory. It might well be argued, indeed, that
Durkheim failed to integrate his assertion that individualism was the
only religion compatible with the complex structure of modern
society (1898) into his studies of modern morality, especially in
Suicide (1897) and *Moral Education* (1925). The absence of any
treatment of responsibility in Durkheim's moral theory is striking in
view of the prominence given to the topic by Fustel de Coulanges's
comments on the relation between collective responsibility and
corporate descent-group organization, and between individualism
and the development of the notion of individual responsibility in law.
Fustel's theme was pursued in the *Année* school by Fauconnet and
Gernet, and outside it by Glotz and Saleilles; responsibility was

also the subject of Lucien Lévy-Bruhl's first work in moral philosophy.

But if Durkheim was inclined to allow his *penchant* for mechanical solidarity to override his insights into the complex structure of modern society, he at least stated firmly that the moral state of society could not be remedied merely by exhortation and education, but required structural reforms (Durkheim, 1897, pp. 444–5; cf. 1901b). In so far as Durkheim saw education as an effective agent of reform, it was because the school could be structured to provide the kind of social experience needed (1925, pp. 235–6). And his analysis of *anomie* (on which La Capra is much more illuminating than Wallwork) rests solidly on structural foundations. Durkheim's fundamental problem was not the nature of the good act, but the nature of the good society. Wallwork's analysis of his involvement with the arguments of moral philosophers (Kant, Wundt, the Utilitarians) makes an important contribution to our understanding of Durkheim, but tends to obscure his more profound concern with the problems of political philosophy. His first thesis made it plain that his conception of a science of morals owed as much to Montesquieu as to the German historical school. His ethical theory needs to be seen in the context of political philosophy and also of the philosophy of law – a topic scarcely explored at all as yet in Durkheim studies.

Wallwork's approach, however, is fully justified in one respect: Durkheim was far more acute and perceptive as an observer of individual moral behavior than as a political theorist. Wallwork gives an excellent analysis of his contribution here both in the early article on 'La Science positive de la morale en Allemagne' (Durkheim, 1887) and in *Moral Education*. His comments on Piaget's debt to and criticisms of Durkheim are particularly interesting. Certainly Durkheim has much to offer moral philosophers, both in his work on socialization and in his intuitive insights into the experience of being in society – especially in his poignant sensitivity to tension between constraint and identification with the group or its ideals.

La Capra's eagerness to relate Durkheim to current preoccupations (Weber, Marx, Lévi-Strauss) makes his book (1972) uneven and at times unreliable, but rewardingly acute and stimulating in many of its perceptions. Both in style ('Durkheim became the Plato of the Australian blackfellows in order to emerge as the Angelic Doctor of consensual society') and his ideas are apt to run away with him. He is too much inclined to tell us what Durkheim might have said on topics he never considered; and his persistent attempt to associate Durkheim's concept of 'collective effervescence' with V. W. Turner's *communitas* (Turner, 1969) gives much of his discussion a misleading bias. (Robertson Smith is completely omitted from his account of Durkheim's sociology of religion.) Turner's *communitas* is certainly the latest version of Durkheim's insight into the experience of ritual, but it is not free from sociocentric bias; *communitas* is seen as opposed to structure and constraint, which is not true of Durkheim's collective effervescence. The best commentary on the latter is the section on dancing in chapter V of Radcliffe-Brown, 1922:

> In the dance the individual submits to the action upon him of the community; he is constrained, by the immediate effect of rhythm as well as by custom, to join in, and he is required to conform in his own actions and movements to the needs of the common activity. The surrender of the individual to this constraint or obligation is not felt as painful, but on the contrary as highly pleasurable. As the dancer loses himself in the dance, as he becomes absorbed in the unified community, he reaches a state of elation in which he feels himself filled with energy or force immensely beyond his ordinary state.

(None of the writers considered here seems sufficiently aware of the importance of Radcliffe-Brown's work as a commentary on Durkheim.)

The good points of the book are a vigorous account of Durkheim's historical context in the society of the Third Republic, and especially his close ties with leading educationalists (Buisson, Liard, Lapie); an excellent discussion of *anomie*; some good comments on Durkheim's distinction between religion and magic, and on the weaknesses of his interpretation of totemism; and very acute observations on the development of Durkheim's ideas in the *Division du travail social* by Mauss and Lévi-Strauss:

> We could easily have emphasized only the negative aspect of the division of labor by calling it a prohibition of tasks; and conversely, outlined the positive aspect of incest-prohibition by calling it the principle of the division of labor of marriageable rights between families. (La Capra, 1972, p. 113 quoting Lévi-Strauss, 1956, p. 277)

'Totemism for Lévi-Strauss amounted to a subcase of the general problem of making differentiation the ground of integration – the very problem which Durkheim had earlier conceptualized in terms of organic solidarity' (La Capra, 1972, p. 115). It would, however, have been useful to discuss here the influence of Radcliffe-Brown, as well as Mauss, in Lévi-Strauss's relation to Durkheim. And the discussion might profitably have been extended to include Lévi-Strauss's *Mythologiques* (1964–71); is there not in Lévi-Strauss's concern with discovering the structure of the human mind a reaction against Durkheim's attempt to provide a sociological alternative to Kantian epistemology?

There is a great deal more interesting work to be done on Durkheim's influence both inside France and abroad (especially in the U.S.). There is also, however, much still to be done on Durkheim's background. None of these books succeeds in giving a clear idea of the mental furniture with which Durkheim grew up. The task is difficult just because he did so much to break the nineteenth-century molds of thought and create the categories and concepts now taken for granted in sociology. But it is very important – especially since Durkheim, for all his originality, was such a polemical thinker – to know to what current models of psychology, law, morals, epistemology, religion, and political thought he was opposing his own theories.

One of the most obvious omissions here is the background to Durkheim's proposal, first put forward in 1895–6 in the lectures on socialism and in *Suicide*, to attack the problems of modern French society by creating a pyramidal structure of occupational groups culminating in a central economic council. One would hardly guess from any of the books under review, even Lukes's, that schemes of this kind were generally in the air at the time (in Britain, a little later, they crystallized in the form of Guild Socialism) and came out of a long tradition of criticism of the laissez-faire economy – a tradition in which similar criticisms were frequently made from left and right; anticipations of Durkheimian ideas can be found in both conservatives (de Maistre) and socialists (Saint-Simon, Proudhon, for example). Far from being an armchair theorist's paper scheme with no basis in reality, Durkheim's proposals was put forward at a time when two competing occupation-based organizations were available as a basis for further development: the Fédération des Bourses du

Travail, set up in 1893, in which local trade unions were combined into local Bourses du Travail, which in turn sent representatives to central meetings of the Fédération; and the Confédération Général du Travail, founded in 1895, which was a federation of national trade unions. The two organizations united only in 1902 – the year of the second edition of *De la division du travail social* with its new preface reiterating the need for occupation-based corporations. (However, the *Histoire des Bourses du Travail* by the anarchist secretary of the F.B.T., F. Pelloutier (1902), with an interesting preface by Sorel, was not reviewed in the *Année*.) The relation between these syndicalist organizations and the political activity of the socialist party – which gained its first significant successes in the elections of 1893 – was a central issue for socialism in the 1890s. In fact, Jaurès had already put forward a proposal virtually identical to that of Durkheim in articles in *La Dépêche de Toulouse* in 1889 (Venturi, 1966, pp. 33–6). He repeated it in a series of articles on the socialist organization of the future published in *La Revue socialiste* in 1895–6, this time citing Durkheim as an authority: 'La décentralisation se fera, comme Durkheim l'a si bien indiqué dans son vigoureux ouvrage sur la *Division du Travail*, non plus géographiquement, comme pour la vie communale, mais techniquement et professionellement' (Jaurès, 1931, p. 347). There seems little doubt that Durkheim's remarks on occupational groups in 1895–6 were the outcome of discussions with Jaurès; and it may well have been Jaurès who was the first to point out the parallels between their ideas.

More detailed research on the debates of the period, especially in Bordeaux, is needed to establish the exact nuances of the position Durkheim was taking up in his lectures on socialism, and the reactions they aroused. It is not clear to me how far, at this date when Jaurès and Guesde were on the whole pursuing a common policy, Durkheim's association with the views of the former implied taking position against the supporters of Guesde in the city and among his own pupils. This may not in any case have been his only preoccupation at the time. It seems to me likely that in *Suicide*, addressed to a wider public (the lectures on socialism were not published until 1928), he may have been taking a position in relation to solidarism rather than socialism. Léon Bourgeois's short term as prime minister also belongs to 1895–6, and his proclamation of solidarism as the political philosophy of the Radicals was delivered at the end of 1895. Durkheim's criticisms of A. Fouillée's *La France au point de vue moral* (Durkheim, 1901b) suggest that while he agreed with the solidarists' critique of modern society, he found their proposed remedies weak and rhetorical. (This was also the judgment of Renouvier, as noted by Hayward, 1958.) The solidarist idea of welfare legislation based on a new legal philosophy was very different from Durkheim's proposals for structural reform legitimated by science. Lukes and La Capra, in their discussion of Durkheim's relation to solidarism, do not sufficiently distinguish between his debt to the earlier solidarist tradition, which has been well established by Hayward (1958, 1960), and his reaction to solidarism as a political program in the 1890s. Thus the proposals in *Socialism* and *Suicide* do seem to mark out a clear commitment both to structural reforms more radical than those contemplated by the solidarists and to a rejection of revolutionary anarcho-syndicalism in favor of the attempt to solve labor problems constitutionally by creating new economic organizations which would be integrated with the machinery of the State.

It is clear that 1894–6 was a crucial period in Durkheim's development. His involvement in the Dreyfus affair is well known; but a more detailed study of the events of these years and Durkheim's life in Bordeaux would be required to determine the relative importance of the Dreyfus affair and the political successes of socialists and radicals in reviving the feeling of urgency and idealism which he had felt in the early years of the Third Republic. It was in the same period that he began to lecture on religion (1894–5) and was, as he himself recorded in a letter, profoundly influenced by the work of Robertson Smith. But one must not leap too hastily from the experience of collective effervescence in the Dreyfus crisis to the genesis of Durkheim's views on religion. What he learned from Robertson Smith was surely that religious beliefs vary with social structure. Smith, himself influenced by the German historical school, enabled Durkheim to extend the lessons he had already derived from them in the field of law and morality into the study of religion and thence to knowledge in general. This lesson was applied to the Dreyfus affair in the defense of individualism in 1898 as the only religion compatible with the structure of modern society ('L'Individualisme et les intellectuels'). The term 'effervescence,' if I am not mistaken (I have not searched systematically), first occurs in *L'Évolution pédagogique en France* (vol. I, 95; lectures of 1904–5, published 1938) in a context which shows the influence of Saint-Simon's concept of 'organic' and 'critical' periods in history (cf. the similar context in Durkheim's 1911 article on 'Jugements de valeur et jugements de réalité,' Durkheim, 1967, p. 134). There is still work to be done on the sources and development of this aspect of Durkheim's sociology of religion; it should perhaps be brought into relation with the keen interest in communication shown in the account of the democratic state in the *Leçons de sociologie* (text 1898–1900, published 1950).

The fact that we have no text of Durkheim's sociological lectures after 1900, and only a fragment of his projected work on *La Morale* (Durkheim, 1920), makes it more difficult to trace the development of his thought in the latter part of his life. Certainly he was much taken up with developing and defending his new insights into the sociology of religion and of knowledge, and with elaborating his ideal-type model of the simple society with details from the increasingly abundant ethnographic data. His faith in the possibility of solidarity in complex societies receded into the distant future (Durkheim, 1912, p. 611). Yet he continued to lecture on law and morals and to give his opinion on a variety of current issues, besides developing his ideas on sociological method and reviewing a wide range of works on the history of the family. Did contemporaries feel that he had turned away from the problems of modern society to locate his Zion among the Australian aborigines? We need a study of the social role of the sociologist in this period: the sociologist's conception of his own role, and his contemporaries' ideas of what he could give them. Durkheim is obviously one of the most fascinating cases; his faith in the validity of his scientific methods and discoveries must be integrated into the collective representations of his time, and the prophetic elements in his personality seen not as an embarrassing skeleton in the sociological cupboard but merely, as he himself might have said, a social fact.

Part two

Economy and society

4 Archaeology and the social and economic history of classical Greece

I

L'archéologie [i.e. antiquarian studies] . . . est la partie la plus intéressante de l'histoire, puisque c'est celle de l'homme dans sa vie publique et privée . . . la connoissance de tout ce qui a rapport aux moeurs et aux usages des anciens. [Millin, 1796]

L'archéologie . . . peut devenir triste, et même très triste. [Robert, 1965b, p. 328]

L'on verrait, on voit déjà, devrais-je dire, des archéologues s'enfermer dans le pur raffinement de leur science. [van Effenterre, 1965, p. 41]

When so much is expected of archaeologists, it is hardly surprising that their colleagues sometimes feel disappointed in their expectations. The excavation of classical sites as a means of learning more about their history, and not merely in search of works of art, may be said to have begun just under a hundred years ago with the excavations of Schliemann at Troy in 1871 and Conze at Pergamon in 1877. Since that time archaeological methods have been constantly in rapid evolution.[1] Both the development of archaeological method and the accelerating pace of change in the Mediterranean countryside increase the discoveries of new sites and the pressure to excavate before they are destroyed. Archaeology also bears an increasingly large share of the task of satisfying the non-specialist's interest in the ancient world, and this demand exerts its own pressure on excavation policy and publications.[2] And ancient historians, who are becoming more and more interested in social and economic history, ask new questions about forms of production and exchange, patterns of settlement, cultural interrelations between the Greeks and Romans and their subjects or barbarian neighbours, and the wide variety of religious beliefs and practices of the ancient world, which require not only the excavation of new types of site (farms, workshops . . .), the examination of material which used to be ignored (bones, domestic pottery . . .), and the excavation of larger areas of ancient cities (residential quarters), but also, above all, enough evidence to permit comparisons and quantitative assessment – not one Troy, but a series of Troys.

These new interests, and the refinement of methods which makes them possible, not only slow down the process of excavation but inevitably lead to specialisation: the technique of excavation and of dating finds becomes increasingly complex, demanding more time and more specialised knowledge and training. This development, among other causes, has led to the disappearance of the old tradition of antiquarian studies,[3] which played such an important part in binding together the various branches of classical studies, and this has left an alarming gap between the archaeologist and the historian. (It is perhaps most obvious in the study of religion.)

This virtual disappearance of a whole tradition of studies is, however, a long-term problem. The most obvious need here is for the special methods and problems of handling archaeological evidence to be more widely recognised as an element in the basic training of any classical scholar – as, for instance, epigraphy is. As yet it seems to be only in France and Scandinavia that such a training is common. But this article is not the place for a discussion of post-graduate training. The present situation is that with a few rare exceptions archaeologists and historians are distinct groups with too little knowledge of each other's interests and problems; questions about economic and social history are formulated by historians, usually in rather abstract terms, and the detailed evidence is scattered in archaeological publications which were not written with these questions in mind. The immediate need therefore seems to be for historians to put their questions to archaeologists in a more precise and concrete form, and for archaeologists to bring out more clearly in publication the historical implications of their finds. This in itself is likely to encourage more historians to make the effort to understand and synthesise archaeological evidence for themselves, and archaeologists to discuss those historical problems which arise directly from the detailed study of the evidence, rather than from abstract analysis, which are at present neglected.

The vague and abstract formulation of problems of economic and social history is, of course, partly due to ignorance of archaeological material and methods. But interest in learning from sociology, anthropology, psychology, economic history and other disciplines new ways of studying the ancient world is a recent growth, and is inevitably still in a confused and experimental stage. The work of J.-P. Vernant, M. Detienne and P. Vidal-Naquet on such subjects as the Greek organisation of space, the *colossus*, or Simonides' contrast of *alētheia* and *doxa*[4] is rich in intimations of new approaches to Greek architecture and art, but so far has provided an assortment of potentially significant examples rather than a precise programme of research into the archaeological evidence. Economic historians are still fighting the old battle of Modernists versus Primitivists – grappling with the problem of finding terminologies and models which will illuminate the economic institutions of the ancient world without introducing misleading analogies.[5] The lack of a firm conceptual basis and accepted categories of analysis has made it difficult to set out confidently in search of new factual evidence.

Nevertheless it seems to me possible and useful to formulate some more precise questions about the economic and social history of classical Greece in terms of the archaeological evidence. I have concentrated on Greece and the fifth and fourth centuries B.C. for two reasons. One is that the conceptual difficulties still make it very difficult to discuss the economic history of any earlier period. More work on Mycenaean documents and their relation to the palace archives of the Near East, and more analysis of the implications for the formation of the religious, political and economic institutions of the Greek *polis* of the collapse of the Mycenaean palaces and the institutions embodied in them, and the momentous experience of the colonisation period, seem to me more urgently needed at the moment, from the historian's point of view, than new archaeological data for Mycenaean and Archaic Greece. The classical period is not free from conceptual difficulties, but the literary sources give us a picture of institutions and attitudes, at least for Athens; they also provide a solid historical narrative of events to be used as a basis for research. We can be sure that the evacuation of Attica in the Peloponnesian war, the political and financial subjection of the Aegean cities in the Athenian empire, or the rise of Macedon, were accompanied by social and economic changes sufficient to leave some trace in the archaeological record.

A second reason for basing the discussion on classical Greece is that communications between archaeologists and historians seem here to be at their worst. The traditional idealisation of Greek art and the traditional primacy of political and military history are both rooted most deeply in classical Greece: the evidence is richer, the accumulated deposit of previous scholarship thicker, the problems far more complex.[6] Collaboration between historians and archaeologists has been more successful in the study of other periods not only because its impulse has come partly from a reaction against the traditional outlook, which tends to be combined with a reaction against this period, but because the problems are simpler. The civilisation of the Roman provinces, for instance, has more recurring patterns than that of the Greek city-states.[7] Where there is less evidence from literary sources there is also more stimulus to attempt to reconstruct history from the archaeological evidence. But we might discover more about the potentialities and limitations of archaeological evidence by exploring the periods for which there is evidence of other kinds by which it can be checked. In any case, our accounts of classical Greece have so far been built on one-sided sources. We are no longer content with history which tells us about Athenian imperialism only from the Athenian point of view, about Greeks but not about barbarians, about cities but not about villages, about temples but not private houses, about philosophers but not farmers. Something can be done – and is being done – to remedy this bias by re-studying the literary sources. But our main hope of learning to recognise the diversity of Greek society and the range of its variations lies in excavation.

II Problems

Any study of the economic history of the ancient world must begin with the question of the relative importance of country and town, autarkic (subsistence or manorial) farming and production for the market, the agricultural basis and the superstructure supported by it. So far the only attempt to apply archaeological evidence to this type of enquiry in Greece has been Kahrstedt's *Wirtschaftliche Gesicht Griechenlands in der Kaiserzeit* (1954).[8] Work in Italy and the Roman provinces, and in prehistoric archaeology, shows that much more can be done. Field-systems can in some cases be detected on air photographs: J. Bradford called attention in 1956[9] to the

remains of probably classical terracing on the southern slopes of
Mt Hymettos and stated: 'It is safe to say, on the evidence of
personal study, that the soil of Attica offers considerable scope for
aerial discovery.'[10] Traces of centuration are visible on photographs
of the areas round Actium, Dyme, Pella and Thessalonica.[11] But
although air photographs are now being used in mapping some
sites in Greece,[12] hardly any attempt has been made to exploit them
for the discovery of new archaeological features. Field-systems, roads
and the density and type of rural settlement (villages or isolated
farms) are all important as indications of the nature of the rural
economy. Excavation of farms and village sites has been very rare,[13]
too rare for a balanced picture of Greek culture as reflected in its
material remains. Excavation of farm buildings could give information about their size and equipment; whether crops were grown for
the market (an oil or wine press would probably not be constructed
merely for household needs);[14] whether the farmer grew his own corn
(did he have a threshing floor?); the influence of urban fashions in
architecture,[15] or the persistence of specialised designs. Animal bones
or outbuildings may give evidence of the livestock kept on the farm.
Pollen analysis may reveal something of the ecology of the region in
antiquity; water supply and erosion can be studied.[16] Storage rooms
and pithoi suggest farming for the household's needs and storage of
the bulk of the harvest, while coins and urban products such as
painted vases show connections with city markets.[17] Rural society
can be studied in village sites and cemeteries: rich landowners
maintaining an elaborate country home, slave-farms run by bailiffs,[18]
or smallholders adopting the tastes of the urban bourgeoisie in
furnishings and tomb monuments[19] have different patterns of life
which should be recognisable in the archaeological data. Changes in
settlement patterns, especially the abandonment of farms or the
contraction or desertion of village sites in the less fertile areas,
provide an index of the demand for farming land.[20] Evidence
for density of settlement would be particularly valuable for the
question of the importance of land-hunger as a cause of colonisation;
and a study of the effect of the concentration of population in
Athens and devastation of Attica in the Peloponnesian war on social
patterns and the structure of agriculture is essential for our understanding of classical Athens.

Aristophanes and Demosthenes shed some light on these changes
in Athens, but for the rest of Greece we have hardly a word in the

literary sources for the classical period. Even epigraphic sources for the organisation of states other than Athens, for public finance, etc., are scanty and have not been systematically studied.[21] For most states the only survey of the archaeological evidence, which might give at least an approximate idea of a level of culture or prosperity, is that in Pauly-Wissowa or *Inscriptiones Graecae*. J. M. Cook recently asked some important questions about the nature of 'city life' in Ionia under the Athenian empire: apart from the absence of public buildings, which is not entirely surprising if the city's revenues were drained off in tribute to Athens, the excavations at Old Smyrna and surface remains elsewhere suggest that the city sites were only thinly occupied in the fifth century, possibly because the landowning class tended to retire, in the face of a pro-Athenian *demos*, to their country mansions.[22] Obviously much more excavation is needed before this can be more than a hypothesis; but the effect of Athenian tribute, political pressure and a considerable period of *Pax Atheniensis* on the social and economic development of the allied cities in the Aegean is another major question of fifth-century history where the scanty evidence of literary sources must be supplemented by archaeological material. The rise of Boeotia, Thessaly and Macedon as major powers in the fourth century[23] equally poses questions about social and economic change to which archaeology can respond. Spartan history demands examination of the perioecic towns of Laconia and the nature of the settlement in Messenia under Spartan domination. And one could go on.

The problems of a city are naturally far more complex than those of a rural site. The most urgent step perhaps is to take stock of the information which past excavation and exploration have already provided. The bibliography of ancient town planning is now growing rapidly, but so far research has concentrated on regularities of plan and overall pattern rather than individual variations. The comparative study of public building in different cities and periods alone provides a large group of subjects for research. The size of building projects and the length of time taken to carry them out is an important element in the study of public finance. The function of the buildings erected at different periods is also relevant to the city's history: buildings for political life and administration, temples,[24] buildings for education, the entertainment of foreign visitors, trade or food storage, theatres, aqueducts, cisterns, drains, roads and fortifications in the city itself and its territory, all give an indication of the pre-occupations of the state at the time when they were set up.[25]

The positioning of inscriptions[26] and of the public and private monuments which formed so large a part of a city's charm and character in the eyes of ancient travellers; the change of taste in this informal yet conscious process of decorating the city with history written in monuments, and the relation of these to changes in architecture and in the financing of public building, can tell us much about social history. In the private sector, though still perhaps subject to the overall plan of the city, there is the question of the distribution of shops, workshops and private houses – their relation to each other and to areas of public building – and the treatment of conflicts of interest between private property and public projects such as roads, drains and defence works.[27] Modern awareness of the problems involved in rebuilding cities should stimulate us to examine the archaeological evidence for rebuilding on ancient sites. After a widespread destruction in war, fire or earthquake one will look for signs of the speed of economic recovery and reconstruction, and of state control of private rebuilding and policy decisions in the re-construction of public buildings. The constant process of piecemeal rebuilding where no major destruction has occurred provides equally important evidence for changes in tenure and land use. The demoli-tion of several small houses to make place for one large one, the persistence of shrines on the same site through successive levels of occupation or the conversion of sacred ground to secular use, the transition of private houses or public buildings to industrial use,[28] all help to build up a picture of the social history of the town. The course of city walls, roads and drains, and their relation to the houses which border them, can show us how the grid principle in city plans was adapted in individual cases to the configuration of the site, the requirements of defence, the orientation and layout of sacred buildings and the claims of property-owners. It would be interesting to know more about the use of areas immediately outside the walls of ancient cities. At Olynthus the grid plan seems to have governed the layout of the rich villas built on the slopes of the hill and the plain. Unfortunately the course of the walls is not known. At Histria there are mud-brick dwellings around the city; at Old Smyrna considerable traces of suburban settlement. The rubbish dump just outside the wall at this site is also interesting.[29] Everywhere there were cemeteries whose layout and relation to the city, to roads and to the geology of the site needs to be more clearly defined. Although on some sites the city spread into the surrounding country-side, *rus in urbe* was probably more common. Greek cities commonly enclosed a large area within their walls, which in parts was thinly settled;[30] density of population and the extent to which gardening and keeping livestock was possible within the city needs study. The houses of landowners who lived in the city on the produce of their farms may be recognisable by the presence of store-rooms and pithoi, agricultural implements, kitchens equipped for roasting whole carcasses, or grinding flour and baking.[31] Prehistoric archaeologists have shown how much can be learnt about diet from domestic refuse; information about butchering methods, the frequency of meat consumption in different social strata and the age at which animals are slaughtered or the place of wild game in the diet[32] is relevant for the interpretation of classical society too. The place of weaving in the household economy is also worth research; loom-weights are re-corded in numerous archaeological reports, but we have no study of their distribution in relation to different areas, periods and classes, and to the literary and archaeological evidence for dyeing establish-ments and the production of ready-made clothing.

The evaluation of the contrast between town and countryside, essential to an understanding of Greece itself, takes on a new dimension in the areas where Greeks settled among other peoples. A considerable mass of information has been collected about the diffusion of Greek objects and motifs,[33] but the background of changing customs, tastes and institutions implied by their movements still needs much study. The whole subject of 'acculturation', included in the 1965 historical congress at the suggestion of an ancient historian, André Aymard, is one of the major problems of ancient history for which archaeological evidence is most essential. We are only just beginning to realise that 'acculturation' is a two-way process.[34] To study it means examining the way in which Greek objects reached barbarian sites, the status of those who acquired them, and the modifications in the institutions of both barbarians and colonies which were set in train by the contact between different cultures. For instance it is an obvious point, but one which has only recently been made, that the economic life of the ancient world included not only the economies of Greece and Rome, which already differ considerably from that of modern Europe, but also other economic institutions which differed radically from these. The 'silent barter' described by Herodotus[35] is an extremely simple form of an adjustment which had to be made wherever Greeks and barbarians met to exchange goods; it demanded a certain amount of flexibility in the institutions of both parties at the point of interaction, and the adaptations of custom introduced at this point would tend to have repercussions on both sides. Karl Polanyi has shown that one of the ways in which a society may adapt itself to exchange relations with a type of economy different from its own is to circumscribe exchange within narrow limits: foreign traders can deal only in a 'port of trade', with authorised agents, and their goods in consequence tend to reach only a limited class.[36] (Where one party is supplying slaves, as was frequently the case in trade between Greeks and barbarians, it is still more likely that political control will play an important part.) This particular model of the 'port of trade' in its details immediately suggests Greek trade with Egypt,[37] and is in some respects inapplicable elsewhere; but it is certainly worth asking whether Greek goods were acquired in other areas by a ruling class, at least in the first generation of trade (and not by Scythian corn-farmers or Celtic miners), and when and how barbarian societies changed to allow a broader distribution of Greek goods and Greek ways. The notion of a 'port of trade' is also generally relevant in that it focuses attention on the wall of contact where two cultures meet and through which cultural osmosis[38] takes place, and on the transformations of culture which occur at this point. It is likely enough that Greek colonies had to develop sufficient flexibility of institutions to serve as intermediaries between the professional traders and markets of Greece and a quite different economic pattern among their barbarian neighbours, and that in consequence their social and economic development was different from that of the old Greek cities. The Russian excavations at Olbia, for instance, have revealed an agora flanked by large fifth-century stoas which seem to have been used for trade, and among the rich private houses near it one at least seems to have belonged to a wine or oil merchant, who had it equipped with a cistern for storing his wares.[39] Commercial public building on this scale is not a common feature in the agoras of old Greece as early as the fifth century, as far as we know (we know very little).[40] It would be premature to argue from this evidence that the state exercised more control over trade in fifth-century Olbia than in Greece, and that merchants enjoyed a high status there, but it is worth looking for more evidence of this kind.

There is also more to be done in collecting evidence from non-Greek sites for the character of their trade with the colonies, and need for a refinement of our conceptual apparatus and increased subtlety in interpretation.[41] A basic requirement is that lists and distribution-maps of Greek objects found on non-Greek sites must be accompanied by precise details of the context in which the objects were found and a rigorous evaluation of the significance of the distribution pattern with regard to the extent of archaeological exploration of the area – in other words, of the statistical basis of the conclusions suggested by the data so far available.[42] The fact that two Attic cups have been found in a Scythian tomb, or that large quantities of Greek pottery and bronzes reached a certain Celtic oppidum, is meaningless to the reader unless he knows how many other tombs or oppida have been excavated, how the offerings in this tomb compare with other grave inventories of the same date, whether the Greek objects in the oppidum belonged to princes or Greek settlers, or were in common use among a population in which Greek habits and tastes were widespread. From this point of view the study of the movement of artefacts or stylistic influence is only a means to the study of changes in tastes and ways of life; changes in the layout of native houses, sanctuaries and settlements, in customs, tools and domestic equipment[43] may therefore be more important than the distinction between Greek manufacture and native imitation. Finally, evidence of mixed settlement is also increasingly frequently discovered – both Greek settlers in native sites and barbarians in, or on the fringe of, Greek cities[44] – and the evaluation of the significance of these cultural minorities poses still more complex problems of interpretation.

The movement of coins, the contexts in which they occur on native sites and the relation of the distribution of coins to that of other Greek objects and other symptoms of Hellenisation also needs much more study.[45] In fact we do not even know at all precisely how the *Greeks* used coins; the question of the reasons for the invention of coinage has recently been re-opened[46] but there is no discussion of the way in which money was used. Coins found in shops (Olynthus), military camps (Koroni), in foundation deposits or votive groups, the storage of coin or bullion in temples or palaces (temple inventories, Persepolis), the habits of hoarders, the range of foreign coinage accepted as currency in different cities, are only a few of the possible lines for research.

The characteristic Greek proclivity for founding 'new towns' provides opportunities for studying acculturation and urbanisation which few societies before modern times can match. Excavation and survey work can show us the pattern of settlement and the life of rural communities before and after a new town is planted in their midst, and tell us how great the change was for those who moved from their old homes into the new polis; but for a full understanding of such sites complementary examination of the surrounding area is essential.[47] D. P. Dimitrov, who excavated Seuthopolis, a Thracian new town of the late fourth century B.C., has made a remarkably successful attempt at reconstructing, mainly from literary sources, some of the details of life in earlier Thracian settlements, but the sites around Seuthopolis which could have told us so much more about the settlers who moved to this particular city, and about its impact on the economic and social patterns of the surrounding territory, have unfortunately disappeared beneath the waters of the R. Turdža.[48]

The use of vases and other artefacts as evidence for trade has been discussed more often by previous writers,[49] and will therefore be treated only briefly here, with emphasis on those aspects of the problem which have received least attention.

As M. I. Finley stressed in his report to the economic history congress of 1962 (Finley, 1965c), it is essential that more attention should be paid to quantitative studies. It is to be hoped that the unique example of G. Vallet and F. Villard in publishing in their volume on the archaic pottery of Megara Hyblaea[50] an attempt to estimate the number of vases of different classes represented by the sherds found will stimulate other archaeologists to pay more attention to the statistical aspect of their material. Such information is particularly important for fabrics such as black-glaze wares, which are less fully published than painted vases; it is impossible to discuss the Attic vase production and trade of the fourth century (when the figures for the production and export of red-figure decline) until more is known about Attic black-glaze.

The fourth century is the most obvious period for research on Greek trade at present, starting from the group of problems which were combined by Rostovtzeff[51] into a theory of an economic crisis in this period caused by loss of overseas markets which, though long overdue for revision, is still frequently quoted. The archaeological picture has changed: Rostovtzeff could take little or no account of the finds from Olynthus and Spina, not to mention sites excavated since the war. Conceptually his thesis rests on shaky ground, both because it is not proved that trade was a sufficiently important element in the Greek economy for its fluctuations to cause economic crisis, and because the evidence for the decline in trade comes almost exclusively from Athens, while most of the evidence for economic crisis comes from other areas. Nevertheless Rostovtzeff pointed to a number of real problems. The fourth century when compared to the rapid expansion of Greek settlement and trade in the fifth century and the Hellenistic period does appear to be an interval of stagnation, if not actual setback. Sicily and the Italian peninsula, with the exception of the Po valley, almost entirely ceased to buy Attic vases. The number of Athenian coins[52] and vases found on oriental sites drops. Colonies and non-Greek settlements began to produce for themselves commodities which they had previously imported from Greece.

On the other hand, we know now that ships continued to carry Attic vases past the shores of Sicily and Italy to Spain, Sardinia, southern France and the ports of the northern Adriatic.[53] It is clear enough that the production of red-figure vases decreased in the fourth century, but far less clear what caused the decline. And more study of the contexts in which colonial and non-Greek products are found is necessary before we can determine whether they were competing with Attic wares for the same market or supplementing them in catering for a greatly increased demand – whether they are a sign of increasing independence from Greece or of increased Hellenisation. A study of buyers' habits in the period of the 'takeover' in south Italy should be a priority.

In general the evidence of vases for social history has remained practically untouched.[54] Both the customer's and the producer's habits and preferences need to be studied. How many vases were made for a particular purpose or destination – and how many of these accidentally found their way elsewhere? Attic vases with *kalos*-names were carried to many areas where they can have meant nothing. A study of vases found in votive deposits and sanctuaries would offer evidence of the variation between vases clearly made to be dedicated in the sanctuary where they were found and those which seem to come from general stock. The uses of miniature vases and the extent to which their production was a specialisation might also be examined. The whole subject of the relation between iconography and shape, and of the different contexts in which vases of different shape but the same function found favour, has hardly begun to be examined. The possibility of identifying vase-painters and workshops offers opportunities to study the working of trade: vases which seem to have been exported in the same shipload,[55] customers with a taste for one painter or workshop,[56] long-term connections between a workshop and a trader who travelled in a particular area,[57] painters' knowledge of the preferences of foreign customers.[58] Above all we need studies of the statistics of use.[59] What was the typical household inventory of vases in each area and period for the rich and for the poor: how does this compare with the typical set of grave offerings? As H. van Effenterre said in his paper on acculturation at the 1965 historical congress (van Effenterre, 1965), we need a 'sociologie du cimetière'.[60] Vases very commonly played a part in burial rites in the ancient world; but in some cases household treasures were buried with the dead, in others special types of vase were bought for the occasion: some were broken at the grave, some placed there holding food-offerings, some stood above ground to mark the grave. The distribution of all these practices needs to be charted.

So far we have discussed only the life of the ancient world in peace. But peace was rare, and war also has its archaeological problems. Archaeologists have long been interested in destruction by war as evidence for chronology, but it has not been studied from the point of view of economic and social history.[61] The extent of the destruction caused by ancient wars in cities, villages and farms is a huge subject for research; the Persian invasion would be an obvious starting point. It is still more difficult to determine the duration of the effects of the destruction. A ten-year period of desertion or squatter occupation of a site destroyed in war would be far from insignificant economically, but might be very difficult to identify archaeologically.[62] The current Swiss excavations of Eretria[63] may show how far it is possible to trace the course of rebuilding there after the Persian destruction in 490, and the relative importance of private initiative and public expenditure and control.

J. R. McCredie, of the American School in Athens, has recently published a survey of forts and watch-towers in Attica[64] which shows the economic importance of another neglected aspect of ancient warfare – expenditure on defence works and the maintenance of garrisons. Comparative studies for other parts of Greece are needed,[65] and evidence from excavation for the duration of occupation in such buildings. Finds of mill-stones, pens for animals,[66] storage vessels, or coins, would indicate whether the garrisons were permanent or short-term, whether they were supplied by a central organisation or had to support themselves or purchase provisions locally. Study of the materials used in building walls and forts and the standard of construction may give an idea of the labour and transport costs involved in building them.

War and other threats (piracy) must have affected the pattern of settlement in ancient Greece. The work of medieval historians and archaeologists on settlement patterns and deserted villages, which is highly relevant to the study of the ancient world, shows that poor land and marginal areas (common enough in Greece) are likely to be the most rewarding for a study of demographic change and rural depopulation due to war or other economic hardship.[67] The recent excavation of a farmhouse by the Dema wall, in a small valley among (now) scrub-covered hills near the Attic-Megarian border, revealed that it was built after the Peace of Nicias, abandoned again when war was resumed, and not re-occupied after 403.[68] Unfortunately the excavators did not examine the other traces of settlement in the area and so the history of occupation of the land is not clear; it may be only the house which was not re-occupied. But it is worth noting that none of Aristophanes' plays after 415 has the rural setting of the *Acharnians* and the *Peace*. We can see traces in the literary sources of the social revolution brought about by the concentration of the population of Attica in the city in the Peloponnesian war, but only years of patient accumulation of archaeological data will enable us to see more clearly the effects of this upheaval in the Attic countryside: the change in settlement patterns and land tenure, and the influence of the experience of city life on the Athenian farmer's tastes and values.

III Methods

The essential basis for any attempt to answer questions about the economy and settlement patterns of ancient Greece is survey work; a systematic record of all traces of settlement and all the evidence available from surface remains for the character, acreage and periods of occupation of each site.[69] This is also the only way of making it possible to examine or preserve antiquities which otherwise are likely to be discovered only as they are being destroyed by modern farming or building,[70] and the only basis for establishing an excavation strategy aimed at choosing for excavation those sites which are most exposed to risk of destruction and likely to yield most information. Archaeological survey work is now beginning on a small scale in Greece, but it is still one of the most backward areas in the world in this respect. The subject was brought up recently in *Hesperia* by William A. McDonald, in his article 'Suggestions on directions and a modest proposal'.[71] There is no need to repeat the forceful arguments presented by McDonald for making survey work a priority in Greece. I would however like to comment on a few points in his article. In the first place it is worth pointing out that if it proves impossible to set up an overall survey under a central organisation, small-scale private initiatives can have far-reaching effects, as has been shown in Italy by J. B. Ward-Perkins: the British School at Rome's survey of Southern Etruria has had a great deal of influence on Italian archaeology.[72] Secondly, I would disagree with McDonald when he says that 'The published results of the surveys might be organised by regions and include all chronological subdivisions. Or they might follow the model of Richard Hope-Simpson's recent publication on the Late Bronze Age habitation pattern in the whole Aegean basin'.[73] Studies of the settlement pattern of a single period over a wide area will certainly be needed, but these should be secondary lines of research based on the main report (when we have it). It is surely essential both for economy of manpower and for comprehension of historical topography that the basic survey, and therefore the definitive publication, should be organised by regions and not by chronological divisions.

I would also stress the immediate responsibility of anyone concerned with the training of students to see that they have experience of survey work as well as of excavation, and the responsibility of every excavator to explore the topographical context of his site and publish the survey results as an integral part of his interpretation of the history of the site. From the point of view of the historian an excavation which is conducted and published without reference to the settlement pattern of its topographical context leaves as many unanswered questions as the presentation of an individual find without reference to its stratigraphic context, and although excavation does not destroy the site's context as it does that of the individual object, one cannot assume in present conditions that the information will remain available indefinitely. The size of the topographic context of a site naturally varies with the size and complexity of the settlement concerned; one could perhaps say as an approximate definition that the context stretches as far as the nearest site of the same type. A farm must be related to the position of neighbouring farms, a village to surrounding villages. A city-state's context is its territory. The excavators of Corinth published a survey of the Corinthia as the first volume of the excavation report, but their example has not unfortunately been followed on other major sites in Greece.[74]

The question of survey work raises in an acute form the problem of the aims and format of excavation publications, which cannot be omitted in a discussion of the relations between archaeologists and historians. Excavation publications do present at the moment a number of problems for the historian who wants to study archaeological material. Preliminary reports appear in a confusing variety of forms ranging from numerous news bulletins presenting slightly different summaries of the same excavations to hard-cover publications arranged by seasons. Even in the publications between these two extremes which give a fairly detailed account of the season's work without being intended to take the place of a final publication, there is no standard form or practice. The custom of publishing preliminary reports seems to have been encouraged mainly with the negative aim of circulating and preserving some record of the work of excavators whose final publications are delayed for decades, or never appear at all. In such cases – and they are unfortunately frequent – any information is of course a gain. But the general tendency to regard preliminary reports from this point of view has perhaps led to neglect of their other possible functions. Even their relation to the final report is not very clear. Should they be entirely superseded by the final publication of the excavation, or can they be designed to supplement it on some points of detail? One important function of the preliminary report is the prompt publication of major finds. Sometimes, however, these are published without a full account of their context, and discussion may continue for years on the basis of an inadequate publication.[75] It is particularly common for inscriptions to be handed over for publication to a 'specialist' who is not in a position to give a full description of the context in which they were found. The preliminary report should surely tell the reader the excavator's further plans for exploration of the site, and for the final study and publication of the material.[76] For instance, will specialists be called

in to study and publish particular groups of finds (bones, architectural fragments, vases)? A clear and concise summary of the
results of the season's work both in terms of problems solved and
new problems raised in the interpretation of the individual site, and
in terms of the wider significance of the finds, is by no means always
provided. Excavations vary greatly in size and complexity, and a site
which can be excavated in two or three seasons requires different
treatment from an excavation which continues for generations; but
this complexity only increases the need for discussion of the function
and form of preliminary reports.

Final publications have been treated recently in a useful little book
published in England on *The Preparation of Archaeological Reports*. [77]
It is addressed primarily to the amateur or inexperienced excavator
of British prehistoric or Roman sites, but its recommendations have
a general application. The emphasis on the study of the history (to
modern times) and geology of the site, and of the ecology, economic
resources and settlement pattern of the surrounding area, is striking
in comparison with classical archaeology, where geological maps are
almost unknown and even clear and accurate maps of contours and
rivers are rare. The study of air photographs and of place-names,
estate maps and other documentary evidence of the later history of
the site, [78] which is taken for granted as part of the preparation for
digging a British site, has hardly been attempted in Greece. It can
scarcely be doubted that our understanding of the pattern of life on
any ancient site could be greatly increased by researches of this kind.

The main problem in publishing an excavation is, as this booklet
recognises, the separation of the 'facts' seen during the course of the
excavation and the 'interpretation', which includes both the reconstruction of the processes of accumulation and collapse by which
the observed stratigraphy of the site was built up, and the inferences
from the excavated part of the site to everything beyond the walls of
the trenches. In practice it is hardly possible to keep the two completely separate, since a description of the observed facts which
contained no element of interpretation would probably be un-
intelligible. But it seems to be a sound suggestion that two accounts
of the excavation are necessary, one designed to present the stratigraphic data in such a way that the interpretation can be checked,
and the other to set out comprehensively in detail the excavator's
reconstruction of the history of the site and of each level and structure
encountered. All excavation reports make some formal division

between facts and interpretation, it is true, but the normal practice
in classical archaeology seems to be to put most of the discussions
of problems of interpretation into the stratigraphic description of the
site,[79] and reduce the interpretative section of the report to a brief
summary of 'historical conclusions'. A fuller account of the excavator's interpretation of the site would no doubt add to the length of
the publication, but it would also increase its clarity. Since the
publication of an excavation demands both synchronic and diachronic description, and since the latter involves the description of
two processes which operated in opposite directions (the build-up of
the deposit and its excavation) a clear exposition is bound to require
some repetition. It may also be worth asking whether in some cases,
particularly where a changing team of excavators is at work on a
site, the description of the 'facts' could not be published year by year
in preliminary reports which would only be summarised (and where
necessary emended) in the final publication.

Repetition is accepted already as necessary in the description of
the finds from the excavation, which are catalogued separately as
well as being recorded in the course of the stratigraphic description
where they have a bearing on chronology or interpretation. The
arrangement of this section of a report is based on material, form and
chronology. The function of the objects receives little attention. Two
suggestions may be made. One is that the prevailing arrangement of
finds by material produces some odd juxtapositions which seem to
have little justification. Mirrors and candelabra have nothing in
common with tools, nails and fishhooks except that they are made of
metal; nor have terracotta figurines with loom-weights, cooking
pots and pithoi with fine painted vases, or altars with mill-stones and
hoppers. In view of the growing practice of allotting different
sections of the catalogue to different scholars for publication, it may
be worth considering whether function is not in some cases a better
principle of classification than material.[80]

The second point is that a site may well produce collections of
material which form a functional group, although not constituting a
closed deposit of chronological significance. The contents of a house,
room, votive pit[81] or sanctuary area form functional groups which
are significant for the use of pottery and other articles, and the
variations in use due to cult, economic status, etc., encountered on
the site. A publication which fails to list and analyse such groups is
taking a remarkably narrow view of the interpretation of the material

culture of antiquity. Such information is probably best presented in tables. Tabulation of the variables relevant to the social and economic analysis of cemetery material (age, sex, type and orientation of tomb, amount and type of grave-offerings, etc.),[82] and discussion of the correlations which may be significant, are also much rarer than they should be.

The purpose of these suggestions is not to encourage the reader of an archaeological report to accept the excavator's conclusions at second hand without examining the evidence on which they are based, but to enable the specialist working on demography, economic life, religious customs or any other topic which requires the comparison of material from a number of sites to see at a glance whether an excavation has produced evidence relevant to his research. Negative conclusions, from this point of view, are as valuable as positive ones. A brief statement in an introductory summary that the skeletons from a cemetery were too poorly preserved to be studied, or that there was no significant variation in wealth among the tomb-groups, can save a great deal of time. There is still an immense amount of work to be done in evaluating the statistical characteristics of archaeological material[83] and synthesising the evidence for economic life, religion and social customs of all kinds; we cannot afford to increase the difficulties of those who attempt such tasks.

IV Obstacles

An earlier version of this paper was discussed at an interdisciplinary seminar of ancient historians, archaeologists and art historians at the Warburg Institute in March 1967. I learnt much from the criticisms of the archaeologists present, but substantial areas of disagreement remained at the end of the discussion. I therefore attempt to report here their reactions.

First and foremost there was the very understandable response that archaeologists are already overworked, have little opportunity to choose where they excavate, and would have to delay publication still further if they were to study every aspect of their material exhaustively before publishing. For archaeologists who work for a national archaeological service the situation is indeed extremely difficult, though the need for survey work is all the greater: good archaeology will never be produced by following the bulldozer and tomb-robber, like birds after the plough. In the present circumstances those classical archaeologists who work in foreign territory and have no direct responsibility for salvage have an increased obligation to select those projects which will contribute most in the long run to the protection of the monuments and understanding of the history of the area in which they work.

A more serious disagreement arose over the question of priorities in the study of the material from different aspects, and indeed over the general conception of the range of the archaeologist's responsibilities. It was argued that classification and chronology must be set on a firmer basis before more general historical questions can usefully be approached; to direct archaeologists' attention to these at present would merely encourage wild speculation. It is the archaeologist's job to recover and present the evidence, scrupulously, scientifically and objectively; if historians wish to make use of it they must learn to understand the materials and methods of archaeology and draw their own conclusions from the excavation publications.

It is certainly essential for economic and social historians, and indeed anyone who wishes to build up a balanced understanding of the ancient world, to be familiar with archaeological methods and the material remains of antiquity. But the distinction made by the archaeologists between discovering and publishing evidence, and drawing historical conclusions from it, is open to grave objections. It reflects an attitude which Louis Robert has constantly condemned in epigraphy:

> Dans quelques milieux, ici ou là, on semble établir une distinction entre le rôle de l'épigraphiste – cet être assez mythique à mon avis – qui publie des inscriptions, et celui de l'interprète et commentateur, qui a la charge de les comprendre. . . . Établissement du texte – et même. très souvent. lecture – et explication ne peuvent se séparer.[84]

Rigour of method and breadth of comprehension of the implications of the material are ultimately indivisible. The interpretation of archaeological evidence for social and economic history is admittedly at present too often imprecise and speculative, but higher standards are more likely to be reached by experiment, discussion and criticism than by waiting until chronology is more firmly established.

It is some time since classical studies ceased to be the dominant model for any study of the past, yet the process of readjustment is slow. Students of other past civilisations are now fully conscious of their autonomy, but classical scholars have some way to go in adapting their methods of research to a situation in which the ancient world is just one of many possible fields for the study of the past. The separation of ancient history from the main stream of historical research, or of the study of classical texts from that of the literature of modern languages, is obvious enough, and only recently have there been moves towards bridging the gap. The separation of classical archaeology[85] from a common tradition of archaeological research which has been established over the last fifty years or so in prehistoric, American, Roman-provincial and medieval (and, most recently, industrial) archaeology, has been less noticed. It is not possible here to go into the history of this cleavage, though it raises interesting questions about the scientific bent encouraged in local archaeology in northern Europe by the early connection of antiquarian research with controversy about the origins of man, the links between archaeology and folklore studies, and, especially in America, between archaeology and anthropology, and the specific character of British and French colonial archaeology in North Africa and the Near East. What needs to be emphasised is that the methods developed by 'non-classical' archaeologists, although they may in part have been devised to compensate for a lack of literary evidence or sophisticated art forms, are still relevant to the classical world. In particular, new methods of studying the terrain by the use of air photographs and the reconstruction of past ecological patterns may help to compensate for the greatest disadvantage of the classical archaeologist who works as a visitor in a foreign country – the lack of the living familiarity with the land and all the phases of its history which is so necessary for the task of 'reading the story of the past from stratified earth'.[86]

5 Town and country in ancient Greece

This paper is concerned with Greek ideas and institutions rather than with archaeological evidence for settlement patterns. Archaeological research of this type is still backward in Greece;[1] and in so far as archaeologists have worked on settlement patterns, the two subjects which have recently attracted most attention – town planning and land tenure – are precisely those in which ideas and institutions imposed a geometrical pattern on town and landscape.

Halbwachs (1938) distinguished three sub-sections in his treatment of social morphology: the religious, the political and the economic. In examining Greek notions of the relation between town and country it will be useful to add two more: military organization, as a special subdivision of political structure with its own characteristics, and the distinction between rural and urban culture, in the sense of education and style of living. It is obvious that societies can vary in their polarization or disregard of the potential opposition between town and country in these different spheres. The city may be regarded as a holy place (Wheatley, 1969; Tritsch, 1929), an enclave of 'burghers' with privileged political status, a centre of commerce and industry, a fortress, the home of education and sophisticated manners; it may equally be associated with sin, revolution, unemployment, vulnerability in war, illiteracy or bad drains.

To the ancient Greeks the city (*polis*) was above all a political conception.[2] In normal usage, *polis* meant a city-state, both territory (*chōra*) and the conurbation at its centre (sometimes also called *asty*) where one would find the basic Greek political institutions – magistrates, council and citizen assembly – and the public buildings in which they were housed. As a type of political organization and settlement the *polis* was contrasted with the *ethnos*, a cultural unit ruled by a king or acephalous, with perhaps some form of loose or intermittent federal organization. Such societies were settled in villages, *kata kōmas*. When Thucydides (1.10, cf. 1.5.1) calls classical Sparta and other Greek states in earlier times '*poleis* not synoecised but settled *kata kōmas*', there is an element of paradox in the description; these communities had the political institutions of the city but lacked the architectural characteristics – walls, monumental public buildings and density of settlement – which were normally associated with them.[3]

The term 'synoecism' which Thucydides uses here (literally, 'settling together') carried implications both of state-formation and of urbanization. The Athenian state came into being, according to tradition, through the creation in Athens of a central government for the twelve towns of Attica which had previously been autonomous, turning to the king of Athens only in moments of danger. The growth of Athens as a city was for Thucydides (2.15) largely the result of this change in political structure. The former towns, however, continued to exist as settlements and local centres of the subdivisions of the citizen body. Most Greek cities had such smaller settlements in their territory, and the distinction between the *polis* and *ethnos* forms of political organization should not be exaggerated.[4] Tribes, phratries and local centres were vital parts of the *polis* with their own cults and autonomy in managing their own affairs; on the other hand, the existence of cities influenced the institutions of those parts of Greece which were still settled in villages. The same segmentary structure can be seen in both types of organization (even if the relation between the tribes of the *polis* and the sub-groups of the *ethnos* remains unclear), despite the greater centralization of government in the *polis*. In consequence, the notion of political autonomy and the use of the term *polis* were apt to fluctuate according to context, and there was no sharp dividing line between city and countryside (*chōra*) either in political status or in religion. The Greek city, unlike the Roman, was not surrounded by a sacred boundary.[5] Some of its gods had their sanctuaries in the city, others in the countryside or villages.

There was indeed a tendency in Greek political thought towards eliminating altogether the distinction between town-dwellers and country-dwellers. Plato, in the *Laws* (745b), prescribed that the territory of his ideal city should be divided into lots of which each household should have two, one near the city and the other near the borders. And Cleisthenes of Athens, in 507 B.C., had already created a new system of tribes and subdivisions designed to eliminate regional factionalism, in which each tribe contained areas from the 'city', 'coast' and 'inland' regions of Attica (Lévêque and Vidal-Naquet, 1964).

But outside Utopia, the attempt to override geographical factors could hardly be entirely successful. Division of the territory into equal parcels of land to be distributed by lot, which seems to have begun with the occupation of conquered land (neighbouring or colonial), and which became part of the general Greek conception of the process of founding or reforming a state, often did not extend over the whole area controlled by the city.[6] The lots of the Spartans occupied an area of the central plain of Lacedaemon, while the rest of the territory was settled by *perioikoi* whose communities were autonomous in local affairs but subject to Sparta in foreign policy. This was probably also the position of some native settlements in territory controlled by Greek colonies.[7] The difference between *perioikoi* ('subjects') and neighbouring allies was often ill-defined. In some colonies there were disputes between the original settlers' descendants and late-comers settled in outlying parts of the territory, who might be in an inferior position both economically and politically. Here the spatial definition of an original *polis* which, one might almost say, extended the idea of town planning to the countryside,[8] led to a later differentiation between this area (called *politike chōra*, polis-country, by the Spartans) and a remoter countryside beyond its borders.[9]

Although the Greek acropolis has often been characterized as a *Fluchtburg*, medieval comparisons, in this as in other respects, are dangerous. Not every Greek city was built on or round a hill. Sparta long remained unwalled, claiming that the spears and shields of her hoplites were sufficient defence. Plato thought city walls only made the citizens cowardly.[10] Although Greek myths told of famous attacks on cities (Troy, Thebes), the tradition of the early *polis* wars (seventh and sixth centuries B.C.) was to stress the conquest of land and the defeat of enemy armies in pitched battle. The members of the Delphic amphictyony swore an oath not to destroy each other's cities or interrupt water-supplies (Aeschines 2.115). Siege warfare and elaborate city fortifications developed only gradually from the fifth century B.C. onwards. Pericles' policy in the Peloponnesian war of concentrating the population of Attica inside the walls linking the city to Piraeus and a supply of food from overseas, and abandoning the countryside to Spartan invasion, was new and unpopular. Until the fourth century B.C., when the use of mercenaries began to spread, the Greek army was composed of citizens and to a large extent of peasants; they fought to defend their land.

The development of Athens in the fifth century B.C. as a large urban settlement depending on imported corn, and the striking contrast between Athens and Sparta in economic, political and military organization, introduced new elements into the Greek conception of the relation between city and country. Right-wing Athenians, like Xenophon and Plato, associated oligarchy, subsistence farming and country life with the courage, physical fitness and obedience required of the soldier; urbanization and seapower led to democracy, mercenary self-interest and weediness. In this contrast between different types of economic activity and ethos, the most extreme form of the urban type was associated with the growing harbour towns, which in a number of Greek states (Athens, Megara, Colophon, several Cretan cities) were situated at some distance from the city itself. An attempt was thus made to detach the developing economic conception of the city from the idea of the city as a political centre, leading to debates in political philosophy on the need to separate the commercial market from the political *agora*,[11] the correct distance to be maintained between the ideal city and the sea (Momigliano, 1944), and the desirability of granting citizenship to traders and craftsmen.

Here again, however, as in the distinction between *polis* and *ethnos*, we have a contrast between different Greek states and not between town and country within the state. The Athenians distinguished the city type, the *asteios* – sophisticated, witty, cunning – from the rustic, *agroikos* (Lammermann, 1935; Ribbeck, 1888); but there is little sign of a grouping of interests, of a conscious solidarity, corresponding to the division of economic activity and manners. Many of the city craftsmen and traders were resident non-citizens, or semi-independent slaves; the struggle of the poorer citizens to emphasize the status distinction separating them from these categories inhibited the development of a breach between town and country.[12]

The situation became quite different later in the Hellenistic kingdoms, where Alexander's conquest led to the creation of a plural society in which the Greek cities differed in ethnic origin, political status and culture from the surrounding countryside. The Romans too granted privileged status to cities and towns. We find the distinction in political status between town and country again in the medieval

'Stadtluft macht frei' (see Nicholas, 1969). Perhaps consideration of the differences between the Greek city-state and the later pattern may provide a starting-point for a comparative discussion of the conditions which make for identification or opposition of town and country. Others have raised the question whether the urban/rural distinction should be treated as a dichotomy or as a continuum (Ward-Perkins, 1972); taking what might perhaps be called a structuralist approach, I have here treated it as a potential contrast which in any given society may be minimized (continuum) or emphasized (dichotomy). In comparing the treatment of the contrast in different societies, it would be necessary to consider (a) the extent of polarization both in 'folk' concepts of town and country and in the measurable clustering or even gradation of settlement sizes and densities; (b) the hardness of boundaries between town and country, both physical (presence or absence of town walls, suburban fringe, etc.) and institutional (discontinuities in legal jurisdiction, political rights, allegiance to religious centres), and the frequency of traffic across the boundaries; (c) the consonance or dissonance of the different types of density (political, economic, religious, military, cultural).

Classical Athens and Hellenistic Alexandria – cities comparable in size, density and level of economic specialization – may serve to represent the ideal types of urban–rural continuum and urban–rural dichotomy. The Athenian countryman had a close and direct relationship with the city; he voted in its assembly, bought and sold in its markets, took part in its religious festivals, sued in its courts, had the same political rights and obligations – including that of military service – as the urban population. As we have seen, the Athenians did their best to ignore the contrast of town and country. Hellenistic Egypt, on the other hand, is a typical example of a plural society in which the boundary between the Greek city and the Egyptian countryside was underscored by structural, social and cultural divisions.[13] Nevertheless, a marked urban–rural dichotomy is neither essential nor peculiar to plural societies. As shown above, it is found also in medieval Europe. What the classical Greek material suggests is that the nature of the country-dwellers' relations with the city and its institutions – direct or mediated through middlemen – is of crucial relevance. The middleman – whether feudal lord, patron or economic entrepreneur – not only derives his position from the existence of a dichotomy, but also helps to preserve it.

Additional note

Several excellent new studies of different aspects of relations between town and country have appeared since the publication of this article, particularly in Finley, 1973b; see also Bingen, 1975. On the territory and relations with the hinterland of Greek colonies see Wąsowicz, 1969, 1975; Martin, 1975; and *Le Genti non Greche*, 1972, *Economia e Società* (1973) and *Metaponto* (in press). On Italy: Gabba, 1972. General survey, with full bibliography: Chevallier, 1974. On the cultural contrast between townsman and rustic, Dover, 1975, pp. 112–14; and Ramage, 1973.

6 Economy and society in classical Athens*

The title of this paper perhaps requires some explanation. It is not intended as a general description of the economy of Athens in the fifth and fourth centuries B.C., but as an attempt to study processes of change in social and economic institutions, behaviour and values at a level at which one can see not only an overall correlation, but also tensions, resistances and interreactions.

But can we separate 'economy' and 'society' in the ancient world sufficiently to discuss their interrelations? Some ancient historians would say that it is impossible. The conception of economic development as a disruptive factor, destroying social relations and creating alienation, is so much a part of the modern world that there is an obvious danger of anachronism in introducing it into the study of pre-industrial societies. It is, however, one of the ideas which we have inherited from the Greeks: Attic texts of the fourth century B.C. show clearly that trading and exchange carried out by professional merchants for profit were regarded not merely as degrading occupations but as a threat to social norms and cohesion.

The main aims of this paper are: first, to discuss the changes in both economy and society which seem most directly related to this reaction, and second, to show how certain avenues of further economic development were blocked, and tensions set up, by conceptions of the appropriate values and behaviour for different status groups. It is therefore concerned mainly with the sectors of the Athenian economy which the Athenians themselves perceived – if only rather vaguely – as 'economic': activities concerned with money, above all; concentrated in the city; involving buying and selling, especially the purchase of food and the production of other commodities for sale. I am not concerned with the question of the quantitative importance of these activities in the total economy of Attica; and I have given little space to other sectors of the economy which have left less evidence of changes and tensions, such as agriculture. I have also said little about differing attitudes towards the economic benefits or costs of the Athenian empire, a subject which would require an article to itself, or about the overwhelming importance of the empire in stimulating economic development in the fifth century.

As is well known, the quantitative evidence for ancient economic history is extremely defective. On the other hand, the evidence for economic institutions, law, and the opinions of different sectors of the population is for some periods rather full. It should be possible to draw some conclusions about possible points of tension or instability in the system by analysing the characteristics and consistency of institutions and values. Important as it is to stress that the Athenian economy must be seen in the context of the social structure and technological limitations of the fifth to fourth centuries B.C., it is also necessary to find a viewpoint which will permit the study of change, of innovation and of resistance to innovation. For this purpose an analytic separation of 'society' and 'economy', or of traditional and 'modern' elements in the Athenian economy, appears to be useful.

The question of the primitiveness or modernity of the ancient, and especially the Athenian, economy has been one of the major problems of ancient economic history since the end of the last century. The debate, which began in the 1890s with Karl Bücher's statement of the primitivist view and Eduard Meyer's and Beloch's modernist counter-arguments,[1] died down somewhat after J. Hasebroek's impressive arguing of the primitivist case in *Staat und Handel im alten Griechenland* and *Griechische Wirtschafts- und Gesellschaftsgeschichte bis zur Perserzeit*,[2] but it is not yet dead. Though the terms in which the problem was posed, and its evolutionist background, cannot be accepted today, the desire to make increased use of comparative studies was at the root of the argument, and we still have to face today the task of finding an interpretation of ancient economic history which accommodates not only primitive technology, small-scale organisation and a general contempt for economic enterprise, but also wide-spread trade, the beginnings of banking and economic analysis, and attitudes characterised by contemporary sources as individualistic and mercenary.

Neither modernists nor primitivists gave a successful account of this combination. Each tended to emphasise the features which suited his own case without explaining those which weighed against it. Nor was it an adequate compromise to say, as Hasebroek, Rostovtzeff and others were inclined to do, that the ancient economy had been primitive until the Hellenistic period and modern thereafter, without explaining the transition: quantitative change was admitted, but the progress made by Hasebroek in understanding the economic institutions of classical Greece had no counterpart in the study of the Hellenistic world.[3] Recently C. Préaux has stressed the need for classical and Hellenistic specialists to collaborate in examining the elements of Greek derivation in the economic policy of the Ptolemies in Egypt,[4] and in so doing has implicitly exposed the poverty of work on economic and administrative questions among historians of fourth-century Greece.[5] The development of a more active economic policy on the part of the state is foreshadowed in fourth-century Greece, in Xenophon's *Poroi* and perhaps in the growth of Rhodes; and the Hellenistic state, as Édouard Will has remarked,[6] still depends to a considerable extent on the activities of private merchants, whose role was defined earlier in classical Athens.

An alternative, more promising combination of the primitivist and modernist viewpoints arose from a less direct comparison between modern and ancient conditions. The concern over the relation between economy and society which was a predominant feature of Western thought from the mid-nineteenth to the mid-twentieth centuries reflected itself in a mounting interest in their relation in antiquity.[7] Already K. Riezler, *Über Finanzen und Monopole im alten Griechenland* (1907), expressed dissatisfaction with both the Bücher and the Meyer–Beloch interpretations. Though he took the view that in Bücher's categories the ancient world should be assigned to the stage of *Stadtwirtschaft* rather than *Hauswirtschaft* (Bücher) or *Volkswirtschaft* (Meyer–Beloch), he was not satisfied in general with the basis of the classification. Following Max Weber and Sombart,[8] he emphasised the importance of 'der wirtschaftliche Geist und die Zwecksetzung des Menschen', in particular the 'Streben nach grenzlosem Erwerb' which, he claimed characterised Athenian economic life in the classical period. Economic requirements and mental attitudes were more developed than institutions and forms of production: his study suggested 'die Umrisslinien jenes grossen Kampfes zwischen Lebens- und Wirtschaftsformen', a contradiction between 'Staatsform' and 'Entwicklungstendenzen des wirtschaftlichen Lebens'. The basic contradiction was between the political

autarchy of the *polis*, which required economic autarky as its complement, and the increasing economic dependence on trade. The lack
of any conception of co-operation between cities on an equal basis
in either political or economic policy meant that attempts to preserve
economic autarky led to domination or war. There was trade on a
'world-wide' scale, but no perception of common economic interests;
each city followed its own immediate advantage, and by monopoly,
seizure, forced loans and other measures prevented the free play of
the market (the point was later developed by Hasebroek in his
distinction between an import interest and a commercial interest in
trade). Furthermore, the development of trade had encouraged the
growth of individualism, aided by the state's exacerbation of the
agonistic character of Greek life. The solidarity of the early autarkic
polis was broken by individualism and class war; class war and
external wars destroyed resources. When Alexander's conquest of the
east made it possible to form larger political units, the Greek *polis*
was too much weakened by poverty and discord to produce the
manpower or creative force which might in these new conditions
have developed large-scale industry.

Riezler's account has several weaknesses, but his sketch of a
conflict between the claims of traditional political and social values
and a growing awareness of economic interests as a differentiated
sphere, both inside the state and in foreign policy, is worth retaining;
and his vigorous attack on the problem of the Greek conception of
the economic functions of the state, despite its extravagances, should
be read as a starting-point for any further research on this neglected
topic.[9] His new approach to the question of the relationship of
economy and society was, I suspect, largely due to his teacher Robert
von Pöhlmann. Friedrich Oertel, in an excellent summary of the
modernist–primitivist debate in his *Anhang* to the third edition of
Pöhlmann's *Geschichte der sozialen Frage und des Sozialismus in der
antiken Welt* (Oertel, 1925),[10] took the question of 'class war' further
by discussing the changes in slavery in classical Athens which tended
to assimilate the slave to the free worker, and thus intensified the
conflict felt by poorer citizens between their social status and their
economic position.

The two themes of conflict – Riezler's idea of contradiction between the autarkic nature of the *polis* and the new economic attitudes
resulting from the growth of commerce, and Oertel's conception of
the tension over status-boundaries between rich citizens, poor citizens

and slaves – were combined by Otto Erb in a brief but stimulating thesis on *Wirtschaft und Gesellschaft im Denken der hellenischen Antike* just before the outbreak of the Second World War.[11] Whereas Oertel had tried to give a balanced assessment of the ancient economy without passing judgment on it, Erb like Riezler presented his conception of the contradictions in the classical economy in an impassioned denunciation of the failure of the Greek *polis*. (The fact that what Riezler had seen as a failure to allow free play to economic development and the progressive forces of the market appeared to Erb as a failure to preserve political and ethical values from the corrupting influence of commerce is sufficiently explained by the economic history of the thirty years which separated the two works.) For Erb, the two contradictions were linked through the 'feudal' ideology of the early *polis*.[12] By tradition, the citizen was a landowner, able to provide for his own needs and play his part as soldier and in other community activities: the economic aspect of life was not differentiated from the framework of family and city. *Homines economici* (slaves, non-citizens or citizens without full rights) and *homines politici* were separate status-groups. But trade introduced a new, individualistic type of economic activity in which no social limit to acquisition was set. In the archaic *polis* the citizen's duties and privileges were based on the use of land granted (in theory) by the state; when the move to the city began, the question whether he was to be 'Rentner oder Sklave' sharpened, and the only form in which the state could provide 'rent' for the poor was by payment for state service. Meanwhile, the rich grew wealthier: private property originally 'Unterhaltsmittel für die Koinonia', was misused as a basis for individualistic acquisition and commercialism, 'Pleonexie und Chrematistik'; and when, in the fourth century, Athens lost her revenue from overseas possessions, the poor used political power to extract money from the rich and thus destroyed capital which might have been used to build up the economy, stifled economic initiative and broke the *polis* society into antagonistic groups.

Édouard Will (1954a) ended his valuable analysis of the history of the modernist–primitivist controversy with an account of Erb's ideas. More recently the question of the contradictions in the economy of classical Greece has been taken up by J.-P. Vernant in his 'Remarques sur la lutte de classe dans la Grèce ancienne',[13] with a reference to Erb's work. Vernant was concerned with the nature of class war in a slave-owning society. He stressed the changes in both society and economy, and in particular the second half of the fifth century as the turning-point when 'l'équilibre économique et social sur lequel repose le régime de la *Polis* apparait dans son ensemble compromis'. The three main characteristics of the *polis* were the unity of city and countryside, the unity of citizen and soldier, and the close link between citizenship and landed property. Fourth-century Athens had lost these characteristics. Urban and rural life were increasingly different, war was becoming professionalised, land was more often sold and the privilege of land-ownership more often granted to non-citizens. I would only add to this summary of Vernant's views that this development in Athens followed on a crisis which had involved the intensification of the first two characteristics – identification of city and countryside, of citizen and soldier – at the cost of the virtual abolition of the tie between citizenship and landholding.[14] Land never lost its 'social' value and virtue, and grants of land in subject territories abroad (cleruchies) were one of the most concrete and essential benefits of empire in the eyes of the Athenian *dēmos*; but by the fourth century the citizen's status was symbolised economically by state pay rather than by landholding. In Vernant's words, 'C'est à travers la médiation du statut politique que la fonction économique des divers individus détermine leur action sociale et politique en solidarité avec tel groupe, en opposition avec tel autre.' The growing wealth of 'slave-owning entrepreneurs' led to conflict between rich and poor because of the traditional social pressure on the rich to display wealth.

C'est sous forme de dépenses somptuaires, et, dans la cité où le luxe individuel est en principe proscrit, par des largesses généreuses au bénéfice de la communauté civique qu'une grande partie de l'argent se trouve relancée dans le circuit de la circulation . . . les conflits entre citoyens se nouent, pour l'essentiel, autour du même problème : au bénéfice de qui se fera cette répartition du surproduit par l'intermédiaire des institutions de la cité? À ce moment, la masse des citoyens, que diversifie la multiplicité de leurs statuts économiques, se trouve polarisée en deux camps adverses; le groupe de ceux qui n'ayant rien ou très peu veulent utiliser les formes de l'État pour taxer les riches au maximum, et les possédants – quelle que soit l'origine de leur fortune – qui sont décidés à résister.

The relation between the 'contradictions' within the citizen body and the characteristics of an economy based on slavery is difficult to determine. Vernant lays the emphasis on the inefficiency of slavery as a system of production (unwilling work, lack of progress in technology, fear of increasing slave numbers). In my opinion there is more to it than that; not only was the existence of slaves and extension of the slave's sphere of action a basic factor in determining the attitudes of the poorer citizens, but slavery also had important effects on the flow of money in the Athenian economy, which have not been sufficiently recognised. To this I shall return below.

Outside Germany, comparatively few attempts have been made to study the 'Wirtschaftsethik' of the ancient Greeks.[15] An important contribution to the study of Athenian conceptions of the economic role of the state was, however, made by Louis Gernet in his work on the corn-supply of Athens.[16] Gernet's method, in economic history as in other fields, might be described as a combination of Durkheim's conception of 'représentations collectives' with Mauss's emphasis on the 'phénomène social total'. The economy can be studied like any other social phenomenon as a system of collective representations, that is, of models of roles and behaviour, conceptual fields and categories, mental associations and disjunctions. In a comparatively undifferentiated society like that of ancient Greece attention must be paid to a wide variety of evidence, from myths and philosophic utopias to anecdotes or the physical appearance, movements or dress associated with a particular status or role (cf. the remark of the pseudo-Xenophontic *Athēnaiōn Politeia* that slaves and metics are as well dressed at Athens as the poorer citizens). Associations must be traced from the economy to other spheres of thought: Gernet's article 'Choses visibles et choses invisibles'[17] discusses the uses of the terms *phaneros* and *aphanes* in philosophy and in the classification of types of property. In studying economic institutions one has not only to assess them from the functional point of view, but to try to see them with the eyes of those who lived them, with the multiple linking threads and the mental blocks which cut across our conceptions of what may seem functionally analogous to our own practice.[18] This is perhaps particularly important in studying the role of the state in the ancient economy: but it is relevant to the study of the economic behaviour of individuals as well. Even 'individualism' is not everywhere the same.

The relevance of the analysis of mental attitudes and traditional institutions in the study of developing economies is now commonly recognised, at least in so far as they constitute 'obstacles to development'. One can perhaps hardly speak of 'obstacles to development' in classical Athens, but the problem of the mixture of 'primitive' and 'modern' elements in the economy of Athens is a related one. The late fifth century in Athens was a period of sudden urbanisation, sharp increase in the volume of trade and the extent of participation in a monetary economy and market transactions, new economic roles and opportunities, and new demands in the field of labour, as well as political and social strains and crises. The Athens Thucydides described in Pericles' Funeral Speech was not living in a Golden Age, but in a period of shattering social change and consequently of changes in values and attitudes, of which Thucydides gave a remarkable analysis.[19] Modern study of the effects of social and economic change should help us to understand the conflicts and strains set up in Athenian society by this process.

It is necessary to admit at the start that we know very little of the economic history of Greece before the fifth century. There is little evidence, and not much solidity in the interpretation of the evidence we have. Moses Finley has given a convincing picture of the gift-exchange economy of 'Homeric' Greece,[20] but the changes which took place between the world of Homer and Hesiod and that of the fifth century remain obscure. Even the fifth and fourth centuries still present serious problems. The economic effects of the Athenian empire are difficult to evaluate even for Athens, still more for the subject cities (a problem which has scarcely been touched). The impact of change during the first fifty, or even the first seventy years of the fifth century is difficult to assess. Through Thucydides and Aristophanes we can perceive something of the impact of the Peloponnesian War, but it is not yet clear how far the changes documented for the war were already anticipated in the earlier years of empire, nor how far trends were reversed in the fourth century.

The autarkic *polis* postulated by Riezler and Erb was in any case a collective representation, an ideal, rather than a historical reality. We find it clearly expressed only by admirers of Sparta, reacting against Pericles' equally extreme conception of the landless city living entirely by trade and sea-power.[21] But the contrast between autarky and trade also corresponded to the individual's change from subsistence farming to city life and the purchase of food in the market.

The autarkic polis was the counterpart of the peasant householder portrayed by Hesiod, struggling to avoid debt and supply his needs with the minimum of contact with others, limiting his desires to the scale of his own resources, suspicious of gold and luxury. It is hardly necessary to refer to the significant use of *oikonomia* – household management – in connection with state finances, or to the importance of the provision of food in economic policy.[22] Corresponding to the representation of the tradeless city was that of the cityless trader. The problem of the relation between social status and economic roles was, as we have seen, a crucial one in classical Athens, and there was an ideal conception of the division of labour according to social status,[23] attested not only by the philosophers but by numerous remarks in the Attic orators and in comedy. Citizens were farmers, slaves supplied domestic services and unskilled labour, while traders were foreigners or metics. The idea that trade and marketing were incompatible with whole-hearted participation in social and political life, expressed by Aristotle in the opposition between natural and unnatural economic activity, *oikonomia* (householding) and *kapēlikē* (commerce), was a deep-rooted one. It can be seen in Homer, in the assumption of a young Phaeacian that if Odysseus is a trader he has no footing in the world of games and gift-exchange shared by nobles throughout the Homeric world, or in the description of Phoenician traders who after spending a year in Syrie left stealthily by night, carrying off the king's son to be sold into slavery;[24] in the Theban law that anyone who had traded in the market within the last ten years could not hold political office;[25] in the hostility against traders as foreigners callously exploiting the hardship of others which flared up in Athens when corn prices rose.[26] A type of interaction in which each party was expected to consider only his own immediate economic advantage was a flagrant contradiction of every conception of social life: the man who lived by such transactions could only be an 'outsider'.

It is in terms of this conception of the division of labour among the three status-groups which made up the city's population that attitudes to work and economic opportunities have to be understood. Other representations are associated with it; in particular, the belief (influenced by colonisation) that in the beginning of the *polis* each citizen had received an equal portion of land, and that if all had gone well land-holdings would still be equal.[27] That they were not was one of the sources of tension in the social structure – one of the points where the lack of correspondence between reality and representation was most obvious. The rich, even in Athens where land signified less than it did in other states, were aware that excessive expansion of their estates was dangerous. Both the political and the economic aspects of changes in patterns of land-ownership during and after the Peloponnesian war require more study. There is some evidence that those who acquired land on a large scale in Attica had their holdings scattered in different demes and did not attempt to consolidate them.[28] Land was 'visible' wealth, and to be visibly rich in Athens after the Peloponnesian war provoked a jealousy which found its outlet in the law-courts: the rich man who had no political power was likely to be frequently threatened with petty suits.[29] Where the poorer citizens felt that they had been deprived of land – a political right rather than an economic one – class-consciousness and revolution could develop. Redistribution of land and the abolition of debt – politico-economic equality and personal freedom from dependence – were the spectres of revolution feared by all Greek cities.

Athens, however, had not been seriously troubled by such claims since the early sixth century B.C. Though the popularity of the cleruchy system in the fifth and fourth centuries shows the continued importance of land (and the pressure of over-population), distributions of cash had to some extent taken the place of land-holding as the symbol of equal share-holding in the *polis*. Kurt Latte has shown that distribution of state revenues was common in the archaic city: there was nothing unusual in the Athenian custom of sharing out the proceeds of the state silver mines among the citizens.[30] (It was because surplus revenue was either distributed or dedicated to a god that Pericles had to create his state reserve fund in the form of a sacred treasure from which money could be borrowed by the state.) In the fifth century the distribution of surplus revenues was stopped, but pay for political and military service to some extent took its place; the distribution of the surplus was revived in the fourth century in the *theōrikon*,[31] which came to be the major symbol of participation in the state's profits – a barometer of the state of public finance, and a political right fiercely guarded against attempts to spend the surplus elsewhere. Demades called it 'the glue of the democracy': it symbolised the fusion of collective and individual income.

For the Athenian *dēmos* was conscious of its receipts as a collectivity as well as of the receipts of the individual as share-holder. We know from Isocrates[32] that the tribute of the empire in the fifth century was paraded talent by talent in the theatre at the Great Dionysia. Old Man Demos, as Aristophanes portrayed him in the *Knights*, liked to have homage paid to him: tribute from subject cities, flattery and gifts from politicians, fines from those condemned in the lawcourts, feasts, festivals and other services from the rich. The expenditure on competitions, sacrifices and other displays of wealth by which in primitive societies the rich win and manifest their prestige was in classical Athens regarded by the *dēmos* as no more than its due; a propitiatory offering to avert hostility rather than a claim to honour. The rich felt unsafe under this relentless pressure to demonstrate their goodwill by spending, especially in the fourth century when the opportunities for enrichment abroad in subject territories were severely curtailed; there is some evidence that, with the exception of a few military 'houses' who still succeeded in recouping their fortunes abroad, few families managed to remain in the wealthiest group for long.[33]

This pressure on the rich has often been ascribed to an increase in the economic differentiation between rich and poor. There may have been a perception of increased differentiation, especially in the hard years immediately after the Peloponnesian war; but it was more than that, and above all it was not a simple reaction against a traditional class of gentry. Political power, by the time of the Peloponnesian war, could be achieved by any man with ability as a military commander or as a speaker; and conversely, social status alone no longer commanded respect in the Assembly. Politics were beginning to become professionalised;[34] the rich man was no longer automatically a member of the political élite. As the heat of competition increased and the *dēmos* – so it seemed to them – made mistake after mistake in the conduct of the war, many rich men opted out. It was this group of rich men without political influence or ambition – a group which included rich metics as well as citizens – which was the object of the attacks of sycophants in the lawcourts, and which was perceived simply in terms of wealth and not as occupying a legitimate place in the social structure.

I have suggested elsewhere[35] that the process of social change in Athens should be seen in terms of structural differentiation of roles, spheres of activity and types of interaction. The dominant importance of political life increased, but the integration of political and economic activity began to break down. The 'representation' of *zweckrational* economic activity as extra-social was no longer adequate.

When the Athenians left their land and village communities to come to the city, as a substantial number of them did in 431 B.C., and as, no doubt, many had done in the preceding fifty years, they came from a life in which political status and economic sustenance were identified in the possession of land, and market transactions played a minor part in a peasant subsistence economy. Market exchange, money and the conception of a differentiated sphere of transactions assessed in purely economic terms were familiar, but had hitherto been encountered only by leaving the local community to visit the city market. The move to the city meant permanent adoption of the economic behaviour associated with traders and markets – which had developed as an independent sphere with its own rules just *because* it had been kept at the margin of social life. Its adoption may well have been accelerated in the Peloponnesian war by the particularly 'anomic' character of an enforced urbanisation in wartime which must originally have appeared as a temporary and unreal interlude, and which was accompanied by the nightmare experiences of the plague in 430 B.C.

Pericles' policy of abandoning the land of Attica and evacuating its peasantry to the city struck at the autarky of the individual as well as that of the *polis*. It raised the pressing question of the substitute for land as the basis of subsistence and symbol of political identity. The answer was to hand, in state pay – for some as jury-men and holders of political office in Athens, but for the majority as soldiers, rowers and garrisons at home or in cities of the empire. This opportunity of state service, in my opinion, effectively blocked any possibility of a development of free wage labour in Athens just when expansion of the city population and economy was at its height. There was an economic demand for more mobile and legally responsible labour, but it had to be filled by modifying the conditions of slavery instead of recruiting free men.[36] Free labour, to judge from our sources, was important for men only in state building contracts, which did not involve subjection to a private employer and took the form of contracts for work (*locatio operis faciendi*) rather than of wage labour. To work for a private employer was regarded as 'slavery'.[37]

This attitude, which may be almost inevitable in slave-owning societies, but which was reinforced in Athens by the possibility of substituting state pay for farming as the appropriate economic basis of citizen status,[38] tended to involve the poorer citizens in a vicious circle. The demand for mobile and legally responsible wage labour to which they refused to respond turned to the slave population, and produced a progressive improvement in the working conditions and opportunities of slaves which further threatened the maintenance of the distinction between slave and citizen in the economic sphere. Slaves and freedmen became foremen, managers of shops and work-shops, captains of trading vessels and bailiffs of estates; slaves acquired legal capacity in lawsuits concerning banking and trade;[39] they increasingly often lived and worked independently, paying a fixed sum to their masters and accumulating surplus earnings, if they could, toward the purchase of freedom; they might be freed under a contract which bound them to continue working for their master as free employees with legal capacity; in banking, where success de-pended heavily on experience and goodwill, a slave could rise to citizenship and the highest level of wealth. Slaves were beginning to be integrated in the community of the *polis* and not only in the household. The problem of creating a class of employees who could act as foremen, managers and agents, without which the scale and scope of business enterprise could not expand, was more satisfactorily solved by the Romans, who had a tradition of client relationships between freedman and ex-owner which was lacking in Greece;[40] but the first steps in this direction were taken in classical Athens.

But what did citizens do? They did not all live solely off state pay even in the fifth century, when the fleet was most active. Some were employed in the extensive foreign trade of Athens, either as traders and seamen or in producing pottery and other goods which were carried abroad. But many of the traders were metics, and production for export never reached large proportions in Athens; many of the ships leaving Piraeus carried cargoes which had come there from other areas, or coin. Production for the local market was probably more important. Attica in the fifth century had a population of over 250,000, and we hear of no rural markets;[41] all, from their experience of military service and the periods of refuge from invasion in the city during the Peloponnesian war, were accustomed to a monetised economy, and those in the city lived entirely by cash transactions. There was plenty of scope for farmers, fishermen, shopkeepers, market gardeners and small craftsmen working alone or with a slave or two, in supplying the local market. The essential for self-respect was that each citizen was self-employed in his own small business. Although Spartans and philosophers thought that craftsmen and shopkeepers should be banned from citizenship, their occupations were not shameful in Athens, even if they gave no cause for pride. (It may be significant of the concern over occupational status that classical Athens is one of the first societies we know in which a distinction between artists and craftsmen begins to be made.)[42]

The slave-owning society of classical Athens thus had little in common with those societies in which slave labour has been employed on a large scale in plantations producing for export. Its prosperity depended on the level of activity of the local market for consumer goods;[43] but the labour input came either from slaves whose consumption was kept to a minimum, or from small-scale producers whose aim was often only to buy a slave to work in their place. The circulation of money was thus quite different from that of a modern economy; the link between capital and labour supplied by wages hardly existed. In these circumstances the state pay and distributions which have been denounced by so many critics of ancient society provided a channel through which the profits of the rich could be redistributed among the poorer citizen consumers. It had economic as well as political significance; and a slump in state revenues meant economic depression as well as political weakness.

For the poor, then, the main problem was to maintain in the face of social and economic change the distinction in economic position between citizen and slave, despite loss of the land which had originally been its basis. The result was an intensification of political activity, especially where the satisfactions of political pay or distributions for the individual, and increased revenue for the collective *dēmos* could be found; and a tendency to prefer increased leisure or political service to expansion of private economic enterprise. Economic and social pressures conflicted mainly in this question of the maintenance of status distinctions; there are few signs that the poor were perturbed by the increasing commercialisation of life which dismayed philosophers.

The effects on the rich were rather different. Slavery was of minor importance, though the lack of legally responsible managers was one reason for the small-scale and disconnected character of business enterprise. It was the conflict between social and economic ends which stood in the foreground. Escalating taxation and liturgy expenses, loss of income from land in the fifth century and of opportunities of enrichment abroad in the fourth, made it difficult to live up to the aristocratic ideal of a liberality untouched by any economic cares beyond those of the conscientious gentleman-farmer. There was a pressure to look for new sources of income. This, it might be thought, was just what was needed for economic development. But though there was an increase in investment in loans to traders, mining and the ownership of slave workshops, such enterprises remained, with the possible exception of mining, marginal and small in scale.

Shortage of capital and credit was not, I believe, one of the most fundamental problems in the classical Athenian economy: the obstacles in mental attitudes and institutions were more serious. There was under-employed capital in the hands of people who for various reasons were unlikely to look for productive outlets for it, though there was a shortage of capital among small men who could have made good use of it, as noted by Xenophon, whose suggestions in the *Poroi* that the state should own merchant ships and mining slaves to hire out to such men, and that corporate mining undertakings should be encouraged, were designed to fill this need.[44] Finley has shown that most of the mortgaging and lending which went on in the landowning sphere was concerned not with productive enterprises but with the fulfilment of social obligations – funeral expenses, dowry guarantees and above all the heavy charges of liturgies. The only firmly institutionalised form of productive loan was the *nautikon daneion* – the high interest bottomry loan.[45]

The fact that hypothecation was used to secure loans for productive purposes in sea trade but not in the case of land requires further examination. It is not perhaps so much a case of a single procedure functioning differently in two separate spheres, but of two different institutions. Although the *nautikon daneion* in Greek law took the form of a loan against security, it was an anomalous form of security. What was hypothecated was the cargo, which on a loan for a two-way trip would be sold abroad and replaced by something else, and/or the ship, which would not return to Athens in precisely the situation where the lender's risk was greatest, i.e. in the case of shipwreck, when in fact the borrower did not have to repay the loan. Hypothecation therefore did not fulfil its normal function of providing security for the creditor; indeed it has often been pointed out that the *nautikon daneion* was a form of insurance for the borrower. The *hypothēkē* – ship or cargo – represented not the creditor's security but his risk, as Pringsheim has shown.[46] It also lacked another characteristic of the normal *hypothēkē*, that of limiting the liability of the debtor. The *nautikon daneion* resembles the institution known to the Italians as the *commenda*, a combination of loan and partnership in which the lending partner contributed a larger share of the capital and/or took a larger proportion of the risk, in return for the other's services.[47] This type of partnership was certainly known in Babylonia in our period, and very probably in Phoenicia (its existence in Palestine in the time of Christ is documented by the Parable of the Talents);[48] it is worth asking whether a knowledge of the commenda derived from eastern traders could have influenced the development of the *nautikon daneion* in Athens. The commenda has characteristics of both loan and partnership, and different societies stress one aspect or the other (emphasis on partnership being found where interest-bearing loans are restricted or forbidden). If the Athenians classed it as a loan, this may reflect some of their attitudes to economic enterprise: recognition of the speculative nature of the transaction, avoidance of direct involvement in trade, and difficulty in conceptualising clearly the forms and problems of single-purpose association, especially those of a partnership in which the contributions were of different kinds.[49]

The *nautikon daneion* and the mortgage of land were not only separated by the values which hindered the entry of land into the sphere of market transactions; they were different institutions, transacted through different relationships, and belonging to different systems of thought and behaviour, even though they could be described by the same general word, *hypothēkē*. The differences between them correspond to a general distinction between modern and primitive credit. Loans are common in many primitive societies; anthropologists have often described the network of debt and credit relationships which bind men together, and the manipulation of loans and interest which bring wealth and power to leading men, and may even lead to the emergence of specialist 'brokers' or duns who spend their time arranging loans or enforcing repayment. Competitive gift-exchange or feast-giving – potlatching – is particularly likely to lead those playing the principal part to draw on as many supporters as possible for contributions to increase the magnificence of their display.[50]

Some traces of similar institutions can be found in Greece. Alkinoos and Menelaos in the *Odyssey* call on their friends and followers to help them in gift-giving,[51] and a few references in later sources to loans of plate look like a survival of the same ethos.[52] In the same way, borrowing to meet heavy expenses in liturgies reproduces the pattern of the primitive loan, which enables the 'big man' to represent his group in splendour or a poor village to enliven the monotony of everyday life by concentrating all the group's spare resources in the hands of single individuals by turns.[53]

In some developing societies, where there is a tradition of strong leadership or corporate activity, such loans or contributions can be made the basis of new productive efforts – investment in communal improvements, or co-operative enterprises.[54] But in other societies the gap between primitive and productive loan is hard to bridge. The Tolai of north-east New Britain, recently described by Dr Scarlett Epstein,[55] have an extensive credit system in their traditional shell-money, *tambu*, but are unwilling to lend cash to each other: they are afraid that the social relationship implicit in the traditional loan system will make it difficult to enforce repayment. The primitive loan, indeed, has two features which make it unsuitable as a basis for modern credit. One is that lending brings prestige which the creditor is likely to lose if he shows impatience for the return of the loan. The second is that he can demand repayment without shame if confronted with a social obligation of the type round which the loan system is built. Such obligations are often irregular and unforeseeable; if regular (*rites de passage*, annual feasts), they belong to a different time-scale from that of economic investment. Often neither creditor nor debtor can be sure how long the loan will last; the debtor often has to borrow again from a third person after a short period in order to repay. The same characteristics – loans for an indefinite period and re-borrowing – seem to be a feature of Athenian land mortgages. In contrast, the mark of the 'modern' loan is that the period of repayment is calculated with regard to the purpose of the loan, and that it is a single contractual transaction and not part of a network of reciprocal obligations.

To some extent the Athenian banks, like modern banks, served to reconcile discrepancies between lenders' and borrowers' needs, and so bridged the gap between social and productive credit. Bankers, often ex-slaves, stood outside the social circle; although the banks were only one-man businesses they were differentiated economic institutions in the sense that transactions with them had no social significance. They provided the flexibility needed to reconcile the different time-scales of productive investment and social obligations;

a man could lend money through a banker in a *nautikon daneion* and borrow from the same banker for a liturgy payment if his debtor had not yet returned to Athens.[56] The 'modernists' were right, in a sense, in citing the Athenian banks as evidence of similarity between the ancient and the modern economy (though the ancient banks lacked the main function of the modern bank, that of creating credit). Although the Athenian bank took the traditional form of a 'household' staffed by slaves, and depended on the ability of a single owner and his friends' confidence in him, the banker like the trader was a sign of structural differentiation: he stood outside the social network, and his role was a purely economic one.

One of the reasons for the low level of development of workshop production and other urban business enterprises was, as I have already suggested, the absence of a suitable personnel in this field to play the part of the banker in cushioning the investor from direct involvement with his investment. To run a workshop in an 'entrepreneurial' spirit would have required supervision by the owner. Instead, the workshops of which we know details were managed by slaves or freedmen, and the owner drew a fixed income from them. There was no interest in expansion. Such businesses might have been acquired accidentally, and their grouping is haphazard.[57] Demosthenes' father owned two workshops, one making beds and the other knives: there was no connection between them. Pasion's bank and shield-factory were equally unconnected and it is significant that while Pasion, an ex-slave, evidently devoted considerable energy and personal attention to the bank, his son Apollodorus (who received Athenian citizenship with his father) acquired three estates, preferred the shield-factory to the bank as his share of the inheritance, and devoted his energies to politics and the showy performance of liturgies, in the style of an Athenian gentleman. As metic traders and bankers became more important to the prosperity and food-supply of the city, the most successful of them were rewarded with citizen privileges,[58] came under pressure for gifts and contributions to the *dēmos*, and tended to adopt the ethos of the rich citizens rather than encourage the latter to venture into new fields of investment. Although Aristotle asserted that 'unnatural' *chrēmatistikē* (money-making) knew no bounds, the general impression given by our sources is that the majority of Athenians were quite ready to give up the effort to make money as soon as they could afford a comfortable *rentier* existence, and that even the few who continued to expand their operations could not pass on the same spirit to their sons.

The result was small-scale, disconnected business ventures, assessed by the security of their returns rather than their potentiality for expansion. Apart from the development of speculation in overseas trade, the most favourable fields for citizen investment seem to have been mining and tax-farming.[59] The difficulties of organising slave employees were no less here, but possibly these activities were preferred because they were more closely connected with the activities of the state. Andocides could speak of bidding up the farming of the Piraeus harbour dues almost as if it were the performance of a liturgy,[60] and Nicias, who was said to have had a thousand slaves at work in the mines,[61] was not the man to do anything inconsistent with the ideal of gentlemanly *aretē*.

It may be noted that Roman 'capitalism' also tended to develop in contexts associated with the state – tax-farming and plantation production of corn for export to Rome. Much of what has been said above about the conflict between economy and society in Athens applies equally to Rome: the difference between Rome and Athens was that Romans had opportunities of stepping outside the tensions and constraints of the city-state to enrich themselves in the provinces.[62] 'Caelum, non animum mutant qui trans mare currunt' is not sound sociology. Mental attitudes, 'representations' and institutions can easily change in a different social climate. The relaxation of social restraints in the provinces led some to commit atrocities, but it also helped to create a tradition of *zweckrational* economic activity and bureaucratic administration. The Athenians too enriched themselves abroad when they could (there is an eloquent decree of Arcesine thanking the historian Androtion for an interest-free loan of money – evidently a rarity – to pay contributions to the Second Athenian Confederacy),[63] but they did not *govern* their empire; financial and other administration was normally left to local authorities. It is worth noting that the author of the second book of the Aristotelian *Economics* found the 'monarchic' and 'satrapal' economies of the east easier to analyse than that of the Greek *polis*, and that it was Xenophon, who knew the Persian Empire, and had commanded an army on a long campaign,[64] who wrote a treatise on city economy containing some very unconventional suggestions for raising Athenian revenues. The economic historian of the Hellenistic world who wishes to analyse the changes in 'representations' and institutions set in process by Alexander's conquest of the Persian empire will have to take into account both contact with the bureaucratic 'satrapal' tradition of administration and the differences in social structure between the Greek *polis* and the Hellenistic kingdom, as well as the difference between classical and Hellenistic conceptions of the State.

Gernet has said that the Greeks did not have a sufficiently clear conception of the State to be able to formulate an economic policy for it.[65] The question needs more study. 'Representations' of the state's economic role existed, but there were several, with little integration between them. The state as householder, caring for its own resources, trying to avoid trade and sordid money-making; the state as protector of the poor and the orphan, and source of cheap corn and cash distributions; the state as army, supported by the contributions of those it defended or the captured property of the enemy; or the state as autocrat, insecurely placed, requiring constant homage of gifts and resorting to trickery in moments of crisis. But a few men did feel sufficiently confident in their position as leaders to formulate a long-term policy: Themistocles, Aristides and Pericles, bent on making Athens the leading power in Greece; Eubulus, skilfully manipulating rewards and sanctions to revive falling revenues after the social war; Lycurgus, marked out by his name for a reformer in the tradition of the ancient law-givers. Specialised, elected financial magistrates with important powers existed in Athens at least from the time of Eubulus, and the idea that economic policy was as necessary as military policy was slowly growing.

But it was Rhodes rather than Athens which turned into the city Xenophon had visualised in the *Poroi*; except that the Rhodians did not make the mistake of thinking that sea-power was unnecessary. Many of the 'modern' features of the Athenian economy, especially the embryonic workings of a supply–demand price mechanism, were due to the centralisation of a large proportion of the trade of the Aegean in a single market. Because of this concentration, the Athenian market was able to exert an influence, even if only occasionally and crudely, on economic decisions taken elsewhere, which would have been impossible if trade had been fragmented among a number of competing centres. But this centralisation was only made possible by the prestige of Athens as the leading power and richest city of the area. Sea-power not only made trade safe from piracy, but also protected traders from being forced to unload and sell their cargoes in any port along the route which lacked corn (Ziebarth, 1929). In the fourth century it was becoming clear that Athens' position was precarious. If Athenian sea-power and prosperity showed signs of decline, trade fell away as other cities tried to take Athens' place. The real advantages she offered in centralisation of the market, provision of credit and an improved commercial law (Gernet, 1938c) were not sufficient to resist the unscrupulous methods of more backward cities or the growing attractions of new rivals.

To sum up: the peculiar historical circumstances of urbanisation and Empire, social change and economic development in classical Athens produced a society and economy containing a number of contradictions. The development of a highly centralised market depended on Athens' position as a sea-power and mistress of an empire whose tribute paid for her fleet and which, by siphoning off wealth and man-power from the other Aegean cities, delayed the development of rival centres. The intense activity of her internal market also depended on the income received by citizens for their political and military services, and by the metic and foreign rowers attracted to the city. Finley, in a recent article on Spartan military organisation, remarked on the paradox that the Spartan state, ostensibly organised as a war-machine, threatened to collapse when faced with war (Finley, 1968c); one might equally say that the Athenians, who prided themselves on their leadership in the arts of peace, had an economy which threatened to disintegrate under peace-time conditions. In these circumstances the burden of production fell on slaves; as the organisation of business and production grew more complex and new forms of enterprise developed in which rich citizens would not take an active interest and poor citizens would not accept employment, the conditions of slavery were modified to fill the need for new kinds of labour. But these changes in slavery increased the poorer citizens' anxiety at the blurring of status distinctions between citizen and slave, and intensified the political activity by which they sought to maintain their political and economic identity. It was this, together with the rapid increase of the market and adoption by disoriented peasants of a 'market mentality', which made the rich and the philosophers feel that political life had been corrupted by greed for money; and this reaction in its turn reinforced the reluctance of the upper class to take an active part in new economic development.

But we need not, like Riezler and Erb, see the period only as one of conflict and social disintegration. It was a creative period for economic institutions and law, as for other fields; and the tensions and contradictions which I have described were at least partly responsible for the increasingly impersonal, individualistic, rational and differentiated character of the economy.[66] This is the 'modern' aspect of the Athenian economy, and it cannot be understood apart from the 'primitive' features which structured it.

I have tried to suggest here that primitive technology and slavery were less resistant to economic change than the mental attitudes of the citizens of Athens, and that ideological 'charters' like the Athenian conception of the correspondence between status categories and economic roles and of the citizen's right to a share in the state's wealth cannot be simply explained as validating the democratic structure of the society, and the exclusiveness of the citizen body, or upholding the claims of a particular social class; these ideas were not only a reflection, but also increasingly a source, of conflict and tension, as the discrepancy between 'charter' and reality widened. They were beliefs held by both oligarchs and democrats, and although rich and poor might be affected by different aspects of the discrepancy, there was both continuity and interchange between their reactions.

There are many subjects here which demand further research. We need to ask how far the Athenian 'representation' of economic life was shared by other Greeks, and how its effects varied in the different conditions of other *poleis* and of the Hellenistic world. Above all we need to make more use of comparative studies of other ancient societies, eastern and western, of later periods in European and oriental economic history, and of modern peasant societies and developing economies. Comparison will not tell us exactly what happened in Greece but, where our sources are so fragmentary, it is an essential stimulus to re-examine our reconstructions by setting them against concrete data from better-known societies, and reminder that the questions which our evidence might permit us to answer are not the only questions to be asked.

Additional note

My concern in this paper with the relation between 'primitive' and 'modern' features in the Athenian economy now seems to me to be a misleading formulation of the problems discussed, as does the emphasis on 'values', derived from the development-oriented economic anthropology of the 1960s. This approach had at least one useful result, in that it led me to an interest in the association of different values with different roles and social contexts (village or city market; assembly or bank) which developed into the work on social structure and contexts of interaction presented in the last three papers in this volume. But the way in which this paper was formulated has probably obscured the extent to which it is concerned with the process of circulation of men, money, and goods in the classical Greek world, and with the relation of this process to diachronic developments in power relations between Athens and other Greek states, in Athenian internal politics, and in the conditions of slavery and the occupation patterns of the free.

Further discussion of the nature of the ancient economy can now be found in Austin and Vidal-Naquet, 1972, as well as in the works by Finley cited in the additional note to chapter 2 above. For attitudes to the sources and use of wealth see also Dover, 1975; on fifth-century Greece in general, Will, 1972, pp. 629–78; on fourth-century Athens, Mossé, 1972. On developments in the law of trade see now Gauthier, 1972; Edward E. Cohen, 1973. On public works and employment by the state, Bodei Giglioni, 1974; on Xenophon's *Poroi*, Bodei Giglioni, 1970. Ph. Gauthier is preparing a new commentary on the *Poroi*.

7 Homo politicus and homo economicus: war and trade in the economy of archaic and classical Greece

Die politische Situation des mittelälterlichen Stadtbürgers wies ihn auf den Weg, ein *homo oeconomicus* zu sein, während in der Antike sich die Polis während der Zeit ihrer Blüte ihren Charakter als des militärtechnisch höchstehenden Wehr-verbands bewahrte: Der antike Bürger war *homo politicus*.[1]

Weber's remark leads in two different directions: the one followed by much of the most important work on the ancient economy of the last fifty years, the other scarcely explored. On the common interpretation, it points to Weber's interest in the historical and cultural preconditions for the development of capitalism; Weber's contrast between *homo politicus* and *homo oeconomicus* has been taken as implying that the classical world, like China (Weber, 1916), could be treated as a test case showing that the genesis of capitalism could not be explained merely by identifying a certain number of basic structural prerequisites, but required a complex study of the interrelations between structure and value-systems. J. Hasebroek's *Staat und Handel im alten Griechenland* (1928) was largely responsible for popularizing a reading of Weber in which the abstract types *homo politicus* and *homo oeconomicus* were identified with occupationally differentiated sectors of Greek society – the landowning political elite and the traders – and the characterization of the conflicting motives and values of these two categories offered by Plato and Aristotle, symbolized in the opposition of *oikonomia* and *chrēmatistikē*, was taken at face value. I myself put forward an interpretation of the economy of classical Athens expressed in these terms (chapter 6 above); and in general over-emphasis on the study of 'values' in abstraction from social structure has been a noticeable weakness in recent work on Greek society.

Weber himself, although he emphasized the importance of religious beliefs in men's assessment of the rewards and consequences attached to alternative courses of action, did not advocate the study of value-systems in isolation. He was even less likely to approve of a dogmatic separation of 'political' and 'economic' rewards; the study of the interrelations of the two was one of the major themes in his last and greatest work, *Wirtschaft und Gesellschaft* (1922). Consequently, his characterization of the differences between the medieval and the ancient citizen needs a more careful reading. He is not saying simply that the ancient citizen was more interested in war than in the activities of the market-place, but that because, in terms of military organization, the ancient city-state belongs to the structural type of the war-band (the whole citizen body being involved in war, with the minimum of functional specialization), the set of institutions which dominates its functioning and gives the key ideal-type which sums up its ethos is (in modern terms) political rather than economic. 'Dominance' here does not mean that there are two conflicting value-systems one of which influences behaviour more decisively than the other, but that the institutions which to us seem characteristically 'economic' – trade, production for the market, the circulation of money, banking – are analytically dependent on and can only be fully understood in terms of the working of other institutions which we would characterize as 'political'.

For the fifth century B.C. the key relationship is of course that between the Athenian empire and Athens' position as the centre of Aegean trade. Earlier, however, a more complicated interaction can be traced between the travels and guest-friendships of nobles, war, raiding and piracy, and the development of trade. In some respects it is fruitful to compare the recent analysis of the relation between war and economic development in the early Middle Ages by Georges Duby (Duby, 1973; cf. Puddu, 1975). Very briefly, Duby sees this relationship developing in three phases: in the first, war, booty, and the exchanges of prestige goods among the upper class contributed to development by intensifying demand and the circulation of goods; later, the growth of the state gave further impetus to development by increasing production of coined money and affording protection to long-distance traders; finally, from the eleventh century onwards, war became increasingly differentiated from a non-military system of production and exchange in which the requirements of the warrior elite were met by increased charges on peasant agriculture, by artisan production in towns and by trade, rather than by plundering expeditions. At this point the life-style of the military elite has become independent of the actual practice of war – for which jousts and tournaments become an increasingly common substitute – and the stage is set for the division of labour between the professional mercenary soldier and a civilian world to whose economy war is an interruption rather than a necessary stimulus. Expressed in general terms applicable also to the ancient world, Duby's message is that trade should be studied in the context of other forms of long-distance transfer of goods, of which war and gift-exchange are the most obviously relevant examples; that the study of transfers of luxury or prestige goods must be related to the dominant institutions of the life-style within which the demand for them is generated; that war is an 'economic' as well as 'political' activity; and that an analytical separation of war from the economic system is only justifiable under specific historical conditions (which may well be peculiar to Western society). The question, of course, is not whether war has economic effects, which it always does, but whether these effects are best analysed as elements internal to the economic system or as the result of forces external to it.

Although war can play an important role in the circulation of goods, its chief economic implications in pre-industrial societies concern the distribution of manpower. In order to understand the place of war in the ancient Greek economy it is therefore necessary to consider the implications of slavery.

Slave labour was used in Greece in the Mycenaean period, and the use of both purchased and captured slaves was firmly institutionalized in the society described in the eighth century B.C. by Homer and Hesiod,[2] although it should be noted that male slaves are rare; the only male slave whose origin is explained (Eumaeus, *Odyssey* 15.403–84) was captured and sold as a child. Ownership of slaves was not confined to the nobles (*basileis*) who held large estates; Hesiod considers an ox and a 'bought woman' the basic equipment for the small farmer's holding (*Works and Days* 405–6 – but there may be a spurious line here), and elsewhere assumes that the farmer will have dependent labourers incorporated into his household, *dmōes* (*ibid.*, 459, 502, 573, 597, 608). The origins of the latter category are not clear, but their name suggests that they were considered members of the household (Benveniste, 1969, pp. 297, 305; Chantraine, 1968, pp. 289–90), incorporated on an individual basis, and consequently at least temporarily assimilated to the status of the chattel slave as a subordinate household member cut off from his own kin group.

The Greek conceptualization of the household, *oikos*, as an autarkic economic unit is closely bound up with the availability of slave labour. In a society where land is owned by individual households and transmitted by inheritance, imbalances in the distribution of land and manpower inevitably arise. Some families have too many children for their land to support, others have too few to work it (cf. Goody, 1973). Sons by right inherited equal shares of their father's property in ancient Greece; daughters were given a dowry in lieu of inheritance, and if this was given in land in early times, dowry transfers would have tended to intensify inequalities in land-holdings.[3] Where no outside source of labour is available, imbalances in the distribution of land and labour are adjusted by connecting the surplus labour of some families to the surplus land of others through such institutions as tenancy, clientship, marriage, fictive kinship or wage labour. Wherever imported slaves, bought or captured, are used to supply the extra labour needed on land which the owning family cannot work with its own manpower, a potential outlet for the surplus labour produced by other families is blocked. Given the scarcity of agricultural land in Greece, the use of slaves in farming meant, at least potentially, the need to drain surplus free labour off the land into emigration or alternative types of occupation.

Although slave numbers cannot have been very high in total in early times, there is evidence which suggests that the predominance of slavery as the preferred form of dependent labour was already established by the eighth century B.C. Other ways of recruiting labour existed but their use was limited. A few men with small prospects of inheriting sufficient land to make them independent were, from the sixth century onwards in Attica at least, incorporated into the families of close kinsmen without sons as adopted sons or in-marrying sons-in-law, but these were a minority; and it appears that even this limited form of redistribution of land and labour was not practised in the eighth century, since Homer and Hesiod both speak of the division of the childless man's property by his kindred, *chērōstai*, as the inevitable and tragic end of the heirless *oikos*, in phrases which strongly assert the independence of the *oikos vis-à-vis* a circle of kin seen as a potential threat to its continued existence.[4] Wage labour is mentioned by Homer and Hesiod (*Iliad* 21.448; *Odyssey* 4.644, 18.357; *Works and Days* 602), and was sufficiently important in Athens in the early sixth century for Solon to use the term *thētes* to denote the lowest of his four census classes, but there is no evidence that wage labour ever developed to the point of supplying employers with a permanent work-force rather than occasional labour at peak periods or for a particular task.[5] Sparta, Thessaly and a few Greek colonies had a subject class of serfs working on the land; we do not know whether the *hektēmoroi* whom Solon liberated from their obligation to pay a sixth of their harvest to their overlords were a similar class or had come into subjection only recently. The main positive argument for assuming that slavery rather than serfdom was the dominant form of dependent labour in most Greek city-states by the eighth century is the remarkable extent of Greek colonization. After the upheavals which marked the end of the Bronze Age, the number of known inhabited sites in the Aegean (excluding Crete) falls in the twelfth to the eleventh centuries to a figure lower even than that for the Early Bronze Age (Snodgrass, 1971, pp. 364–7), yet by the early seventh century Greeks are solidly established throughout the islands and coastal regions of the Aegean, are well embarked on the colonization of Sicily and southern Italy, and are beginning to settle in the Black Sea. This astonishing expansion needs some explanation. The tradition that each adult male colonist received an allotment of land in the new settlement makes it clear that the Greek city was already by the eighth century conceptualized essentially as a union of property-holding households, in which kin groups intermediate between city and *oikos* were of only secondary importance. With private ownership of land by individual households solidly established and with only limited openings for the absorption of surplus labour from poor households into the work-force of larger estates, the problem of 'land-hunger' becomes a question not of overall population density but of the resources available to individual households. Furthermore, the evidence of Homer, the prominence of animal sacrifices in Greek religion, and the tradition recorded by Aristotle (*Politics* 1305a 21 ff.) that the seventh-century tyrant Theagenes of Megara won popular support by slaughtering the flocks of the rich, all suggest that stockrearing may have been much more important in Greece in the eighth and seventh centuries than it was in the classical period. If so, it would be quite possible for rich households to farm extensive landholdings with a small force of slave herdsmen – as Odysseus does in the *Odyssey* – while the smallholder was already, as Hesiod advised (*Works and Days* 376–8), limiting his family to one son because land could only be acquired by inheritance. A significant proportion of households could have been pressed by land-hunger, and ready to emigrate in order to acquire land, well before all the cultivable land in Greece was being intensively farmed.

The possibility of using slaves where extra labour was required, as well as generating a flow of permanent migrants from Greece to new settlements abroad, also set young men free for shorter periods of travel. A father did not need his sons to work his land; their presence in the *oikos* was a potential threat and a source of friction, since their interest was to persuade the old man to relinquish land on which they could marry and found a new household. Hesiod advises men not to marry before the age of thirty (*Works and Days* 695–6) and refers to quarrels between son and father as one of the most wicked of crimes against the family (*ibid.*, 331–2). Solon thought it necessary to enforce by public prosecution (*graphē*) a father's right to maintenance from a son to whom he had passed on property *inter vivos* (A. R. W. Harrison, 1968, pp. 77–8; Ruschenbusch, 1966, Fr. 55–7). Aristophanes' *Wasps*, later, gives a lively picture of friction between a father and his co-resident unmarried son, though in an urban setting. Even men who would eventually inherit property, therefore, were left in an ambiguous and marginal status between the age of recognition as a social adult at sixteen or eighteen and full incorporation into the community as a married household head with the right to hold office, at the age of thirty or over (Kahr- stedt, 1936, p. 18).[6] During this period a young man was not expected to take an active part in debates in the assembly (Xenophon, *Memorabilia* 3. i. 6), although he could vote; in a sense the only sphere in which he could exercise his citizen rights fully was in fighting.[7]

Recent studies (Vernant, 1962, 1968a; cf. also Greenhalgh, 1973) have strongly emphasized the contrasts between hoplite warfare and the earlier mode of fighting represented in the *Iliad*. The hoplite army was recruited by the city and not by individual leaders, and its success depended on the solidarity and discipline of a block of identically equipped troops rather than on the exploits of heroes who stood out from the rank and file in equipment and skill as well as in courage. The structure of the hoplite army provided a new image of the structure of the city, and one which lent itself to democratization, since hoplite status was open to any man who could provide himself with armour. Hoplite fighting involved a steadily increasing proportion of the citizen population, in warfare which was normally restricted to short-term campaigns against neighbouring states and which developed strongly ritualized conventions. Only Sparta, with her serf class of Helot labourers, managed to conduct lengthy campaigns in the eighth and seventh centuries in Messenia; and the poetry of Tyrtaios (West, 1971, Fr. 1; cf. Fr. 10) and the legend of the Partheniai (Pembroke, 1970) suggest that this was not accomplished without strains.

Concentration on the hoplites has, however, obscured traces of the persistence of the Homeric *hetaireia* right up to the time of the Persian wars. Alongside the seasonal rhythm of production and destruction in hoplite warfare ran the longer-term cycle of a man's life, with youth as the period of search for wealth abroad, followed by home production in the *oikos* between approximately the ages of thirty and sixty. It was in the young men's world of unofficial enterprises and liminal status, I suggest, that the ethos and structure of the Homeric *hetaireia* continued to flourish.

When Telemachos decides to travel from Ithaca to Pylos to seek news of his father, he secures the loan of a ship from a friendly young nobleman, Noēmōn, and has no trouble in recruiting twenty *hetairoi* to serve as his crew (*Odyssey* 2.212 ff.). The line 'Come, give me a ship and twenty *hetairoi*' recurs at 4. 669, and may well be a formulaic expression; the term *hetairoi* is also used elsewhere in Homer of a ship's crew (Gray, 1974, p. 108). There has been much discussion of the meaning of *hetairos* in Homer (see especially Jeanmaire, 1939, pp. 97–111; Andrewes, 1961), but in the majority of cases it need denote no more than participation in a common enterprise, in a relationship which has elements of equality but which does not exclude leadership by those who stand out among their 'comrades' by virtue of birth, character or resources. In this instance, Telemachos' companions gain nothing from the voyage except free wine and food *en route* and meat provided by Nestor (*Odyssey* 2.349 ff.), and a change of scenery. Had they travelled further afield, into territory where their leader had no guest-friends, there would have been booty as well (*Odyssey* 9.39 ff., 14.245 ff.; Gray, 1974, pp. 122–30). Some Greeks took raiding-parties into country close enough to home to bring retaliatory attacks (*Odyssey* 16.424 ff., 21.15 ff.). This was the 'seafarers' life' which the illegitimate and therefore landless Archilochos left behind him when he quit Paros to become a hoplite and landholder in the colony of Thasos (*thalassios bios*, West, 1972, Fr. 116; cf. Latte, 1964; Russo,

1975, p. 714; *Odyssey* 14.222–6). Hesiod's father may have lived in the same way before settling as a small farmer in Boeotia, although Hesiod himself thinks of seafaring only in terms of brief trading voyages with a cargo, presumably, of farm produce to sell in the nearest city (*Works and Days* 618–94).

Hesiod seems to assume here that if his brother Perses trades in this way he will have his own small boat; but the *gnomē* 'Praise a small ship, but put your goods in a large one' (*ibid.*, 643) seems better suited to the trader who loads his wares on another man's vessel. A recent study by Benedetto Bravo (1974) has called attention to the fact that of the two most common early terms for the trader, *emporos* and *phortēgos*, the former certainly and the latter possibly implies collaboration between traders and others. The *emporos* is a passenger on another man's ship, the *phortēgos* can be one who carries another man's goods.[8] This is scarcely surprising. Any man might own a small boat capable of crossing the Gulf of Corinth, but to build, equip, and man a 'broad, cargo-carrying ship of twenty oars, fit for open-sea crossings' (*Odyssey* 9.322–3)[9] required both material and social capital. Representations of ships on West Greek vases of the eighth and seventh centuries confirm that the ships which visited or sailed from the Greek colonies in southern Italy and Sicily were of the same type as those portrayed on the vases displaying the warrior exploits of the Athenian elite in the Dipylon cemetery (Gray, 1974, pp. 22–6; see also Humphreys, 1977). These were the ships which Greek aristocrats owned and used in war, diplomacy, visits to religious festivals and games, and travels abroad to contract or keep up personal alliances – especially when in exile, a not infrequent phenomenon in the archaic age. Attic antiquarians recorded rather indistinct memories that until 507 B.C. Attica had been divided into forty-eight districts called *naukrariai*, each of which had to provide when necessary one warship and two horsemen; clearly the responsibility for providing ships and horses fell on the richest families in each district. In an age when political success depended on personal resources and prestige, noblemen travelled abroad to make influential friends, to contract marriage alliances with leading families in other states, and to gain fame by winning at the Olympic, Pythian, Nemean or Isthmian games; some voyaged further afield to see the wonders of the East (Solon) or to serve eastern monarchs as mercenary soldiers (Alcaeus Fr. 27 in Lobel and Page, 1955; Page, 1955, pp. 223–4). Sappho's brother visited Egypt (Herodotus 2.134 f.). The Alcmaeonidae of Athens, whose fortunes were reputedly founded on a magnificent gift of gold-dust from the king of Lydia, and who had married into the family of the tyrants of Sicyon, undertook to organize the rebuilding of the temple of Delphi in the late sixth century – when cut off from their lands in Attica by the hostility of the tyrant Peisistratos – and used their network of alliances to such good effect that they were able to face the building with marble, although the sum allocated to them by the Delphians for the work had been calculated on the assumption that all of the stonework would be of *poros* limestone (Herodotus 6.125–30, 5.62). Private ownership of longships is likely to have continued until the development of the trireme, which as a highly specialized war machine with a crew of two hundred men required resources which few could muster.[10] Even so, private triremes were commissioned by the athlete Philip of Croton in 510 (Herodotus 5.47) and by Alcibiades' great-grand-father Kleinias in the Persian wars (Herodotus 8.17).

It was the aristocracy, in the first place, who wanted gold and ivory from Egypt, bronze from Etruria, Phoenician textiles, and slaves from Sicily and the Black Sea. Little but an ideological hairline divided the noble who voyaged in order to come home loaded with valuable gifts (*Odyssey* 3.301–2, 4.80–92, 19.282 ff.) or to exchange iron for copper (*ibid.*, 1.182 ff.) from the 'commander of sailors out for gain (*nautai prēktēres*), always thinking about his cargo' (*ibid.*, 8.159 ff.). The latter did not necessarily restrict his activities to peaceful trade, and the former differed from the trader principally in seeking goods for his own consumption (or use in gift-exchange!) rather than for resale. As Bravo suggests, a rich man might send his dependants to trade for him, either on his own ship or on craft belonging to others. In the fourth century, grants of immunity from harbour dues in Olbia at the mouth of the Dnieper cover carriage by the beneficiary's son, brother (if sharing an un-divided estate) or servant (*therapōn*). Equally, if a young nobleman could give a passage on his ship to a diviner (*Odyssey* 15.277 ff.), he might have done the same for other specialist *dēmiourgoi* (*ibid.*, 17.382 ff.) like the smith who travelled with tools, wares, and raw materials on the ship wrecked off Cape Gelidonya in south-west Turkey in the late Bronze Age (Bass, 1967), or for a trader with goods for sale. The *hetairoi* who rowed his ship might take goods for exchange, or hope to acquire them abroad by raiding, piracy or military service.[11] The life of overseas adventure could absorb men of varied origins, left them free to choose their mode of operation (some crews would rob even Greek passengers, Herodotus 1.24) and might bring them any fortune from shipwreck to the huge treasure brought back from Tartessos in Spain by the Samian Kolaios and his crew (Herodotus 4.152; note that the dedication is made by the whole crew, not Kolaios alone). Some men may have spent their lives at sea, but many must have embarked with the hope of acquiring enough mobile wealth and slaves to bring them a secure status as hoplites, a good marriage, and a respected position in the local community when they settled on their fathers' land. Even those who had no land to inherit could presumably hope to acquire it if they amassed sufficient wealth in their travels.[12] Archaic Greece was a poor country; less sophisticated in culture and craftsmanship than the civilizations of the East, less rich in metals than the barbarian regions to the West. Much of its mobile wealth was brought in from overseas, and much of it was probably acquired by force or friendship rather than market exchange. This mobile wealth encouraged social mobility; not, as used once to be suggested, through the creation of a 'merchant class' distinct from the traditional hoplite peasantry, but by providing young men waiting to inherit small farms with an opportunity to equip themselves as hoplites, and perhaps, in some cases, to acquire more land. Because such expeditions brought back slaves who could be added to the family workforce, even the growth of artisan production in Greece which was stimulated by increased trade and mobile wealth is not likely to have affected more than a small minority of free householders. Essentially archaic trade and warfare provided men with a complement to agriculture rather than an alternative.

The most obscure point in the development of Greek trade is the second half of the sixth century. Trade undoubtedly intensified considerably at this time, but it is still not clear whether this led to significant increases in the urban artisan population and greater professionalism in trade. The first Greek representations of large 'roundships' which clearly relied entirely on sail and could carry bulk cargoes with only a small crew belong to the end of the sixth century (British Museum B. 436; Casson, 1971, figures 81–2).[13] The design may have been influenced by the Phoenician *gauloi* which could be seen off Greece and in the eastern Mediterranean at this period (Herodotus 3.136–7, 6.17; Masson, 1967, pp. 39–42).

The large merchant vessel implies the existence of the *nauklēros*, the merchant shipowner who takes charge of a trading expedition not through his ability to recruit a band of *hetairoi* but because he has capital equipment (the ship, very possibly a slave crew) and expert knowledge of pilotage and trading conditions. Such a man could emerge either from the *emporoi* who travelled as traders on ships piloted by others, or from a career as pilot and steersman (*kybernētēs*) to an aristocratic galley-owner. As with other positions requiring expert knowledge – poet, sculptor, holy man, doctor – different routes were open: birth, patronage, inclination, talent. But it is still doubtful how far this development had progressed by the end of the sixth century. A. W. Johnston (1974) finds evidence that in the late sixth century merchants handling trade in Attic vases were operating on a sufficiently large-scale and regular basis to have developed the use of 'merchants' marks' on orders reserved for them; but it is not yet clear what these marks really imply, nor how long any single trader remained in business.

Given the unsatisfactory nature of the evidence, any interpretation of the economy of archaic Greece is bound to be provisional and open to discussion. One may however legitimately ask that such an interpretation should integrate data on trade into a holistic view of the circulation of men and goods rather than taking it, *à la* Adam Smith, as a primary phenomenon sufficiently explained by the uneven geographical distribution of raw materials. What I am suggesting in the first part of this paper is that archaic Greek trade should be seen as part of a much wider context of exchanges between the Aegean and the world beyond, in which the import and export of manpower were of greater moment than the exchange of goods, and upon which a rigid distinction between 'trade' and the transfer of goods through war, raiding, hospitality, and gift-exchange cannot be imposed. At the basis of this model is the nexus of relationships between private property in land, the import of slave labour, and the consequent generation of a stream of surplus free manpower which finds its place partly through definitive emigration, but also in temporary activity outside the home city-state in war, seafaring and trade.

In the second half of the paper I argue that the Athenian empire represents a different and more complex way of integrating surplus free manpower into the economy of the city-state by means of profits derived from war and trade. War and trade are still intimately connected in this model; but instead of being complementary activities carried out by the same personnel, they are differentiated and linked by money, the market-place, and the exaction of tribute by Athens from her subjects.

In contrast to the hypothetical and doubtful character of any discussion of archaic trade, it can be stated with confidence that the Persian wars marked a watershed. Greek cities hurriedly built triremes to match those sailed by Phoenicians and Ionians in the service of Persia, and consequently the number of privately owned pentekontors available for long-distance trading voyages is likely to have declined fairly sharply. At the same time the threat of Persian invasion led to an extraordinary demand for food imports in Greece (the Aeginetan cornships seen by Xerxes in the Hellespont, Herodotus 7.147, can scarcely be taken as evidence of regular trade on a large scale in earlier years); and when the Persians retreated the Greek fleet followed them in the first of a long series of campaigns which took men far from home, lasted through the winter instead of being restricted to a short campaigning season, and posed new problems of provisioning. The historian Ion of Chios personally heard Kimon tell a story which implies that by the time of the capture of Sestos and Byzantion in *c.* 476 the Athenian commanders were already paying their soldiers a regular living allowance (*trophē*) and using the proceeds from the sale of booty or prisoners' ransoms to pay part of the cost.[14] (The probability is that Athens' allies continued to rely on the old-fashioned custom of giving each man a share of the booty and leaving him to provide his own keep, and that this was one of the main reasons why allied cities found it difficult to continue providing ships and crews for League expeditions.) Consequently a new market for bulk trade in food was available, in the fleet when on campaign and at other times in the enlarged urban population of Athens, for which military service became a primary occupation, supplemented by casual work in city and market (cf. chapter 6 above). Athens soon took action to improve security at sea for cornships; Kimon expelled pirates from Skyros in *c.* 465, settlements of Athenian cleruchs were planted along the homeward route from the Black Sea in the Gallipoli peninsula, on Lemnos, and Imbros, on the island of Hagios Eustratios (Halonnesos; [Demosthenes] 7.2–4), at Carystos in Euboea and in Andros on the other side of the Cavo d'Oro channel between that island and Euboea (Brunt, 1966b). Other Athenians were settled inside the Black Sea at Sinope and

Amisos, and the strength of Athenian sea-power was paraded in a ceremonial visit of the fleet to the Black Sea, in the 440s or 430s. Policing of western waters could be left to the Greek cities of Sicily, but the Athenian fleet may have visited Sicily and Naples as early as the 450s (Lepore, 1968, pp. 170–86).

These changes provided sufficient conditions for a rapid increase in the number and size of functionally specialized merchant ships designed to carry bulk food cargoes to feed the Athenian fleet and the city population of Athens. The ship fresco from the Tomba della Nave at Tarquinia, dated by the style of its paintings *c*. 450–40 (Moretti, 1962; Casson, 1971, figure 97), shows a massive vessel of similar design to those of representations from Greece (Casson, 1971, figures 81–2) and Cyprus (*ibid.*, figure 94, sixth to fifth centuries) – but with two masts. A new cycle of production and exchange came into being, regulated by the Athenian demand for cash tribute from her allies and for food, slaves, and other goods to be purchased in the market by the Athenian *dēmos*, who received the tribute as military pay (and, to a lesser extent, after 451, pay for civic service) – and by the Athenian political elite whose profits from empire far exceeded those of the *dēmos* (Aristophanes, *Wasps* 655–724). When the war against Persia came to an end and tribute money began to pile up unspent on the Acropolis, Pericles (whether by happy accident or financial genius I should not care to say) put it back into circulation by employing substantial numbers of men in the construction of public buildings.

The Persian wars and the continuous Athenian military activity which followed thus radically changed the place of war and trade in the Greek economy. Previously only Sparta had made war a major element in her economic system, keeping young bachelors quartered in central men's houses as a threat to the subject Helot labour-force and very probably hoping to acquire much of the armour needed for her hoplite army as booty. Her peculiar economic system had enabled her to field a larger force, for longer periods, than any other archaic Greek state. In the fifth century Athens too found a way of making military activity the central pivot of her economy. But the structural parallels between the citizens of Sparta, freed to fight as hoplites by the labour of their Helots, and the citizens of Athens, paid to row in the Athenian fleet by the tribute of their subject cities, was to some extent obscured by the role of trade and market exchange, and of the state, in the economy of Athens. Whereas the

Spartan Helots, although 'owned' by the state rather than by individuals, paid over their produce to individual Spartiates and in kind, the subjects of Athens paid a collective tribute to the Athenian state, and in money. Athens claimed in theory to spend this money for the military protection of her 'allies', and military activity in Athens was consequently defined as abnormal, a response to danger; whereas full-time military training was considered the normal activity for Spartan men. Thus while Spartan citizens appear as a warrior elite, the Athenian *dēmos* tend to be characterized by their non-military activities in the market – especially in the works of fourth-century writers who were used to an economy in which full specialization in trade and associated urban occupations was more common (contrast the fifth-century *Constitution of Athens* attributed to Xenophon, which gives full weight to the *dēmos*' activity in the fleet). The Athenian economy was seen as one in which money produced money via the exchange of commodities, and generated a new attitude to the empire as a source of profits, while the dependence of the circulation of money on the state's disbursements of tribute, and on the pressure on the allies to acquire money in order to pay tribute, was overlooked.[15] I have argued elsewhere (chapter 10) that this misrepresentation of the Athenian economy in ancient sources was facilitated by the fact that all members of Athenian society experienced the assembly and the market-place as separate social contexts with sharply differentiated norms of behaviour, as well as by the economic interests of upper-class Athenians in the latter stages of the Peloponnesian war and thereafter. Comparison of Athens with Sparta was taken to suggest a connection between oligarchy, military success, and an agricultural and non-monetarized economy. The clear-cut division of labour in Sparta between warrior and Helot categories also prompted the view that Athens' failures in the Peloponnesian war were due to the fact that the producing classes had been allowed to take political decisions which should have been left to the landowning rentier elite. In reality, for most of the fifth century all classes in Athens were involved equally in an economy based on empire and trade, the *dēmos* living by state pay and petty trading while the rich made larger profits from empire and used them to finance trading voyages, mining, urban property development, slave-staffed enterprises of various kinds or further exploitation of subject communities. It was probably not until 428 that the costs of imperialism began to bear at all heavily on the rich.

If the Athenian empire and the wars of the fifth century led to changes in the volume and organization of production, it was not in Athens but in the cities of the empire and the other communities with which she regularly traded. Athens' demands for corn seem largely to have been met by areas outside the empire, Thessaly and the northern coasts of the Black Sea, and Egypt, in all of which the growth of trade is likely to have meant intensified demands on the subject peasant populations by the ruling strata (Gernet, 1909a; Wąsowicz, 1975). But the details of this process are not known. Wine, probably oil, resin, wool, cheese, linen, hides, wax, are likely to have come from the harbours of the empire (Knorringa, 1926). Athens' demands were for agricultural products and raw materials: artisan production grew in Athens and Piraeus, not in the other cities of the Aegean. The cleavage of interests between landowners with oligarchic sympathies and an urban population living by trade and seafaring – including fishing and serving in the Athenian fleet – may have been earlier and more pronounced in the empire than in Athens. It is interesting that in 413 the imposition of tribute was replaced by a 5 per cent tax on trade in all the harbours of the empire, shifting the main burden of financing the war onto those directly involved in trade and tax-farming, who had most to lose by Athens' defeat (and to some extent, of course, onto the population of Athens itself).

Despite the limited growth of the cities of the empire during the fifth century (J. M. Cook, 1961), they represent better than the atypical achievements of Athens or Sparta[16] two developments which were to remain characteristic of the economy of the Greek city throughout antiquity. First, the city as a centre of trade becomes a mechanism for converting agricultural produce into money paid to the ruling military powers as tribute or tax. Only in areas with navigable rivers could the countryside be effectively exploited without cities. Second, the intensification of trade, supported in the first instance at Athens by cash payments for military service and performance of civic functions, gradually developed the potential to support full-time specialization in urban occupations rather than the part-time contributions of men also serving in war. In Athens in the fifth century there was no need for a division of labour between the pacific and the predatory sectors of the economy. Agriculture was disrupted, for much of the last three decades of the century, by Spartan invasions; the high level of activity in the market was mainly sustained by pay received from the state, and provided part-time occupation in the market for free men also receiving state pay, and increased opportunities for slaves (see above, chapter 6), rather than a self-supporting urban production cycle capable of absorbing surplus population off the land. If anywhere, it was in the cities of the empire that those who shared in the profits of war, through serving as rowers, differentiated themselves from their fellow-citizens who stayed at home and paid tribute. But in the fourth century in Athens a change is perceptible. Immediately after the defeat in 403, the cessation of military pay clearly meant a general crisis in the economic life of the city, and the *dēmos* clamoured for the resumption of military activity. But later there are signs of the development of a more stable peace-time economy. By the time of Demosthenes – after half a century during which the city's frequent failures to supply generals with adequate funds to pay their troops are well attested – the ordinary citizen was reluctant to leave his home occupation for military service. Mercenaries had to be employed in the army (Demosthenes 3.35; 4.16, 20 ff., 46 f.); there is also evidence that rowers were becoming differentiated into a skilled quasi-professional group who could command extra pay, and an urban rabble who could not be relied upon ([Demosthenes] 50.7, 11–19, 35; cf. Jordan, 1975, pp. 213–15). Although the areas best known as a source of mercenary soldiers were poor and mountainous districts such as Crete and Arcadia, Athenians too served as mercenaries abroad. Isaios 4 concerns the estate of an Athenian mercenary soldier who died in Acre (according to a plausible textual emendation) leaving two talents – equivalent to about 18,000 days' pay at contemporary rates (Parke, 1933). The *miles gloriosus* makes his appearance as a stock figure in comedy in the second quarter of the fourth century (Webster, 1953, p. 39). War still made its contribution to Athenian wealth, but this came rather more from the freelancing activities of individual specialists, and less through the mediation of the state, than in the period of the empire. It remains doubtful how far the development of trade in the Greek cities of the fifth and fourth centuries can be interpreted as the beginning of a self-sustaining urban economy. Military force and taxation continue to be central for the understanding of the circulation of men and goods throughout antiquity. But the closer examination of the relation between war and trade in the fourth century and later must be left for another occasion.

Part three

Structure, context and communication

8 The social structure of the ancient city

A report to the Social Science Research Council, written in collaboration with Professor A. Momigliano, who has kindly allowed me to reprint here his contribution as well as my own.

General premises

Some years ago Mrs S. C. Humphreys and I decided to embark on a project which we liked to call 'A new *Cité antique*'. We were concerned with the question of the relations between family, religion and political institutions in the ancient world and we wanted to see how much of Fustel de Coulanges's *Cité antique* (1864) could survive a thorough re-examination of its presuppositions. It soon became evident that our research involved two different subjects: (1) the structure of the family in the ancient world in its relation to changes in political and economic institutions, (2) the relations between political and religious institutions with special consideration of the problem of freedom (and dissent) in politics and in religion. Though we have continued to work in the closest collaboration, it was natural to reserve the study of (1) to Mrs Humphreys because of her special interest in anthropology, and to reserve (2) to myself who had a longer experience of research on institutions and intellectual life in Antiquity. Therefore this report presents our results separately, but on the understanding that we join in common responsibility for methods and results. Despite the separation of subject-matter, research has proceeded throughout the project in close collaboration and with constant discussions at each stage of formulation. Our theoretical and methodological concerns in this project have also been developed in joint seminars held at the Warburg Institute on the history of methods in philology (1969–70) and on history and anthropology (1970–1). One of our main practical aims has now been achieved in the creation of a new Combined Studies degree in Ancient History and Social Anthropology at University College London (starting in October 1973). This course will make it possible for both of us to use and develop further the experience and new approaches resulting from this research project in training undergraduates and graduate students.

Both of us have devoted considerable attention during this period of research to the history of studies of ancient society from the nineteenth century onwards. Mrs Humphreys has already published articles dealing with two key figures in the relations between ancient history and anthropology in this century: Karl Polanyi, who transmitted the sociological approach in economic history of Bücher and Max Weber to M. I. Finley and Leo Oppenheim in America; and Louis Gernet who maintained the Durkheimian tradition in France and played an important part in the formation of a new anthropologically-oriented school of research under his pupil Jean-Pierre Vernant. Mrs Humphreys has also completed an extensive study of the development of kinship studies, with special reference to the problems of the ancient world, from the works of Maine, Bachofen and Fustel de Coulanges in the 1860s to the present day. Perhaps the most important results arising from this study are: (1) an emphasis on the importance of Mommsen's techniques of analysis as the basis both for the main advances made in the study of kinship by ancient historians (Ed. Meyer, G. De Sanctis) and, through the rediscovery of Max Weber by anthropologists in the 1950s, for the development of renewed interest in historical studies, political institutions and the ancient world among anthropologists; (2) a new evaluation of the importance of the problem of local government and local organization (municipal or kin-based) in nineteenth-century social thought and its central position in the development of studies of kinship and social structure. J. G. Droysen's *Die Attische Kommunalverfassung* (1847) is a particularly interesting and little-known text; the problem was central for Lewis H. Morgan, Durkheim, Tönnies and many others.

For my part, I have tried to define the set of presuppositions which led scholars and historians – such as Fustel de Coulanges himself, J. Bernays, J. G. Droysen, and U. Wilamowitz – to choose their fields of research and to make their value judgements. One of the facts which have forcibly imposed themselves on my attention is the impact of Jewish problems – past and present – on the historical consciousness of the nineteenth and twentieth centuries. If Fustel was more generally concerned with the distinction between Aryans and Semites, Droysen, Bernays and Wilamowitz were directly concerned with Judaism and Jews. This is an aspect of the sociology of knowledge which should be more thoroughly investigated by students of French and German thought.

I must finally point out that this report deals only incidentally with my extensive recent research on the origins of the Roman Republic. In a series of papers from 1966 onwards I have proposed a new model of archaic Roman social structure. This model takes into account the status-distinctions which in different contexts divided Roman society in such a way that no contrasted pair of status-categories coincided completely with another pair (seniores-iuniores; adsidui-proletarii; classis-infra classem; patricii-plebei; patres-conscripti; patroni-clientes). This model has attracted much attention and has been the object of much discussion; almost all the recent work by A. Alföldi consists of polemic against it. Both Mrs Humphreys and I have made a cautious use of this model, where it seemed safe.

A. M.

PART I FREEDOM OF SPEECH ·AND RELIGIOUS TOLERANCE IN THE ANCIENT WORLD

I The problem

More than a hundred years ago Fustel de Coulanges had one of those moments of vision which are so rarely given to the historian. He *saw* the connection between the structure of the ancient state and the nature of ancient religious beliefs. His vision, as he was at pains to emphasize, was strictly confined to the Aryan nations. He accepted the new notion of Aryan cultural unity and had no desire to be involved in the theological controversies which any extension of his model to the Semitic nations would have implied.

Today, not unexpectedly, it is the student of the Near East who can derive most immediate advantage from Fustel's *Cité antique*. We know infinitely more than Fustel could ever know about the city life in the Near East which preceded and accompanied the great empires. The archives of El-Amarna, Ugarit and Mari have added new chapters to the history of the cities of Syria in the second millennium. On the other hand the student of Greece and Rome cannot exclude himself from these new developments. The decipherment of Mycenaean Linear B has presented us with the task of interpreting a Greek archaic society in which monarchy and religion combined in a manner hitherto unknown to us. Recent research has also uncovered the role of religious and mythical thinking in the military and political organization of the Greeks even of the classical age. Every new discovery of evidence on archaic Italy has produced new questions about the relation between State and religion: it will be enough to refer to the discovery of the sanctuaries of Lavinium and Pyrgi. The Roman State always took care of its gods, because the gods took care of the State. The Christianization of the Empire was revolutionary in many other aspects, but very conservative in reasserting the principle that the sovereign takes care of the god who protects him and his State.

What is, however, by no means self-evident is how at a given period, in a given civilization, the right to express opinion and to take decisions on political matters is correlated with the right to worship in one's own way and to express opinions on religious matters. The mere formulation of this problem implies the assumption that the mutual interaction between religion and politics never amounts to identity of the two spheres. This assumption I consider to be correct. I think we must respect the basic fact that politics represent relations between men, while religion represents relations between men and god(s). Though we may soon find ourselves in difficulties in coherently maintaining this point of view, the opposite point of view – the identification of the religious and of the political sphere – would lead us into utter confusion. A slave may be in a condition of religious equality with his master, but cannot be in a condition of political equality with him.

It is therefore legitimate to try first to characterize separately decision-making institutions (and freedom of speech on political matters) on one side, and religious institutions (and freedom of discussion on religious matters) on the other side. A correlation of the two series has to be attempted as a second stage of the research: it will here be sketched in the conclusion.

In an inquiry of this kind there are of course general factors to be taken into account which raise further problems. For instance, though it is obvious enough that the rise of individualism makes it more difficult to ensure political unanimity or religious conformity, it requires extensive and difficult research to define what is individualism at any given moment of any civilization. No attempt has been made in the stages of research represented by this report to enter into the complexities of this question. But the writer has just published a small volume on the *Development of Greek Biography* (Momigliano, 1971a) – followed by a paper 'Second thoughts on Greek biography' (Momigliano, 1971b) – on one specific aspect: how in Greece the rise of individualism expresses itself in two specialized literary genres, biography and autobiography.

II Political assemblies and freedom of speech

(A) Preliminary remarks

For the study of decision-making bodies in Antiquity the common distinction between councils of advisers and popular assemblies is good enough. More sophisticated distinctions, such as that between elite council and arena council (the arena council being further subdivided into community-in-council, or assembly, and arena council *stricto sensu*, when a council faces a public), have been found of little service for the Ancient World. The terminology, theory and practice of political assemblies – and more specifically of freedom of speech – in modern Western Europe is genetically connected with Greek and Latin ideas and institutions. It is therefore not very difficult to recognize in the Greek and Roman World the institutions and ideologies which are the classical counterpart of modern political institutions and ideologies. The difficulties encountered by the researcher mainly depend on the state of the evidence, which is scarce, unevenly distributed, and related to social and political conditions which are seldom well known. The discovery and interpretation of data relating to the ancient civilization of the Near East (Egypt, Mesopotamia, the Hittite Kingdom, Persia, Phoenicia, Judaea) present far more serious problems because – with the partial exception of the biblical texts – genetic connections with modern ideas and institutions are not apparent. The very notion of decision-making becomes ambiguous: for instance, what is deciding in a theocratic society? The notion of assembly is, however, clearly recognizable in the Ancient Near East and can serve as a convenient starting point for the inquiry.

(B) The Near East

The existence of councils of elders and of general assemblies of citizens in individual cities of Mesopotamia since the third millennium B.C. has, in my opinion, been established by Th. Jacobsen and other historians. They have shown that the gods themselves formed a society with some democratic features. Among the Hittites, the king had to reckon (at least until King Telepinus, c. 1500) with a central political assembly and not only with the local assemblies of individual cities. Popular assemblies (not to speak of councils of elders) operated in the world of the small city-states of Syria-Palestine during the second half of the second millennium: we know of rebels who used political assemblies to spread their call to subversion. Political assemblies existed, more particularly, in Phoenician cities, and their organization in Carthage (for which we have the information of Aristotle) may have been influenced by Greek models.

On the other hand, Egypt is a typical land of regular bureaucracy where there was no place for formal assemblies. More surprisingly, there was certainly no assembly and probably no central council of elders among the Persians during the Achaemenid period. All this is by now fairly well known. It raises rather than solves problems about mechanisms of decision-making and the nature of public opinion in each country. The whole matter of public opinion in Mesopotamia – especially during the great Assyrian Empire – seems at present to be ill-defined. In Egypt the insistence on the power of words, which is characteristic of the crisis of the first intermediate period (2200–2000 B.C.), is replaced by the idealization of silence at least from the fifteenth century B.C. onwards. The biblical evidence allows an extensive study of political assemblies and decision-making in Israel, though we are often in doubt whether our evidence about pre-monarchic institutions (and even monarchic ceremonies) reflects actual events or later idealization and theorization. Here it will be enough to emphasize the two elements which particularly characterize Hebrew political institutions. The contractual character of leadership is a notion which underlies much biblical thinking about judges and kings and has its counterpart in the notion of the covenant between Yahweh and Israel. This implies that the divine kingship which modern scholars have tried to introduce into ancient Hebrew thinking can only be a marginal phenomenon. Prophecy is one of the essential channels for the maintenance and reassertion of the covenant between Yahweh and Israel. It is also the most powerful expression of freedom of speech among the Jews. When prophecy lost momentum, the notion of an unchangeable Torah became the centre of Jewish life: this implied a profound reorientation. To confine ourselves to the political consequences, it meant that in the post-exilic period decision-making was transferred to a priestly aristocracy.

(C) Greek political assemblies and freedom of speech

To characterize Greek and Roman political assemblies in relation to (ancient) oriental and (medieval) western political assemblies is not difficult. After the Mycenaean age the Greeks never had to face kings with overwhelming divine rights or priests with political power. In Greek cities, issues were settled by smaller or larger groups of equal warriors. Decisions were taken with reference to oracles and priestly rules, but the decision-making process was rarely a mere acceptance of divine orders. On the other hand the notion of representation, which plays an increasing part in medieval assemblies, was never clearly formulated in ancient times (though there were some assemblies in the Greek world which were *de facto* representative). Clear-cut division of the members of an assembly according to status is apparently never to be found in Greek assemblies. Even in the Roman Senate the patricians seldom voted separately from the plebeians.

Taxation is both a major item in the agenda of medieval parliamentary transactions and a sign of the contractual nature of the relation between king and subjects. Neither taxation nor contractual relationship plays any conspicuous part in the ancient assemblies of Greece and Rome. But the element of decision-making in matters of peace and war, in the elections of magistrates, and in the enactment of laws, which is a salient feature in the assemblies of Greece and Rome, emerges only slowly and painfully in the development of medieval assemblies.

The student of Greek assemblies is immediately faced by the question of the value of the *Iliad* and of the *Odyssey* as historical evidence. The poems of course express the idealization of a vague past. But one is entitled to ask what relation this political ideology bears to the institutions of Greek society at any given moment. The tentative answer is that only the *Odyssey* provides a description of political assemblies which can be fitted into what we know of Greek society in the eighth to the seventh centuries B.C.

Another traditional question – whether Macedonian assemblies (and in general Macedonian institutions) resembled those of Homeric society – must be answered negatively. What we know about Macedonia in the fourth to the third centuries points to a military monarchy in which the soldiers are peasants who, though they have little real power, yet have the right to address the king either individually or collectively. The elite soldiers (the *hetairoi*) depended of course on the king: they were very different from the Homeric *hetairoi*, companions bound by a reciprocal tie of loyalty and friendship.

In archaic Greece the notion of liberty (*eleutheria*) did not include freedom of speech. Indeed an important notion of Greek archaic ethics, *aidōs* (modesty, respect), implied that silence and reticence were characteristic of the good man. Decision-making was basically an aristocratic affair performed by councils of elders. The functions of general assemblies in archaic Greek cities are difficult to assess. It is not impossible that in the eighth to the seventh centuries B.C. Sparta – which later, in classical Greece, represented an oddity, institutionally speaking – played a considerable part in attributing decision-making power to the general assembly (*ecclēsia*) and in regulating its articulation with the Council of Elders. In Sparta itself the full citizens, being absorbed in the task of keeping serfs and 'allies' under control, never developed the potentialities of their assembly. Government by political assemblies – including judicial functions – must have been developed elsewhere, perhaps in the colonial cities of Asia Minor and Sicily. In the fifth century Athens provided the most famous and influential model of it – what we call Athenian democracy, with its characteristic demagogues. Though the details of this development are far more obscure than is usually realized (we do not know, for instance, where and how counting of votes was introduced) there is no doubt about the impact of government by assemblies on the life of the Greeks from the sixth and fifth centuries B.C. onwards. The intellectual creativity of Greece (including the theatre and philosophy) is unthinkable without the extraordinary amount of freedom of speech in the assembly. On the other hand it is precisely in Athens that about 430 B.C. legislation was introduced for the first time to make it an offence to deny the gods of the city and to teach new doctrines about meteorological phenomena.

It is interesting that in the fifth century the Greeks had two words for freedom of speech: one (*parrhēsia*) emphasized the right to say everything, the other (*isēgoria*) the equality of freedom of speech within a certain sphere, which might even include slaves. The term *parrhēsia* spread from Athens. When during the fourth century the governing class in Athens was effectively reduced to a minority of wealthy people, they emphasized the right to say all they wanted rather than equality of freedom of speech. With the further decline of democratic institutions towards the end of the fourth century, *parrhēsia* became more of a private virtue (the courage to speak frankly) than a political right. Freedom of speech was consequently developed in these circumstances as a refined art in social relations. The social rules of speech in Greece are altogether a most promising field of research. At the same time the autocratic governments of the post-Alexandrian era inevitably produced a revulsion among educated men against the flattery and degradation inherent in tyranny. This too was expressed in the term *parrhēsia*. The Greek ideal of *parrhēsia* influenced the late Republican and Imperial developments of the Roman notion of *libertas* (as is obvious, for instance, in Tacitus), but the original Roman *libertas* is quite another matter.

(*D*) *Roman political life and freedom of speech*

Republican Rome was an aristocratic society in which patricians and plebeians, patrons and clients, rich (*adsidui*) and poor (*proletarii*) were kept apart by law and custom. The important point, however, is that patricians, patrons and rich men were not necessarily the same persons. The different categories of civic status varied in their relevance and implications in different institutional contexts. This gives the social structure of early Rome its special physiognomy and characterizes its multiple political assemblies. Legal regulations and customs concerning decision-making have to be interpreted by taking into account this intricate system of status-categories. The ultimate result of such an analysis certainly confirms the aristocratic character of Roman government, but emphasizes the admission of foreigners into citizenship, the rapid transformation of slaves into full citizens, the greater scope for political influence of women, the imperialistic orientation of the whole social fabric. *Libertas* in Rome was connected with citizenship rather than freedom of speech. The prevailing attitude seems to have been that only persons in authority had a right to speak freely. Thus decision-making tended to be gerontocratic and favoured the incorporation of kinship and clientship in the political sphere. Yet the very ambiguity of Roman terminology about freedom of speech reflects the introduction of new elements which the old aristocracy was ultimately unable to control. To save themselves, the aristocrats supported a military monarchy, which we call the Principate.

Just because the Principate *de facto* abolished Roman political assemblies – with the exception of the Senate – the connection of freedom of speech with political freedom became generally recognized in the first century A.D. Burning of books and desultory persecution of philosophers particularly affected the intellectuals and the members of the senatorial class (who were often authors of books). After the first decades of the second century freedom of speech ceased to be an important issue even for the Senate. The case for freedom of speech became part of the case for the toleration of the Christians. Eventually it also became an issue within the Church in relation to sects and heresy. The organization and development of the Councils of the Church has to be seen as an attempt to settle questions of dogma and discipline within the framework of a new type of aristocratic assembly. The emphasis on the individual freedom of speech – *parrhēsia* – of the believer and especially of the saint towards God and emperor kept open another substantially aristocratic way of approach to decision-making and self-expression.

III Religious dissent and impiety

(*A*) *The great monarchies of the ancient Near East and the Jews*

Both in Egypt and Mesopotamia an offence against the gods was likely to have consequences for the community at large. There is no special problem about the mechanism of divine punishment. An individual god can act as both judge and executioner or may delegate the execution of his sentence to subordinate entities. Punishment is often decided by a council of several gods.

What is difficult for the outsider to grasp is the exact nature of the relations between gods and men in a situation where the welfare of the community is supposed to depend almost exclusively on the behaviour of the king. In Mesopotamia the matter was at least simplified to the extent that the king was normally regarded as a human being, though he was chosen by the gods and might attain divine attributes and prerogatives. He was responsible for the conduct and property of the slaves of the god – namely his subjects. Consequently he was controlled in his conduct by omina and rules of purity. The ordinary man seems to have done very little in the religious sphere to contribute to the welfare of the community. He seems to have reacted with an intense concentration on his individual affairs and by attempts to foresee (and to avoid) whatever the future held in store for him personally.

In Egypt the king was god and could do no wrong. The ordinary man only had to trust the king and obey him. If he was close enough to the court to hope for a career, he was taught the rules of the game by suitable literature. Otherwise he was left free to concentrate on the next life – the only life which did not quite depend on the king and his officers. Death was the one sector which was left open to private initiative.

In such situations, religious dissent was bound to be unimportant, unless the king himself chose to innovate. The only dissenter about whom we have any information is, not surprisingly, a king of Egypt, Akhnaten. It is characteristic of the situation that he did not meet any serious opposition when he set up his new religious and political capital at El-Amarna. It is equally interesting that there was no serious resistance when after his death his new monotheism was rapidly obliterated.

There was more scope for religious dissent among the Persians. Zoroastrianism developed as a religious reform with a well-defined doctrinal apparatus. The Achaemenid king was never a god. Our difficulty is that we know so little about the occasion, the place and the chronology of the Zoroastrian reform. The Achaemenid empire undoubtedly displayed broad toleration of the gods – or at least some of the gods – of its subject populations. On the other hand, toleration was not so deeply rooted in the Achaemenid values as to exclude repression of cults which were considered unfriendly. When we reach the better-documented period of the Sassanids, the situation is totally different. It is an intolerant state which persecutes Christians and Manichaeans. But this is a part of the problem of intolerance in the third and fourth centuries after Christ to which we shall return later.

Pre-exilic Judaism is in a situation by itself because what we know of it from the Bible is a minority opinion: an orthodoxy which was seldom or never realized. This minority opinion is based on the assumption that the Hebrews are directly answerable to Yahweh. Therefore the king is not supposed to confess for his people. Confession of sins is presented as collective: 'We have sinned'. However, at different moments, and in different writers, the emphasis on the nature of sin and on individual responsibility (within the national solidarity) underwent a change. What remained fairly constant was the emphasis on justice as the basis of the relation between god and man. God is just and man must be just. Those who wrote the pre-exilic books of the Bible certainly had a reality before them. But it is almost impossible to reconstruct in detail the religious situations against which the biblical writers reacted. When after the exile the minority became a majority and organized itself in a priestly state, we find schism (Samaritans) and sects.

(B) The Greeks

The Greeks knew *asebeia*, as opposed to *eusebeia*, which is the proper behaviour towards the gods, parents (and one's native land), and the dead. The word *asebeia* first appears in the sixth century B.C. It was a technical term in Attic law. On the whole it was an offence against established religious customs rather than a denial of accepted dogmas. But Diopeithes' law of about 430 B.C. made possible the prosecution, and in certain cases the condemnation, of philosophers living in Athens during the fifth and fourth centuries B.C. Thus the risk of being incriminated for *asebeia* was particularly great in fifth- and fourth-century Athens where freedom of speech in political matters had apparently grown into freedom of speech about everything (including the gods). The Athenian prosecutions of the philosophers are the historical precedent – and the paradoxical justification – for the penalization of religious opinions advocated by Plato in the *Laws*. Plato contributed to the notion of heresy in so far as he contributed to the idea of intolerance and inquisition. But even in Plato the corporate body primarily concerned with the repression of impiety is not one of priests or of theologians, but one of ordinary citizens. Greece never knew the official interpretation of a religious doctrine by a church, and Plato was Greek.

Freedom of cult and of religious opinions remained a basic feature of the three centuries after Plato. Persecution of philosophers for their religious ideas is occasionally encountered also in the Hellenistic period, but rarely. Hellenistic society was characterized by an extraordinary variety and mobility in its theologies and cult associations. Sanctuaries were attacked to obtain money, but this had always happened. The two main episodes of religious persecution are outside the sphere of proper Hellenism. At the beginning of the second century B.C. the Roman authorities persecuted devotees of Bacchus as if they were a danger to the State. Even more conspicuously the Jews had to defend their cult of Yahweh against an attempt to transform it into a cult of Zeus. This attempt at Hellenization came as much from Seleucid kings as from Hellenized Jews: later the Jews of Palestine forcibly converted some of their gentile neighbours. In the social struggles of the late second and first centuries B.C. we meet revolutionary armies with cults of their own, but we do not hear of holy wars.

(C) *The Romans*

The oldest meaning of *pius, pietas* seems to have been 'what is acceptable to the gods'. In the ordinary Latin of Republican and Imperial times, *pius* characterizes proper behaviour towards gods, parents and other relatives, and the Roman State; also respect for treaties. *Impius, impietas* indicated of course the opposite, and normally expressed strong disapproval, though there are strange exceptions in inscriptions which seem to use *impius* in the sense of 'unhappy'. The influence of Greek *eusebēs/asebes* largely helped to accentuate the subjective, personal aspects rather than the ritualistic connotations of *pietas* and *impietas*. Virgil, more than anybody else, made *pius* an attribute of the ideal Roman, and consequently *impius* an un-Roman qualification. *Pietas* became an attribute of the emperor. But *impius, impietas* never became important words of Roman political ideology. They primarily remained associated with domestic and religious life. There was never a crime of *impietas* in Roman law, notwithstanding some texts to the contrary, such as Tacitus, *Annals* 6.47. The Christians were never persecuted for impiety. The interesting question is whether the Romans ever knew *why* they persecuted the Christians.

IV Religious dissent and heresy

(A) Early Christianity

Whatever reason the Romans gave themselves for persecuting the Christians, they were operating within the ideology according to which a State protects its own gods. This in its turn presupposed a society which recognized foreign gods provided that they did not disturb local gods. Even the Jews fitted into this situation, though as a marginal and unstable case. In the first century B.C. they had developed a variety of sects which had learned (more or less) to tolerate each other as well as foreign cults. Jewish proselytism was altogether a modest phenomenon. The Jewish god being a national god, it was implicitly acknowledged that other nations would do well to go on with their own gods. The Greek word *hairesis*, 'choice', was adopted by Greek-speaking Jews, such as Philo, to indicate Jewish religious sects.

In these Jewish texts and in some Christian texts, *hairesis* means one doctrine among others; it does not mean the wrong choice, the choice that is inspired by the devil and destroys the unity of a religious society. This latter meaning (heresy as the wrong choice) makes its first appearance in two of St Paul's most authentic letters (I *Corinthians*, *Galatians*). Here a whole new set of presuppositions is introduced by connecting the idea of heresy with the idea of salvation. The creation of a non-political society based on faith which does not recognize the values of ordinary political society is new in itself. So is the right to exclude from this society anyone who does not conceive of salvation in the same terms. A clear distinction between heresy and schism is not to be found before the end of the fourth century. The notion of heresy which developed in the first two centuries – say from St Paul (who did not invent it) to Tertullian – included at least five elements: revelation, dogma, apostolic tradition, authentic interpretation, and the right to exclude the dissenter. It shaped Christian society as an orthodox corporation permanently aiming at converting the outsider and at excluding the dissenting insider.

(B) Judaism and Zoroastrianism

Judaism and Zoroastrianism were involved in this process. Both the Zoroastrian *zandik* and the Jewish *min* – the counterparts to the Christian heretic within their respective religions – seem to be later than the Christian heretic. Middle Persian has the word *zandik*, which later passed into Arabic to indicate the unbeliever, the heretic, the Manichaean. *Zandik* seems originally to have meant the man who prefers the *zand*, that is the commentary, to the text of the *Avesta*. The term does not seem to be earlier than the third century A.D., which is the time of Mazdean intolerance towards Christians and Manichaeans.

Judaism had passed through a period in which different sects coexisted. The picture is not complete without referring to sceptics and Epicureans. The rule of Herod was the result of inevitable compromise and an admission of foreign influences. The trial of Jesus probably represented a profound departure from this line of toleration, the importance of which was not realized by contemporaries. But it was the war of 66–70 that produced a complete transformation of Jewish society. The Sadducees were virtually eliminated by the Zealots, and the Zealots were massacred by the Romans. The only group which survived, though with terrible losses, was that of the Pharisees. They had to reorganize themselves and their ideas, but they succeeded in establishing a new orthodoxy as binding on the believer as the worship in the temple of Jerusalem which had preceded it. It is in this new climate that the notion of *minuth* – which we translate by heresy – became important. It is clear from the Gospels that excommunication from the Synagogues was practised as early as the first century A.D. About the end of the first century the prayer for the extirpation of the *minim* was inserted into the Eighteen Benedictions. A saying by Rabbi Akiba about criteria of orthodoxy brings us back to the same time: which is also the time of the prototype of the Jewish heretic, Elisah ben Abujah.

The notion of heresy did not provoke among the Jews the searching questions about the relations between theology and philosophy which it produced among the Christians. Christian theologians faced Greek philosophy much sooner than Jewish theologians.

Religious intolerance spread into the pagan world. By the end of the third century A.D. it had become a distinctive feature of both the Roman and the Persian empires. The conversion of Constantine was momentous because, after a brief period of general toleration, it provided the possibility of combining political persecution of dissenters with the excommunication of heretics. In the persecution of Priscillianists in the late fourth century the State took it upon itself to eliminate the whole body of heretics.

V Conclusion: the interrelation of religion and politics in the ancient world

It is obvious that the more the sovereign claims to justify his power by divine right, the less liberty his subjects have to question his decisions. The divine right of kings is inevitably in permanent conflict with the freedom of speech of the subjects. In Egypt protest was possible only in periods of crisis and was later replaced by the ideal of silence. In Israel the voice of the prophet made itself heard within a weak political organization. The Hebrew king never achieved undisputed divine rights except in the pages of modern scholars. In Persia the kings justified their absolutism by claiming to possess the divine truth.

In Greece divine kings, if they ever existed, had long disappeared by the time of Homer. Decision-making developed within the framework of aristocratic and, later, of democratic institutions. In Republican Rome the ruling aristocracy controlled the priesthoods and used them to reserve decision-making to themselves; but they never (or only exceptionally) claimed divine inspiration or divine rights. In Republican Rome, as in Greece, decision-making was essentially a non-charismatic business transacted in assemblies. When Caesar and Augustus replaced the Republic by monarchy, the divine rights of the monarch slowly reasserted themselves. The transition to the notion of Christian Emperor by the grace of God was relatively smooth.

Divine monarchy created special obligations for the sovereign to ensure the happiness of his subjects. Paradoxically, it favoured considerable freedom of religious beliefs for the unimportant subjects. The situation was different in Israel, where sin was a collective responsibility and where every individual was bound by the Covenant between Israel and Yahweh. The weak Jewish kings, however, had to listen to the prophets speaking in the name of Yahweh against the State authorities. In the late Hellenistic period a certain amount of reciprocal religious tolerance among sects allowed Jews to live surrounded by Greeks.

In Greece aristocracies could easily tolerate religious sects in their midst. But Athenian democracy, which supported uninhibited political freedom of speech, soon discovered that it was unable to save its own gods from the consequences of freedom of speech and took some rather ineffectual steps to punish impiety. The aristocrats of Republican Rome seldom had to fear religious dissent. But the Roman emperors, who were not concerned with the religious beliefs of the majority of their subjects, had to face a confrontation with the Christians who tried to convert everyone and (potentially on everyone's behalf) questioned the divine status of the emperors. If the Jews refused to worship the emperor, that could be interpreted as a barbarian peculiarity and therefore tolerated in normal circumstances. The struggles against Druids and Jews had straight forward political causes: they were struggles against ordinary rebels and criminals. Christianity posed social questions of a different order.

Where sects or schisms were allowed to develop, they represented *ipso facto* a new experiment in social coexistence and affected social life (Magi, Pythagoreans, Rechabites). Christianity was the first religion to claim supranational universality and at the same time to challenge the right of other beliefs to exist. As such, Christianity was bound to deny the divine nature of pagan kings, but was ready to attribute divine rights to Christian kings. Christianity not only excluded the unbeliever, but also excluded the believer who believed in the wrong way. Heresy was a principle of discrimination which had to be accepted by Christian kings. Thus religion came overtly to be regarded as a regulative principle of political life – a departure from the Greek and Roman practice of the thousand years that had gone before, yet not a simple return to the theocracy of the Eastern Empires.

A. M.

PART II KINSHIP IN GREEK SOCIETY, c. 800–300 B.C.

I Aims

We decided at an early stage in our research that I should concentrate my work on the place of kinship in Greek society during the period of the independent city-state – from Homer to the end of the fourth century B.C. Inevitably I have concentrated on Athens, which provides far more evidence than any other Greek state; but a better understanding of Athenian social structure helps in appreciating the significance of variations attested elsewhere.

There were several reasons for this choice. In the first place,

Fustel's perception of the connection between changes in the structure and function of kin groups and the political and economic development of the Greek city was obviously still valid in general terms. His views on the nature of Greek kinship and kin groups equally obviously required serious modification. Secondly, to approach the general problem of the structural evolution of the Greek city from the point of view of kinship was particularly appropriate for one of the main methodological aims of the project – to contribute to a closer integration between ancient history and social anthropology. After stimulating extensive discussions in the half-century following the publication of *La Cité antique*, the topic fell into neglect among classical scholars as a result of their reaction against the influence of Frazerian anthropology. It has been recognized for some time that a new study based on modern anthropological theory is needed to clear up the confusion of ideas created by this situation. At the same time kinship still represents the most extensive and solid body of anthropological theory, and thus provides a more strategic starting-point for the development of techniques of analysis suited to historical data than more experimental branches of the discipline.

II Substantive conclusions

For a study of the forms and functions of kinship groupings in ancient Greece it was found convenient to distinguish four institutional contexts: the official subdivisions of the state (tribe, phratry, deme, etc.), the aristocratic conical clan (*genos*), the bilateral kindred (*anchisteis*) and the household (*oikos*). These groupings and the clusters of rules governing their structure and articulation are the nodes of the kinship structure of Greek society: they overlap, but are distinguished by functional specializations as well as by the different ways in which genealogical relationships are selected and structured in them. This division of the kinship institutions of ancient Greek society into sub-systems, and consequent distinction between the principles of internal organization of each sub-system and its modes of external articulation, is particularly important for the study of social change and of variations between Greek societies.

The relation between tribe, trittys, phratry and *genos* in ancient Athens has been a central problem in the study of ancient kinship

since Fustel de Coulanges. Eduard Meyer and De Sanctis already
saw at the beginning of this century that the *genos* had to be separated
from the other three groupings, despite Aristotle's statement that
the *genos* was a segmentary subdivision of the phratry. (This statement only survives in a quotation without context which concerns
the Athenian state in the time of its legendary founder Ion, not its
constitution in Aristotle's own day.) Fuller information about
descent groups in other societies makes it possible now to support
Meyer's and De Sanctis's view with new arguments. An appreciation
of the resemblances and differences between these Greek groups and
descent groups elsewhere described by anthropologists can contribute to the understanding of both.

(1) *Tribe, phratry, etc.* Membership of tribe and phratry was always
a requisite for citizenship and, even before the concept of citizenship
existed, for social personality. For Homer the man who has no
phratry is also homeless and outside the law. Tribe, phratry and
other official subdivisions of the State are recruited by patrifiliation
and organize society in sets of superimposed segments: each tribe
consists of three trittyes in Athens, each trittys contains a fixed
number of phratries (perhaps three: this suggestion is based on the
fact that *trittys* originally means a group of three, not a third part).
The numbers of these groups are fixed; they are not internally
structured by genealogy (all members have identical rights and
obligations), and they do not show the processes of fission and
fusion characteristic of the segmentary lineage system as a political
organism. They are administrative (and military) divisions. Only
inside the phratry do we find the formation of smaller groups
(*thiasoi*) recruited from within the phratry, apparently on a voluntary
basis, which probably had significance for the internal political
processes of the group and were labile in composition. (The special
case of the place of the *genos* inside the phratry is discussed below.)
In anthropological terminology tribes, trittyes and phratries are
patrilineal clans and sub-clans made up not of lineages but of
individual households and associations with a mixed basis of
recruitment. What their early history may have been, in periods for
which we have no sources, is extremely difficult to estimate; particularly since clans in 'tribal' societies have been much less studied by
anthropologists than lineages. The relation between the tribe as
sub-division of a city-state and the 'peoples', *ethnē*, which made up
the loosely-organized non-urban federations of northern Greece also

remains very unclear. We do not know how these latter groups were structured.

(2) *Genos* It is fairly generally agreed now that the *genos* organization was predominantly if not entirely confined to the nobility. Evidence from different parts of archaic Greece shows that it varies in form in relation to differences in the rules for succession to political and/or religious office. Where succession is hereditary the *genos* is internally structured by descent in the form of a 'conical clan', with genealogical precision concentrated round a few leading lines with a direct interest in succession and less attention paid to the relative ranking or even criteria for inclusion or exclusion of junior branches. Where, on the contrary, offices are filled by election from among the members of a single *genos* (Corinthian Bacchiadai) or from a noble stratum defined by membership in one of a number of *genē* (pre-Solonian Athens), the criteria for membership must be strictly defined but descent will be less important in the internal structure (except where individual *genē* also possess rights to hereditary religious office – as they did in Athens). The *genos* was not directly recognized by the State as a corporate subdivision of the political body, and fission and fusion were thus free to occur: there is one documented case of fission in an Athenian *genos*.

Since both *genos* and phratry were recruited patrilineally it seems to follow that no *genos* extended outside the bounds of a single phratry. Whether this is so or not, there is some evidence that it was not uncommon for a *genos* to assume a dominant position inside a phratry. Given the predominance of the aristocracy in politics, law and religion in the early Greek city – and their increasing need for popular support as elective office and assemblies began to grow in importance – this situation is not surprising. One current explanation is that the two forms of organization grew from a single source, representing the result of a process of stratification within the system of patrilineal clans in which the less successful branches of the conical *genos* became gradually absorbed into the undifferentiated phratry. However, the Mycenaean Linear B documents reveal a fairly elaborate system of military status-grades and administrative offices which was clearly capable of generating and supporting a stratification of nobles and non-nobles. The Homeric poems seem to show a simplified form of this status distinction and it remained important until the introduction of hoplite fighting gradually brought about a wider distribution of political power.

Although in the Dark Ages after the collapse of the Mycenaean kingdoms many individuals no doubt crossed the status boundary between nobles and commoners, in both directions, it does not seem impossible that the idea of the boundary survived from the Mycenaean period – along with the dim memories of past glories which were the 'charter' of the aristocratic patrons of epic poetry. It seems better therefore to treat phratry and *genos* as separate phenomena, distinct in both form and functions despite the intimate connection due to overlapping membership; and to regard the *genos* in its various forms as resulting from a combination of the status distinction between nobles and commoners and the rules for succession to office.

This analysis of the form, functions and articulation of phratry and *genos* in Athens may have implications for the study of kin groups in early Roman society. The question is whether the Roman *gens* was originally a division of the whole society (equivalent to the Greek phratry) or of the patriciate only (like the Greek *genos*). Etymology is of little value except in so far as *gens* like *genos* ('family' – a non-technical word with a wide range of uses) suggests a genealogically-structured group. The Roman *gens* however had jural functions which the Greek patrilineal *genos* did not. This in itself would create an emphasis on genealogical structure within the *gens*. Roman law already by the time of the Twelve Tables presupposes that all Romans belong to a *gens*. Momigliano has recently argued (1969b) that the distinction between patricians and plebeians did not harden until after the fall of the monarchy in Rome. On this view it would hardly be possible to maintain that the Roman *gens* began as a patrician form of organization which was later imitated by plebeians. Instead, the *gens* (which in some cases exhibits stages of fission marked by the use of hereditary cognomina) seems to represent the lineage level of kin grouping which is absent in Athens. This point deserves further study.

(3) *Kindred* Roman analogies led Fustel and Maine to assume that the Greek rule of inheritance was originally agnatic, and that the residual inheritance rights of matrilateral kin were a later extension parallel to the introduction of *cognati* by the praetor's edict in Rome. This view also was refuted by Ed. Meyer and De Sanctis (following B. W. Leist), but still finds adherents. Analogy in fact, for what it is worth, points the other way. Ancient India and Germany seem to have had the same form of ego-centred bilateral

kindred as Greece, while there is no Indo-European parallel to the
rigour of the Roman doctrine of agnation and *manus*. A significant
point is that there is no evidence for a rule of exogamy in Indo-
European corporate groups based on kinship. The close relation
between political and jural structure and functions in descent groups
studied by anthropologists in Africa is certainly facilitated by rules
of group exogamy. Intra-lineage marriage would tend to disturb the
ordered pattern of genealogical structure. It may be suggested, as an
implication of this research which requires further investigation, that
both in Indo-European and in Semitic societies the absence of the
exogamy rule in unilineal descent groups facilitated the differentiation of the political and jural functions of kinship and may thereby
have had an influence on social evolution (cf. Humphreys, 1972).

Political procedure developed in Greece at the expense of kinship.
This is most obvious in the replacement of hereditary political
office by election or appointment by lot; but rejection of personal
interests and ties as irrelevant and illicit is a general feature of the
definition of political roles and norms of behaviour in political
contexts. Study of the functions of the personal, ego-centred kindred
requires consideration of the extent to which these norms were
observed or, to put the question the other way round, of the evidence
for manipulation of ties of kinship and affinity in politics. The
evidence available is very limited even for Athens, but suggests that
coalitions of agnates may sometimes have played a dominant role
in the smaller subdivisions of the city, phratries and demes. But
kinship was not the only possible basis of alliance within these
groups. In the central political elite too there are scattered signs of
intermarriage between powerful families and kin coalitions, especially
in circles with oligarchic sympathies. However, alliance is not
justified in terms of kinship solidarity, but by reference to values and
ideology. Kinship (including affinity) provided an easily available
basis for group-formation and the communication of attitudes, but
political co-operation with kinsmen was optional and had to be
justified in impersonal terms; and the solidarity between kinsmen in
politics was no different from that between friends. Though
prosopographical research in Athenian history can provide valuable
insights into the composition and boundary-maintaining processes
of the political elite, it is not the key to Greek politics. The absence
of the *cursus honorum* marks a significant difference between Greece
and Rome here. There was no place in Greece for the display of

kinship solidarity by helping junior kinsmen up the early stages of the political ladder.

The bilateral kindred (*anchisteis*) extending to second cousins had rights of intestate inheritance and claims on heiresses (*epiklēroi*, brotherless girls) in Greek law. Some fifty speeches by the Attic orators of the late fifth and fourth centuries B.C. dealing with suits in family law provide evidence on the working of kinship in this sphere. This body of material, which has not previously been systematically analysed from the point of view of the study of kinship in Attic society, can be treated as a series of 'case histories' illustrating norms of kinship solidarity and the strains to which they were subject. The norms of solidarity are stronger in this private context, where there is no competing rule of impersonal behaviour, but optionality is still evident. The material of course is biased; only serious disputes reached the lawcourts, after attempts at a peaceful settlement through private arbitration had failed. Nevertheless many speeches claim frankly that closely related households had been on bad terms for many years before resorting to law. Speakers blame quarrels on their opponents, but make little attempt to disguise their existence. Only in the case of disputes within the nuclear family was there strong social pressure to compromise and maintain at least an outward appearance of amity.

The optionality of kinship, outside the nuclear family, is a phenomenon commonly observed in studies of kinship in complex societies. In the Athenian case some important factors in this loosening of kin ties seem to be urbanization and the increasing number of non-citizens in the urban population of the late fifth and fourth centuries, together with new though still limited opportunities for social mobility. Institutions such as the transfer of one son from a household with several male heirs to a related family with none, by adoption or uxorilocal heiress marriage, had an obvious rationale in peasant farming communities. Consensus about the upper and lower limits for a reasonable-sized landholding supported these measures for a limited redistribution of plots within localized kin groups by adoption and intermarriage. But when kindreds were scattered through the city, and urban property and cash came to overshadow farmland in a good many estates, attitudes inevitably changed. The religious values associated with the provision of an heir to 'continue the *oikos*' were not strong enough alone to prevent abuse of adoption and a growing resistance to the obligatory marriage of heiresses to elderly next-of-kin (a prominent theme in New Comedy).

Men could conceal their affairs from kin much more easily in the city. The Attic law of marriage and legitimacy was oriented to the definition of the citizen: strictly speaking, only citizens could marry and produce legitimate children. Nevertheless non-citizens' unions were recognized as a sort of 'common-law marriage'. With considerable numbers of non-citizens (resident aliens and freedmen) in the urban population, and limited control by kindred, unions with non-citizens and attempts to pass the offspring as citizen and legitimate became increasingly common. They form a significant proportion of our legal cases. Such unions tended especially to occur in cases where kin had already dissociated themselves from a man whose associational and/or occupational status was lower than their own. Discrepancies between civic and economic status were in general likely to encourage such unions; for a poor citizen to 'marry' a richer metic offered advantages for both sides. The effects of increasing social mobility are also evident, especially from the late fourth century onwards, in a heightened concern with friendship. The socially mobile man needs to detach himself from his less successful kin and construct himself a new primary group of friends selected because they share the identity he wishes to assert.

(4) *Household* It is easier to analyse the evidence for the isolation of the nuclear family in the urban society of classical Athens than to assess the reality and operational bases of what Glotz called 'la solidarité de la famille' in earlier periods. The nuclear family already appears to be the normal residential and economic unit in the Homeric poems, despite the large extended family households of Priam in Troy and Zeus on Olympus. The Greek kinship terminology associated with Priam's household in the *Iliad* suggests that the extended family had been a historical reality, but it seems to have belonged to an earlier period. Several of the kin terms particularly applicable to a family in which both sons and daughters of the king continue to reside in his household with their spouses after marriage drop out of use after Homer. The solidarity of the kin group in the early Greek city-state should not be exaggerated: Hesiod advises the peasant to keep on good terms with his neighbours because they will come running to help quicker than kinsmen in an emergency.

The difference between earlier and later Greek society, in terms of the functions of kinship, perhaps lies not so much in changes in the structure of the household and its relations to a wider kin group as in the changing significance of the household itself as a context of interaction. In the Homeric world a man's prestige is entirely bound up with his *oikos*: his ancestry, his wealth and the use he makes of it in distribution to dependants or gift-exchange with equals, his personal alliances with other kings through marriage or guest-friendship. The suitors who covet Odysseus' kingdom seek it through exhausting his wealth and wooing his wife. Although Homeric nobles hold assemblies and dispense justice publicly to the *dēmos*, their own struggles for dominance tend to take place in the banqueting-hall rather than in the agora.

The development of more elaborate political institutions removed political interaction from the context of the household and placed it firmly in the centre of the city as context of public interaction. Even the use of wealth to acquire prestige and support by distribution and gifts was channelled through the institutions of the city. The development of the city meant – especially in democratic Athens – a sharp distinction between public and private life, between the impersonal, egalitarian interaction of the open agora and the enclosed, intimate, hierarchic relationships of the *oikos*. A feeling of conflict between the norms of citizen behaviour and the personal loyalties of the family is obvious in the debate between Antigone and Creon in Sophocles' *Antigone*, or Plato's elimination of the family for his Guardian class in the *Republic*. Aristotle's distinction between *oikos*-oriented and market-oriented economic activity (*oikonomia* and *chrēmatistikē*) contrasts household and agora in a different way; but to claim that private interests and public good only required a return to a traditional subsistence economy to effect their reconciliation was in fact a confession of their incompatibility.

Ancient sources are apt to be more informative about values than about the structural bases on which they rest, and classical scholars have too often been content recently to embark on detailed studies of values without adequate sociological ground-work. I have attempted to examine the structural bases of the conflict of values between *oikos* and *polis* by examining their articulation in law, economic institutions, religion, social life and socialization. It is not easy to formulate precise theoretical criteria for deciding whether the integration of private life and the family into the wider society is adequate or defective; but it can be shown that there was hardly any place for the family as such in Athenian public life or in the religion of the city, that the combination of hierachy and intimacy demanded in *oikos* relationships presented a strong structural contrast to the competitive, egalitarian and impersonal interaction in the public sphere, that Athenian family law tended to generate conflicts within the *oikos* rather than solving them, and that the social life of the male *andrōn* within the household reversed the norms of decorum of both *polis* and *oikos*.

III Sources and methods

(*I*) *Literary sources and the sociology of knowledge*

Attic drama represents a special case in the problems of handling the source material for this study both because kinship and the family play an exceptionally important part in it – which, in view of the dominance of public life in classical Athens, is unexpected – and because the plays exhibit a highly systematic and consistent pattern of family relationships. The underlying structure unconsciously reflected by the poets is clear, while their more conscious motives for selecting family themes are more problematical. The pattern of tensions, conflicts, avoidance and solidarity in the relationships of the nuclear family is constant throughout the work of the three tragedians and Aristophanes in the fifth century, and recurs in the New Comedy of Menander at the end of the fourth century. Same-sex relationships are tense or conflictual, and so is the relation between husband and wife (even in Menander where the love of young couples struggling against family opposition to their marriage is frequently portrayed); brother and sister, father and daughter are closely united, while the relationship between mother and son is ambiguous but may turn out happily in the end. The treatment of the father–son relationship is particularly revealing: open quarrels in both Old and New Comedy, tension and avoidance in tragedy. Other Athenian sources confirm this indication of strain in the father–son relationship, especially Plato's dialogues. Upper-class fathers' lack of confidence in their ability to control their sons is indicated by their anxiety to put their sons in the hands of professional teachers, and by their acceptance of the pattern of institutionalized homosexuality in which a younger man (*c.* 25–35) as the adolescent boy's lover took the father's place as his model of adult male behaviour. These solutions to the problem only exacerbated it.

(Analysis of the functions of institutionalized homosexuality in Athenian society tends to support Xenophon's statement that homosexuality was disapproved of in Sparta where the functions of Athenian homosexual relationships – facilitating avoidance between father and son, creating links between successive age-sets – would have been redundant. In the Spartan regime the structure of the men's house, *syssition*, cut across the age-set system, and conflicts of economic interest or authority between father and son could hardly arise.) Tragedy in Athens reflected both the tension felt between norms of public interaction and the demands of private life, and the internal conflicts generated by intra-sex and intergenerational struggles for dominance and economic resources within the family. If the *oikos* was problematic as a component of the city, it was also problematic in itself.

The emergence of a clear pattern from the analysis of family relationships portrayed in tragedy and comedy is a rare case in which literary, fictional texts, studied as a group, unconsciously reveal aspects of the structure of the society in which they were produced. The other sources which provide evidence for Greek conceptions of social structure and the place of kinship in society (epic and lyric poets, philosophers, historians) present more serious problems of method. Diversity of time, place, social milieu and subject-matter makes it essential to relate these sources not only to the structure of the society in which they were produced, but also to the position of each author and the expectations of his public.

The epic poet attached to the context of the noble household presents a different view of society from that of the lyric poets who compose for public occasions or private, single-sex convivial gatherings. Early prose writers and sophists, travelling from city to city to lecture, were constrained to present their ideas in a sharper, more rigidly structured form than later philosophers who could develop and refine themes and methods gradually in the more specialized and less competitive atmosphere of a philosophical school. There is an observable trend from concentration on the noble *oikos* as the most significant unit of social structure in Homer, through pre-occupation with contrasted social categories (human/divine, male/ female, old/young, rich/poor, etc.) in the archaic and classical periods, to a new focus on the individual's personal network of kin and friends from the late fourth century onwards. These changes are partly due to changes in the position of the intellectual in society,

and in the constraints imposed on him by the context in which his
ideas were communicated and by the expectations of the audience.
But changes in intellectual roles and communication-contexts are
in themselves indicative of changes in social structure. The fact
that the function of expressing collective representations, of describing and advising, and criticizing society, passed from epic to lyric
poets and then became divided between dramatic poets, philosophers
and historians indicates shifts in the balance between public and
private contexts of interaction.

This analysis has general implications for the use of individual
writers as evidence for collective representations and categories of
thought in complex societies. It is also, obviously, relevant to the
problem of the 'discovery of the individual' and of the concern with
types in classical Greek literature and art. Much of what has been
taken for emergent individualism in archaic Greek poetry should
rather be classed as efforts to define the role of the poet or experiment
in the depiction of types. It is doubtful whether it is legitimate to
speak of the emergence of the individual before the development in
the late fourth century of the conception of society as a set of ego-
centred networks. (Momigliano's work on the development of
Greek biography points towards the same dating.) Even here,
though there is a new interest in questions of inner psychology, the
process of constructing a social identity through association with
like-minded friends is equally important. On the one hand biography and autobiography, on the other hand the philosopher's
interest in ego-centred networks and the concept of the friend as a
'second self', both reflect increasing social mobility and new opportunities outside the traditional framework of the city-state; a man
can choose his life and his friends, and his choices become significant
and worth discussing. The new interest in fortune, *Tychē*, belongs
to the same pattern.

(II) Interaction contexts and the study of social change

Anthropologists have only recently begun to expand their research
beyond the limits of the traditional fieldwork technique, which
tended to confine them to synchronic analysis of a single small
community. The historian is at present better placed for studying
both changes in social structure over long periods of time and
variations within a single culture. Admittedly deficiencies in the

evidence for ancient Greece impose severe limitations; only for Athens from the early sixth century onwards is the evidence reasonably continuous, and even here there are serious gaps and problems of interpretation. Nevertheless it is possible to make some contribution in both fields.

The first step in this type of research is to identify suitable units of analysis – units which can provide access not only to the more permanent and stable aspects of social structure, but also to the sensitive and labile areas where small shifts of balance are capable either of generating change or of absorbing it. The social science which has advanced furthest in the study of processes of change seems to be linguistics. In the study of semantic change the essential fact is the existence within a single linguistic unit of different groups and contexts with their own speech conventions; there is a continuous process both of elaboration and change within such contexts and of passage of individuals and influences from one context to another (Meillet, 1906).

Since a method of analysis derived from linguistic models is being proposed, it is appropriate to begin with examples taken from the study of kinship terminology. To treat kin terms *en bloc* as a single system to be compared with the structure of rights and obligations based on kinship permits some crude correlations (differences between the Homeric terminology and that of classical Athens correspond to different residence patterns), but obscures the problem of the coexistence of alternative terms and throws no light on the actual process of change. It is necessary instead to realize that in classical Athens (where the evidence is reasonably detailed) there are four overlapping kinship terminologies associated with different contexts: the terms of address and intimate reference used in the home, terms of common public reference, precise terms used in legal contexts, and poetic terms. There is a complex interdependence between these four sets of terms. Changes initiated in one context may extend their influence to others.

A common sequence appears to be for separate terms for patrilateral and matrilateral kin to be replaced in intimate address and reference (where the context of use would tend to make the distinction redundant) by a common term of respect or *Lallwort*; in suitable structural conditions, where the difference between patrilateral and matrilateral kin is becoming less strongly marked, this single term may spread into general public use and eventually generate in the legal sphere (which was not tolerant of archaic-sounding language in Athens) new terms of precise reference formed by modifiers (sequence *patrōs/mētrōs* > *theios* > *theios pros patros/mētros*).

Change in the three prosaic terminologies may affect even the poetic terminology which depended for its separate existence on the use of terms discarded by everyday language as obsolete (consciousness of a distinction between poetic and prose language adding speed to the process of obsolescence). For example, the emergence in everyday speech of a single reciprocal term for affines, *kēdestēs*, in place of the contrasted pair *pentheros* (wife-giver)/*gambros* (wife-taker) led Sophocles and Euripides to treat the two latter terms as simple alternatives, each reciprocal in use. Poetic language also formed a reservoir from which occasionally terms could be recalled to express concepts or distinctions absent in prose terminology: Herodotus used the poetic *kasignētos* when speaking of classificatory siblingship among non-Greek peoples, and Hellenized Lydians in the early Roman period revive Homeric terms – presumably to express distinctions in their native terminology for which the Greek *koinē* of the period provided no equivalent.

These examples suffice to show that the Athenian of the classical period was expected to use and understand, in different contexts, kinship terminologies which differed not only in vocabulary but also in structure. Exactly the same point applies to norms of behaviour towards kin and the rights and obligations associated with kinship. Phratry, *genos*, kindred and household each have their own rules, structure and patterns of behaviour. There is in each case a central cluster of coherent structural principles defined and upheld by law or strong religious and moral beliefs. Since the same people are involved in all four groupings, some integration between them is a functional necessity for the society. But the degree of consistency in norms of behaviour required within a single grouping or interaction-context is higher than that required for the articulation of different contexts. The latter may be achieved to a considerable extent by spatial or temporal segregation and functional specialization. Changes may occur either because this separation breaks down or because it is carried too far. Changes in the articulation of phratry and *genos* depend on the degree of recognition of *genos* membership as relevant in the phratry context. On the other hand, too great a separation and lack of interaction between kindred and household in urban conditions tended to create problems in both spheres.

Insulation of the aristocratic homosexual interaction-contexts of gymnasium and symposium in classical Athens both from public political life and from the family seems to have encouraged an insulated elaboration or 'involution' which had problematic consequences in both public and private life. (There are further methodological implications here for the study of involution in ritual contexts: Athenian homosexuality has a marked tendency to ritualization, in the wider sense of the term.)

The concept of the *context of interaction* as a basic unit of social structure has proved valuable in several different aspects of this research: in analysing the component parts of the Greek kinship system, kinship terminology, the conflict of values between city and household, and the sociological factors influencing different presentations of social structure in literary sources. In a sense it represents a return to Malinowski's concept of the 'institution', but in a revised form. Malinowski's pupils found it difficult to achieve a clear presentation of the articulation of different institutions. The concept of social structure developed to meet this difficulty by the Radcliffe-Brown school emphasized the most permanent elements in society: jural rules, corporate groups, offices, well-defined roles. Difficulties inherent in the fieldwork situation and lack of interest in processes of change influenced this orientation. We still have to find a framework of sociological analysis which will incorporate both permanent and labile, both highly-integrated and loosely-articulated parts of the social system.

This research thus represents an experiment in combining the analysis of permanent corporate units (defined as corporate groups, corporate categories, colleges, offices and commissions: Smith, 1974) with that of more loosely defined groupings and sets of behavioural norms. The concept of 'interaction context' includes both. Corporation analysis proved to be an excellent method of studying the form and articulations of kin-based corporate groups (tribe, phratry, deme, *genos*, etc.), especially the relation of variations in the form of the *genos* over time and in different parts of Greece to variations in the rules for succession to office. But the extent to which significant contexts of interaction are dominated by corporations and structured by their constitutive principles varies from one society or period to another. In particular, while corporation analysis may give access to a high proportion of the major aspects of social structure both in 'tribal' societies of segmentary-lineage type and in the structurally differentiated modern society, it may be suggested that there are intermediate levels of complexity where its use is more limited. The Greek city is characterized not only by the development of centralized political institutions (with a consequent decrease in the functions of identically based segmentary groups such as tribe and phratry) but also by the multiplication of specialized roles and arenas of interaction – rather than specialized organizations. It thus represents an intermediate level between the tribal society composed of multifunctional identical segments (Durkheim's 'mechanical solidarity') and the stage of full structural differentiation in which each functional sphere has its own corporate organization (organic solidarity). For a society of this type the study of relations of complementarity or conflict between the behavioural norms associated with different contexts of interaction is essential.

This approach appears to be valid also for the study of variations in the social structure and kinship systems of different Greek states. Spartan society has a much tighter and functionally more extensive set of corporations (age-sets and men's houses, civic status categories, etc.) than Athens. There are few areas of loose integration; the articulation of Spartan society is almost completely specified by the rules which constitute its corporate groups and categories. In other regions political procedures and differentiated economic roles and contexts of activity were less fully developed than in Athens, and interaction in private contexts had greater importance, with consequences for marriage patterns, the political use of wealth, etc. The potentialities and implications of this type of analysis will have to be further developed in later work.

S.C.H.

9 'Transcendence' and intellectual roles: the ancient Greek case*

The problem put before members of the *Daedalus* conference ('wisdom, revelation and doubt', 1975) raised, as will be clear from the variety of the contributions, problems of perspective, definition, and method as well as substantive questions. To single out 'transcendence' as a common feature in the Jewish, Greek, Chinese, and Indian civilizations of the first millennium B.C. (and others) implied: (1) a scrutiny of our own motives and presuppositions in making this choice; (2) the question of the method to be used in a comparative study of intellectual and religious creativity, and of the relation between everyday life and a transcendent reality, whether conceived as abstract thought or supernatural Being; and (3) different substantive orientations determined by the form in which movements toward transcendence appeared in different civilizations.

The problem of perspective I have treated only tangentially, suggesting that what we call rational discourse is not a cultural specialty of the West but a necessity for any complex and mobile society. The argument needs much closer scrutiny and could not be developed here, but it represents at least one possible line of defense against the charge of ethnicity – the strength of which has yet to be tested – for those who would like to claim the Greeks as early moderns and not merely early Europeans.

In method I have deliberately chosen the level of social structure for my approach. It seems to me the closest level to the plane of ideas on which systematic analysis is at present possible. Our understanding of patterns of combination or contrast on the level of ideas has as yet barely progressed beyond pure intuition even for individual cultures, let alone comparative studies. We are, however, in a position to make some fairly solid generalizations about correlations and implications on the plane of social structure. Furthermore, literary texts, which constitute the primary type of source for the problems we are considering here, can tell the sensitive observer much about the constraints exercised on the authors by their social context. In fact, the ground here has been very well prepared by traditional philology, even if the question has not been formulated specifically in these terms. Consequently it is possible, starting from the analysis of social roles and the expectations associated with them, to 'plot' a certain number of approximately fixed points on the level of ideas. To use a metaphor, we can chart some of the channels and obstacles in the riverbed down which the stream of creative thought flows, even if we do not have a theory of hydrodynamics sufficient to explain the form of each eddy in detail. The same metaphor indicates that we are still operating at a relatively superficial, though critical, level of analysis: there is no question here of examining the geological processes by which the streambed was formed. I have aimed only at making a coherent and comprehensive analysis on one level, that of the constraints exercised on creative thought by the norms associated with social roles and contexts of communication. Naturally I do not believe either that thought is wholly determined by these constraints or that changes in social roles and contexts of communication cannot be further analyzed.

My focus on intellectual roles arose partly from this methodological orientation and partly from the nature of the Greek data. Our comparative discussion showed the importance of making a distinction (first suggested by J.-P. Vernant) between transcendent power and transcendent – or possibly immanent – order. In Greek thought the latter is predominant. The historian of ancient Israel or of Christianity before the twelfth century must study the wiring systems and lightning conductors that tapped or diverted the irruptions of supernatural power into social affairs; the historian of ancient Greece is confronted instead with a succession of cosmologies, a search for order and meaning that required the gods themselves to be subject to a predestined pattern. It is not a very long step from Homer's Olympus to the carefree, wholly detached gods of Epicurus.

Two suggestions may be made about the reasons for this predominance of cosmology over theology in Greek thought. In the first place, polytheists need a cosmology more than monotheists. Hesiod's *Theogony* and the massive work of synthesis of local legends contained in the epic cycle were matched by an equally remarkable effort of synthesis on the plane of cult, by which the diverse maiden-goddesses of different parts of Greece merged their identity, at least partially, with that of Artemis, Athena, or Persephone; the mother-goddesses became Demeters, the *Kouroi* took the name of Apollo or Dionysos, and so on. The Jews found their national identity in the cult of Yahweh; the Greeks constructed theirs in the Olympic pantheon. Secondly, the idea of calling on Heaven to redress the balance of power on earth was incompatible with the structure of the aristocratic society of archaic Greece, based on the premise of equal access to the same sort of power for all members of the governing class. To concentrate the ambiguities, tensions, and doubts surrounding a message from a transcendent power on a personal recipient – true or false prophet? – would have destroyed the balance of *polis* politics. The most that the gods could be allowed to communicate was an impersonal arbitration, which was more explicitly ambiguous than the pre-twelfth-century ordeal analyzed by Peter Brown (Brown, 1975) and, like the verdicts of human arbitrators, could be rejected. We do not therefore find the contraposition of religion and the state, or the emancipation of political affairs from religion, appearing as an issue in ancient Greek sources; the process of secularization was not traumatic. On this point ancient Greece stands with China in opposition to the Judeo-Christian tradition; the question put to us has revealed a cleft in the *collegium trilingue*.

I

'Transcendence,' whether it takes the form of divine revelation or of theoretical cosmology, implies a search for authority outside the institutionalized offices and structures of the seeker's society. Even its most concrete form, the law code, implies a transfer of authority from the holders of office to the written rule. Transcendental impulses therefore constitute, by definition, an implicit challenge to traditional authority and indicate some dissatisfaction with it. The notion of transcendence has a relation to Weber's notion of charisma, but directs our attention to some possible sources of charismatic authority rather than to its exercise. I am concerned here, however, not with all attempts to base authority on transcendental sources of legitimation, but only with those cases in which the source of legitimation is a new, comprehensive, universalistic account of the universe seen as divine or natural order.

The man who has such a vision need not have any practical ambition to change society. He may be seeking only to find a secure anchorage for his own thought. Our emphasis on the vision, rather than on any action that may result from it, implies that the individuals with whom we are concerned are intellectuals: in Durkheim's definition,[1] men performing roles in which comprehension (*intelligence*) is both means and end. Furthermore, the conditions of historical research limit our inquiry to those intellectuals whose beliefs and theories made sufficient impact on their contemporaries and immediate posterity to be considered worth preserving, and were preserved in written form.[2] It is therefore necessary to consider the effects on the form and content of these theories of the conditions in which they were communicated and their mode of preservation.

Study of the social position of the Greek intellectuals from Homer to Aristotle, and of the contexts in which they communicated their views, has suggested to me that there were factors both in the social structure of the Greek cities between the eighth and the fourth centuries B.C. and in the conditions of communication experienced by Greek intellectuals that favored the development of transcendental theories. I do not claim that the genesis of such theories can wholly be explained by reference to social structure, but I see no other starting point for a cross-cultural comparison. I also think it particularly important for the study in which we are engaged to examine the position of the men who 'stand back' to look at society and present a new image of it, and the conditions under which they communicate their views. Studies in the sociology of knowledge too often move directly from social structure to *Weltanschauung*, without considering that differences of social status both affect men's experience of social structure and delimit their means of expressing it.[3] I propose, therefore, to trace in some detail shifts in the status of intellectuals, the differentiation of intellectual roles, and changes in contexts of communication in ancient Greece, beginning with the Homeric bard and ending with the formation of philosophical schools in fourth-century Athens. These two termini represent, on the one hand, the intellectual integrated into the structure and value-system of the aristocratic household (*oikos*) and the ruling class of eighth-century Greece and, on the other hand, the emergence of corporate intellectual organizations with recognized functions of teaching and research, and their own criteria of intellectual performance. Aristotle professionalized philosophy in Athens.[4]

This gradual development of intellectual roles, from partial incorporation in the *oikos*, through a period of independent but not clearly defined status, to the beginning of the formation of functionally differentiated groups and organizations, is not unique in Greek society; it is only one example, the most clearly attested, of a general process of social evolution occurring in Greece between the post-Mycenaean Dark Age and the Hellenistic period. A general movement can be seen from the domination of the *oikos* as the framework of social organization and interaction out into the open spaces of city life,[5] in which roles were defined by context (market, assembly, temple, battlefield, law court, competitive arena) rather than by full-time specialization; and it is only some time later, in the late fifth and the fourth centuries, that specialized occupational roles acquire more definite contours and begin to assume importance as social categories and as a focus for the formation of permanent groups.[6] This is a stage in the process of evolution from simpler to more complex forms of social structure that has not received much attention. The differentiation of intellectual roles in Greece is part of this process, even though the fact that the intellectuals were able to theorize the changes in their own position makes their case in some ways unique.

II

From the time when we first meet them, in the Homeric poems, Greek intellectuals were free to innovate and to criticize. Myths and traditional tales were not fixed in form; seers could speak severely to rulers, and Homer is always ready to laugh at the gods even if he is careful to respect the values of the aristocracy. The intellectual and his audience were not tied by any compulsion other than the willingness to speak and to listen.

The poet in the Homeric world is one of a small number of specialists who occupy an intermediate position between nobles and *dēmos*. Like heralds, seers, shipwrights, and doctors (*Odyssey* 17. 382–6), poets may travel from one part of the Greek world to another and find a welcome everywhere because of their skills. The welcome will come from the *oikos* of one of the leaders of the community, and it is here that the poet will sing. He is a hanger-on of the noble *oikos*, but dignity is conferred on him by his possession of an uncommon skill and of knowledge derived from divine inspiration. The Muses have taught him about the great deeds of the past and the affairs of the gods. Some training in music and poetry is already part of the young noble's education – Achilles and Patroclus can pass the time singing 'the deeds of men' in their leisure from the fighting outside Troy (*Iliad* 9. 186–91) – but at home the 'big man' would have a professional bard to entertain the guests in his hall. Odysseus has Phemius (*Odyssey* 1. 325–84, 22. 330–53), Alcinous in Phaeacia has Demodocus (*ibid.*, 8. 83–92, 487–531).

The accounts of poets' performances in the *Odyssey* only show, of course, that this was Homer's conception of the role of the poet in the idealized heroic past. But the aspects of Greek (and Trojan) society selected for attention in the *Iliad* and the *Odyssey* fit the situation of the poet as portrayed there. Women as well as men listen to the poet in the Homeric *oikos*; even in the war-centered *Iliad*, domestic scenes (both terrestrial and Olympian) are given a place, and in both *Iliad* and *Odyssey* women are portrayed with a delicacy rarely reached again in Greek literature.

Society is seen from the point of view of the noble *oikos*, with its far-flung network of guest-friendships and marriage alliances and its accumulation of stored wealth representing in concrete form the gift exchanges of past and future. The exchange of gifts and courtesies is minutely described. The poet enters fully into the affection, trust, and gentleness of relationships within the *oikos*: not only family members but also guests, slaves, and animals (Achilles' horses, Odysseus' dog Argos) are included in this intimacy, and the relations of the gods with the heroes they protect have the same quality. In the milieu of the *oikos* differences of status and even of kind are played down. By contrast, the institutions that brought nobles and *dēmos* together in public in eighth-century Greece make few appearances in the poems, and the status distinction between nobles and *dēmos* is strongly marked. The ordinary mass of soldiers barely appears in the *Iliad*; phratries are mentioned only twice; there is only one scene of judgment, on the shield of Achilles, and only two assembly scenes in which the *dēmos* plays a role of any importance; in one of these the commoner Thersites is beaten and mocked for speaking, while in the other Telemachus attempts to get support from the *dēmos* against the suitors and fails. The world the poems portray is the idealized past of the upper class, and its values are not questioned. Perhaps there is a momentary gleam of mockery in the comment on Glaucus' exchange of armour with Diomede – 'he must have lost his wits, to exchange gold armour for bronze' (*Iliad* 6. 234–6) – but otherwise the upper-class ethic is unchallenged. The poet can laugh at the gods, but not at the *basileis*. He identifies himself with the interests of his audience: he does not allow his own personality to intrude, except when he invokes the Muses.[7] He maintains a distance between himself and his patrons only by confining his account of their world to the past.

This identification with the point of view of the noble *oikos* strongly suggests that the poet (or poets) of the *Iliad* and *Odyssey* did not feel their situation to be radically different from that of the bards Demodocus and Phemius in the latter poem. Nevertheless it is possible that by the second half of the eighth century, the date usually assigned to the Homeric epics, poets were also performing in competitions held during funeral celebrations or public religious festivals. Hesiod, who cannot be much later than 'Homer,' won a prize at the funeral games of Alcidamas, king of Chalcis. The long, elaborate Homeric epics would perhaps be more suited to this context than to the less formal performances in the noble *oikos* described in the *Odyssey*. The bard singing in the *oikos* had to adapt his performance to the mood of the audience. His formulaic technique of composition allowed him great flexibility in expanding or reducing the length of each episode of his song. Public competition gave the poet more control over the length and proportions of his presentation. He had a new claim on the attention of his audience; paradoxically, the fact that their judgment of his poem had to be delivered formally made him less dependent on pleasing them.[8]

The situation of the public competition was perhaps also more suitable for catalogue-poetry than was the *oikos* context. A catalogue must be complete, and it displays the poet's unique possession of knowledge learned from the Muses. Hesiod's *Theogony* was, we know, composed for a competition; and Hesiod not only sees Boeotian society from the point of view of the *dēmos*, instead of that of the nobles, but also sees it in a perspective that implies greater distance between the poet and his audience. Hesiod's vision includes both past and present. In the *Works and Days* he criticizes the nobles for their injustice, but he does not blame them alone for the ills of the Iron Race: men's present troubles are part of a pattern stretching

back to the deeds of Prometheus. The contrast between Hesiod's
point of view and that of Homer is so striking that one can hardly
avoid seeing Hesiod as a deliberate rebel against the conventional
values of epic.

The story of Pandora sums up in a single image the rejection of
two essential values of the Homeric world, women and gifts. A gift
to Hesiod is either a bribe, a debt, a tax, or a trap. Women are a
necessary evil. Wives, brothers, neighbors are not to be unquestion-
ingly trusted.[9] Kings and nobles may be courteous to each other –
Hesiod does not confront Homer on his own ground – but they
neglect their duty to society as a whole. The poet who no longer
trusts the rulers must look beyond them, to the gods. Hesiod can
hardly have been the first village poet. But the institution of public
competitions in poetry may have made it possible for the first time
for the poet still attached to village society to confront the poet who
had left his original station to become a hanger-on of the noble
oikos.[10] For our present inquiry, however, the most significant
difference between Homer and Hesiod is perhaps one of structure[11]
rather than values. Hesiod's *Theogony* and *Works and Days* are
neither sophisticated narratives like the *Iliad* and *Odyssey* nor mere
lists like the 'Catalogue of Ships' in *Iliad* ii; they have a simple but
shaped structure, the pattern of a genealogy in the *Theogony* and
the rhythm of the farmer's calendar in the *Works and Days*.[12] The
myth of the Five Races of Men in the *Works and Days* also has a
strongly marked structure unparalleled in Homer. The Gold, Silver,
Bronze, and Hero races are, like the lands visited by Odysseus in the
Odyssey, mythical models of 'alternative societies,' in which the
poet plays with fundamental rules and distinctions of Greek culture,
abolishing first one and then another. But in Odysseus' travels there
seems to be no pattern in the passage from the idle Lotus-eaters to
the cityless, cannibal Cyclopes and thence to the incestuous family of
Aeolus, the perpetual daylight of the Laestrygonians, also cannibal,
the confusion of men and animals in the house of Circe, the perpetual
night of the Cimmerians, and the land of the dead; and the implicit
contrast between these aberrant societies and the normality of
Ithaca is left unstated. Hesiod's myth, on the contrary, is made up of
a series of symmetrical identifications and oppositions. The Gold and
Silver races represent childhood, leisure, and freedom from all
physical ills; the Bronze race and the Heroes represent manhood,
war, and the physical dangers that go with them; the Iron race is

identified with old age, work, and sickness. The Gold race and the heroes are just, the Silver and Bronze men unjust; in the Iron age justice struggles against injustice, but with little success.[13] The scheme of the four metals is reinforced by patterns drawn from Greek life, the three main age categories of the Greek city,[14] and the social contexts of leisure, war, and work. The contrast between the harsh reality of the Iron age and the previous worlds is repeatedly emphasized. So is the separation between gods and men, which Homer and his audience liked to minimize.

It was virtually inevitable that a poet who adopted a critical attitude to the ruling class should reject its claim to be closely related to the gods, and transfer his respect to the latter; but whatever predecessors Hesiod may have had, his belief in a pattern in human society sustained by Zeus and Justice was surely felt by him to be a new message. The account at the beginning of the *Theogony* of his meeting with the Muses on Mt Helicon and personal 'call' to poetry seems to indicate that he needed to emphasize this transcendental source of authority, both because he combined the roles of farmer and poet in a way which may have been unusual and because he felt that he had a personal message to deliver. The *Works and Days* has Hesiod's personality so firmly stamped on it that any rhapsode reciting the poem in the future had to take on the *persona* of Hesiod, brother of Perses, for his performance.[15]

It is commonly thought that Hesiod wrote his poems down, and so insured the preservation of those personal touches that might have been lost in oral transmission. Even after all possible allowance has been made for anticipation of Hesiod's themes in earlier poetry now lost to us, it is not difficult to believe that the *Theogony* represented a theological *tour de force* on a scale never achieved before, and that the vision of Justice in heaven, in human society, and in the seasonal rhythm of the farmer's labor presented in the *Works and Days* was new. Systematization and novelty are, as we shall see again later, interconnected. The man who has a new message for his audience must structure it in such a way that it makes a clear-cut impression on their minds. The *Iliad* and *Odyssey*, composed for an audience familiar with the legends of the Trojan war and the conventions of heroic society, display the poet's art in his ability to transport his audience from the battlefield to the household of Hector or Zeus, to digress from the line of the story and pick it up again smoothly, to pass swiftly from one emotional mood to another.

The poet could play this game because the audience was ready to cooperate with him. A poet playing a new game could not count on the same level of cooperation; he had to explain what he was trying to do.

Writing brought into relief a division between creation and performance, which in traditional oral epic had normally been unneeded. It is also likely at first to have favored the diffusion of short poems more than that of long epics. After Hesiod, the role of the creative poet who says something new about and to his society passed from epic to lyric poetry. Epic poetry gradually passed entirely into the keeping of the rhapsodes as the gap between creative poet and professional memorizer widened. Together with the introduction of writing, innovations in music and changes in city life may have influenced this transfer of interest. Greek writers on the history of literature attribute changes in both lyre and flute music to the early lyric poets;[16] there is an element of *argumentum e silentio* in these statements, but it is intrinsically likely that increased interest in lyric poetry led to new developments in music and meter and these, in turn, increased the demand for new songs to replace traditional hymns and refrains. Before the introduction of writing, poems composed for solo singing at banquets, or for various types of choral songs and dances, sometimes combined with solo performances, depended on popular favor alone for circulation and survival. They were not the responsibility of any specialist. Topical witticisms might circulate widely but would be quickly forgotten; subtleties of phrase and detail in dancing-songs might be eroded in transmission. The poet lost control over his song when he had sung it once; anyone could learn and repeat it. Writing changed this situation. The lyric poets of the seventh century, although still composing in the first instance for oral performance, are conscious that their words will travel and will last. Archilochus describes the newly colonized island of Thasos for those who have not seen it and calls a poem criticizing a friend a 'message-scroll' – even if one may wonder whether the poem was really as confidential as the term suggests.[17]

The lyric poetry of the archaic age reveals to us more ephemeral aspects of Greek social life than the epic, but at the same time challenged the poet to charge the ephemeral with permanent significance. The response of the lyric poets to this task of immortalizing the mood of a particular moment and social context, and to the problem of marking each poem recognizably as the creation and property of its author,[18] has led scholars to talk of an age of 'the discovery of the individual'; but the Romantic associations of the phrase are misleading. It might be more revealing to speak of the poet's discovery of the city and of the type. The focus of political life was moving from the noble household to council and assembly-place; displays and distributions of wealth also were less *oikos*-centered, more often channeled into public contexts: funeral cortèges and marriage processions, sacrifices, religious festivals. The poet, too, composed his choral songs for public contexts. In the *oikos*, the dividing line between men's and women's quarters hardened as the male members of the household became more concerned with public institutions. Poetry still had its place in the *oikos*, but was no longer addressed to a mixed audience that included the women of the household. Symposium singing was for men alone (or for men and courtesans). The symposium was already beginning to specialize in political activities excluded from the institutionalized contexts of council and assembly: the launching of lampoons and criticisms of leading figures, intended for a wide circulation in the city (Archilochus), and calls to revolt (Alcaeus). Women sometimes responded by creating their own parallel groups (Sappho).

Both in public and in private contexts performances of lyric poetry tended to be dominated by a homogeneous group (choir or audience), which gave the poet a new opportunity to throw himself into a single part. Whereas the epic poet was expected to display his gifts by portraying a variety of characters and scenes, the lyric poet had to fit a shorter song to a more clearly defined context, performing group, and audience; the context often required him to sustain and explore a mood rather than to vary it. (The consequent changes in the roles attributed to gods in poetry deserve study.) Choral lyric regularly includes first-person references to the character and interests of the chorus, although it may also include accounts of myth in which the chorus's own personality is muted and its voice merges with that of the poet. Monodic lyric could be sung, in the first person, in a character other than that of the poet: Archilochus' song 'Not for me Gyges' wealth' was sung in the *persona* of 'Chares the carpenter.'[19]

Love-songs and war-songs do not have to be composed in the bedroom or on the battlefield. The new hope of immortality or of a rapidly spreading fame brought by the introduction of writing frequently led the poet to insert his own name or some other token of identification into his works, but at the same time encouraged him to look beyond the immediate situation to the unity of all human experience. The lyric poets are conscious of speaking with a voice that is more than the word of a single individual. Even in his private quarrels, Archilochus is well aware that his mockery is a weapon that can shame his victim before the whole city. The poet who praises a victorious athlete confers the accolade in the name of society and records it for all time.[20]

Although some of the lyric poets traveled and apparently lived by their profession (Alcman, Arion, Xenophanes), lyric composition required no special training of memory and was open to anyone who had received the basic upper-class education in music and letters.[21] The poet had his place in all spheres of city life cult, war, leisure, politics. Alcaeus and Theognis remain embedded in their own aristocratic milieu, bitterly resenting the rise of tyrants and *novi homines*, but the poet's role as possessor of a special 'wisdom' – *sophia*, originally denoting the poet's technical skill, was gradually taking on a deeper moral implication[22] – could also enable him to stand back from faction and address both parties in the role of adviser and mediator. Hesiod and Tyrtaeus already approach this position, but it was Solon who provided the ideal model of the intellectual as sage. He first appears to us as a rebel using poetry in a new way, for a direct appeal to the citizenry calling for action disapproved by the ruling group. There was evidently no precedent for the use of poetry in a political context in the *agora*; Solon pretended to be a herald gone mad. His appeal was successful; Athens won control of Salamis, and the power of his verse won such respect that he was later invited to mediate between nobles and *dēmos* in a revolutionary crisis and make new laws for the city.

The lyric poets of the seventh and early sixth centuries did not strive for transcendence; they were content to explore the new opportunities offered by the growing institutions of the city and the changing world in which they lived. But they founded their new interpretation of the poet's role on two claims *that helped to determine later Greek conceptions of the intellectual: that the poet speaks to posterity as well as to his immediate audience, and that he has something of value to teach and is not a mere entertainer.

The integration of the poet into the aristocratic city of the archaic age was disturbed in the sixth century by the concentration of power in the hands of tyrants. The flow of political and social life split into three channels: the poet had to choose between accepting patronage at court, committing himself to political activity as a rebel, or deliberately withdrawing from politics. It is at this time that the Scylla and Charybdis of Greek intellectual life, concentration on technical skill for its own sake and abandonment to mysticism, make their first appearance. There were Orphic poets as well as composers of symposium-verse on the traditional themes of love and wine at the court of the Pisistratids in Athens. The mystic enhanced the dignity of the poet's role by claims to divine revelation, the symposium-poet by stressing his mastery of his art and capacity to create an immortal beauty. By the time of Pindar, the poet can accept not only the patronage of tyrants but even a money payment without any loss of dignity.[23]

It is, however, the other stream, the choice of the intellectuals who withdrew from political life, that most concerns us here; these thinkers, most of whom adopted prose rather than poetry as their medium, sought a new pattern in life outside the traditional structures of the city-state.

The choice of prose may have been influenced by the increased importance of assembly debates in the city and indicates the value attached to informal discussion with friends and pupils by these thinkers. It may also indicate lack of interest in a wider public. But as the new cosmologies became more programmatically anti-mythical, and poets concurrently tended to move away from description and comment to the greater detachment of myth and allegory, prose became the medium of rationalism and gradually excluded poetry from the fields of the philosopher and historian.

Miletus, the home of the first philosophers, was ruled by a tyrant in the time of Thales, the founder of the school,[24] and her position throughout the sixth century was a difficult one: the weight of the decision whether it was possible for the Greeks of Asia Minor to resist the great land powers, Lydia and Persia, must have pressed heavily on her citizens. For almost the whole of the century, after withstanding Lydian attacks, she maintained friendly relations with the barbarian powers while the rest of the East Greek cities succumbed one by one. Thales advised the formation of a united state of Ionia and was disregarded (Herodotus 1. 170). His kinsman and pupil Anaximander made the first Greek world map, about the middle of the century; this interest in geography, like that of Hecataeus fifty years later, when Miletus finally emerged as leader of the Ionian revolt against Persia, is not to be detached from the political problem of the feasibility of Greek resistance. To some intellectuals in other Ionian cities emigration to the west seemed the only solution. Xenophanes left Colophon when it was taken by the Persians, Pythagoras left Samos under the tyranny of Polycrates: both detached themselves physically as well as intellectually from a disrupted society.

Other influences no doubt played their part in the genesis of pre-Socratic philosophy. Thales may have learnt astronomy from Oriental teachers; if it is true that he made his reputation as a sage partly by explaining the solar eclipse of 584 B.C., his fellow citizens would have been predisposed to expect further rationalistic explanations from him. It is clear also that both the style of discussion practiced by the first philosophers and their conception of the order and symmetry of the world of nature were influenced by the political institutions of the sixth-century Greek city.[25] Yet I would still suggest that the immediate impulse toward the search for justice in nature came not from the establishment of a new form of justice in the city, but from its disruption.

The writings of the pre-Socratics are preserved only in fragments, and the reports of their doctrines given by later sources are not entirely to be trusted, but the comprehensive sweep of their cosmologies is not in doubt. Anaximander ranged from the creation of the world out of infinity to a map of its contemporary configuration and divisions, transforming theogony into cosmogony and the traveler's tale into the imaginary voyage round the known world. Hecataeus used the latter form again in his *Journey round the World* (*Gēs periodos*), and in his *Genealogies* tried to systematize the history of the Greek states as Hesiod in the *Theogony* had systematized their theology. Even if the pre-Socratics addressed themselves to a narrower public than Hesiod, they had the same problem of communicating a new vision and may have been influenced by this difficulty to give their theories an easily grasped structure resting on simple principles, symmetrical correspondences, and striking contrasts. Early maps made the three continents equal in size and assumed the Nile's course to be the mirror-image of that of the Danube. The Pythagoreans drew up parallel lists of paired opposites: limit and infinity, odd and even, right and left, male and female, light and darkness, etc. The idea that the universe was constituted out of a small number of opposed pairs of elements seems to go back in some form to Anaximander and had a long and successful career in Greek science. It has been suggested that such uses of analogy and polarity in early Greek philosophy can be seen as survivals of primitive thought patterns and the influence of myth. But myths do not usually display their structure so obtrusively. The emphatic use of symmetry and correspondence is a feature of ideology rather than of myth; myth, though it contains an important element of fantasy, does not aim to startle the audience by its novelty.[26]

Even the medium and context in which this new kind of communication took place had to be created. No suitable public context as yet existed, and even in private contexts philosophical discussion must have been new. The fact that the first philosophical books were prose works suggests rejection of the conventions and atmosphere of the symposium in favor of a sober meeting at which the philosopher expounded his views to interested listeners, arguing his case and in all probability allowing his hearers to interrupt with questions and objections.[27] In the latter feature the philosophical meeting surely differed from the only comparable teaching situation of the time, the instruction of initiates in religious sects.

Reason, revelation, and art formed a triangle within which the intellectuals of the sixth and early fifth centuries had to select their course. The model presented by the mystery religions continued for some time to exercise an attraction for philosophers. The Pythagorean groups of southern Italy can well be characterized as belonging to a sect rather than a school; Pythagoras taught not only a doctrine but a way of life. Indeed, the commitment demanded of Pythagoreans went beyond that required by Greek religious sects, which tended to concentrate their teaching on the adept's ritual purity and future existence, and limit their reunions to ritual occasions. Communal meals and regular companionship, however, were in all probability a feature of the life of the Pythagoreans from the beginning, and this, combined with a numerical strength of several hundred and common beliefs that included respect for law and order in the city, inevitably disturbed the precarious equilibrium of city politics. Three hundred or more[28] men who associated constantly and were committed to thinking alike, drawn mainly or entirely from the upper class, could scarcely in the Greek city-state avoid having some of the functions of a political party. The Pythagoreans seem to have dominated the government of Croton until their fellow citizens turned against them about the middle of the fifth century. At some point, possibly as a result of this setback, a division developed within the school between those who made the life of pure contemplation their ideal and turned to research in mathematics and others who held to the traditional tenets of the sect and a less specialist model of the good life. In the sixth century, although intellectuals as individuals were making a status for themselves in Greek society, there was as yet no place for the intellectual group. The numbers of the Pythagoreans and the role of revelation in the origins of the school led to an emphasis on discipline and agreement which both cut them off from communication with other intellectuals and made their integration into the city problematic. Even in the fifth and fourth centuries the extent of their discoveries in mathematics and music and of their relations with philosophers of other schools is obscured for us by the constant, introverted process of revision of the tradition about Pythagoras which accompanied every new development.[29]

In Heraclitus of Ephesus (*fl. c.* 500 B.C.) the relation between revelation and philosophy took a different turn. He is said to have rejected the role of political 'sage' and lawgiver offered to him by the Ephesians, and retired first to the temple of Artemis and then to the mountains. He knew the doctrines of Pythagoras, Xenophanes, and the Milesians (including Hecataeus) presumably from books (fr. B 40), and seems to have been content to diffuse his own ideas solely through writing.[30] He dedicated his book in the temple of Artemis, and many have detected in his fragments the urgent tone of a man with a vision to communicate. Whereas the Milesians had tried to trace the constitution of the universe back to an origin seen as historical process, Heraclitus conveys the experience of piercing through the illusion of sense-data to perceive a different underlying reality, perpetual flux. Two fragmentary references to oracles, 'The lord of the oracle of Delphi neither speaks out nor conceals, but gives a sign' (B 93), and 'The Sibyl, uttering from an inspired mouth a message without wit, beauty or adornment, has a voice which carries over a thousand years because of the god' (B 92), suggest that the oracular style of Heraclitus' own writings was a conscious imitation, and that he saw his book not as an attempt to convince the reader by argument, but as a set of clues sufficient to guide the wise man to the vision experienced by its author. He emphasized that his opinions were reached through self-questioning and not derived from any teacher (B 101). Discussion was not a part of his conception of the philosopher's role.

The element of concealment in the isolated, oracular individual Heraclitus and the silent school of Pythagoras was exceptional. Parmenides, like Heraclitus, was concerned with a new conception of the reality underlying phenomena rather than with causal explanation; he explicitly used the language of revelation and presented his vision in verse. Nevertheless, his revelation of the unity of Being was a solution to a problem of logic; it rested on the presupposition that argument was a central part of the philosopher's life. In general, the pre-Socratics and Sophists are characterized by their readiness to expound their views to all, in contexts ranging from the informal discussion shared with a small gathering of friends and pupils to the public lecture, and by their competitive relation to one another. Although Anaximander was the pupil of Thales, Anaximenes of Anaximander, and Zeno of Parmenides, each emerges as an independent personality with a reputation of his own, not borrowed from that of his master. In the case of Leucippus and Democritus, whom the historiographic tradition does not distinguish, it is clear that the disciple was the greater of the two. Philosophical schools with a continuous tradition did not as yet exist, with the exception of the Pythagoreans. In the fifth century, philosophers, like other intellectuals, traveled from city to city, expounding their views in the houses of leading citizens or in the public gymnasium. They were the traveling *gurus* of ancient Greece, each with his own theory to expound and his own reputation to build. The type of the philosopher was not yet fixed, the audience's expectations were plastic; the only necessity was, as Louis Gernet has said, that the philosopher should not look like everybody else – and, one might add, should not think like anybody else.[31]

In these circumstances some of the features that, it was suggested above, characterized the first cosmologies, remained prominent in philosophical theories for a considerable time: each theory had to be comprehensive in scope, clearly articulated in structure, and sufficiently simple and striking in its basic tenets to make an immediate impact on the audience. Extremist positions were attractive: everything changes, nothing changes. There was a tendency for each new theory to bear a simple structural relation to that of the proponent's leading predecessor or rival: total reversal, rearrangement of an accepted set of elements, a different answer to the same

question. Although the emphasis was on disagreement and independence, common ground was nevertheless created by this competition and, despite differences in style and personality, by a
common readiness to submit each theory to the test of argument.
Criticism of rival views was an inherent necessity of the situation.
Even so, when argument and criticism began, in Zeno's work, to
take precedence over cosmology, they had to be clothed in the
striking garb of paradox. In the later part of the fifth century the
ability to defend a paradoxical thesis, 'to make the weaker argument
appear the stronger,' became a major item in the stock-in-trade of the
Sophists. The technique of argument became a subject for displays –
parodied in Aristophanes' *Clouds*, preserved in written form in the
Dissoi Logoi (*Double Arguments*), Antiphon's *Tetralogies*, and the
pseudo-Xenophontic *Constitution of Athens*, in which the rationality
of democracy is taken by an oligarchic writer as the paradox to be
defended.[32] Plato's Socrates, like the Unjust Argument in Aristophanes' *Clouds*, finds a sparring partner who will uphold a conventional view and demonstrates its weaknesses. In the *Protagoras*
Plato presents a contest in argument, before an audience, between
Protagoras and Socrates; mention is made of Protagoras' previous
experience of such contests, and the difference between a contest
and an informal discussion is noted (335 ff.).

In the democratic city of the fifth century, philosophers and
Sophists could not entirely stand aside from politics. Even
Anaxagoras, who seems to have concerned himself solely with
cosmology and is said to have claimed that his fatherland was the
heavens, not Clazomenae, was attacked in Athens as an associate of
Pericles. This example shows, however, the crux in the relation
between the philosopher and the city. The philosopher's point of
view was too comprehensive for the Assembly, and advice given
outside the framework of democratic institutions was suspect. The
majority of philosophers and Sophists in the fifth century were
excluded from direct participation in city politics because they led a
life of travel or had settled in a city that was not their own; the same
conditions compelled them to look for a general approach to politics
that transcended the particular affairs of individual cities.

Two alternative solutions were found. One was speculation on the
origins and nature of political institutions, the basis of law, the
requirements of the ideal state. The other was development of the
technique of argument as a political skill that the Sophist could

teach. The Sophists no doubt varied in their sincerity or cynicism. They had opportunities to display their rhetorical skill on general political themes when invited, as they often were, to serve as ambassadors; many of them presumably seriously hoped to make their pupils good citizens. But it soon became clear that they could only teach the technique of argument and, above all, of persuasion; in the fourth century the science of argument was already divided into two branches, logic for the philosopher and rhetoric for the politician.

Other compromises between the detachment of the intellectual and the interests and concerns of the lay audience appear in the development of other specializations in which practical experience was systematically organized with the help of concepts and theories drawn from philosophy: medicine, geography, and history. Structural symmetry is marked in medicine and geography, which had similar problems of systematizing a mass of observations collected from very varied sources. This was true of history also, and history too had its rigid frameworks; but historical narrative put less strain on the audience than most of the new prose works. History drew on the tradition of poetry as well as philosophical theory; it had the poetic aim of immortalizing great deeds as well as the scientific aim of explaining political and military success or failure.

The main importance of historiography for our theme, however, lies in the unique combination of intellectual detachment and acceptance of the framework of the city possible to the historian. Greek society and culture in the early fifth century were in an anomalous state. Cultural unity had always been strong; since Homer, the intellectuals had lived on this unity, which enabled them and their works to travel from one city to another, and had constantly reinforced it by their use of the common symbols. But the nation was still politically fragmented, though, since the Persian wars, uncomfortably aware of the possibilities of union. The *polis* was still the only social framework available; the traveling poet or philosopher did not find a wider society, but only a series of variations of the same small unit. The intellectual was predisposed by his status in society to transcend the limits of the city, but Pindar and the pre-Socratics, by doing so, had detached themselves from city affairs altogether. Both Herodotus' and Thucydides' histories escaped this dilemma, in different ways. Herodotus found in the Persian wars a historical theme centered on a moment of Greek unity and therefore fit to stand as a modern alternative to the Panhellenic world of myth, which had allowed the poets to transcend the limits of their patrons' interests and allegiances.[33] At the same time, as a Greek of Asia Minor, Herodotus knew only too well that the Greeks were not alone in the world. They had to be set in a perspective that included not only other powers but also other cultures. Here he could draw on the Sophists' emphasis on the relativity of culture.[34] Thucydides, on the other hand, faced squarely the problem of the city-state as a political unit and found in the Peloponnesian war a theme which allowed him to combine the study of the internal organization of the *polis* with that of its external relations in a wider field of forces.

By the middle of the fifth century, Athens was not only politically but also culturally more than one city-state among others: mistress of an empire and cultural center of Greece. The question of the role of the intellectual in the city therefore affected Athenian intellectuals particularly closely, both because they had to face the question of the justice of Athens' policy and because their audience was made up of fellow citizens. Democratic Athens expected participation and comment from its citizens. It was a society in which books had a wide circulation,[35] but public oral communication was still the essence of communal life. The dominant contexts of communication, assembly, law courts, and theater, were all forms of drama; in each of them a small number of protagonists performed before a mass audience of judges. Each had its own rules and conventions, a formal solemnity; number by itself created distance between the anonymous audience and the performers.

In the archaic city the poet's role as mediator and spokesman was in part at least a function of the lack of communication between the *dēmos* and the political elite. But after the expulsion of the Pisistratid tyrants in 510, Athens developed, in council, assembly, and law courts, institutions that insured confrontation and discussion. The range of topics debated there was wide: but it was not limitless. Gradually tragedy, comedy, and philosophy took up positions offering possibilities of scrutiny and criticism that lay outside the scope of the political institutions of democracy.[36]

An early form of tragedy performed by a single actor and chorus had been introduced under the tyrants, but nothing is known of it. The second actor was introduced during the first generation of the democracy, by Aeschylus. His earliest extant play, the *Persae*, is dominated by the theme of *hybris*. Xerxes is the tyrant punished by the gods for his ambitions. Aeschylus and Pindar share this conception of the poet's function of reminding the powerful that their power is limited and feeble in comparison with the designs of the gods.

The fear of the recurrence of tyranny was a common Greek concern. But we can follow its effects in more detail in Athens than elsewhere. The problem of preventing the rise of new tyrants was one not easy to handle in the framework of assembly and law courts. Miltiades was tried for giving the *dēmos* bad advice after the failure of his attempt to sack Paros in the year following his victory at Marathon; but this trial was exceptional. Impeachment was not used again to attack a popular leader until the attempted trial of Alcibiades for the mutilation of the Hermae in 415.[37] Instead, the Athenians turned to ostracism, which was used for the first time in the year after Miltiades' trial[38] and continued in use until the unsuccessful attempt to ostracize Alcibiades two years before the affair of the Hermae. It is reasonable to conclude that the trial of Miltiades had aroused a dangerous amount of faction. Ostracism did not require the formulation of any specific charge against its victim, allowed no opportunity for public argument, and brought no dishonor. Was it mere coincidence that in the decade when ostracism was first used – and used, in the *dēmos*' enthusiasm for the new weapon, almost every year – competitions in comedy were also first instituted? In both institutions the power of public opinion is deliberately harnessed as a force of social control; the elite voluntarily submit themselves to the risk of temporary exile and public ridicule. Both institutions provide an opportunity for the expression of suspicions without formal trial or the possibility of defense. Aeschylean tragedy expressed fear of tyranny and warned against ambition in general terms; comedy singled out individual leaders for criticism. 'There goes our squill-headed Zeus, Pericles, with the Odeion for his skull-cap – since the ostrakon missed him!'[39]

Tragedy and comedy had, of course, many other aspects. The texts we have were only one element in a spectacle that included costume, music, and dancing. Satyr-plays may well have been more ballet than drama, and it would not be difficult to think of Aeschylus' *Persae* as a sort of opera. His later *Suppliants* may have contained an Amazonomachy in ballet form between fifty Danaids and fifty Egyptians,[40] and there is a tradition that the entry of the chorus of the *Eumenides* caused a panic in the audience. Sophocles seems to have cared less for spectacle, but Euripides' musical innovations were notorious, and the dancing in the *Bacchae* must have been extremely striking. Comedy offered even wider scope for choreographic and musical invention. Both were visually richer than earlier poetic genres; this offered the poet new opportunities, but at the same time influenced his choices.

Drama left less to the imagination of the audience than earlier monodic or choral poetry. This concreteness made it easier for the poet to represent complicated situations and relationships, but forced him to reconsider his own relation to performers and audience. Dramatic representation of the protagonists of myth and strong characterization of the chorus in costume, dance, and music increased the distance between the poet and his creation. How was he to make his own voice heard? Comedy solved this problem by deliberately playing on the ambiguous relation between poet and chorus, allowing a fully characterized chorus to step out of character at a certain point in the action and speak for the poet.[41] The tragic poet could not expose the illusions of the stage in this way. He might choose to use his chorus mainly as spectators of the action, accompanying it with gnomic comments which could be taken by the real spectators as indications of the reaction the poet expected from his audience; this type of choral comment, common in Sophocles, is not far removed from the tone of Pindar's odes, and the chorus that makes it is not strongly characterized. But a discrepancy still remained between the point of view suited to a chorus taking part in the action of the play and that of the poet who stood outside and created it.[42]

This is particularly obvious in the case of Aeschylus; the plots of his trilogies carry the main weight of the poet's comment on life, showing how time reveals a foreordained pattern in human and divine actions and relationships.[43] The task for the poet's wisdom is to represent this pattern, in dramatic action, rather than to comment on it. What he presents is a vision of cosmic justice which resembles that of Anaximander: a perpetual, depersonalized cyclical process in which aggrandizement alternated with compensation. It is not the justice of fifth-century Athens, and to ask whether it is the justice of the society that created the myths Aeschylus used is a digression.[44] The notion of justice had been borrowed from social institutions by the pre-Socratics to serve as a metaphor for their transcendental vision of natural processes in the universe, and was then reintroduced into the sphere of social relations by Aeschylus as the basis of a transcendental theology. This interplay of philosophy and poetry is in my opinion crucial for understanding Aeschylus.

Aeschylus played a major part in the genesis of tragedy; if he was limited, in shaping tragedy into a medium that could express his conception of life, by the presuppositions of rival authors and the expectations of his audience, we are no longer in a position to detect the traces of such constraints. It is different with Sophocles and Euripides. In their work the element of reaction against earlier conceptions of tragedy, inevitable in a competitive situation, must not be overlooked. Sophocles exploited Aeschylus' notion of drama as the representation of pattern in human relationships without his accompanying belief in a transcendent justice working through time to harmony. He emphasized instead the inability of the human actor to perceive the pattern in which he is caught. This change of attitude enabled him to develop his dramatic technique with much greater sophistication. Instead of the slow rhythm of changing fortunes of an Aeschylean trilogy, he presents a series of swift reversals, each revelation – or lie – changing the relationships among the characters. The poet, standing outside the action, no longer sees a pattern of justice, but only the limits of human knowledge. There is a touch of irony in that the conventional wisdom of the simple pious chorus and the insight of the poet converge.

But the separation of the actor's perception of the situation from its true meaning in a pattern of relationships hidden from him also led the poet to focus his attention more closely on the actor's reaction to his experiences. Sophocles sees the human actor as being not only unconscious of the structure of the situation in which he finds himself, but also essentially solitary in the midst of his relationships. There is in his values what one might call a heroic individualism.[45] The individual's stand in defense of his own rights and duties, regardless of the claims of others and the conventions of status, is not yet a value rewarded by society or the gods; the interests of society require compromise. But the individual who refuses to compromise and to admit that he may be wrong, though he pays dearly for his individualism, stands out like the oak among the reeds in the fable. It is characteristic of the difference between Aeschylus and Sophocles that the only extant Aeschylean tragedy that emphasizes this isolation of the suffering hero is the *Prometheus*, in which the hero knows his future destiny. Prometheus can contemplate his own sufferings with dignity because he knows how it will all end. Sophocles' heroes – with the exception of the aged Oedipus – achieve the same dignity without the foreknowledge.

By the time of the institution of radical democracy in 461, tyranny was no longer Athens' most immediate danger. If there was *hybris* in the city, it was in the temper of the assembly itself and its leaders, who now felt strong enough to intervene in Egypt and defy the Peloponnesian league simultaneously. To contemplate this course without disquiet required faith not only in Athenian seapower but also in the capacity of democratic institutions to arrive at an accurate forecast of events by rational argument; it required a strong belief in the courage, resolution, single-mindedness, and foresight of the citizen body. Thucydides, professionally committed to the belief that failure could be rationally explained and therefore could have been avoided, showed his awareness of the tragedy in Athens' position[46] but had to base his history on the assumption that her ambitions were realizable. Sophocles' heroes have the courage, resolution, and detachment from private social ties expected of the Athenian as citizen, but they lack foresight. But while warning his fellow-citizens of the limits of human reason, Sophocles also rejected the pragmatism of the Socratic tenet that there is no virtue without knowledge. His heroes' virtues are disastrous, but still noble.[47]

While tragedy criticized the basic assumptions of the decision-making process and comedy fastened on the absurdity of particular decisions and the weaknesses of individual leaders, philosophy asked new questions about the education of citizens and above all of political leaders. The rationalization of politics left plenty of scope for intellectual questioning. But the philosophers, when they turned back from the contemplation of the cosmos to human society, had to re-think their own role in the city. Socrates is memorable for his personal encounters with Athenian norms rather than for his analysis of them. In the first place, he made a sharp distinction between the laws of Athens, to which he gave unconditional loyalty, and her conventions, which he flouted freely. Reason is the transcendent standard on which this distinction is based; obedience to law can be rationally justified, obedience to convention cannot.

Like the Cynics, Socrates also combined with his rejection of social conventions disregard of the physical habits and desires of his own body. Ascetic self-control and superiority to the desires of the ordinary man, including the desire for wealth and power, became a permanent part of the Greek philosopher's self-image.[48] This does not, however, imply superiority to the claims of the state. The *daimonion* that guided Socrates' life was not the 'inner voice' of the Protestant conscience. In the first place, Socrates had to believe that it was external to him. In the second place, though its instructions led him to behavior that his fellow-citizens found eccentric and incomprehensible, it did not lead him into conflict with authority. His protest against the condemnation of the generals who commanded at the battle of Arginusae was not inspired by the *daimonion*, but made in the same spirit of obedience to law that led him later to accept his own death-sentence.[49] To uphold the laws of Athens was not in Attic eyes a matter of individual conscience but the common duty of all citizens,[50] even if Socrates held to it in circumstances that called for exceptional resolution. There was no call for the *daimonion* to intervene here; and Socrates certainly did not believe that every man had a *daimonion*. His *daimonion* explained the paradoxical life he found himself leading as a philosopher in the interests of intellectual consistency, in the attempt to strip his behavior of superficial conventions and arrive at the essential core of virtue; a life of search for the answers other men claimed already to know.

It was not only philosophers who required a new concept of virtue. Attic society was becoming more complex and more mobile; the old aristocratic conception of *aretē*, in which class attributes, status obligations, and more abstract moral qualities were inextricably mingled, was no longer adequate. Virtue had to be democratic, the same for all men; at the same time it had to be rational, adaptable to all circumstances. Specification of virtuous acts was always vulnerable to argument. (Aristotle's doctrine of the Mean attempts to solve this problem.) Should a son always obey his father? Even if the father is a fool? Status no longer seemed enough to define duty.

Comedy had already begun to occupy itself with these questions in the fifth century: Aristophanes' *Clouds* and *Wasps* play with the relation between son and father, the *Lysistrata* and *Ecclesiazusae* with the relation between men and women. By the time of Menander the conflict between individual inclinations and the rights and obligations attached to kinship statuses is a stock theme, with the obligatory marriage of the heiress to her next-of-kin singled out as especially ludicrous. Similar themes occur in Euripides' plays,[51] but for the tragic poet the test was not so much to question the accepted norms of the world of myth as to make them dramatically credible. In his attempt to do this, Euripides broke away from the tradition of Aeschylus and Sophocles to focus on the content of relationships rather than their structure. Electra's hatred of Clytemnestra is no longer sufficiently explained by the murder of Agamemnon; it must also be portrayed as a clash of abrasive personalities. The essential part of the *Alcestis* is the portrayal of the relationship of husband and wife. The *Hippolytus, Ion,* and *Bacchae* study three modes of relationship between worshiper and god.

Two influences are at work here. On the one hand Euripides is reacting to changes in the structure of Athenian society. Increased spatial and social mobility in any society tends to weaken status-based obligations, such as those attached to particular positions in a kinship system, and replace them with more flexible ties based on similarity of interests and compatibility of personality. 'Kinship becomes optional.'[52] Such a change will evidently lead to increased interest in the personal content of relationships, encourage the idea that marriage should be based on personal selection, and give friendship a new importance as the model of a personal relationship founded entirely on choice. All these ideas are shared by Euripides and Menander, while friendship was given a central role in ethics by philosophers, especially from Aristotle onwards.[53] On the other hand, besides reacting to changes in social structure, Euripides was also keenly concerned with the conventions and presuppositions of tragedy, the medium through which his reactions were expressed. Athenian audiences by his time included highly sophisticated literary critics and tragedy was a well-developed genre. In Euripides' plays it is frequently hard to draw a dividing line between the challenge to conventional social norms and the challenge to conventional ideas about tragedy.[54] His scrutiny of the content of personal relationships fitted the changing structure of Athenian society in the Peloponnesian war, but it was also an effective strategy for a new-style tragedy which, while still operating within the traditional framework of myth, gave the impression of applying a penetrating, skeptical realism to beliefs accepted without question by earlier poets.

Euripides' obvious concern with the conventions of the genre in which he wrote can, again, be seen both as a product of the development of the genre itself and as indicative of the greater prominence of common-interest associations in the increasingly mobile Athenian society of the later fifth century. One can see in ancient Greece a gradual evolution from the definition of specialized intellectual roles, with a privileged position in certain social contexts, to the formation of informal intellectual associations,[55] and finally, in the late fourth century and the Hellenistic period, the development of permanent organizations: philosophical schools in Athens, the Museum in Alexandria, the Panhellenic association of Dionysiac artists. It is only with this last stage, when intellectuals have their own functionally specialized organizations recognized by society, with their own financial resources, governing body, and representatives to defend their collective interests,[56] that the role can be said to be fully institutionalized. This process of evolution was not peculiar to intellectuals, although the presence of many non-citizen intellectuals in Athens certainly encouraged an emphasis on community of interest that transcended distinctions of political status. By the late fifth century, traders and bankers were beginning to form their own network of business ties and to be perceived as a group with distinct interests, although they scarcely developed a functionally specialized corporate organization even in the Hellenistic period. Politics, too, with the development of rhetoric, was becoming more specialized: by the fourth century the deliberately plebeian style of politics affected by the demagogues of the Peloponnesian war was beginning to disappear from the Assembly, though still to be found among military leaders. The fifth-century debate over the education of political leaders in itself indicated that success in politics was coming to be seen as the outcome of a conscious decision to embark on a political career. So does the use of the term *apragmōn* for the man who kept clear of political activity; it was the justification of the upper-class citizen who preferred a quiet life to the pursuit of honor and prestige in the political arena. The oligarchic speech-writer Antiphon created a new kind of reputation for himself as a political expert who advised others, but never spoke in the Assembly or sought office.

Antiphon was one of those who in 411 B.C. attempted to replace the government of the Assembly by a more oligarchic constitution. This short-lived venture, followed by the more extreme and disastrous *coup* of 404, both crystallized in the minds of the right-wing upper class the idea of an oligarchic alternative to democracy and made it appear unlikely that any future attempt to set up such a government could succeed. This is the situation in which Plato grew up. His family belonged to the core of the Athenian aristocracy and, the *Seventh Letter* tells us, he took it for granted that he would start to play a part in politics as soon as he came of age. He joined the Thirty, among whom he had kinsmen, in 404, but was soon disillusioned. The condemnation of Socrates by the restored democracy horrified him; and even if he had still wished for a political career in Athens, his association with the Thirty and with Socrates would have been difficult to live down. He had to rethink his position in Athenian society and justify his choice of the philosopher's role and the intellectual life (*theōrētikos bios*) in intellectual, political, and moral terms. This justification was elaborated gradually in works that seem to be directed to his own intellectual circle rather than to a lay audience. The theory is comprehensive, uniting in a single chain of reasoning the movements of the planets and the details of kinship terminology in the ideal city; but whereas in the pre-Socratics the comprehensive, cosmic scope of philosophical theory seems to be partly a response to the competitive situation of the philosopher and the audience's demand for a complete, clearly structured image, in Plato's case it seems to be his own need for integration that determines the range and unity of his theory.[57] It is the last confrontation between the intellectual and the city. Aristotle has not the slightest hesitation about the philosopher's role. Logic, ethics, political theory, and metaphysics were for him separate branches of philosophy, united only by the school's aim to cover the field systematically and by the demands of theoretical consistency and elegance of method. Social institutions and transcendental Ideas both have their place in the curriculum, but the effort of integrating them in a single theory has disappeared.

III

The story of the dialectic between transcendence and acceptance of a fixed status and limited sphere of activity in society does not, of course, end with Aristotle. But the period of the independent city-state in Greece provides enough material for some tentative generalizations.

No society is entirely imprisoned in the boundaries of time, place, social structure, and daily routine. In all societies men step outside their usual roles in ritual, endow their corporate groups with perpetual life, and believe in entities that exist outside space and time. Such transcendence of the limits of ordinary human experience and perception may well, however, be integrated into society by being assigned a special place in the rhythmic alternation of the sacred and the profane, or in the division of labor. Since transcendence always represents an implicit relativization of the normal social order and a potential challenge to it, those who have an interest in maintaining the social order will seek to contain and integrate transcendence in this way – to routinize it, one might say. Nevertheless, there are still moments when a new vision of society from a transcendental perspective stands out clearly as a challenge to established patterns of thought and behavior and, though it does not completely transform them, effects irreversible changes. It is some of these moments that we are studying here.

The question of the differences between the transcendent vision of the holy man and that of the secular intellectual will require a cross-cultural comparison. I can only offer here some tentative notes on the absence of the holy man, who derives his authority from divine revelation, in archaic Greece.[58] In the first place, Greek religion was polytheistic and Greek concepts of the ways in which the gods communicate with men were influenced by a monarchic model of the world of the gods. It was not Zeus himself, but lesser deities, who spoke and appeared to men. Zeus gives signs and omens, but not oracles[59] or revelations. This in itself limited the authority of revelation. Secondly, the aristocratic society of the archaic period preferred oracles to omens. Omens could only be interpreted by a specialist *mantis*; such holders of charismatic authority were a welcome check on the power of kings, but a disruptive element in the aristocratic competition for power, based on rotation of office. The interpretation of oracles could be decided by public debate; while omens were plain statements in a language that only the specialist knew, oracles were riddling statements in a language known and accessible to all.[60] Consequently the Greeks were predisposed by their experience of oracles to submit all revelations to public discussion and arguments about interpretation. The claims to divine inspiration made by poets and philosophers did not imply that their statements could not be questioned. A divine revelation could only achieve absolute authority if it was protected by secrecy.

It seems to be possible to distinguish four major moments in the development of the Greek intellectuals' conceptions of society and cosmos: Hesiod's vision of Boeotian society as part of a theological order, the pre-Socratic vision of a natural order in the universe, the search for a new moral order carried on simultaneously in the fifth century by tragic poets and philosophers, and Plato's demand for a radical transformation of society in accordance with a transcendental standard. Criticism, detachment, internalization, alienation. Hesiod's ideal order is an image of the social system he knows with deviance eliminated; he does not question the rules and boundaries of the social structure, but only the behavior of individual actors. The pre-Socratic model of the regular, eternal order of nature shows human society to be, by contrast, short-lived, contingent, and arbitrary; social norms and boundaries are relativized, but the possibility of alternatives is not yet seriously considered. It is not until about the middle of the fifth century that poets and philosophers begin to search for a new meaning in human actions and new definitions of virtue that transcend the norms of status and the accepted definitions of success and happiness. At the same time historians provide new models of political action that take account of the decreased significance of the boundaries of the city-state. It is this double movement toward the internalization of values and the conceptualization and realization of structures larger than the *polis* that is continued in the later fourth century. Plato's resistance to this trend stands out as exceptional; he insists that the philosopher must either transform the structure of the city, while maintaining its boundaries, or withdraw entirely from political society.

The preconditions for the contemplation of society from a transcendental perspective in ancient Greece are found in the position of the intellectual in society and the nature of his audience. His special skill gave him a privileged, though interstitial, place in his own society; and as a master of language he necessarily had the ability to recreate social relationships and manipulate them in thought. He also had, from the beginning, an audience that stretched as far as the Greek language was understood. The shared experience to which he appealed in communicating with his audience had to be one that transcended local and temporary interests. Homer, living in a society in which the network of relationships between aristocratic families in different cities was a major factor in political life, could move from one noble *oikos* to another, singing of the shared past of the heroic age, the over-arching power of the gods, and the common conventions of courtesy and gift-giving. Hesiod and the lyric poets were more immersed in local affairs, but the introduction of writing gave them a new audience in the future. The poet becomes an essential part of the process of communication within the city; at the same time he is detached from the immediate configuration of interests, no longer by a special knowledge of a common past and of the world of the gods, but by a special responsibility toward the future. His function is no longer to remember great deeds, but to immortalize them. An idealized image of equilibrium between the intellectual's claim to a transcendental authority and his place inside the city is reflected in the story of the Seven Sages. Their wisdom can be compared and is honored by Apollo of Delphi, whose authority transcends both city boundaries and human perceptions; but it is manifested in their capacity to give good advice within the framework of the city.

Nevertheless, one of the Sages, Thales, advised the formation of a league of cities to resist the pressure of the great land powers of Anatolia, and his advice was ignored. It became more difficult to have confidence either in the solidity of the external boundaries of the city or in the intellectual's freedom to disregard its internal divisions. Internal conflicts and external threats provided a basis for the monopoly of political power by tyrants; external dangers, in Ionia, made it necessary to take the measure of the states and cultures of the East. Mathematics, astronomy, and cosmogony replaced myth and religion as the basis of the intellectual's cosmopolitan culture. It was some time before the negative, relativistic attitude to social norms implied in this new transcendental vision developed into constructive study of the technique of argument and the nature of virtue. Meanwhile the procedures of political discourse had also changed, and so had conceptions of the nature and composition of *polis* society.

In fifth-century Athens the emphasis was on unity rather than internal divisions. Increasing social mobility was bringing the ordinary man's social experience nearer to that of the intellectual. In the archaic city the poet had presented the point of view of different groups and categories – nobles and *dēmos*, warriors and women – to the public as a whole. He had been part of a diffuse process of communication in which distinctions between topics suitable for the *agora*, the symposium, or other contexts were weak and easily overridden. In classical Athens the conventions of Assembly and symposium were more rigid; different modes of discourse had their separate compartments. The conception of the city as made up of groups of different age, sex, status, and interests, which appears in lyric poetry and also in ritual, gave way to a less supple division between citizens, equal and united in interests, and others. The interests of women, old men, young men, or groups from a particular village are now a subject only for comedy. The intellectual's own communications are assigned their formal context. They are still essential to the city, but they have a new function.

The dialogue in tragedy and philosophy is no longer between different parts of the city, but between the individual and society; not because the individual must defend his own rights, but because he has a responsibility to judge the quality of life in the community. Classical Athens was a society that did all its thinking out loud, and the thoughts that could not be properly expressed in the Assembly had to be aired elsewhere: worries that could be hidden by joking in comedy, deeper anxieties in tragedy, questioning of accepted conventions and values in the debates of philosophers. Socrates was conscious of thinking for the whole of Athenian society. Plato thought for himself and his pupils, and, from his time on, Greek intellectuals addressed themselves primarily to other intellectuals – except when they had to make themselves intelligible to the Romans.

It has, I hope, been clear from the above account that at every point the intellectual's comment on his society was subject to influence from a variety of directions: his relation to his rivals or predecessors; his audience's expectations, their conception of his social role, the conventions of genre and the topics appropriate to a particular social context or historical moment, their interests and the extent to which he and they share a common social experience; his own conception and experience of his place in society; the demand for novelty and the difficulty of communicating new ideas; his concern with the technical problems of art and argument, or with the mysterious processes of motivation and inspiration; the tensions between his need for approval and his need to maintain his own independence. The technical and conceptual problems of presenting the interaction of all these factors in a structural analysis are formidable. I have been able only to present a narrative description accompanied by analytical comments.

Two points seem to me to emerge from this account as particularly worth study from a comparative point of view. One is that new transcendental visions are, if I am not mistaken, likely to be presented by persons in a precariously independent, interstitial – or at least exposed and somewhat solitary – position in society; they are therefore particularly likely to occur in societies sufficiently differentiated to have specialized social roles with distinct bases of authority, but not complex enough to have integrated these roles into functionally differentiated structures. This might suggest that the reason for the absence of 'transcendence' in Egypt and Mesopotamia is the encapsulation of religious and intellectual specialists in the organization of the temple or palace. The second point concerns communication. One of the factors influencing the intellectual to adopt a transcendental perspective appears to be the need to make his work comprehensible to an audience widely extended in space and continuing indefinitely into posterity. How far is our own appreciative response to these works – and especially to the rationalism of the Greek philosophers – due to the authors' deliberate intention of transcending limitations of social structure and temporal horizons? How far is this successful transcendence due to content and how far to form, to the structuring of the communication in such a way that it contains within itself enough information to make it immediately comprehensible?[61] Is this a common quality of rational discourse and of 'classic' works of art?

10 Evolution and history: approaches to the study of structural differentiation*

I Social change, evolution, and history

The proportion of historical studies among the contributions to this seminar raised implicitly the question of the relation between historical studies of social change and a theory of evolution. It is of course true that nineteenth-century evolutionary theory was a way of seeing the world in historical terms: but surely no one proposes to revive evolutionism as a way of classifying societies on a historical scale running from the Lower Savagery of the Palaeolithic to the Higher Civilisation of the industrialised West. Nineteenth-century evolutionists put forward linear models of a unified world history; what implications have the change from unilinear to multilinear concepts of evolution and the sophistication in the use of non-historical comparative typologies developed during the functionalist period for the relation between evolutionary anthropology and history?

The historian may well feel tempted to start by remarking that social change can be studied in the field, while evolution cannot. Some anthropologists may disagree. Yet the term 'evolution' has traditionally implied concern with long-term processes and it also, I would suggest, implies a significant distribution in time of processes of social change: the processes which originally produced the incest taboo, the city, writing, or the State cannot be observed today.

No doubt it is possible to devise formal analytical categories which can handle both the emergence of culture and the modernisation of the Third World, but analogy with the development of synchronic structural theory suggests that the study of processes of change occurring in relatively simple societies may have a useful contribution to make. I am not personally much convinced that the comparative study of processes of social change – the comparison of

242

structures seen dynamically and not statically – will produce results which could appropriately be called a theory of evolution, but this is perhaps not very important at present: we can surely agree that such a study is worthwhile in any case.

Of the two case studies incorporated in this paper, the first deals with structural differentiation and the conceptual articulation of social functions (politics, religion, the economy); the second with the relation between structural differentiation and thought during the period when the early Greek thinkers transformed a religious cosmology into a scientific and philosophical account of the world. The ancient world provides abundant material on structural differentiation as well as evidence for processes of historical 'breakthrough' which offer a challenge to comparative theory.

Studies of social change in the modern world deal with the impact of highly complex societies upon simpler ones and consequently provide only a limited range of evidence for the study of structural differentiation. As Gershenkron (1962) has conclusively demonstrated, processes of development and modernisation in the modern world take place in a constantly developing environment, and changes in this environment modify the form of the process. The sequences of the process of economic development in a country industrialising with the help of foreign capital today are not the same as those of the Industrial Revolution in England. Similarly, the process of structural differentiation in a primitive society undergoing modernisation in a world which already has banks, factories, newspapers, universities, political parties and trade unions bears little resemblance to processes of structural differentiation in pre-industrial societies. In the latter the units created or modified by differentiation were simpler and in general changed more slowly, and combined in more varied ways. One of the questions most relevant to the problem of evolution, perhaps, is whether we can say that some of the structural configurations found in archaic societies had greater evolutionary potential, were more adaptable and more favourable to further differentiation, than others.

Study of the variety of structures exhibited by archaic societies and of the slow differentiation of new roles and organisations in them prompted the considerations of the concepts 'articulation' and 'setting' which form the second section of this paper. Particularly in using the concept of the social setting as a framework for interaction, I have tried to work with a conception of social structure which combines the on-the-ground reality of concrete social organisations with the models of appropriate behaviour which actors carry in their heads. For me, as a historian, the analysis of social change is not completed until its meaning to actors has been analysed. History is not merely a source of new specimens to be added to the anthropologist's repertoire of societies used in synchronic (or timeless) comparative studies; it is about processes of change and how people live in changing structures with models which accommodate and legitimate change. One of my main reservations about the concept of evolution in social anthropology is that it leaves aside this question of meaning in human action. To insist on the consideration of meaning does not imply that change is always intended, or even always perceived; what has to be shown is how objective changes in behaviour, perceived or not, are meaningfully related to previous patterns. The breakthrough in the biological theory of evolution came with the explanation of the mechanism underlying the process; so far no comparable development has occurred in social anthropology. Functionalism has signally failed to explain *how* societies adapt. Since in the history of social anthropology evolutionism and functionalism have appeared – however paradoxically – as opposed tendencies, I hope that the return to an evolutionary point of view implies an attempt to solve this problem. It may well imply also a divergence between studies focusing on processes of change triggered by alterations in a society's environment (physical or social) and those concerned with endogenous processes of elaboration and drift. An adequate theory of social change must however be able to account for both.

The third section of the paper contains an analysis of the process of structural differentiation in ancient Athens seen from the point of view of the resulting articulation of functionally differentiated institutions and conceptualisation of their reciprocal relations. Athenian society provides an example of a loosely-articulated social structure in which different social settings were free to develop their own norms and conventions. The dominant status of political values did not prevent the relatively autonomous elaboration of other values in non-political contexts. This loose articulation of the social structure permitted both the development of new roles and interaction-settings and the relatively free passage of actors from one setting to another which formed the preconditions for the development discussed in the fourth section of my paper: the new cosmologies replacing the implicit logic of myth with explicit reasoning put forward by Greek intellectuals in the sixth and fifth centuries. It might be possible to develop this line of research further to study the function of intellectuals in Athens as a source of explicit models of the integration of an increasingly complex society and culture. For the present, however, I have confined myself in the concluding section of the paper to more formal and methodological questions concerning the relation between evolution towards more complex social structures and the degree of choice available to actors.

II Articulation and setting: tools for the analysis of structural differentiation

Structural differentiation has been a central theme in studies of social evolution since the time of Spencer, and structural-functionalism equally recognised the utility of classifying societies as simpler or more complex according to the diversity of their component units – roles and corporations, the latter being defined as presumptively permanent regulatory units, i.e. units which outlive their members or incumbents and submit them to rules: lineages, formally constituted associations, estates and corporate status categories in general (e.g. slaves), offices, colleges, councils, etc. (see Smith, 1974). The assessment of complexity should include consideration of the way in which these units are articulated as well as their variety; the mode of articulation may be especially important in influencing the way in which further differentiation takes place in the structure, and for this reason is considered at some length here.

All societies must organise the flow of their personnel into roles and groupings in such a way that individuals are not normally required to perform incompatible roles simultaneously. Although most societies use a number of modes of articulation in combination, different modes predominate in different structures and contribute to their characteristic configurations. The following list of examples is not intended to be exhaustive, and concentrates mainly on articulation in relatively simple social structures.[1]

Segmentary articulation, that is, replication of units of similar form and functions arranged in a pyramid of increasingly inclusive units, occurs over the greater part of the scale of societal complexity, being exemplified by the relation between central and local government in modern states as well as in the segmentary lineage systems of acephalous tribes. As these examples indicate, segmentation may or may not be accompanied by organisational hierarchy. Hierarchically ordered segmentary systems are more complex than those which rely solely on differences of situational relevance to decide which unit shall act in a given case.

One of the simplest modes of articulation in societies which have more than one type of corporate group has been well described by F. Gearing (1958) as the 'structural pose': the whole society changes formation simultaneously as it moves from peace to war, from ritual to political debate, or from one type of economic activity to another.

For functionally differentiated organisations to operate simultaneously and continuously, other modes of articulation must be found. All (male) members of the society may serve in each organisation for a limited period, either based on an age-grade system or some other form of rota allocation; in either case the selection of those due to serve may be made individually or by groups. (The rota principle is also used, as an alternative to simultaneous change of structural pose, to allocate leisure periods within a serving or occupationally specialised group.) In relatively undifferentiated societies individuals may also be left to divide their own time between spatially segregated organisational settings requiring different roles and behaviour-patterns: farm, village centre, hunting country, town market.

Different roles, statuses, and contexts may or may not be differentially ranked in the value-system of the society. Age, sex, jural or ritual statuses may so far outweigh any others that there is no context in which they are not relevant; and the ideologies supporting such ranking may vary considerably in their degree of elaboration. In the Indian caste system strong emphasis seems to be laid on the relevance of the rules of ritual purity to personal interaction in all contexts, although this does not imply that caste hierarchy is preserved in power relations outside the ritual sphere. Helot status is likely to have been much more pervasively relevant in ancient Sparta than slave status in Athens. The ranking of roles and statuses may be closely linked with the ranking of types of activity. In a militaristic society it may be impossible to argue publicly that public finances are insufficient for war. Late Antique holy men could cow even emperors; but such a concentration of value in a single charismatic role could hardly have been tolerated if the role had not also been firmly associated, normally, with a peripheral position in society. Beyond village level, the Holy Man operated as an outsider (Brown, 1971). The question of the range of relevance and the ranking of religious, political, and economic values and statuses is problematic in many societies: I return to this point below in the discussion of structural differentiation in ancient Athens (see also the discussion of religion and law in the twelfth century A.D. in Brown, 1975). Value-ranking may, further, assign alternative patterns of behaviour and types of relationship to different stages of the individual's life cycle, as in the case of alternative mating patterns in some West Indian societies (Smith, 1962a), or homosexuality in classical Athens.

A fuller study of the relation between modes of articulation and value-systems cannot be attempted here. All that has been done is to point to a few cases where values appear to play a crucial role in articulation. The extent to which principles of articulation are explicitly asserted and elaborated ideologically seems to be very variable.

The examples so far given illustrate alternatives to articulation through full-time occupational specialisation. As occupational specialisation develops it seems to be accompanied by the development of an increasing number of what one might call 'service' institutions, specialising in exchange, communication, and arbitration. Even in simple forms occupational specialisation requires some system of redistribution or mechanism of exchange: palace 'rationing', market-place, or the formal redistribution of the village harvest in the Indian *jajmani* system.

Such service institutions may have either a central or a peripheral place in the social structure; they may be a part of the apparatus of the state (lawcourts, planning ministries), or their efficacy may depend on segregation from the everyday context of social relationships. Appeal to oracles takes disputes into the realm of the sacred; market-places provide a detached social setting, with its own rules of interaction, for 'disembedded' economic transactions (see, for example, Benet, 1957).

The concept of social structure as an articulated set of roles and corporations used above to define complexity might serve for the study of the process of differentiation in modern developing societies where new roles can be rapidly institutionalised on the basis of pre-existing models and new corporations set up by well-established mechanisms. In archaic societies, however, the process of institutionalisation could be very slow. In a sense the differentiation of the role of philosopher in ancient Greece can be said to begin with Hesiod in the eighth century B.C.; the process was fully concluded only with the establishment of fully organised philosophical schools four centuries later. Thus, although much structural differentiation does take the form of fission of existing corporations or creation of new, functionally specialised corporations of existing types (as in, for example, the proliferation of collegiate commissions in classical Athens as functionally specialised committees of the Council), there are other forms of differentiation which can only be studied by looking behind roles and corporations to find the matrix in which they develop.

Linguists working on phonetic change have found that the structuralist concept of language as a homogeneous system governed by unambiguous rules has to be replaced by a more flexible notion which takes account of variation in speech norms between one social context and another, in relation to the character of the social setting and the status of the speakers. Language is seen as containing 'variable structures . . . determined by social functions' (Weinreich *et al.*, 1968, p. 188). The emphasis in recent work has been mainly on the marked differences between formal and informal speech, and on the influence of speakers' models of correct or modern pronunciation on their performance, especially in formal test situations. Speakers are aware of differences in speech between classes and age-groups. Their model of linguistic rules is stratified, takes account of change over time, and allows for situational variation (Labov, 1972; cf. also Bailey, 1972).

Social stratification and social mobility naturally occupy a large place in sociolinguistic studies in modern societies. In an early study on semantic change using a similar approach, Meillet (1906) had already observed that 'seule, la considération des faits sociaux permettra de substituer en linguistique à l'examen des faits bruts la détermination des procès', and had emphasised that every social grouping has its own shared culture which includes particular turns of speech. Every occupation, recreation, deviant group has its own vocabulary created partly by assigning special meanings to words with a wider connotation in the language at large, and partly by borrowing or inventing new terms. Common interests and frequent communication provide the optimum conditions for the elaboration of this common culture and the acceptance of innovations. At the same time communication between members of different interest-groups makes it possible for such innovations to be spread beyond the setting in which they were originally introduced, often losing specificity in the process.

Let me give an example from anthropology. The term 'sibling', an Anglo-Saxon word which seems to have gone out of use in the early Middle Ages, was reintroduced with the meaning 'brother or sister' by physical anthropologists working on the characteristics of twins; they had learnt the word from Karl Pearson, who besides his statistical work in the Galton laboratory at U.C.L. had made a study of the early kin terms of the Germanic languages in which he asserted that 'sib' and 'sibling' came from a root meaning 'to suckle' (Thorndike, 1905; K. Pearson, 1897). Social anthropologists borrowed the word from the physical anthropologists some time later (Lowie, 1920, p. 26). Lowie was, of course, German; Pearson had studied in Germany in his youth and retained throughout his life a strong interest in German history and culture. Thus this innovation which has such obvious functional utility is the result of a complex chain of interactions across ethnic and disciplinary boundaries.

It is surely clear that this conception of rules of behaviour as linked to specific social settings, associated with differentially valued reference-groups, and evolving because people accept innovation from those whom they regard as associates in a common enterprise or as prestigious, has wide applications outside the sphere of language. It provides an approach to the study of processes of social change which can accommodate both the cases where change results from a conflict of interests, stressed by transactionalists, and the equally important cases where groups innovate, consciously or unconsciously, without conflict, because their shared values and aims lead them to do so. Even traditionalistic societies may develop an involuted elaboration of their norms (cf. Goldenweiser, 1936; Geertz, 1963) through a series of innovations which are accepted as being entirely in accordance with tradition.

An institutional setting, as understood here, is a concrete interaction-context defined for actors by spatio-temporal segregation and/or symbolic scene-marking devices, and associated with a particular set of roles and behavioural norms. Such settings vary in their degree of closure and in the specificity of their norms. Sacred places, 'total institutions' (Goffman, 1961), convivial gatherings of various kinds, theatrical performances, military settings, and the meeting-places of secret societies and deviant groups all exhibit relaxation or reversal of some of the norms of everyday public life with varying degrees of closure and tendencies to involution in their behavioural norms. In the ancient world the stylised conventions of the Athenian gymnasium and symposium are cases in point. Similar elaboration of rules and conventions, however, may also be found in political assemblies, lawcourts, market-places, places of work, etc.

III Structural differentiation in ancient Athens

As the above examples show, some institutional settings are dominated by and identified with corporate groups, while others are not.[2] Freedom to elaborate and innovate in different settings may be controlled by the mode of articulation of the institutions concerned, the proportion of corporation-dominated settings and the corporate structure of the society (cf. Smith, 1974, p. 261). Ancient Greece provides valuable material for the study of such differences, because different Greek city-states articulated very similar sets of institutions in different ways. The reorganisation of Spartan society in the sixth century B.C. placed the greater part of all social settings under the control of one or another of a set of interlocking corporate groups (men's houses, military units, age-sets) with explicit and well-integrated norms which left little place for innovation (see Finley, 1968c). Athens had a much less rigid social structure in which a considerable number of social settings with well-defined norms of behaviour were neither regulated by the State, corporation-based, or explicitly integrated into a comprehensive scheme of values: the market-place, the gymnasium, the symposium, the philosophical discussion, the workshop, the bank. The corresponding occupational roles – trader and shopkeeper, athletics trainer, entertainer, pimp, courtesan and parasite, philosopher, craftsman, banker – were not linked to any organised corporate units. Roles and settings developed together. In the theatre, tragic poets at first took major parts in their own plays, and the idea of acting as a special skill, deserving public recognition in the form of prizes as much as the gifts of the poet, was slow to develop; actors' awards began only about 440 B.C. Jokes based on parody, reversal, and inappropriate application of contextual norms are frequent in the fifth-century comedy of Aristophanes: assembly debates conducted by women (*Ecclesiazusai*), demagogic speeches in the idiom of the market (*Knights*), mock trial (*Wasps*), sale of children disguised as pigs (*Acharnians*), discussion of treaties in terms appropriate for food (*ibid.*). In the late fifth century upper-class young men at symposia parodied the Eleusinian mysteries and the conventions of the assembly and the philosophical discussion.

Symbols were used to mark the transition from one setting to another. Gluckman (1962b; cf. Kuper, 1971) has suggested that such ritualistic definition of social settings is likely to be found in comparatively simple, small-scale societies where the same persons circulate through all settings. (See however Goffman, 1956 for examples, on a more limited scale, from complex societies.) By the use of role-defining oaths as *rites de passage* the Athenians both marked the assumption of political roles and reiterated the norms governing behaviour in political contexts, particularly the obligation to leave aside all personal interests. Oaths of this kind were taken not only to mark the acquisition of citizenship and the beginning of military service at eighteen, but also whenever a citizen took office as magistrate, councillor or juror. Role-defining oaths were also quite frequently taken in the Greek world by mercenary soldiers entering service, and by armies before a particularly critical campaign or battle. There is really no reason to suppose that there is only one reason for the accumulation of ritual around social settings. Where the setting is one in which opposed interests conflict, the ritualisation of procedural conventions helps to limit conflict and tensions and to provide common ground on which opposed parties can agree (or about which they can disagree as a way of evading more serious issues). Furthermore, elaboration of these symbols of agreement may occur either because the parties involved legitimately wish to present themselves as the representatives of the community as a whole or because they wish to disguise non-democratic processes of decision-making behind democratic forms.

In archaic and classical Athens we can observe the process of elaboration of political procedure and norms governing interaction in a variety of settings. Some norms, like the rules of political procedure, are formally enacted; others are based on tacit understanding and enforced only by informal sanctions. It is with the latter, and especially with the conventions concerning the articulation of political, religious, and economic activities, and of the corresponding categories in Athenian thought, that the following discussion is mainly concerned. Athens, as has been said, seems to provide an example of a loosely-articulated social structure in which heterogeneous social norms applicable in different settings were integrated only by the segregation of the settings and the conventions – few of them enforceable by law – which associated different values and behaviour-patterns with different contexts.

Occupational specialisation developed only slowly: it is not until the late fifth and the fourth centuries that Greek thinkers begin to show concern over the question of the division of labour, and occupational roles become a target for ridicule in comedy. Antiochos of Syracuse (Jacoby, *F.G.H.*, 577 F.13), Herodotos, Hippodamos of Miletos, and Plato were fascinated by the idea of occupational castes; and we shall presently return to the debate over the fitness of urban workers for political responsibility. It seems that it was only in the later fifth century that specialisation developed in Athens to a point where different occupations began to be perceived as blocs in the society and not merely as isolated or part-time skills. The earlier assumption – which remained influential – had been that all citizens performed all roles in turn, moving from one context to another. Roles based on charismatic inspiration (poet, seer) or skilled crafts (potter, shipwright, smith) were not sufficiently numerous in the archaic period to affect the predominantly agricultural character of the society. This free circulation of persons through the roles belonging to different interaction contexts, on the implicit assumption that the appropriate norms and values would be respected in each case, prevented the development of an explicit, institutionalised hierarchy of roles and functions, and left the question of their ranking to subsist unresolved.

I believe that the analysis of this form of role-specialisation, associated with social settings rather than with particular performers or with organisations, and of its effects on the process of social differentiation in Athens, can throw some light on Athenian thought about the articulation of social functions and the relation between the individual and the State. Greek influence on our own categories of thought makes it sometimes easy to overlook peculiarities in the structure of Athenian society and social thought which are worth singling out for discussion.[3]

The main point to note is the progressive exclusion from Athenian political contexts of appeals to divine authority or to economic discontents. Assembly and Council were the dominant social settings of the city, and the fact that their activity was thus limited to merely administrative regulation in matters of religion and to public finance and taxation in the economic sphere tended to lead Athenians to overlook the central role played by the State both in the relations between men and gods and in the economy. (Aristotle – not an Athenian, but resident in Athens – is even weaker on religion than on economics.) Context influenced classification: the fact that public finance was discussed in assembly and council while other economic matters, with the exception of the corn supply, were not, prevented the development of a unified conception of the economy, and a parallel selectivity in the handling of religious matters in the same context tended to encourage a separation in thought between public cult and private devotions.

No attack on the primacy of political life was mounted from the side of religion before the rise of Christianity, though earlier developments in religion and philosophy prepared the ground. Revolts motivated by economic distress, though rare in Athens, were common elsewhere in Greece; but they aimed only to redistribute wealth and power within the existing institutional framework, and drew their justification from the dominant value of the political sphere, justice. The only attempt to create an alternative base of authority from which to criticise the values, norms, and operation of the political sphere came from the intellectuals – poets, philosophers, and historians.

The relation of the intellectuals to political authority is relevant in this connection because we find here what is lacking in the relation between politics, religion, and economics: the monopolisation of specialist roles by a limited number of individuals who thereby relinquish their opportunities of holding other roles and circulating freely through all social settings. Greek philosophers, like medieval holy men or nineteenth-century nonconformist industrialists, lost on the swings what they gained on the roundabouts. The way in which they developed their alternative basis of authority (which involves notions as fundamental to us as science, liberty, and conscience) was conditioned by the norms of the political settings from which they excluded themselves; in the first place by their acceptance of an association between secularisation and rational argument which was already well developed in political contexts by the late sixth century B.C., and in the second place by the need to find a different perspective and idiom from that of political debates.

Let us now look more closely at these two aspects of differentiation in Athens – the purely contextual differentiation of politics, religion, and economics, and the role-specialisation of the intellectuals.

(a) *Politics and religion*

It is clear that the gradual elaboration of rules of procedure and criteria of relevance in the context of political assemblies and councils in Athens, between *c.* 600 and *c.* 350 B.C., meant a progressive elimination of appeals to divine authority and religious feeling from the political sphere; and it is noteworthy that the process of secularisation here seems to have been carried out with far less polemic than in the intellectual transition from myth to philosophy. The relation between religion and politics is worth examining in more detail: it illustrates very well the peculiar characteristics of the process of functional differentiation in ancient Greece which were outlined above.

Leading roles in the religious sphere in ancient Athens can be divided into six classes. (1) The annually elected magistrates of the State (whose offices went back at least to the seventh century B.C.) each performed certain sacrifices and rituals; one of them, the *archon basileus*, had a special responsibility for supervising the organisation of religious festivals and presiding over the judgment of cases concerning religious matters. The 'kings' of the four tribes, Geleontes, Hopletes, Argadeis, and Aigikoreis, supported him in these functions. (2) A certain number of priests were also appointed annually in the democratic State, beginning with the priests of the eponymous heroes of the ten new tribes created by Cleisthenes in 507 B.C. (3) Other priesthoods created in the period of democracy were held for life by women appointed by the State. (4) But the life priesthoods which already existed in the seventh and sixth centuries were owned by descent groups (*genē, sg. genos*); these had their own complex norms of appointment, which tended to work in favour of hereditary succession. (5) Experts on religious law (*exēgētai*) were also appointed by the *genē*; from the time of Solon, however (early sixth century), the State had a second board of *exēgētai* selected by the Delphic oracle from candidates elected by the whole *dēmos*. (6) Finally, a charismatic commission as mantis, seer, and expert in matters of religion, could be held by anyone who could command sufficient credence.

Instead of a gradual separation of religious and politico-military offices and bases of power, we find that both were gradually thrown open to a wider range of candidates. Although by the later fifth century appeals to religious feeling in political debates were exceptional, it was never considered inappropriate for a politician to take a leading part in ritual or for a priest to hold political office. (The evidence on this last point has not been systematically collected, but it is a presupposition of the *genos* system that priesthoods and political office may be combined. Hipponicus, son of Callias of Alopeke, was both Torchbearer of the Mysteries of Eleusis and general in 426–5; Lycurgus of Boutadai was priest of Poseidon Erechtheus and director of Athens' finances in the 330s. Only in the case of the Hierophant of the Mysteries is it possible that taboos may have prevented the combination of religious and political office.)

If Homer is a reliable witness, at an early stage in Greek history the political authority of kings *was* sometimes challenged by seers. The model of the absolute, divinely inspired certainty of the prophet had its place in Greek culture; it is enough to refer to the figure of Tiresias in Sophocles' *Oedipus Rex*. But prophets were rare in the aristocratic *polis*. The appeal to oracles in the archaic period was characteristically an appeal to a divine authority located outside the boundaries of the State. We hear more of seers in the late sixth and the fifth centuries, but their claims to influence rest on learning and mastery of the technical aspects of ritual rather than on inspiration (they are the democratic counterpart of the aristocratic *exēgētai*), and their position is ambiguous: the *mantis* is a stock subject for jokes in Old Comedy, and Plato's religious expert, Euthyphro, complains (*Euthyphro* 3c), 'When I say anything about sacred matters in the Assembly, foretelling the future, they laugh at me as though I were a madman.' After the rules of rational discourse in political meetings have been fully established, we find attacks on the introduction of religious values into political contexts as a manifestation of superstition, lower-class ignorance, and lack of emotional control (Momigliano, 1973). But during the process of elaboration of the rules there is no sign of a split in the upper class between religious and rationalist factions. There seems to have been a mutual agreement progressively to limit the use of the long-range weapon of appeals to divine power. Even the intellectuals, for whom the secularisation of the cosmos and of the past involved a serious struggle with traditional beliefs, seldom found themselves radically at odds with society and traditional institutions on the issue of the relation between religion and politics; their criticisms of the irrationality of the political sphere were directed at the purely secular failings of tyrants in the sixth century and of the Athenian democracy in the fifth.

The combination of minimal specialisation in the religious sphere with the progressive exclusion of religion from political contexts may well have been one of the major preconditions for the development of something approaching a personal religion, alongside the public rituals of the city, in Greece. The growth of mystery cults in the sixth century might well be studied in relation to the elaboration of political institutions at the same period: the chronological relation between the increased popularity of cults which denied the relevance of social stratification and changes in the bases and political correlates of stratification is obscure. In classical times, it is clear that the segregation of religion from politics – which *de facto* implied subordination – meant that religion was increasingly regarded as a part of private life.[4] Furthermore, every level of organisation and every type of social grouping had always been represented in cult and had its own appropriate rituals: household, village, phratry, tribe, age and sex categories, occupations. A man's cult allegiances therefore expressed his identity and interests; as Athenian society, from the time of the Peloponnesian war onwards, became more urbanised, mobile and differentiated, many new voluntary associations with their own cults were formed; the range of choice increased, and this may have further encouraged the feeling that religion was a matter of personal idiosyncrasy rather than ascribed group-affiliation.

Public cult meanwhile became increasingly a matter of spectacle and the financial administration required to provide it. The tyrants in the sixth century and the democracy which followed the reforms of Cleisthenes in 507 B.C. had a common interest in bringing cult finances more firmly under State control and limiting the use of personal wealth in this context by rich men hoping for electoral favour. Competitions between tribal teams or choruses, a large number of which were instituted under the tyrants and during the first half of the fifth century, divided the cost of the performance between four or, after Cleisthenes, ten backers and the credit of victory between the backer and the actual performers. The liturgy system, instituted probably in 502/1, regulated the distribution of these financial burdens and the corresponding political advantages and laid down minimum rates of contribution. But in addition to regulating the use of private wealth in public cults, the fifth-century State, with its huge revenue from empire, could make private contributions appear insignificant by its own level of spending. A rich man could still win popularity by his generosity, and might sooner win an opportunity to show his capacities in office, but the city did not depend on his wealth. There is a marked distinction here between the city as a whole and its constituent communities, the demes, which did rely very largely on the wealth of their richer members and consequently tended to be dominated politically by them.

(b) *Politics and economics*

Research on kinship in ancient Greece suggested to me the importance of the increasing separation of public and private life in classical Athens. Political life, normally, belonged entirely to the public sphere; privacy tended to be equated with secrecy. Political manoeuvring carried on in private, 'behind the scenes', features in the fifth-century sources only when revolution is being planned. Religious life, as we have just seen, tended to be split into a public and a private aspect, but this separation was not problematic. (It was Socrates' critical examination of traditional values rather than his personal *daimonion* which disturbed the Athenians.) In the case of economic affairs, however, the boundary between public and private life did create tensions and value-conflicts.

In public life formal rationality in economic matters was fully accepted. Private contributions to the State's expenditure were, as we have seen, regulated through the liturgy scheme. Public accounting had begun in the temple treasury, where the need to keep the property of the god separate from that of his servants could not be questioned. (On the Acropolis, the property of Athena Polias had been supervised by a board of periodically elected treasurers, and not by the priestess, at least since the sixth century. In small country shrines where priests had more financial responsibilities the situation was sometimes different.) Pericles built up Athens' reserve fund in the fifth century by giving money to Athena: a purely secular reserve would have been too easily dissipated. There was no feeling of conflict between economic rationality – as being 'materialistic' – and religion. It is quite characteristic that the reform programme of Lycurgus in the 330s comprised both the reorganisation of Athens' public finances and a revival of traditional religion.

Our sources convey, however, a strong feeling of opposition between the economic and political spheres, in the form of anxiety over the intrusion of economic motives classed as private into public political decision-making. Although the economic consequences of alternative courses of action for public finances were carefully considered, it was a principle of the articulate Athenian Right that the economic consequences for individuals were a matter of purely private concern and should not be taken into account. Whereas economic calculation in the public sphere was associated with the ceremonial dignity of temple inspections and the formal presentation of accounts to Council and Assembly by outgoing magistrates, in the private sphere it was associated with the haggling, jostling, and trickery of the market-place. In economic transactions between the State and individuals, the progress made in regularising the State's receipts and expenditure did not lead to any corresponding increase in predictability for the individual. The demands of the liturgy system on the estates of the rich continued to be irregular in both cost and timing. Similarly, it was difficult for soldiers and rowers to know in advance when they would be called for service and how long the campaign would last. The surviving public financial records from the fifth century show clearly enough the very considerable difference in State expenditure between years of peace, in which tribute money accumulated in the Acropolis reserves, and the years of heavy fighting in which these reserves were depleted. The effects of war service on labour supply and of wage payments to troops on consumer demand were felt throughout the economy. It is scarcely surprising therefore that the *demos* did not disregard their economic interests when war policy was discussed.

The Athenian elite's refusal or inability to recognise that the State was a large-scale economic enterprise exerting a dominant influence over the whole economy has parallels in later history. Their emphatic separation of public finance and private economic interests is reflected in the Janus-head faces of mercantilism and classical economic theory: the one centred on the financial well-being of the State, the other on the behaviour of individuals in a market, while both equally distinguish the economic transactions of individuals from the legislative intervention of the State. There is therefore considerable historical interest in tracing the history of the boundary between economy and polity in ancient Greece.

In the Solonian crisis of the early sixth century B.C. in Athens, political and economic issues were closely related to each other. Checks on the economic exploitation of the poor by the rich went hand in hand with the extension of a minimum of political rights to all citizens; civic status and rights were correlated with different forms of military service and therefore (since the soldier provided his own equipment) with wealth. The further stages in the democratis-ation of the Athenian constitution were, however, achieved without any threat of revolution from below, by action initiated from within the upper stratum of Attic society. Economic issues played no part in the reforms of Cleisthenes and Ephialtes; and Pericles' economic interests were focused almost entirely on tribute, democratic political institutions, and the fleet. In the fifth century the State dominated the economy by participation, but this domina-tion was largely unrecognised and did not lead to any attempt at regulation by law. Economic inequalities were allowed to subsist while the process of democratisation in politics continued, with the sole exception of the introduction of pay for political service to ensure that economic stratification did not completely nullify the attempt to achieve political equality.

The growing use of slave labour and, in the fifth century, the increasingly important role of the State as an employer of labour, were crucial factors here. Rich and poor rarely confronted each other in the fifth century as employers and employed. Those em-ployed by the State were regarded either as self-employed contractors (working on public building projects) or as citizens performing their political duties (as soldiers, rowers, jurors, etc.). Competition for economic resources was deflected away from the private sphere into competition for control over the economic activities and policy of the State. This competition took, of course, a political form, and was staged in the assembly; its economic component was subordinate and, in the opinion of the literate upper class, illegitimate – an intrusion of mere irrational individual appetites into the rational dialectic of public decision-making.[5]

Further work is required to determine the extent to which this model of the relations between polity and economy in Athens is applicable to other Greek city-states, where the State's participation in the economy was in general far less significant. The subordination of economy to polity was of course equally definite, though differently articulated, in Sparta; and the subordination of private to public life was far more rigorous. It was Sparta which inspired Plato entirely to eliminate private life as the Athenians knew it from the social organisation of the Guardian class in his *Republic*; by eliminating property, the family, and the differences in education and way of life between men and women, he hoped to eradicate inequality and irrationality.

Most other cities were less successful than Athens and Sparta in freeing the State from dependence on the economic resources of wealthy individuals, and consequently tended to be both more oligarchic in government and more liable to experience revolutions and counter-revolutions motivated by clearly economic aims. However, even here Athens and Sparta provided institutional models and ideologies and, in the classical period, dominated the political and economic environment of their neighbours. The articulation of polity and economy in Athens and Sparta was not typical, but it was decisive.

The idea that citizens should be equal and similar in the political contexts of the city as they were on the battlefield in the hoplite phalanx thus led to a progressive hardening of the boundary between public and private life. This distinction between the public and the private, primarily concentrated in the political sphere, cut across the economy and men's relations with the gods. The consequence was that the economic and even to some extent the religious activities of the State came to be seen as sub-sections of the polity, while the economic and religious activities of the individual citizen were not considered to be the concern of the State, provided that they did not clash with the requirements of the public sphere. This proviso was, as we have seen, problematic already in the fifth century in the case of the citizen's private economic interests. In the case of religion it was perhaps inevitable, given the increased size, urbanisation, mobility, and heterogeneity of classical Athenian society, that the distance between primary-group rituals and public ceremonies should widen. In a secular State, this could easily bring a shift of focus, for the devout, from public safety to personal protection or salvation.[6] It furthermore enabled the intellectuals to accept traditional religious forms in the public sphere while developing new beliefs – rationalistic, metaphysical or mystical – in private.

The dichotomy between public and private religion helped to prepare the ground for martyrdom.

(c) *Individualism and intellectuals*

These conclusions perhaps suggest a new approach to the relation between the State and the individual in ancient Greece. Except in Sparta, the individual was only required to subordinate his own interests to those of the community in specifically political contexts. The dichotomy between public and private life, though it admitted little questioning of the primacy of the former (while the *polis* maintained its independence), left considerable freedom in the private sphere. The attempt to maintain a clear-cut distinction between political and non-political activity carried with it a *laissez faire* attitude to the latter and so set up the balance which would later tip to support the individual's claim to non-interference as a right. Although there is confusion and exaggeration in the claims for a 'discovery of the individual' in ancient Greece, some of the preconditions for the later development of individualism were created in classical Athens.

The freedoms of the non-political domain included freedom of thought and speech – at least within limits. This leads directly to the question of the position of the intellectual in Greek society. It is only in the case of the intellectuals that we have to deal with an influential category of *persons* standing outside the political sphere, rather than a class of *arguments* excluded from political debates. There were three bases of the intellectual's claim to a transcendental authority independent of the political sphere: art, reason, and revelation. The first is by its nature removed from possible conflict with political authority, and seems to have been stressed particularly by poets who stood in a somewhat dependent relation to their patrons (Homer, Pindar). But the primacy of reason over revelation in Greek intellectual history demands a closer consideration of the relation of the intellectual to the political sphere, and of the articulation of politics and religion.

As has been said, politically oriented prophecy of the Jewish type was very rare in Greece. Poets and philosophers who claimed special knowledge of theology described an eternal, ordered pattern in the universe; they did not transmit messages from supernatural beings. Even in the *Iliad* and *Odyssey* the interventions of the minor gods in human affairs are limited by the power of Zeus, who does not intervene in person; and the idea that even Zeus is powerless against fate is already present. Hesiod goes further, associating Zeus with an abstract principle of justice in the cosmos. Men and gods are irretrievably separated and estranged – the sacrifices men offer to the gods re-enact the deceit which caused the estrangement; the justice in the world of the gods is contrasted with the injustice in the world of men.

To some extent Hesiod appears to be reacting against the conventions of heroic epic. Homer presented his noble *basileis* as intimately associated with the gods, and often of divine parentage or ancestry; the association, by implication, emphasised the close ties between the gods and Homer's noble audience. Hesiod would not concede this to the *baslieis* of eighth-century Boeotia. Yet even Homer does not take his gods very seriously. If the eighth-century peasant could feel alienated from a religion dominated by the aristocracy, the *basileis* themselves were little inclined to let the gods get the upper hand. In a situation where each leading family had its own priesthoods and responsibility for a different element in the cult and festivals of city or countryside, a balance of power on earth required a balance of power in heaven – a balance guaranteed by the sovereignty of Zeus, who is bound by fixed principles and decisions taken in the past, whether his own or fate's. To claim a special relationship to a god implied involvement with the power-struggles of the upper class. There is some evidence that families of ritual specialists and seers were in fact absorbed into, or were a component in, the aristocracy, at least in Attica and Elis.

If the field of communications between gods and men was problematic, the business of communication between human groups was, on the contrary, full of opportunities. Poets were in demand, in the archaic age, both as bearers and creators of a shared culture which reached as far as the Greek language, and as privileged intermediaries between nobles and people in their own communities. Because poetry was not the language of political debate, poets could make comments excluded by the rules of the political arena. The ritualisation of poetry in classical Athens only increased this trend, restricting personal attacks to comedy, while tragedy raised the fundamental questions about the nature of Athenian society for which there was no place in the debates of the assembly.

In the seventh and early sixth centuries it was perhaps still possible that the intellectuals might have been, like the religious specialists, absorbed into the ruling elite. The legend of the Seven Sages, though it clearly reflects the unity of archaic Greek culture and the focal role of Delphi, also implied that there was a place of honour open to the intellectual in his own city. Power-struggles within the aristocracy had brought many cities to the point of exhaustion and breakdown; they were prepared to accept tyranny, the dictatorship either of the victor in the conflict or of a compromise candidate. Two of the Sages, Thrasybulus and Periander, were tyrants. Solon was offered the tyranny in Athens and accepted the position of lawgiver instead.

It was commoner, however, for intellectuals to find themselves subordinated to the tyranny of others, and to react either by emigrating or by turning their attention away from Greek society to wider horizons, to geography and cosmology. The Ionian natural philosophers found in the structure of the universe and the arguments of the lecture-room the principle of equality and procedures of debate which had disappeared from the city. Those who travelled to escape tyranny found themselves still cut off from politics by the fact of being strangers. Notions of citizenship were being formalised; the cities were beginning to turn in upon themselves.

The change in Greek politics brought about first by tyranny, and then by the increased formalisation of political procedures which followed it, was decisive for the independent stance of the intellectual. From the late sixth century onwards the ambiguities surrounding the position of the charismatic sage and of the poet – mediators between nobles and *dēmos*, between past and future – begin to dissolve. One might almost say that the intellectuals, from being middlemen, move into the position of outsiders. They are outside city politics and comment on them from every point of view which an outsider can take: comparing Greek institutions with those of barbarians, pro-pounding theories of the effects of climate on national character, setting the city-state in a wider context by writing histories of wars, satirising, asking fundamental questions in philosophical debate and in tragedy about the meaning of conventional values. Even though in Athens most intellectuals are citizens and not foreigners, they exert their influence through non-political media.[7]

This detached stance, though related to growing formalisation in the political sphere, was also encouraged by differentiation among the intellectuals themselves. Philosophers, doctors, and historians distinguished themselves from poets by their use of prose; their polemic against traditional myths provoked poets into finding new insights in the old stories. Conventions of genre divided up the intellectual's field of action. The large city audiences of the fifth century could be reached only through a formalisation and ritualisation of the context and techniques of communication.

Eventually, after the magnificent balance between formal discipline and profound, radical reflection achieved in classical Athens, the intellectuals of the late fourth century B.C. began to turn in upon themselves, to address themselves to a small band of disciples and fellow-professionals rather than to society as a whole. They drew apart from the city, justifying themselves with the idea of the *bios theōrētikos*, the contemplative life, as the highest type of occupation. But the true turning-point, as suggested above, came earlier: at the point when – approximately in the sixth century – philosophers and poets were offered a choice between a political role as sages and avoidance of politics. The majority chose to make their comment on society outside the political arena, and by this choice acquired the freedom to say what they liked – at the price of having their remarks considered irrelevant to political decision-making. Of course the fifth-century sophists did, indirectly, influence the character of Greek politics very considerably. There was even a somewhat abortive attempt to develop a literature of political pamphlets. But the boundaries of the different contexts of theatre, assembly, and lecture-room, and the conventions of genre associated with each, created a *prima facie* presupposition of non-interference. Just as the Athenian was expected to forget his private interests in the assembly, he was also expected to forget Aristophanes' jokes at the expense of prominent politicians. The sophists' criticisms of traditional religion and values were difficult to accommodate because they claimed to be telling a truth valid everywhere, in the temple as much as in the lecture-room; but even here the impression of intolerance produced by the prosecution of philosophers in fifth-century Athens does not imply any general restraint on free intellectual discussion. Parody of sacred rites or mutilation of sacred objects was of course another matter: this was considered a direct attack on the gods and the reaction was correspondingly sharp.

By choosing to speak outside the political context, Greek intellectuals set themselves free to travel – as some poets had done from earliest times. In the period of the sages, some (Pythagoras,

Epimenides) appealed to religion as the source of a wisdom which did not require knowledge of local conditions. But the majority worked to develop a new style of context-free communication, truth proved by argument instead of authority, general theories which encompassed the whole Greek world. The philosophical discussion and sophistic demonstration had, of course, their own conventions; but there was a new effort to make discourse status-free, to state explicitly, or question, hitherto unstated assumptions: to cut out the multiple channels through which an act of communication can be socially coloured, and let the words speak for themselves. This was the invention of formally rational discourse. The new idea of truth, the new role of the full-time intellectual, who lived by writing and lecturing, and the general increase in social and geographical mobility in the classical period, led to a new search for more abstract, situation-free definitions of values and norms and for a personal integration able to unify the manifold contexts of experience. The impact of Socrates on his contemporaries was surely due above all to their recognition that his disregard for conventions was inspired by a profound search for personal integrity and coherent values.

IV Differentiation and communication: the evolution of thought

I should like to pursue further the suggestion of a connection between structural differentiation, together with increasing mobility, and the development of individualism (or at least some of its pre-conditions) and of formally rational discourse, by connecting it up with the work of Basil Bernstein on the relation between communication and social context. I have analysed more fully elsewhere (chapter 9) the process of differentiation of intellectual roles in Greece, stressing the mobility of intellectuals from the sixth century onwards and the spiritual and/or physical withdrawal from involvement in city politics of the early Ionian philosophers, which may well have been connected with the rise of tyranny. Intellectuals were expected to innovate continuously; their writings travelled even when they did not, and many of the early philosophers in any case lived the life of wandering gurus on lecture-tour; they faced a variety of audiences of whose local affairs they had limited knowledge, and who had not much idea what the new speaker would have to say. Certainly the fact that the early philosophers became dissatisfied with the mythical and religious tradition which did form a common culture for all Greeks, and began to seek for a new kind of cosmology, cannot be explained by looking solely at the conditions in which they communicated their ideas. But the emphasis on formal rationality in argument, and on a relational cosmology which made explicit statements about the processes connecting one type of phenomenon with another, brings Bernstein's work readily to mind.

Some preliminary remarks on the aspects of Bernstein's work which are most relevant to the present theme seem to be required. If I understand him correctly, the essential difference between restricted and elaborated codes lies in the degree to which the message communicated is made verbally explicit (elaborated code) or left implicit and inferred from the hearer's understanding of a culture shared with the speaker and of information conveyed by the speaker's social status, tone of voice, body movements, etc., and by the context of communication (restricted code). The elaborated code is thus – in the extreme, ideal-type case – a single-channel, context-free mode of communication, the restricted code multi-channel and embedded in its context. Consequently, elaborated codes require a more highly differentiated lexicon (see further below) and syntax than restricted codes. Restricted codes will be used in small-scale, homogeneous societies or groups, elaborated codes between members of complex societies who occupy different social positions and consequently differ in social and cultural experience.[8] In addition, elaborated codes are found especially where the boundaries between functionally differentiated groups are weak and communication across boundaries relatively frequent: this was the case, I have argued above, in Athens, and the same is true of the Ionian cities.

It seems legitimate to see an analogy between the difference, on Bernstein's definition, between restricted and elaborated codes, and the differences of form between the mythology and religious cosmology of archaic Greek culture and the formally articulated arguments of Greek philosophy and science; and consequently legitimate to postulate a connection between the 'elaborated code' of this formally rational discourse and the increasing differentiation and mobility within Greek society in the period when it was developed, i.e. the sixth and fifth centuries B.C.

The central importance of the relation between speech and context is well illustrated by an example of restricted-code use given long ago by Malinowski (1923, pp. 310–12), in a case where social class is irrelevant. Men co-operating in a familiar technique have no need of an elaborate syntax but use a restricted number of stereotyped, laconic phrases – even if the operation is one where new decisions have to be made quickly in response to a changing situation, as for example in small boat sailing. Understanding of the context makes verbal explanations redundant.

Malinowski went on to contrast such situations with the context-free discourse of modern science – but later (1935, vol. II, p. 58) corrected himself, saying that the difference was 'only a matter of degree'. Even the language of modern science cannot be separated from its social context. Nevertheless, the relative distinction may be an important one. As Bernstein has recently stressed in making a distinction between speech code and speech variant (1973, pp. 11 ff.), the basis of the classification of restricted and elaborated codes is the way in which information is transmitted (how much by speech and how much by context); the form of articulation of speech is only an indicator of coding, and may also have other significations. The formal characteristics used in some of the earlier test work as indices of the use of an elaborated code (complex sentence structure, etc.) may carry their own social significance as status markers, may be part of the accepted style expected of all speakers in certain formal contexts (seminars, lectures). (In such contexts speakers may also, perhaps, be required to handle a subject-matter which itself consists of verbal constructs – definitions, theories, etc. The relations between the concepts of science, whether made explicit in a particular discourse or not, can only be learned from scientific texts and not directly from experience. Most communication on such topics is likely to require an elaborately organised form of speech, however small and intimate the group concerned.) Consequently the formal features which distinguish the explicit, exploratory use of speech from the repetition of acceptable formulae are not the same in all contexts.

These difficulties, however, concern the recognition of elaborated rather than restricted codes. There seems to be good evidence on the relation of speech to context in simple societies illustrating the formal characteristics used by Bernstein as indices of restricted-code use in small, homogeneous groups. Take Malinowski's observations on Kiriwinian (1935, vol. II, p. 36; cf. also Lee, 1959): 'The relation of the words, as well as the relation of the sentences, has mainly to be derived from the context. In many cases the subject remains unmentioned, is represented merely by a verbal pronoun and has to be gathered from the situation' (cf. Finnegan, 1967, pp. 75 ff.). Malinowski also comments (1935, vol. II, p. 66) on the lack of terms for general concepts, as opposed to the proliferation of particular terms in areas significant to the islanders (e.g. agriculture). This perhaps suggests that in lexicon and taxonomy, as in syntax, it is differentiation into hierarchically organised structures and not mere multiplication of options which marks the elaborated code, if one compares simple and complex societies; the difference probably would not be perceptible in comparing elaborated and restricted codes within a complex society, where the multiplicity of different activities makes general terms necessary for reference to occupational fields other than the speaker's own.

The essential point, however, is the use of implicit rather than explicit relations between words and sentences singled out by Malinowski. Labov's attack (1969) on Bernstein for failing to recognise the 'logic of non-standard English' in fact demonstrates that this logic, though perfectly adequate for vigorous expression of a simple argument, *is* implicit. Steps in the argument omitted by the speaker are supplied by Labov. The example (a New York Negro boy's statement of his reasons for not believing in Heaven) is too simple and brief to prove much; it does show that lower-class speakers in complex societies can produce effective context-free discourse (which should not in my opinion have been doubted), but it is not an example of fully explicit reasoning.

The distinction between implicit and explicit logic is related to Max Weber's distinction between substantive and formal rationality. (In both cases we are dealing with ideal types, and in concrete instances the distinction will be merely relative.) Take law as an example. A substantively but not formally rational system of law, based on equity – on the court's feeling for the just solution in each particular case – can only work smoothly and acceptably where norms are homogeneous and the circumstances surrounding each case are widely known. The decision is rational because it is an acceptable expression of shared norms in a particular context. More complex societies, however, require a formally rational legal system in which a common set of principles, from which applications to particular cases can be deduced, must be explicitly stated. The rationality in this system lies in the explicitly specified relation of lawcourt decisions to each other rather than in their relation to the circumstances of each individual case.

Most of the experiments of the Bernstein group have been concerned with specifically linguistic phenomena; but one, carried out by Dorothy Henderson, deals with the implicit logic of conceptual categories in a way which is very relevant to the present discussion. Henderson (1970) asked mothers to select the definitions they would use in explaining the meanings of words to their seven-year-old children. In each case they were offered a choice of four explanations: (a) a general definition, (b) an antonym, (c) a 'concrete explicit' example, and (d) a 'concrete implicit' example.

Cool
(a) It's a little bit warmer than cold.
(b) It's the opposite of warm.
(c) It's when something is no longer hot to touch.
(d) It's what you feel when the sun goes in.

Mix
(a) To put things together.
(b) It's the opposite of separate.
(c) It's what you do when you put different paints together to make different colours.
(d) When I make a stew the food is all mixed up.

The important point here for us is the difference between the last two types of example. (Working-class mothers chose more concrete examples and, within these, more of the 'concrete implicit' type.) In the 'concrete explicit' type the relevant feature of the experience offered as an example is explicitly pointed out. In the 'concrete implicit' type the child is left to infer it; the speaker assumes that the mixed-ness of stew and the coolness of the sun going in are equally obvious to everyone.

Henderson's 'concrete implicit' examples show the sort of implicit logic pointed out by Lévi-Strauss in the classifications underlying totemism and myth. (Note also the deliberate play on such implicit classifications in riddles, well developed in many primitive and folk cultures; cf. Finnegan, 1970.) Mythical thought, in contrast to scientific thought, is characterised by the use of concrete entities (*zoēmes*) rather than abstractions, and by the fact that their relationships are inherent in them and not separable from them, are left implicit and not explicitly stated. Anthropologists found myths, judged by nineteenth-century standards of formal rationality, illogical, until Malinowski pointed out the substantive rationality in the relation of each myth to its institutional context; Lévi-Strauss's treatment of myth can be seen as an attempt to provide a general structural-functional theory in which the *ad hoc* adjustments by which myths are adapted to different cultural contexts can be seen as manifestations of underlying laws of human behaviour.

Despite the revolution in the study of myth achieved by Lévi-Strauss through looking away from the relation of each myth to its context, to focus on the relation of myths to each other, his work demands a return to the study of myths in context. He has himself stressed the importance of this task (Lévi-Strauss, 1960). Because the symbols of myth are *zoēmes* and not arbitrary signs, and because their relationships are left implicit and not explained in the myth, the structural analysis of a myth can only be validated by showing its continuity with its cultural context. Furthermore, it is surely *because* myths are embedded in their cultural context that they are transformed when they cross cultural boundaries. The process of transformation can only be understood by studying it in context.

The evidence available for this task is at present lamentably inadequate. Most myths have been published only in translated plot summaries, stripped of all their contextual and auditory dimensions, supplemented to make explicit what was not stated in words by the narrator (compare the literal and free translations in Malinowski, 1935, and see Finnegan, 1967); most were recorded in artificial conditions, many from informants speaking the recorder's language and not their own. Lévi-Strauss's definition of myth as sense divorced from sound (1971) certainly fits most of the data he was using. Even those anthropologists who took care to collect verbatim texts were unable to publish more than a handful of them, and it is only very recently that attention has been paid to the context and mode of narration (cf. especially Finnegan, 1967, 1970).

Nevertheless, the limited evidence available suggests that myth resembles Bernstein's definition of a restricted code in three ways. In the first place, narrators of myth make extensive use of para-linguistic and kinesic channels of communication. Change of voice, sometimes accompanied by movement and/or music, or even developing into dramatic representation, gives colour to the personalities of the characters in the story (which are also coloured by the audience's knowledge of their exploits in other tales, as pointed out by Jacobs, 1960), and vividly conveys their emotions. (Contrast the quantity of words expended on these two functions in any modern novel.) The audience may be drawn into the narration by joining in the songs which punctuate it. (Cf. Bernstein's concept of 'sympathetic circularity' in restricted codes? The frequent use of repetitions in myth-telling might also be considered here.) Context radically influences the mode of narration; the same incidents may be classed as sacred lore, clan history or children's story, according to the context of narration and the status of the speaker (Firth, 1961; Finnegan, 1970) – a phenomenon which has surprised Western observers who expected to find differences of content between the three 'genres'.

Secondly, besides being a multi-channel mode of communication in which context and paralinguistic and kinesic signals play a part as well as words, myth is also, as Lévi-Strauss has shown, characterised by superimposition of codes within its purely verbal level. Different sets of categories – for example, modes of cooking, animals, meteorological phenomena – play out, in the same story, their own relations of contrast and association, without being explicitly harmonised with each other. The structural parallels between them detected by the analyst are only unconsciously apprehended by narrator and audience. Here again, where an elaborated code transmits an integrated message through a single channel, the restricted code juxtaposes several channels and leaves their relations implicit.

Finally, myth overtly displays at the verbal level a simple linear structure. It takes the form of a narrative: a string of incidents happening one after the other, the causal relations between them seldom explicitly stated. (It is probably this lack of causal connections in the narrative which, more than any other feature, led modern students to characterise myth as 'illogical'; lack of causal connections is also one of the traits by which nonsense verse is characterised.) Similarly, Bernstein's restricted-code speakers prefer parallel to subordinate clauses and use 'and', 'then', and 'but' rather than less common conjunctions, whereas elaborated-code speakers use a wide range of subordinating devices to build up complex sentence structures.

Geoffrey Lloyd (1966) has analysed in detail the development, in the early stages of Greek philosophy, of concepts and modes of argument which made explicit the relationships of contrast and homology implicit in earlier cosmologies (cf. also Parry, 1970). Much recent work on the history of science in the sixteenth and seventeenth centuries has likewise shown how modern science emerged through the process of making explicit, systematising, and testing patterns of thought inherited from magic and from pre-scientific visions of the world. I have myself tried to show, for ancient Greece, how the development of philosophy corresponded to changes in the place of the intellectual in Greek society and the introduction of new forms of communication in which the assumptions shared by speaker and audience were fewer and new ideas had to be presented in more explicitly structured arguments (chapter 9). During the time of transition between the first adumbration of the philosopher's role in the sixth century B.C. and the permanent establishment of philosophical schools in the fourth century, the basis of shared assumptions underlying communication between the philosopher and his audience was very limited; and these two centuries were a period of remarkable concentration on the formal properties of argument and classification, culminating in Aristotelian logic and taxonomy. It was also in the same period that the range of the philosopher's knowledge was greatest, and its subdivisions least marked. Plato represents the high-water mark of the 'integrated code' here; with Aristotle we are already moving from 'integrated code' to 'collection code' (Bernstein, 1971b), different topics being treated in different books and the integration of the whole teaching into a single cosmology receiving less emphasis. Aristotle in the 'esoteric' works we have is already addressing himself to students in his own philosophical school, who may already have some grounding in philosophy, rather than to a general public; almost nothing of his 'exoteric' writing for a wider audience has survived.

This last point indicates that if the distinction between restricted and elaborated codes can be applied to the evolution from mythical to scientific thought, the development traced will not be wholly rectilinear. Although some steps in the evolutionary process have irreversible effects – the introduction of writing is the most obvious example – trends towards restriction and towards elaboration may well succeed each other in an evolutionary spiral (I am assuming for the sake of the argument a society which is growing steadily more complex), as new social boundaries are drawn, harden, and later are again called into question. Kuhn's concept of paradigm-development and paradigm-change seems to fit in here (Kuhn, 1962). As a paradigm becomes established, the boundaries between the relevant and the irrelevant harden, and they are reinforced by parallel divisions in the structure of groups and organisations. Within each division the shared culture acquires greater density: communication becomes easier, more can be taken for granted. To some extent rivalry between or within groups may take over the function of ensuring explicitness of argument, when it is no longer necessitated by the novelty of a new paradigm and lack of a shared culture in the public to which it is addressed. Indeed explicitness of argument may become a general norm of scientific roles and contexts. As I suggested earlier, the abstract and verbal nature of the subject-matter of a developed science may make this inevitable. Nevertheless explicitness is never complete and the inclination not to state explicitly, and not to question, what everyone in the group knows, is strong.

'Strong framing' of knowledge, with well-institutionalised boundaries between subjects – which may be backed by educational specialisation from an early age – increases the need for elaboration and explicitness in any communication across boundaries. The effort has to be made, if shared culture is not to turn into shared illusion; and the reason why we may hope, in a complex society, that we are sharing belief in truth along with our errors, is that the complexity of the society does make full cultural homogeneity impossible and elaborated-code communication necessary.

V Differentiation, choice, and change

The preceding discussions of the articulation of functionally differentiated institutions in Athens and of communication-codes both imply a concern with the difference between restrictive and flexible social forms at approximately the same level of structural complexity as well as with the process of evolution from simpler to more complex structures. The difference between Athens and Sparta in the classical period lay in the articulation of the different elements in the social structure rather than in the variety of units involved. And groups may surround their area of discourse with 'strong framing' and accept statements on the basis of the status of the speaker and the context of speech, rather than explicit argument, in the most complex societies.

This indicates some of the difficulties of reviving the concept of social evolution in the present day. In the nineteenth century theories of social evolution combined three elements: the assumption of development towards increasing complexity, the search for laws determining a unilinear sequence of stages in this development, and belief in progress. The position now seems to be that studies of the correlates of increasing complexity do not imply any faith in progress, that the search for regularities in processes of social change is not associated with the assumption of a unilinear sequence and need not be associated with the idea of evolution at all (Smith, 1960, 1974), and that studies of the pre-conditions and genesis of developments which we still value as progressive (the incest taboo, sedentarisation, the city, the state, philosophy and science) coincide only partially with studies of social evolution in the formal sense of increasing complexity.

The axis of our comparisons thus seems to be shifting from the contrast between simple and complex societies to the contrast between adaptable and inflexible ones (for parallel developments in evolutionary biology see Huxley, 1954). But how do societies adapt? To answer this question, we need further research on two topics in particular: forms of social integration or institutional articulation, and the ways in which change is legitimised. Human societies both utilise institutionalised mechanisms of adaptation and are composed of thinking individuals whose actions are influenced by their perception and interpretations of what goes on around them.

The study of communication obviously provides a link between the two problems. Bernstein's work on communication as a mechanism of social integration – and of social control – continues the work on exchange in homogeneous and in differentiated structures begun by Mauss (1925a). Communication in a restricted code, like gift-exchange, is part of a *fait social total* in which medium of exchange, social context, and status of actors are linked together. Elaborated-code communication, like 'general-purpose' money (Bohannan, 1959) or complex forms of marriage (Lévi-Strauss, 1966) enables actors to handle a much wider range of situations with an instrument which they perceive as differentiated, not attached to particular settings and statuses. Such mechanisms of exchange and communication facilitate adaptation not only because they are relatively (not absolutely) context-free, but because they are thought of as being context-free and available for use in new circumstances. 'Elaborated codes . . . contain the potentiality of change in principles' (Bernstein, 1973, p. 200).

Thus the institutional study of adaptive mechanisms in society leads back inevitably to the question of the actors' perceptions and experience. We cannot compare the capacity of different societies to change, and the amount of choice allowed to their members, without asking how change and choice are perceived.

As well as developing more dynamic and variable models of social structure in their own work, anthropologists need to recognise that actors too have dynamic and variable models of the structure of their society. The ideal-type traditional society whose members believe that nothing ever changes would be extinct by now, if it ever existed. Actors' models are not synchronic maps of a total social structure of the type produced by structural-functionalist ethnographers, but diachronic in scope and uneven in coverage. They are based on concrete experience of social settings and the norms of behaviour attached to them, and at the same time they shape the actor's perceptions of his experience. The study of processes of structural differentiation raises particularly interesting questions about the perception of changes in social structure. Sometimes the introduction of a new institutional setting creates the conditions for the rapid development of new clusters of norms – as in the case of the introduction of dramatic competitions in classical Athens; sometimes it is a new role which develops and only slowly becomes attached to particular settings (the Greek philosophers: see Gernet, 1945). The study of the process of differentiation of political, economic, and religious functional spheres (which of course have different boundaries in different societies) prompts questions about the conceptualisation of these functions and their articulation. Here, if anywhere, it should be possible to demonstrate the relation and interaction between the boundaries of institutional groupings and of conceptual categories. If the study of social evolution is no longer an end in itself, it is still an important approach to the understanding of societies in time and in change.

Notes

1 Anthropology and the classics

   *This paper was delivered to the annual meeting of the Council of University Classics Departments in January 1974.

1   The study of *mētis* was also influenced by G. Dumézil; it was an attempt to study Greek concepts of sovereignty as well as the treatment of ambiguity in Greek myth.

2 History, economics and anthropology: the work of Karl Polanyi

1   Desai, 1968 (with earlier bibliography); Gershenkron, 1967; Conrad *et al.*, 1967; Vilar, 1965.

2   Gershenkron, 1967; Goodrich, 1960; Mair, 1957, especially pp. 9–22, 'Applied anthropology and development policies' (1956).

3   Polanyi, 1957a, pp. 68, 71; Mauss, 1925a. Talcott Parsons's 'structural differentiation' (Parsons, 1951, chapters 4–5; Smelser, 1959a) is a much more precise and useful formulation of what Polanyi calls 'disembedding'.

4   Polanyi, 1957a, pp. 241–2, 248–50. This does not mean that *only* activities concerned with the supply of material means are included in the economy.

5   For householding, cf. Polanyi, 1944, p. 60; 1966, chapter 5, 'Householding: land and religion'; for other definitions, Polanyi, 1957a, p. 250. I use the term 'market exchange' instead of Polanyi's 'exchange' to avoid ambiguity, since reciprocal gift-giving may also be regarded as a form of exchange.

6   Cf. Seton Watson, 1911; Valiani, 1966; Ignotus, 1961. I am not attempting here a biography of Karl Polanyi; some further details of his background may be found in the obituaries by his daughter Kari Levitt (1964) and by Bohannan and Dalton (1965), and in Zeisel, 1968. Cf. also Duczyńska, 1963, and the account of Polanyi's activities as a leading member of the Galilei Circle in Tömöry, 1960 (I should like to thank Dr L. Peter for telling me of this book, and Dr M. Boskovits for translating parts of it for me). [See further now the excellent account in Salsano, 1974.]

7   For the Law syllabus see Surányi-Unger, 1930, written under the Horthy regime and almost completely ignoring the previous unofficial left-wing sociology; Becker and Barnes, 1952, pp. 1078–81; Lukács, 1955; and the account of Sorokin's university years in Russia in his autobiography (Sorokin, 1963). [On Lukács see now Lichtheim, 1970.]

8   Mannheim, 1934.

9   I know no comprehensive study of the influence of Marx and Marxism in sociology, but cf. Parsons, 1928–9; Adler, 1957; Hughes, 1958.

10   Polanyi, 1922. His concern, at this time as later, was with the quality of social life rather than the details of economic organization. For the quite

276

different issues with which economists at the time were concerned see Dobb, 1965.

11 Polanyi, 1934c; cf. 1934b, 'Lancashire im Fegefeuer'. (Polanyi continued to write for the *Österreichische Volkswirt* from England during the latter part of 1933 and in 1934.)

12 Polanyi, 1932; cf. 1944, pp. 33–4.

13 Polanyi, 1934a. R. Firth's comment on a New Guinea co-operative society's subscribers' meeting provides a striking parallel: 'The public character of this presentation, its formal, almost ritual atmosphere, and the organization involved, all show the serious committal to community purposes which marks so many of the large-scale economic enterprises of the New Guinea people' (Firth, 1964, p. 202).

14 Popper, 1945, vol. I, p. 190, n. 30.

15 Popper, 1945, vol. I, pp. 26–7. This interest in nominalism can be traced back to the discussions of the Galilei Circle, in which the theories of Ernst Mach were an important influence. The Circle's second publication was a translation by Polanyi of part of Mach's *Analyse der Empfindungen* (Mach, 1910). If I am right in supposing that Polanyi tried to apply Mach's method in the social sciences, this is a new example of the wide range of Mach's influence – which deserves further study.

16 Polanyi, 1959, p. 165; cf. 1957a, p. 245.

17 Polanyi, 1960, p. 330.

18 Popper, 1945, vol. II, pp. 89–90, with p. 308, n. 11. Polanyi's emphasis on operations probably owes something also to George A. Lundberg's sociological theory of 'operational definitions'; Polanyi may have come into contact with Lundberg when he was at Bennington College in 1943. But he was already familiar with a similar methodological approach from his study of Mach.

19 I have to thank Jean Floud for directing me to the work of Löwe and Heimann. Heimann admired *The Great Transformation* (Polanyi, 1944), which he cites several times in his own works (Heimann, 1947, 1955, 1963), though for its historical analysis rather than its policy. Löwe evidently did not; he never refers to it, nor does K. Mannheim. Löwe's pupil Robert Heilbroner (1962) seems to me, *pace* Dalton (1968, p. xii, n. 4), to be little influenced by Polanyi.

20 Parsons, 1940. Polanyi also had much in common with the American 'institutionalist' economists, though I doubt if institutionalism directly influenced his work to any significant extent.

21 For the teaching activities of the Galilei Circle see Tömöry, 1960. Polanyi's admiration for English socialism is clear in his articles for the *Österreichische Volkswirt*.

22 On Fascism see Polanyi, 1937, and Polanyi, Lewis, and Kitchin, 1935. For debate on the compatibility or incompatibility of planning and freedom, cf. the work in this period of, for example, Heimann, Popper, Mannheim, Michael Polanyi, and F. A. von Hayek.

23 Hildebrand, 1946.

24 E.g. Sorokin, 1941, 1948; Mannheim, 1943. On Mannheim and Utopianism see Shklar, 1966. Manuel (1966b) shows that Utopianism is not, as is often claimed, defunct. Polanyi (admittedly a very minor figure as a Utopian) is of some interest as standing midway between the old economic Utopianism and the 'Utopias of love', if one may so call them, discussed by Manuel. The Hippies might be regarded as the Utopian movement corresponding to this new type of Utopian theory (cf. Eisenstadt, 1965).

25 Polanyi's account of reciprocity (1944, pp. 54 ff.) is based on Malinowski's *Argonauts* (1922); his conception of redistribution was of course derived from Thurnwald (1932, pp. 106–8; cf. Polanyi, 1944, pp. 261–70).

26 E.g. Kelter, 1935; Lacour-Gayet, 1945; Mund, 1948; Einzig, 1949; Simiand, 1934. For the conception of the later Roman Empire as a 'totalitarian' economy see the bibliography in Heichelheim, 1948, pp. 1123 f. (chapter 8, n. 1), and Frank, 1940, p. 303.

27 Laum, 1914, 1924, 1933. His *Schenkende Wirtschaft* (1960) relates aid for underdeveloped countries to primitive gift-exchange. Cf. also below, n. 157.

28 See the preface to Polanyi, 1957a.

29 The unpublished *Towards a New West* belongs to 1958, the work of organizing *Co-Existence* began in 1960. See Polanyi, 1962; Levitt, 1964; Medow, 1965.

30 Sievers, 1949. Polanyi is compared to Adam Smith and Marx.

31 Polanyi, 1957a, in its published form, dates mainly from the years after Polanyi's retirement in 1953 (cf. the preface). He still published in 1947 an article, 'Our obsolete market mentality' (Polanyi, 1947), on the views he had developed in *The Great Transformation* (1944).

32 It also reflects, of course, the move to a world which was politically less liberal; Polanyi's wife, having belonged to a Communist Party, was not allowed to enter America (they made their home in Canada).

33 Dalton, 1962, 1964. Cf. Polanyi, 1944, pp. 159 ff.

34 Polanyi, 1960.

35 Polanyi, 1964 is a briefer version of Polanyi, 1966, chapter 10.

36 Polanyi, 1959, 1957b.

37 Dalton, 1959, Cf. Dalton, 1960, 1961, 1962, 1963, 1964, 1965a, 1965b, 1966, 1967.

38 Cf. Steiner, 1954; Bohannan, 1955.

39 Bohannan, 1959.

40 Sahlins, 1965a, 1965b, 1960, 1968, [1972].

41 Cf. especially Nash, 1965, 1966; Belshaw. 1965. For other work on markets see below, n. 74.

42 Godelier, 1966.

43 Meillassoux, 1960, 1964. He contributed to Bohannan and Dalton, 1962, and announced a further programme of study of African economic systems in 1966 (p. 445). [See now Meillassoux, 1971, 1975, 1976.]

44 Smelser, 1959b; see also Smelser, 1963.

45 Cf. Moore and Feldman, 1960, especially Hoselitz, 1960; also Moore, 1967. It is particularly clear in the case of Moore that to an American sociologist with a background of institutionalist economics Polanyi simply represents a convenient extension of familiar theories to the field of non-market economies. (Cf. also Usher, 1944, and Clark, 1948, p. 5.)

46 Leeds, 1961; Sinha, 1968.

47 Cf. also Will, 1954a.

48 Rostovtzeff, 1933. The same formulation still occurs in anthropological discussions, e.g. Firth, 1967a, pp. 97, 111. Note Dowd's more precise distinction (1967) between growth as quantitative change and development as structural change.

49 There were only three reviews of Polanyi, 1957a by ancient historians: Heichelheim, 1960; Leemans, 1958; de Sainte Croix, 1960. Polanyi replied in 'Ports of trade' (1963).

50 Cf. the discussion and bibliography of Vidal-Naquet, 1965. On land, Finley, 1952, 1953, 1957a, 1968b. On labour, Finley, 1959, 1960a, 1964, 1965a, 1965b, 1968d.

51 See also Finley, 1955. The implications for Greek economic history of Mauss's 'Essai sur le don' (1925a) had previously only been explored by Louis Gernet (see below, chapter 3).

52 Finley, 1965d, cf. 1965c.

53 Burford, 1969; Austin, 1970.

54 Cf. Oppenheim, 1964; Mallowan, 1965; Gelb, 1967.

55 Already in Oppenheim, 1954; cf. 1964, chapter 2, and 1967.

56 Oppenheim, 1964, p. 129; Saggs, 1962, pp. 279–80.

57 Cf. Polanyi, 1963, p. 41.

58 Bibliography to 1965 in Firth, 1967; add Scott Cook, 1966; Cancian, 1966; Godelier, 1966. [See now H. Schneider, 1974; Godelier, 1973.]

59 Cf. Mair, 1934.

60 Polanyi, 1944, pp. 64 ff.; 1957a, pp. 256 ff.; 1966, p. xxiii.

61 In ancient history by Kraay, 1964; cf. Vidal-Naquet, 1968b; Will (1954b, 1955) also stressed the non-commercial features of early Greek coinage (following Laum, 1924, 1952; see also Gernet, 1948a). He particularly emphasized taxation and the early function of money as a standard of value in judicial contexts. See also P. Grierson, 1961 and other papers in *Moneta e scambi*, 1961.

62 Cf. Bohannan, 1955; Douglas, 1967; Godelier, 1966, pp. 274 ff.

63 Cf. M. Lambert, 1963.

64 Polanyi, 1944, p. 61; influence of the 'Modernist' school in ancient economic history, especially, probably, Heichelheim, 1938 (chapter 7) and 1930. On Greek banking see now Bogaert, 1966, 1968.

65 Benet, 1957; cf. Benet, 1961.

66 It was, however, as is shown by Maunier, 1927, a very calculating form of reciprocity.

67 Polanyi, 1957a, pp. 68 ff. Polanyi's distinction is explicitly related here to Tönnies's *Gemeinschaft* and *Gesellschaft* (Tönnies, 1887) and Maine's 'status' and 'contract' (Maine, 1861), with Hegel and Marx associated with the 'sociological background' of the distinction.

68 See especially Polanyi, 1960.

69 Polanyi, 1957a, p. 87. The weakness of this account of the Greek economy is mainly due to a confusion between the disembedding (structural differentiation) of the economy and the formation of a system of interconnected price-making markets.

70 Kraeling and Adams, 1960, pp. 216–18.

71 Polanyi, 1957a, p. 255.

72 Cf. also Solomon, 1948; Hoselitz, 1960.

73 Polanyi, 1957a, p. 255.

74 See especially Bohannan and Dalton, 1962; Firth and Yamey, 1964; Mintz, 1959; Skinner, 1964–5; Nash, 1965, pp. 125–7.

75 Uchendu (1967) makes some useful preliminary distinctions. Mead (1937) deals with marketless societies.

76 For temporary price-fixing in periods of scarcity, cf. Bohannan and Dalton, 1962, pp. 196, 422; Gluckman, 1965, pp. 190–2.

77 As Polanyi stressed, the sale of cooked food plays an important part in many primitive markets. In Dahomey wholesalers watched the market and adjusted their prices to leave the market women a 20 per cent mark-up (Herskovits, 1938, vol. I, p. 55).

78 [Aristotle], *Constitution of Athens* 51.3. Cf. Francotte, 1910, pp. 291–312. For fixed prices, Schulhof and Huvelin, 1907; Feyel, 1936.
79 Bauer, 1954, p. 391. The studies in Bohannan and Dalton, 1962, however, show that there is considerable local variation in the degree of formal organization of associations and pricing.
80 Twitchett, 1966, 1968.
81 Cf. Francotte, 1910, pp. 291–312.
82 But this is seen as a group situation rather than an individual one.
83 Tardits and Tardits, 1962.
84 Mintz, 1961; Yamey, 1964, p. 383; Dean, 1962–3 (a study of the influence of tribal affiliations, age and sex, not personal ties); Uchendu, 1967.
85 Baldwin, 1959; de Roover, 1951; Dempsey, 1943.
86 The speaker in [Demosthenes] 34.39 emphasizes his generosity in selling voluntarily at the usual price (*tēs kathestēkuias timēs*, five drachmas) and not at the market price of sixteen drachmas; the *kathestēkuia timē* therefore is not a fixed price, though it *may* be the price 'set' by the State on this occasion for re-selling corn purchased with its own funds. *Estēkuia timē* as fixed (maximum) price occurs in *P.Teb.* 703, 174–81; cf. Welles, 1949, p. 34, n. 71 (a reference I owe to O. Murray).
87 Huvelin, 1897, especially pp. 194 ff., 383 ff.; Laurent, 1932.
88 Sahlins (1965b) raises other questions about the study of 'prices' in gift-exchange.
89 But in his article on the port of trade (1963), Polanyi classes the medieval European *portus* also as a port of trade. Cf. Weber, 1923, pp. 188 ff. (pp. 213 ff. of English translation).
90 Belshaw, 1965, pp. 92 ff.
91 Leeds, 1961.
92 Polanyi, 1957a, p. 116.
93 Polanyi, 1957a, p. 263.
94 Revere, 1957.
95 On Hittite attitudes to the sea see now Hoffner, 1967, p. 182; on Bronze Age Crete, Starr, 1955. Even in the fifth century the Athenians failed to demonstrate that sea-power could prevail against land-power, and it is not clear that Pericles aimed to do more than show Sparta that Athens was invulnerable (Thucydides 2.65.7). Alexander conquered a large part of the Persian empire without having control of the sea. See further Momigliano, 1944.
96 Herodotus 5.36; Thucydides 1.143.3–5. The account of the campaign of Sphacteria, Thucydides 4.26, shows how difficult it was for ancient warships to keep up a blockade.
97 La Foire, 1953.
98 E.g. Bücher, 1893; P. J. Hamilton Grierson, 1903; Wilamowitz-Moellendorff, 1880, pp. 195–202 ('Der Market von Kekrops bis Kleisthenes'); Lehmann-Hartleben, 1923, pp. 14 ff., 31 ff.
99 The Greek *agora* was both assembly place and market, a central focus of the life of the city. And the city was not marked off from the countryside by a different political and jural status: there was no distinction between *castrum* and *bourg*. The medieval model of the market which springs up outside the city is not applicable here. The oriental equivalent of the Greek *agora*, however, seems to have been just outside the city gates; cf. Seston, 1967a, 1967b. Assyrian sources refer to selling at the gates of the city.
100 Cf. Wood, 1935.
101 Polybius 3.22.8–9.

102 Cf. Finley, 1965c, pp. 26–7, 34, and chapter 4 below (pp. 117 f.). There is a great deal of re-thinking to be done about corn production and distribution in the ancient world, and Polanyi's distinction between redistributive and market institutions should play an important part in it. Fixed prices in 'administered trade' must be studied in this context of royal or state monopoly. The citizen freeholdings of the Greek cities and Rome were small islands in a world in which tenure was normally of the redistributive or 'Asiatic' type (i.e. the peasant paid taxes, and the privileged classes held large estates ultimately derived from the State). Until the spread of state intervention under the Roman empire, the redistributive system was linked to the market institutions of the cities by the independent shipper and the tax-farmer, and by the profit-making activities of the kings (see Will, 1966, pp. 148–78, for the symbiosis of Ptolemaic state control and Rhodian private trade). Plantation farming for the market, like the 'capitalistic' business associations of tax-farmers (and the Babylonian 'bank'; cf. Szlechter, 1947),' developed in a predominantly redistributive situation and must be studied in this context. The mixture of redistributive and market forms of organization is complicated for us by the emphasis on the latter in ancient thought, which was not interested in the situation of the barbarian or the provincial peasant, as well as by our own preconceptions. For similar problems in Chinese economic history, cf. Twitchett, 1968.

103 The separation of Aztec trade and markets may have been exaggerated by Chapman (1957); R. McC. Adams (1966a, pp. 163 f.) has questioned her account of the separation of trade and tribute. The reasons for the difference in the goods handled by fairs and by local markets in the Middle Ages seem to be purely operational.

104 Cf. Belshaw, 1965, pp. 92 ff.

105 Polanyi, 1966, pp. 104–69; see also Johnson, 1966. Curtin (1967), in his review of Polanyi, 1966, underrates the originality of Polanyi's approach.

106 For the formal definition see Robbins, 1935; substantive definition in Godelier, 1966, pp. 27 ff.

107 Polanyi, 1957a, pp. 243–70 ('The economy as instituted process'). Cf. M. Weber, 1922 (1956 ed., pp. 31, 44–5; translation, 1964, pp. 158, 184), and n. 113 below.

108 Frankenberg, 1967; Cohen, 1967. The contrast between Firth and Polanyi should not be exaggerated; Polanyi's and Dalton's strictures on the misuse of economic theory were not aimed at Firth, and Firth (1967b) argues for a careful use of economic theory in combination with awareness of social factors. Firth, Cohen, and Manning Nash (Nash, 1968) agree that the theoretical controversy is of little importance.

109 Cf. Joy, 1967. He warns, however, that 'the venturesome should look for guidance from economists specialist in the relevant field. Textbooks – and economists in the wrong field – are likely to prove unhelpful and disappointing'.

110 Firth and Yamey, 1964.

111 See pp. 72 f.

112 Gombrich, 1960, p. 120: in the Greek world 'The image has been *pried loose from the practical context* for which it was conceived and is admired and enjoyed for its beauty and fame, that is, quite simply *within the context of art*' (my italics); cf. Gombrich, 1955.

113 Gluckman, 1965, pp. 251 ff. The formal/substantive distinction is used with different implications in legal theory generally, in Kantian philosophy, in

Weber (in the form of the distinction between formal and substantive *rationality*) with regard to both law and economics (cf. Dieckmann, 1961), as well as by Polanyi in the economic context; the interrelations of the different uses are obviously extremely complex. It is perhaps worth noting here that Weber's 'substantive rationality' carries no implication of universality or common ground for comparative studies; Weber is inclined to stress the multiple possibilities of substantive rationality, whereas Polanyi avoids the epistemological problems of basing comparative studies on substantive and not formal categories by the positivist claim that the possibilities empirically turn out to consist of 'only a small number of alternative patterns for organizing man's livelihood'; Polanyi, 1957a, p. xvii; cf. p. 250.

114 T. K. Hopkins, 1957; H. W. Pearson, 1957a.
115 Smelser, 1959b.
116 For the economic model on which this theory is based, see H. W. Pearson, 1957b; cf. T. K. Hopkins, 1957.
117 Cf. Godelier, 1966, p. 256.
118 Mauss, 1947, p. 101.
119 Cf. Gluckman, 1965.
120 Parsons, 1966, pp. 34, 18. In the case of 'valued objects' there is, I think, always an element of 'evaluating' as well as of 'valuing'.
121 Polanyi, 1957a, pp. 190–2.
122 Cf. Godelier, 1966, p. 251, n. 57. Maunier (1927, pp. 41–2) records that in 1922 one Berber group decided to ban *taoussa* (ritual exchange) during a famine.
123 Foster, 1965 (cf. Kaplan *et al.*, 1966). His theory is certainly suggestive for the interpretation of both ancient and modern Greek peasant society (Hesiod; Friedl, 1962); but cultural traits shared by all peasants are notoriously hard to find (R. Redfield, 1956). For an attempt to define the 'peasant economy' along different lines see now Thorner, 1964.
124 Polanyi, 1957a, p. 290.
125 Polanyi, 1957a, p. 339.
126 Wittfogel, 1957; criticism relating to Mesopotamia and Mexico in R. McC. Adams, 1965 and 1966a; to Ceylon, Leach, 1959. Cf. Vidal-Naquet, 1964b; Godelier, 1965.
127 D. North, 1965.
128 Parsons, 1966.
129 See Godelier, 1966, pp. 251 ff.; M. Harris, 1959; Sachs, 1966. Suggestions for the study of surpluses in Dalton, 1960.
130 Cf. however J. Suret-Canale's criticism of Meillassoux (Suret-Canale, 1967), and Godelier, 1966, pp. 84 ff.
131 Douglas, 1962 is an exception.
132 See above, p. 44.
133 See Douglas, 1967; Mair, 1934.
134 Polanyi, 1944, pp. 153 ff. Cf. Lukács, 1923, pp. 229–60, 'Der Funktionswechsel des historischen Materialismus'.
135 Polanyi, 1922. He was critical of some aspects even of the Marxist interpretation of the development of the market economy (Polanyi, 1944, pp. 153 ff.).
136 Benet, 1957, p. 215. Polanyi added in *City Invincible* (1960) that householding is formally the same as redistribution (pp. 307–8 in Polanyi, 1968). It is worth noting that this resemblance may be used as the basis for an ideological justification of a redistributive system, as in Dahomey.

137 Polanyi, 1944, p. 60; Bücher, 1893, pp. 108 ff.
138 Polanyi, 1966, p. 72. Previously Polanyi had entirely omitted inheritance systems from his comparative economics.
139 But this system is as much reciprocal as redistributive; cf. Neale, 1957 and Ishwaran, 1966.
140 Since Smelser was discussing Polanyi, 1957a, he did not consider house-holding.
141 Cf. above, n. 40.
142 See Bohannan, 1955.
143 Cf. Mead, 1937.
144 Sahlins, 1965a also has a rich appendix of ethnographic material.
145 E.g. Polanyi, 1957a, pp. 255–6.
146 See Argyle, 1966 for a more critical and cautious account of the evidence.
147 See Finley, 1957b.
148 Starr, 1961, pp. 79 ff.; Finley, 1957a.
149 See the discussion of gift-prestation in ancient Thrace by Mauss (1921).
150 Herodotus 5.47, 8.17.
151 This is hardly due to Hesiod's own position as an immigrant's son, but the mobility of the colonization period has to be taken into account.
152 Twitchett, 1968 provides interesting comparative material.
153 Demosthenes 3.29, 23.207.
154 Gernet, 1950. The change was part of a general trend to classify legal proceedings by the matter concerned instead of the status of the actors.
155 This analysis owes much to that of Erb (1938). Rodinson (1966, pp. 45–73) has drawn on Polanyi's ideas in a similar way in his account of the dis-embedding of the economy in medieval Islam, as P. Brown pointed out to me.
156 For a different application of the concept of structural differentiation to the history of the ancient world see K. Hopkins, 1968, 1965; Weaver, 1967.
157 Laum, 1951–2; Duncan-Jones, 1963.
158 Cf. Pringsheim, 1950 and the discussions by Gernet (1951c, 1953c). The problem of the origins of contract was a central one for the *Année sociologique* school to which Gernet belonged (cf. Mauss, 1925a; Davy, 1922, etc.). The material from the ancient Near East is even richer than that from Greece; cf., for example, Cassin, 1955.
159 See now Dupront, 1966.

3 The work of Louis Gernet

1 On the work of Vernant, Vidal-Naquet, and Detienne see Darmon, 1970 and the introduction by B. Bravo to Vernant, 1970. See also Kirk, 1970, 1974; Detienne, 1975.
2 For biographical information see the accounts by friends and colleagues in *Hommage à Louis Gernet* (1966), the obituary by H. Lévy-Bruhl (1962), and the introduction by Vernant to Gernet, 1968. Bibliography of Gernet in *Hommage*, 1966 and Gernet, 1968.
3 Simiand, 1910, p. 563; Gernet, 1909a.
4 Cf. Durkheim, 1893 and 1901a. For recent bibliography on the question of responsibility in Greek law see Maddoli, 1967.
5 Fondation Thiers, 1911, pp. 14–15; cf. also Mauss, 1921.
6 Fondation Thiers, 1911, p. 7; Gernet, 1917c.
7 Mauss, 1925b, pp. 21–2.

8   Lévy-Bruhl, 1966, p. 14. Most of these (together with P. Fauconnet, H. Hubert, A. van Gennep, P. Roussel, A. Piganiol, and others) contributed to Simiand's *Notes Critiques*. Cf. Andler, 1932, chapter 5; Mauss, 1928; Bouglé, 1936.

9   See Appendix I to this chapter.

10 Glotz was sympathetic to the work of the *Année sociologique* school, although he did not collaborate with them directly. Both in *La Solidarité de la famille* (1904) and in *La Cité grecque* (1928), he modified Fustel de Coulanges's views on the evolution of Greek city society by arguing that the solidarity of kin groups weakened, and individualism increased, as the power of the State grew: a thesis which bears an obvious relation to Durkheim's *De la division du travail social* (1893). (On Fustel, Glotz, and Durkheim see now Momigliano, 1970). Gernet's *Pensée juridique* (1917b) contains some pertinent criticism of Glotz, 1904, but is still influenced by it to a considerable extent. Durkheim had reviewed it (1905). Glotz (1906) stressed the interest of Greek law for the comparative study of social development (p. 287); see also Glotz, 1907.

11 Gernet, 1910a, reviewing Croiset, 1909.

12 Gernet, 1925, p. 500.

13 The Hellenistic section was written by André Boulanger, who had already published a study of Orphism (1925). See also Boulanger, 1923, pp. 163–209.

14 On the rivalry between history and sociology see especially Berr, 1911; Febvre, writing on Simiand in 1930 (Febvre, 1962, p. 188), says, 'Lorsqu'à vingt ans, avec des sentiments mêlés d'admiration et d'instinctive rebellion, nous lisions l'*Année sociologique*. . . .'

15 Berque, 1956; see also Maunier, 1932.

16 Berque, 1936 (not available to me), 1937, 1955; review of the latter, Gernet, 1957b.

17 Cf. Smith, 1962b; for current attitudes to history among social anthropologists see also I. M. Lewis, 1968.

18 Gernet, 1934.

19 Jeanmaire reviewed for the *Année sociologique* in the 1920s, but was closer to the Frazerian anthropological tradition than to Durkheimian sociology (obituary by Gernet, 1960a); he sought to illuminate Greek data by comparison with the institutions of primitive societies, rather than to study them in relation to a general sociological theory. Jeanmaire, 1939 (cf. Gernet, 1944) deals with initiation rites and secret societies (see now Brelich, 1969); Jeanmaire, 1951 (cf. Gernet, 1953a) compares Dionysiac rites with African *zar* and *bori* cults, and with shamanism.

20 His editions for the Collection Budé of Lysias (1924–6), Antiphon (1954a), Demosthenes (1954–60, 1957a) and Plato (1951a) were highly respected; articles on Greek law were reprinted in a collected volume (1955a). It is unfortunate that he left no pupil to continue his work in this field.

21 *Hommage à Louis Gernet*, 1966.

22 See especially Vernant, 1962 and 1965a. I should like to thank Vernant and Elena Cassin for their kindness in discussing this paper with me.

23 Gernet, 1928.

24 Except in Thrace (Gernet, 1932a, p. 101). That there were survivals of 'the totemistic way of thought' in Greece was claimed by Jane Harrison (1912, pp. 128–33); the theory has been maintained by George Thomson (1941, 1949). Granet accepted the idea of totemism in China: 1926, pp. 150–62,

'Manger ou ne pas manger son semblable', and pp. 602–6 (but the word does not occur, to my knowledge, in his later works).

25   Granet, 1919, 1922a; 1929, pp. 175–96 ('Les coutumes paysannes'). See also Appendix I to this chapter.

26   Gernet (1928) leaves it open whether the phratry is the combination of (exogamous) units which meet in festivals, or the smaller unit. (The theory of exogamy and 'group marriage' put forward in this article was probably inspired mainly by Granet's work and is not supported by any convincing Greek evidence.) In this article Gernet emphasized (rightly, in my opinion) the 'caractère "démocratique" assez accusé' of the phratry. However, in 'Dionysos et la religion dionysiaque' (1953a) he derived the phratry from '"hétairies" ou compagnonnages guerriers', following Glotz (1904, pp. 85 f.) and Jeanmaire (1939, pp. 133–44). See now Andrewes, 1961; Roussel, 1976.

27   Gernet, 1928 (1968, pp. 21–2). The potlatch was already associated with chiefship by Davy in Moret and Davy, 1923, followed by Georges Dumézil (1924). Mauss considered this view too narrow (1925a; 1966, p. 269, n. 2). As evidence of the potlatch in Greece Gernet cited the feast of Tantalus, referring to Dumézil.

28   The idea that the family ancestor cult was not the earliest form of religion was not peculiar to the Durkheim school (cf., for example, Schurtz, 1902, p. 356). Fustel's theory of the primacy of the ancestor cult depended on his belief that the family was the earliest form of social group (on family and *gens* in Fustel see Momigliano, 1970, p. 91, n. 10). I hope to study elsewhere the impact on ancient historians of the substitution of the horde as the primal social group, under the successive influence of Bachofen, Australian ethnography, and Morgan's explanation of classificatory kinship terminologies.

29   Gernet, 1968, pp. 154, 171; cf. 1932a, pp. 69–75; Granet, 1926, pp. 606–11; 1929, pp. 219–29. 'Confréries' are not mentioned in Granet, 1919, which moves directly from the segmentary organization of the rural milieu to the centralized government of the cities. Mauss had lectured on secret societies in 1905–6, using Schurtz, 1902, which also incorporated secret societies into an evolutionary scheme (Mauss, 1969, vol. III, p. 59).

30   Gernet, 1932a, pp. 84 ff.; 1948a (1968, pp. 119–30); 1945 (1968, pp. 426–8). Cf. Vernant, 1962, p. 111; Detienne, 1967, pp. 16–17, 41–4.

31   Gernet, 1938a; cf. 1968, p. 427. See also Jeanmaire, 1939.

32   Gernet, 1932a, pp. 94–6. Note also the remark in his review of M. I. Finley, *The World of Odysseus*, that there is in Homer 'un certain jeu dialectique entre un passé que le poète ne connait pas et un présent que, de parti pris, il élimine' (1956c). Archaeological evidence now seems to show that the Greek cults at hero-tombs are post-Homeric (J. M. Cook, 1953).

33   The most extensive Durkheimian treatment of hero-cults is Czarnowski, 1919.

34   See Gernet, 1937b, on *phernē*, and 1932a, pp. 137 f.

35   Gernet, 1920. Cf. (for the earlier stage) Gernet, 1932b, and Durkheim's discussion of adoption, 1893, pp. 185–8.

36   Gernet, 1932a, pp. 97–129.

37   Cf. the analysis of *hybris* in 1917b.

38   Gernet, 1945; 1932a, pp. 135–40. Cf. Vernant, 1962, pp. 61 ff.

39   Gernet, 1917b, *passim*; see also 1968, p. 325 (1924). For the importance in the development of legal concepts of the 'surexcitation collective' experienced at religious festivals (an idea obviously inspired by Durkheim,

1912: cf. below, nn. 85–6), see especially 1917b, p. 60. For kin groups Gernet, 1909b, 1937c, 1927. On *Volksjustiz*, Gernet, 1924, 1936b, 1937b (on *phōr*), 1959.
40　Gernet, 1937a, 1948b; 1917b, Appendix III, 'La Désignation du jugement' (pp. 448–51).
41　Gernet, 1932a, pp. 95–6; 1955a, pp. 17–18 (1948b); cf. the discussion of *isonomia* in Lévêque and Vidal-Naquet, 1964; Vernant, 1963; Detienne, 1965.
42　See the discussion of *adikēma* in Gernet, 1917b, and pp. 432–6; also Gernet, 1959, 1951b (especially p. 255 in Gernet, 1968), and 1956a.
43　Cf. Mauss, 1935b. In revising 'La Création du testament' (1920) for republication in 1955a, Gernet dropped many of the references to comparative material. It is worth noting also that in his postwar work on law (1951b, 1956a, etc.) he was more concerned with the law of contract (Durkheim's 'restitutive sanctions') than with penal ('repressive') law, though his remarks on the establishment of some forms of contract by means of a 'détour par le délictuel' (1959).
44　'Der Dichter in Marcel Granet nur allzu oft den Kritischen Philologen zum Schweigen bringt. Sein Werk liest sich wie ein interessanter Roman, aber es ist auch zum grossen Teil nichts anderes'; Forke, 1930, on Granet, 1929. References to hostile reactions in America in Ware, 1934. Discussion of the comparative method in Granet, 1952, pp. 16 f.
45　Gernet, 1955c; cf. 1956b, p. 246.
46　See Ullmann, 1951, pp. 154–69, and Öhman, 1953, on the history of the 'semantic field' method, beginning with R. M. Meyer, 1910 and the definition of the term 'Bedeutungsfeld' by Ipsen (1924, p. 225).
47　Gernet, 1917b, pp. iv–xiii; cf. 1955a, p. 62, n. 1 (1937a).
48　Gernet, 1909b (but see now Chantraine, 1960).
49　See Colby, 1966. So far the 'New Ethnography' school has dealt only with vocabulary sets which are syntactically homogeneous – a serious limitation.
50　Cahen, 1921. He was associated with the *Année sociologique* school: see the obituaries by Mauss (1925b, pp. 4–5) and Meillet (1927). Cf. also Febvre, 'Frontière' (1928) and 'Civilisation' (1930), and Benveniste, 1969.
51　'Frairies antiques' (1928) also contains a semantic discussion of *eranos*, *pherō*, *phernē*, *symballesthai*, *telos*, etc.
52　Gernet, 1968, p. 46 (1928); cf. Benveniste, 1951.
53　Meillet, 1906.
54　This orientation is already evident in Mauss and Hubert, 1899. Cf. V. Karady's introduction to Mauss, 1968, pp. xxx–v, xliv–viii.
55　See especially Mauss, 1934, 1947. Mauss also did much of the work on the statistics of Durkheim, 1897.
56　Mauss, 1927a; cf. also Halbwachs, 1938. Although Radcliffe-Brown used the distinction between morphology and physiology (e.g. 'On the concept of function', 1935), Mauss's conception is closer to Malinowski's institutional analysis than to Radcliffe-Brown's structural-functional approach.
57　Mauss and Beuchat, 1906.
58　Quotations from Gernet, 1968, pp. 418–19, 425. The reference is to Empedocles Fr. 129, Diels and Krantz (1951). The idea of shamanism was introduced into Greek studies by K. Meuli (1935); see now Dodds, 1951, chapter 5, 'The Greek Shamans and the origins of puritanism', and Cornford, 1952. Cornford was influenced by N. K. Chadwick, *Poetry and Prophecy* (1942).
59　Mauss, 1935a.

60 Cornford, 1921, 1935; 1952, pp. 188–201. See also Appendix I to this chapter.
61 There is a brief discussion in Gernet, 1945 (1968, p. 427); for a general history of the problem of survivals see Hodgen, 1936.
62 Though Gernet noted (1938b) that this tendency was weak in Greek law; tradition, *mos maiorum*, was not theorized as a source of law in ancient Greece. This question has not received much attention in anthropological studies of law. The theory of primitive legal formalism (which now appears to have been an over-hasty generalization from Roman evidence) is only one aspect of the wider problem of the way in which time, and especially the past, is conceptualized in different legal systems. Cf. Gernet, 1956a, 1937a.
63 Marc Bloch, 1925. The brief section on law in Halbwachs, 1950, pp. 147–53, does not fulfil Bloch's requirements.
64 Durkheim, 1893, 1901a; cf. also Huvelin, 1907; Gurvitch, 1963, pp. 59–174, 'La Magie, la religion et le droit'. Note however Gernet's insistence (1968, p. 178: 1951b) that 'une recherche positive ... ne peut se faire que dans des milieux définis. On ne se soucie pas, en pareil cas, d'une histoire générale de l'humanité que commanderait une loi d'évolution: il s'agit d'une analyse qui porte sur tel ou tel civilisation'.
65 Tarde, 1890, 1893.
66 Mauss, 1935b, p. 73.
67 Gernet, 1968, p. 245 (1951b); cf. 1955a, p. 12 (1948b), 'si les rites comme les procédures sont un langage'; also (from a different point of view) Timpanaro, 1963 ('A proposito del parallelismo fra lingua e diritto').
68 Mauss, 1909, p. 78; Granet, 1922b.
69 Gernet, 1968, pp. 99–100.
70 Gernet, 1968, pp. 130–1 (1948a). The same point is made by Granet, e.g. 1922a, p. 82.
71 Gernet, 1968, pp. 120, 125. See also Gernet, 1933; Granet, 1926, pp. 43, 596–7; Detienne and Vernant, 1969.
72 Gernet, 1932a, pp. 196–241, 'Les Représentations'.
73 Cf. Gernet's discussion of Plato (1948c), and Pocock, 1968.
74 Gernet, 1953c.
75 Cf. Gernet, 1933; Pembroke, 1967.
76 Gernet, 1968, p. 359 (1953c).
77 This is true even of Halbwachs's *Morphologie sociale* (1938), but I am thinking particularly of the tendency of Granet and Gernet to present early Chinese and Greek society by the successive description of a series of institutional complexes or 'milieux', each with its characteristic form of social grouping. Mauss showed his awareness of the inadequacy of Durkheimian theory from this point of view in 'La Cohésion sociale' (1932).
78 Cf. above, nn. 39–40.
79 Gernet, 1932a, pp. 242–85, 'Les Milieux de la vie religieuse'.
80 Gernet, 1932a, pp. 268–85. Certainly Gernet makes many sensitive and penetrating observations about aspects of Greek religion which escape his main scheme (*ibid.*, pp. 196–204, 304–23; 1955d); but he lacks a sociological theory which can integrate these into his view of the place of religion in Greek society.
81 Gernet, 1932a, p. 255 (my italics).
82 Cf. the references cited above, n. 39, and Gernet, 1948a. But for Gernet religion is only *one* of the sources of law.

83 In the narrower sense of 'le sentiment que la société a d'elle-même' (Durkheim, 1912, pp. 329–30). On the various meanings and development of Durkheim's conception of the *conscience collective* see Gurvitch, 1963, vol. II, pp. 1–58.
84 Durkheim, 1950, pp. 60 ff., 95–7.
85 Gernet, 1917b, pp. 117–18; 1955a, pp. 66–7 (1937a). He had argued in 'L'Approvisionnement d'Athènes en blé' (1909a) that the Athenians did not have an abstract conception of the State, but only a number of imperfectly co-ordinated 'representations' of the city as a collectivity. Cf. also 1955a, p. 18 (1948b): 'c'est surtout à des moments privilégiés de vie collective qu'on a chance d'apercevoir la signification originelle des pratiques considérées comme efficaces pour la création et la défense du droit. En raison des représentations multiples que suscitent et entretiennent les jeux, il se pourrait que les jeux sont *un* des milieux où se sont définies les notions et les attitudes qui sont explicatives de la procédure la plus ancienne.'
86 Gernet, 1917b, pp. 434–6; cf. 1968, pp. 258–60 (1951b), 262, 287 (1956a). By employing the notion of collective consciousness in the field of politics and law rather than religion, Gernet was implicitly focusing on the relation of perception of group identity and social structure to the performance of collective or 'member' roles in goal-oriented action, instead of the phenomena of 'collective effervescence' and symbolic expression of values which have attracted most attention in Durkheim's presentation. Seen from this angle, the Durkheimian idea of the generation of new norms in moments of heightened collective life is not so far removed from the interaction theory developed by Talcott Parsons and others through work with small groups. For Gernet the collective consciousness in this sense is, like Marx's class consciousness, a basis for action. Recent anthropological studies of ritual are also tending to stress the aspect of mobilization for collective action (Gluckman, 1962a; Turner, 1968).
87 Abstract, universalistic rationality increases with social complexity through 'le conflit et la synthèse entre les représentations qui émanent de groupes différents ou répondent à des moments différents de la société' (Gernet, 1917b, p. 435).

4 Archaeology and the economic and social history of classical Greece

1 Surveys of recent developments in method are common: I have especially used Courbin, 1963. [See now Binford, 1972; Redman, 1973; Finley, 1971.]
2 These pressures on the archaeologist should be examined in the whole context of the organization of national archaeological services, their relation to university teaching, etc., which lies outside the scope of this paper.
3 Cf. Momigliano, 1950, 1964.
4 Vernant, 1965a; Lévêque and Vidal-Naquet, 1964; Vidal-Naquet, 1964a; Detienne, 1964, 1965.
5 Finley, 1965c. The present paper owes a great deal to Finley's work on ancient economic history and especially to the suggestions for research listed at the end of his report to the 1962 conference in economic history (*loc. cit.*).
6 Cf. the comments of R. McC. Adams (1966b) on a similar situation in Near Eastern archaeology. On the other hand, there is a flourishing debate between archaeologists and historians on the history of early Rome

(e.g. Gjerstad, 1965, 1966, 1967; Momigliano, 1963, 1967; Dohrn, 1964; *Entretiens Hardt*, 1967).

7   Hence planned selective excavation directed to the solution of historical problems is also much more feasible. See, however, the cautions of Richmond (1943, pp. 478 f.).

8   But see the important article of Gajdukević on the economic history of the Bosporan region (1966) [also Gajdukević, 1971; Wąsowicz, 1975]. Kahrstedt's work should be followed up by new surveys of the evidence on the ground. Archaeological evidence for the rural economy has been better studied in Italy, from the early article of Carrington (1931), inspired by Rostovtzeff, to the British excavations at Francolise (Ward-Perkins, von Blankenhagen, and Cotton, 1965); cf. particularly Ruggini, 1961, as well as Kahrstedt, 1960. Cf. also Lemerle (1963) on the relations of town and countryside from the fourth to the twelfth centuries A.D.; Collingwood, 1929; Hatt, 1959.

9   Bradford, 1956.

10 Bradford, 1957, p. 31.

11 Chevallier, 1958. For air photography of classical sites since Chevallier's *Bibliographie* (1957), see Schmiedt, 1961; Castagnoli, 1961; Chevallier, 1961; Schmiedt, 1957, 1966. [See now Schroeder, 1974.]

12 Bradford, 1957, pp. 277–86; Kondis, 1958; Jones, Sackett, and Eliot, 1957 (the Dema wall); *Chronique des fouilles*, 1966, p. 897 (Lefkandi); Mellink, 1967, p. 170 (Pergamon); Wiseman, 1967, p. 14, n. 9 (Corinth).

13 Boardman, 1956, 1959; Jones, Sackett, and Graham, 1962; Levi, 1963, pp. 514–17 (Iasos). [Jones, Sackett, and Graham, 1973; general survey, Pečírka, 1973. For the programme of archaeological survey and farm excavation in the territory of Metapontum carried out under the direction of D. Adamesteanu, see Adamesteanu, 1973, and *Metaponto* (in press).]

14 Zawadski, 1960–1.

15 The Dema house differs from the farms of south-east Attica described by J. H. Young, 1956a; cf. the bibliography of Attic houses in Jones, Sackett, and Graham, 1962 (pp. 102–3) [also Jones, Sackett, and Graham, 1973; Pečírka, 1973]. The distribution and function of towers as farm buildings needs further study and excavation: cf. J. H. Young, 1956a; Ormerod, 1924; Manganaro, 1965, p. 300 (Young's Leros I); Paraskevaïdis, 1964; Holloway, 1966, p. 84 (Agora Inv. I. 6991); McCredie, 1966; Dimitrov, 1958.

16 Ward-Perkins, 1964.

17 For the contrast between manorial farming and cash-cropping see Plutarch, *Pericles* 16.4. Coin hoard at Pindakas; vases (especially *lebēs gamikos*) in the Dema house.

18 Cf. n. 8 above.

19 In Attica study of tombs may clarify both the migration of powerful families to the city (progressive concentration of tumuli in the Kerameikos?) and the spread of city fashions to the demes, for which grave stelai should be a fruitful subject of research. Work such as that of J. Frel (1966) on identifying the sculptors of Attic stelai will also increase our knowledge of the interaction of city and country. There is much to be learnt still about the demes as economic, religious, and cultural centres from sanctuaries, theatres, etc. For land owned by the demes see Andreyev, 1967. [Also D. M. Lewis, 1973. In my opinion the fact that the prices of public land sold by auction in the inscriptions discussed by Lewis are all multiples of $12\frac{1}{2}$ drachmai does not reflect a fixed price per stremma of land, but the practice

attested in Attic leases of computing the capital value of land at 12½ times the annual rent.]

20 See below, n. 66. The development of 'industrial' areas such as the Attic mining district will also have affected settlement patterns. (For the current excavations at Thorikos see Mussche *et al.*, 1967 ff.)

21 See however Burford, 1969. The period just before the Persian wars is particularly interesting in the development of public finance: e.g. Herodotus 6.46 (Thasos).

22 J. M. Cook, 1961.

23 Momigliano, 1934, p. 59; Biesantz, 1965 for an attempt at an archaeological contribution to the social history of Thessaly.

24 The complex of functions fulfilled by Greek temples and sanctuaries, and the buildings associated with them, needs further study. For the connection of temples with public finance see Will, 1955 [de Franciscis, 1972; Bogaert, 1968]. Bergquist, 1967 has a useful collection of material but a limited conception of 'function'.

25 Martin, 1956, 1951; Delorme, 1960; Neppi-Modona, 1961 is useful for data, but little has been done to study Greek theatre-building from the point of view of social history (or that of demography); see however Frézouls, 1961. For roads see J. H. Young, 1956b. On the need for a closer relation between archaeology and epigraphy, see Susini, 1966.

26 Schefold (1966, p. 109) suggests that the archaic Eretrian law *I.G.*XII. 9. 1273–4 was originally fixed in the archaic walls near the harbour gate; but cf. Vanderpool and Wallace, 1964.

27 R. S. Young, 1951b; Travlos, 1960.

28 Ghirshman, 1967, pp. 3–7 (Susa); Mellaart, 1967; conflict between the orientation of the temenos of Artemis Leukophryne and the agora at Magnesia on the Maeander: Martin, 1951, pp. 404–6; Crosby, 1951 [Vallet, 1973, 1975].

29 Histria: Coja, 1962 [see now the general survey in Wąsowicz, 1969]; Old Smyrna: J. M. Cook, 1959, p. 15 and plate I; p. 46.

30 Eretria: Schefold, 1966 [and Kraus, 1972]; Agrigento: Dunbabin, 1948, p. 314.

31 Robinson, 1946, p. 200. Sparkes (1962) shows the range of material on cooking equipment but does not discuss chronological development or social variations. Dembinska, 1963 would be a useful model for a collection of the literary and archaeological evidence on food in ancient Greece. A villa with its own baking facilities next to the forum of the Magdalensberg settlement: Vetters, 1966.

32 E.g. Cook and Heizer, 1960. Practically no attempt has been made by classical archaeologists to study skeletal remains as evidence for diet, health, etc.

33 For the eighth to sixth centuries, Boardman, 1964 [important new discussion of early trade and colonization: Ridgway, 1973]. A comparable survey for the fifth and fourth centuries is badly needed. Chapter 2 of Rostovtzeff, 1941 remains the best general treatment of the fourth century. Cf. also Benoît, 1965; Hatt, 1966 (chapter I, 'Les Celtes et la Méditerranée'); Clairmont, 1955, 1956–8.

34 Dupront, van Effenterre, *et al.*, 1965. See also Mannoni, 1950; Courtois, 1955; Mansel, 1961; *Greci e Italici*, 1962; *Kokalos*, 1962; *Le Rayonnement des civilisations*, 1965; Berciu, 1966a, 1966b [*Le Genti non Greche*, 1972; Humphreys, 1973].

35 Herodotus 4.196. [Farias, 1974 doubts the historical reality of the practice.]
36 Polanyi, 1957a, chapters 8–9; see chapter 2 above.
37 Herodotus 2.178–9 [cf. Austin, 1970].
38 van Effenterre, 1965, p. 39.
39 Gajdukević, 1964; Slavia, 1960. [See now Wąsowicz, 1975.]
40 There was a commercial stoa in the Piraeus in the fifth century (schol. Aristophanes, *Acharnians* 547), but none has been found in the Agora (Aristophanes, *Ecclesiazousai* 684–6 does not imply a stoa exclusively used for corn-dealing). The interpretation of the North Building at Corinth as a commercial stoa (Stillwell, 1932, pp. 212 ff.) seems conjectural.
41 At present imprecise use of terms like 'close contact' or 'hellenization' can produce considerable variations in the interpretation of the same evidence.
42 E.g. Gjerstad, 1967, p. 262: 'In a comparison with the amount of Greek pottery imported by the principal cities in Etruria it becomes evident that the overseas trade of Rome was of the same dimensions as that of the biggest Etruscan cities (Villard, *La Céramique grecque de Marseille* [1960], p. 124).' This shows how easily statistical information is misused; Villard stated clearly that his figures were only significant for the proportion of imports in different periods, not for the amount of pottery imported.
43 Duval, 1952, pp. 67–9 ('La Maison gauloise et ses survivances').
44 E.g. Grammichele (Dunbabin, 1948, pp. 122–5); Spina and Adria; Tell Sukas (Riis, 1962, pp. 137–40); cf. also n. 34 above.
45 Christ, 1967, pp. 91–100; P. Grierson, 1965–6.
46 Will, 1954b, 1955; R. M. Cook, 1958; Kraay, 1964.
47 Cf. the report of exploration of pre-Roman farming sites near Lullingstone villa, Meates, 1966.
48 Dimitrov, 1958, 1961; Danov, 1962.
49 Will, 1958; Vallet and Villard, 1961; R. M. Cook, 1959.
50 Vallet and Villard, 1964. Delougaz (1967, pp. 148–9) reports that a new method of recording which 'aims at a total quantitative as well as qualitative analytical recording' was devised for the Protoliterate pottery from Choga Mish in the Susiana plain.
51 Rostovtzeff, 1941, chapter 2, 'The ancient world in the fourth century B.C.'.
52 Schlumberger, 1953.
53 See the list of proveniences in Beazley, *A.R.V.*[2] (1963); Jannoray, 1955; D. M. Bailey, 1962.
54 Metzger, 1951, 1965; M. A. Levi, 1958. [Webster (1972) attempts to answer many of the questions formulated here, but his view that many vases specially commissioned by Attic patrons reached Etruria through 'second-hand trade' is difficult to accept. In particular, there is no reason to suppose that vases with *kalos*-names were only produced on special commission; they are the ancient equivalent of tee-shirts printed 'I love Ringo'.]
55 Boardman and Hayes, 1966, pp. 21, 59. [The conclusions which can be drawn from merchants' marks are discussed by Johnston, 1974; see also Johnston, 1972.]
56 Beazley, 1945, pp. 153–8.
57 I have the impression from a superficial analysis of the data in *A.R.V.*[2] that these connections may have been more common in the fourth century. It is likely enough that developments in shipbuilding and in the organization of trade (the *nautikon daneion*) would have led to more regularity in traders' movements, but more study is needed.
58 Langlotz, 1957.

59 It is therefore important that the basic description given whenever a vase is discussed (provenience, museum number, publications) should include precise details of the context in which it was found, where this is known.

60 Jacoby's two articles, 'Genesia' (1944a) and 'Patrios nomos' (1944b), are of major importance. Cf. also R. S. Young, 1951a [Kurtz and Boardman, 1971]. Accounts like that of F. Cumont (1949) show how far we are from knowing the distribution (chronological, regional or social) of different customs, rites, and beliefs, and from assessing the extent to which the accounts of the literary sources corresponded to actual behaviour. In such an enquiry funerary art must be seen as part of the total social pattern. Much might be learnt from a sociological study of funerary art in later periods, where art-historical studies have been highly developed (Panofsky, 1964, chapter 3–4; Pope-Hennessy, 1958, pp. 41–54, 'The humanist tomb'; see also Giesey, 1960). L. Robert's studies of the language of tomb inscriptions are essential. Cf. also Susini, 1966.

61 Finley's pupil A. H. Jackson is now preparing a thesis on the legal and economic aspects of war in Greek history. [Jackson, 1970.]

62 It is also difficult to date archaeological material sufficiently closely to determine the effects of war on trade; cf. however Woolley, 1938, pp. 22–3, on Greek trade with Al Mina while Athens was at war with Persia.

63 Schefold, 1966.

64 McCredie, 1966; cf. Winter, 1966 [and Garlan, 1974].

65 See the bibliography on towers, n. 15 above.

66 Mill-stones: Fabricius, 1935, p. 14. Pens: J. M. Cook, 1959, p. 5; but the fort above Old Smyrna was perhaps a private *tursis* rather than a state post?

67 Antoniadis-Bibicou, 1965. Cf. also Bradford, 1949, 1957; Tchalenko, 1953; Stiesdal, 1962; Pesez, 1967. The figures in Randolph, 1687 may be worth signalling as evidence of the proportions demographic fluctuation could assume in the islands: only about 3,000 inhabitants on Andros, 5,000 on Naxos, but more than 20,000 on Tenos, which was in Venetian hands (for modern figures see Philippson, 1959); in Euboea, 'since the Turks have had possession of it, most of the Greeks are fled from the villages and towns'. Latifundia and other phenomena comparable to the enclosure movement in England were probably not an important cause of rural depopulation in ancient Greece. The smallholding tradition persisted strongly throughout the classical period (cf. Asheri, 1966), and Kahrstedt (1954) thinks that even in the Roman period the formation of large estates did not involve population movements. But there was a considerable shrinkage of settlements in the Hellenistic period, the causes of which need to be examined.

68 Jones, Sackett, and Graham, 1962. The farm excavated by the same team at Vari (Jones, Sackett, and Graham, 1973) was also only occupied for a short period (in the second half of the fourth century).

69 Catling, 1962; Tchalenko, 1953; cf. also the publications of the British School of Archaeology at Rome, cited below, n. 72, and R. McC. Adams, 1965.

70 Ward-Perkins, 1961, pp. 1–2; 'There is a brief moment, after the plough has passed and before the disc-harrow has done its work, when it is possible to record a great deal which has not been seen since antiquity and will never be seen again. It is the capture of this fleeting opportunity that is the object of the School's current programme of field survey.'

71 McDonald, 1966; cf. McDonald, 1964.

72 Ward-Perkins, 1955, 1961; Ward-Perkins and Frederiksen, 1957; Duncan, 1958; G. D. B. Jones, 1962–3; Ogilvie, 1965; W. Harris, 1965. For related treatments see *Vie di Magna Grecia*, 1963; Wetter, 1962; Stiesdal, 1962; Johannowsky, 1963; 'Schedario topografico', 1966 and 1967. The Fondazione Lerici and the University of Rome now have an annual course on surveying (Chevallier, 1966). Italy had in any case a strong tradition of topographical studies (Beloch, Ashby, Fraccaro, Lugli . . .) which has been lacking in Greece. Recently however the American School of Classical Studies at Athens has produced an excellent series of studies on the topography of Attica (J. H. Young, 1956a, 1956b; Vanderpool, 1965, etc.; Eliot, 1962; McCredie, 1966 [Traill, 1975]. Is it too much to hope for a systematic revision of the *Karten von Attika*?

73 Hope-Simpson, 1965.

74 Fowler, Robinson, and Blegen, 1932; see also Payne, 1940, chapter 1. J. M. Cook has done more in this direction than any other postwar excavator in the Aegean, but his accounts of the territory of Old Smyrna (1959) and Castabos (1966) do not compare with the publications of the British School at Rome. (Cook also initiated the British School at Athens' survey at Knossos; see Hood, 1958.) For Thasos see Bon, 1930. [We now have two excellent Bronze Age surveys, Warren, 1972 and McDonald and Rapp, 1972; but the position for classical sites has hardly changed, though M. H. Jameson is directing a survey of the Argolid (Jameson *et al.*, 1976). Renfrew, 1972 illustrates the gap even for the Bronze Age between the questions archaeologists are now asking and the evidence so far available to answer them. Regional archaeological surveys are now being published for Italy in the series *Forma Italiae* (1967 ff.). See also the series *Ancient Greek Cities* produced by the Athens Center of Ekistics (1970–3).]

75 The publication of the dedication to the Dioscuri and the thirteen altars found at Lavinium without an adequate description of their stratigraphy is a typical example (cf. Castagnoli, 1959, 1962; Montini, 1959; Alföldi, 1965, pp. 265–71).

76 It is equally important that final reports which appear in instalments should include information about the form the whole publication will take. The plan of publication for *Mégara Hyblaea* is given in Carcopino, 1965, but not in the introduction to either of the volumes so far published (Vallet and Villard, 1964, 1967).

77 Grinsell, Rahtz, and Warhurst, 1966.

78 Ahrweiler, 1965; Antoniadis-Bibicou, 1965; Topping, 1966. P. Faure's work on Cretan caves and mountain sites (Faure, 1964 and recent issues of the *Bulletin de correspondance hellénique*) is admirably comprehensive both in chronology and in range of interests.

79 I do not know how far this is due to the practice of recording excavations in diary form (cf. W. Y. Adams, 1966, p. 159) rather than card-indexing information during the excavation (as was done at Olynthus: Robinson, 1946, pp. viii–ix). M. E. Mallowan's decision to return to a diary-like form for the final publication of *Nimrud and its Remains* (Mallowan, 1966) has been both praised (Maxwell-Hyslop, 1966) and criticized (Munn-Rankin, 1967).

80 Functional classification in *Olynthus* and in *Corinth*, vol. XII (1952). Contrast, for example, *The Swedish Cyprus Expedition*, IV, 2 (Gjerstad, 1948), pp. 130–83, 'Arts and crafts'.

81 D'Agostino (1965) comments on the failure to list the contents of votive pits in his review of *Mégara Hyblaea*, vol. II (Vallet and Villard, 1964).

82 Hood, Huxley, and Sandars, 1959, p. 225; Burger, 1966.
83 W. Y. Adams (1966) remarks that sampling is 'one of the most universal and
    least understood problems in archaeology'. Cf. Cook and Heizer, 1960,
    especially the paper by Spaulding.
84 Robert, 1966, pp. 412–13. Cf. W. Y. Adams, 1966, 'If no one else is ever as
    fully competent to publish archaeological data as is the original excavator,
    it is doubly certain that no one else is as fully competent to interpret them';
    and Leroi-Gourhan, 1963, p. 50, 'Au cours de la fouille, l'archéologue doit
    tout voir et tout comprendre. Or, s'il est un principe fondamental de la
    recherche, c'est bien qu'on ne voit et qu'on ne comprend que ce qu'on est
    déjà préparé à comprendre et à voir'.
85 And possibly post-neolithic Near Eastern archaeology; cf. W. Y. Adams,
    1966; R. McC. Adams, 1966b. Egypt has always held a rather exceptional
    position, with a strong tradition of 'treasure-hunting' archaeology con-
    tinuing alongside pioneer work from an early date in physical anthropology
    and archaeological surveying (a good account of the latter in Trigger,
    1965). [See now Butzer, 1976.]
86 Thompson, 1966, p. 100.

5 Town and country in ancient Greece

1 See chapter 4 above. The available archaeological material is collected in
   Philippson, 1950–9, and in Pauly-Wissowa, *Realencyclopädie*: see names of
   ancient cities and regions. Cf. also Robert, 1965a; L. and J. Robert, 1954.
   Important discussions in *La Città e il suo territorio*, 1968.
2 For reasons of space I can only give here a simple outline which does not do
   justice to the complexity and variety of the data. The bibliography touching
   on the subject is immense; see (apart from the studies cited below) the
   recent collection of basic articles in Gschnitzer, 1969, and Kirsten, 1956.
3 Bolte, 1929. The circumference of Sparta was about six miles.
4 Gschnitzer, 1955 contains valuable observations, but starts from the hardly
   justifiable assumption that the etymology of state-names indicates the
   historical process of state-formation. The analysis of Kachin society by
   Leach (1964) might well be applied to the relation between *polis* and
   ethnos organization in Greece.
5 The prohibition of burial within the city imposes itself only gradually: see
   R. S. Young, 1951a; Vallet, 1968. For the Romans, the concept of *urbs*
   might indeed be defined by performance of the correct foundation rites
   (Varro, *De Lingua Latina*, 5.143), though this was perhaps a juridical as
   much as a religious way of thinking. The earliest Greek description of city-
   foundation begins with a wall: Homer, *Odyssey* 6.9 ff.
6 Asheri, 1966. Areas marked out in 'lots' have recently been explored in the
   Crimea (Chersonesos, near Sebastopol) and in the territory of Metapontum
   in southern Italy. See Wąsowicz, 1966; Uggeri, 1969; Pečírka, 1970;
   Pečírka and Dufkova, 1970.
7 Cf. especially *La città e il suo territorio*, 1968.
8 For the beginning of Greek town planning (eighth to seventh centuries
   B.C.) see now Drerup, 1969; Vallet and Villard, 1969.
9 For the opposition between mountainous frontier territory as 'bush' and
   cultivated land see Vidal-Naquet, 1968a, 1970.
10 *Laws* 778d–779a, with a reference also to the fortification of frontiers. On
   Greek warfare, fortifications, etc., see Vernant, 1968a [and Garlan, 1974].
   On early city walls Drerup, 1969. Fortifications may have played a greater
   part in Mycenaean warfare.

11   Aristotle, *Politics* 1331a 30 ff. Note also that the beginning of structural differentiation of law from politics made it possible to treat litigiousness as an urban vice (Aristophanes; Polybius 4.73.6–10), and often to associate it closely with commerce.

12   See further chapter 6. The urban/rural boundary did not coincide with the opposition between rich and poor even when upper-class Athenians attempted to separate hoplites from sailors. The political philosophers' idea of the peasant proprietors as a 'middle class' (Mossé, 1962, pp. 247–53) was based on the traditional identification of citizenship and the right to own land. Aristophanes' frequent play on the urban/rustic contrast belongs mainly to the years when the rural population of Attica was evacuated to the city, and is cultural rather than political; on the false picture of Aristophanes as champion of a conservative peasantry see Gomme, 1938.

13   For the *chora* of Alexandria see A. H. M. Jones, 1940, p. 20.

6   Economy and society in classical Athens

*I should like to thank Moses Finley, Jan Pečírka, David Asheri, and John Davies for much helpful discussion and criticism. It should not be assumed that they agree with the views expressed here.

1   Bücher, 1893, 1901; Ed. Meyer, 1895; Beloch, 1912–27 (especially vol. III, 2, 1923, pp. 419–49). See Oertel, 1925 and Will, 1954a.

2   Hasebroek, 1928, 1931.

3   Rostovtzeff's attempt to explain the vicissitudes of incipient capitalism in the ancient world as a result of the expansion and contraction of markets (cf. especially Rostovtzeff, 1936) ignored most of the institutional problems. A detailed study of Rostovtzeff's assumptions and models as an economic historian would be of considerable interest. See Einaudi, 1950.

4   Préaux, 1961, 1954; Welles, 1949; Vidal-Naquet, 1967.

5   See however Aymard, 1953; Bengtson, 1953.

6   Will, 1966, pp. 148–77.

7   Cf. Salin, 1944, and chapter 2 above. The trend reached its extreme in the work of Nazi sympathizers such as B. Laum (1933) and J. Brake (1935).

8   Sombart, 1902, chapter 3; cf. the review by Simiand (1903). Sombart worked out his typology of economies in more detail later, in *Die Ordnungen des Wirtschaftslebens* (1925; see Westrate, 1963).

9   See the review of Riezler by Gernet (1910b). It might be useful to compare the economic activities of the state in Greece with Chinese materials: cf. Balazs, 1960.

10   Pöhlmann, who was something of a *Kathedersozialist*, took the original line of accepting Marxist doctrine on the origins of capitalism and the class war, and arguing that the Greeks had already passed through the whole process and demonstrated the drawbacks of socialism. Hence he combined an extremely modernist interpretation of the Greek economy with an unusually critical view of Greek society (cf. his sharp remarks on nineteenth-century German idealization of Greece; Pöhlmann, 1902). He differed from Marx in separating the State from class interests and held that class war could be avoided by a combination of economic reform with the concentration of political power in the hands of a monarch and bureaucracy free from class bias. George Grote's democracy and his *laissez-faire* economics were equally anathema to him (Pöhlmann, 1902, 1890). The *Geschichte* in its earlier form (Pöhlmann, 1893) provoked a sarcastic response from Kautsky (1895). See also Salin, 1923.

11 Erb, 1938.

12 This strange use of the term 'feudal' (which does not affect the essentials of Erb's argument) appears also in Hasebroek, 1931, p. 216: 'es ist das Charakteristische griechischer Demokratie im Gegensatz zur abendländ-ische Demokratie, dass die aufsteigende demokratische Schicht nicht einen depossedierten Adel demokratisiert sondern vielmehr umgekehrt sich selbst feudalisiert, d.h. mit ihrem politischen Aufstieg auch in die gesamte Mentalität und alle Lebensformen des depossedierten Adels hineinwächst, am restlosesten in Sparta'. Cf. also Jeanmaire, 1939.

13 Vernant, 1965b; see also Welskopf, 1960; Lauffer, 1958.

14 In the sense that during the Peloponnesian war the State programmatically declined to defend the rural estates of its citizens (cf. also Xenophon, *Economicus* 4.6–7). The extent of the disruption caused by the war may be difficult to assess in substantive economic terms, but the ideological shock is amply documented. The increased frequency of alienation of land was no doubt related to this development – though like Finley (1968b) and Gernet (1968, p. 365: 1955b) I do not believe that alienation was earlier prohibited by law in Attica.

15 With the exception of studies of attitudes to work and technology on which see, for example, Aymard, 1943, 1948, and the works cited below, n. 23.

16 Gernet, 1909a. The importance of Gernet's work on the economic role of the State was stressed by Simiand in his review (Simiand, 1910).

17 Gernet, 1956d. See above, chapter 3.

18 Barth (1966, 1967) has stressed that social change cannot be understood if categories and institutions are regarded as monolithic and not admitting variation. But while granting that the individual in changing circumstances has a choice between a number of more or less established forms of be-haviour, it still remains essential to see how changing circumstances are perceived in terms of 'collective representations'.

19 Description of the plague, Thucydides 2.47.3–53; analysis of *stasis*, 3.82–3.

20 Finley, 1954, 1955. Cf. also Gernet, 1928, 1951b.

21 Cf. Momigliano, 1944. On *autarkeia* see Laum, 1933; Gigon, 1966.

22 Hasebroek, 1928; Gernet, 1909a.

23 On Greek conceptions of the division of labour in the city see Vernant, 1955, 1957; Vidal-Naquet, 1965, pp. 138 ff.; Pečírka, 1967; K. Hopkins, 1967.

24 *Odyssey* 8.159–64, 15.403–84. Cf. the remarks of Jeanmaire, 1956, pp. 19 ff., on the association of *kerdos* and *mētis* in the economic field; also Heinz-Otto Weber, 1967.

25 Aristotle, *Politics* 1278a 25.

26 Seager, 1966 (Lysias 22).

27 See Asheri, 1966; Welskopf, 1960; Finley, 1968b; Fuks, 1968. That the Athenians had no foundation-myth of this type themselves did not prevent them from sharing the ideal.

28 Lysias 7.24, 17.5; [Demosthenes] 50.8 (Apollodorus); Aeschines 1.97, 101 (Timarchos). But some scattered estates were due to the intricacies of inheritance, e.g. Isaeus 11. 40 ff. On the effects of adoption see Gernet, 1955a, p. 125 (1920). The extensive estate of Ischomachos in Xenophon's *Economicus* cannot be taken as evidence for Attic conditions; Xenophon had experience of large estates outside Attica and as Marcel Caster (1937) has shown he was interested above all in the art of ruling, which had to be exercised on a large scale. (See also Taragna Novo, 1968.)

29 Xenophon, *Memorabilia* 2.9; *Economicus* 2.5–6. Cf. the remark of Isocrates, *Antidosis* 159–60: 'When I was young it was safe and dignified (*asphales kai semnon*) to be a rich man; now one has to defend oneself against the charge of being rich as if it were the worst of crimes.' The justifiability of the complaints of the rich has been studied by Cloché (1941). See also the fine analysis of the attitudes of professional orators to fee-taking in Dover, 1968, pp. 155–8.

30 Latte, 1947. Division of confiscated property in the fourth century, Plutarch, *Moralia* 843d.

31 Buchanan (1962) has defended Boeckh's figure for the *theōrika* against A. H. M. Jones (1957, pp. 33–5). In arguing for the unimportance of state pay in classical Athens Jones ignored payment for military service. While accepting his point that few lived entirely on state pay, I differ from him in regarding it as an important determinant in the formation of the citizen's 'representation' of economic options, at least in the fifth century. The effects of greatly decreased revenue and military activity in the fourth century are not at all clear. We *can* see a drop in population: 21,000 adult male citizens and metics in 321 as against an estimated 40,000 citizens and well over 10,000 metics in 431 (A. H. M. Jones, 1957, pp. 8–10).

32 Isocrates, *On the Peace*, 82.

33 See Davies, 1967, 1968, 1971; the latter provides a basis for a more accurate assessment of changes in the role of land in the economy of Athens and in the composition of the wealthiest class.

34 Cf. Eisenstadt, 1964.

35 See chapter 2 above.

36 Cf. Pseudo-Xenophon, *Constitution of Athens* 1.11.

37 Xenophon, *Memorabilia* 2.8.3–4. In Xenophon's *Economicus* it is taken for granted that the farm overseer (*epitropos*) will be a slave. Free overseer in Menander, *Geōrgos* 46, 57. See Finley, 1959. A fluctuating labour force was particularly necessary in the building industry: cf. Brunt, 1966a and, for Greece, Burford, 1969, pp. 110–12. In harvesting, where temporary labour was also required, we hear of slave gangs working on the same basis of *locatio operis faciendi* ([Demosthenes] 53.21), and of the employment of free *women* (Demosthenes 57.45); the prestige of free women could be sacrificed rather more easily than that of the men. But there is a reference to male agricultural labourers in Theophrastus, *Characters* 4.3.

38 Claude Mossé (1962) has put forward a similar view of the relation between state pay and avoidance of dependent wage-labour, but thinks that the roots of the trouble lay in an economic depression in the fourth century which restricted the demand for labour and the citizen's opportunity of finding work. In my opinion the prosperity of the Athenian economy in the fourth century fluctuated with the strength of Athenian sea-power: I have indicated briefly elsewhere (above, chapter 4) why Rostovtzeff's theory of a general economic crisis due to the loss of overseas markets in the fourth century needs re-examination. I disagree with Mlle Mossé, therefore, both in taking a more optimistic view of the economy of fourth-century Athens, and in holding that the citizen's attitude to wage labour was determined during the Peloponnesian war rather than afterwards.

39 Gernet, 1950. Cf. for Rome Jacota, 1966. Does the law cited in [Demosthenes] 35.51 envisage the loan of money by slaves to shippers?

40 J. Lambert, 1934; Kaser, 1938; Szlechter, 1947 (pp. 311 ff., 'La Société entre le patron et l'affranchi'); Treggiari, 1969 (pp. 68–81). On Cosentini 1949–50 see also Kaser's review (Kaser, 1951). For claims on freedmen in

Greece, and the difference between Athens and other Greek cities, see Gernet, 1955a, pp. 168–72, 'La *dikē apostasiou*' (1950).
41 Megarians and Boeotians visited the Athenian market (Aristophanes, *Acharnians* 729 ff., 860 ff.).
42 Schweitzer, 1925; Kris and Kurz, 1934; Gombrich, 1955.
43 Cf. M. Weber, 1923, pp. 122–3. In the slave-owning regions of the Americas, though production for export was predominant everywhere, the extent to which a local market in foodstuffs, etc., developed is an important variable. See Genovese, 1965; Smith, 1954; Dowd, 1956; Mintz and Hall, 1960; Mintz, 1955.
44 Cf. also Aristotle, *Politics* 1320a 30.
45 Finley, 1952, pp. 56, 83–7.
46 Pringsheim, 1916, pp. 4–8, 25 ff.; Condanari-Michler, 1939.
47 Paoli, 1930; Paoli and Biscardi, 1966; Udovitch, 1962. The class of lawsuits dealing with *aphormē* (starting capital) has been taken as evidence for the commenda in Greece, but there is no evidence that the lender bore any risk. The interpretation of the Law of Gortyn, col. 9. 43 ff., as a reference to commenda contracts is highly conjectural (cf. Willetts, 1967, *ad loc.*). Hasebroek (1923) is probably wrong in claiming that sources speak of partnership between lender and borrower in the *nautikon daneion*. In Ptolemaic Alexandria the *nautikon daneion* was secured by guarantors instead of hypothecation (Wilcken, 1925; Bilabel, 1926, no. 7169).
48 Szlechter, 1947, pp. 68–72, 'Les contrats de société à l'époque néo-babylonienne. . . . La société en commandite'; Derrett, 1965; E. Lambert, 1906–7.
49 The evidence on Greek business partnerships is collected in Endenburg, 1937; Ziebarth, 1896, pp. 12–26, is still useful.
50 E.g. Codere, 1950; Balandier, 1961; Pospisil, 1963; Barić, 1964.
51 *Odyssey* 15. 80–5; 8. 387–95; 13. 14–15.
52 Thucydides 6.46.3; [Demosthenes] 49.22 (for the entertainment of Jason and Alketas; cf. Mauss, 1921).
53 See Gernet, 1928 and 1951b on *eranos*; Glouskina, 1960; Hands, 1968.
54 Belshaw, 1967.
55 Epstein, 1969.
56 For Greek banking see Bogaert, 1968. Bank loans for 'social' payments, [Demosthenes] 49.6, 17, 22; cf. Finley, 1952, pp. 83–7. The fact that there was a special suit for *aphormē* may suggest that the borrower had more control here over the date of repayment (Lipsius, 1905–15, p. 737).
57 Babylonian business 'houses' of the period provide a striking contrast (Cardascia, 1951); the Babylonians developed multiple interlocking operations centred on land, the Greek banks were based on simple differentiated operations separated from land.
58 Grants of permission to own land have been studied by Pečírka (1966).
59 The first three types of lawsuit singled out in the fourth century for rapid procedure – *dikai emmēnoi* – were those concerned with trade, tax-farming, and mining (Gernet, 1938c).
60 Andocides, *On the Mysteries* 133–4.
61 Xenophon, *Poroi* 4.14. For the theory that Sosias, who leased Nikias' slaves, had previously been his slave and foreman see Lauffer, 1955, pp. 1178–80.
62 Keith Hopkins has recently given a stimulating new analysis of Roman Republican society in sociological terms (K. Hopkins, 1968; cf. also Carney, 1962), but we need more study of the structural variations in

contemporary sub-systems within the society, with reference both to class groupings (see Gagé, 1964) and to politico-geographical context. In particular I should like to know how far economic activity outside Rome (for members of Roman, not provincial society) was more easily differentiated from political and social norms (distribution and display: see Frederiksen, 1966) than that within the city. Three aspects of the question may be distinguished: (1) the use of political power to accumulate wealth, (2) the pattern of investment in land, tax-farming, etc., (3) awareness of the economic problems of government. As C. Préaux has seen (1961, p. 229), such questions are part of the general problem of 'colonialism' in the ancient world.

E. Badian promises a book on provincial administration in the Republic. See meanwhile Badian, 1958, 1968; A. H. M. Jones, 1940; Wilson, 1966; Brunt, 1965; Nicolet, 1966. For Roman investment in Italy, Toynbee, 1965. See also Ruggini, 1968. Interesting suggestions of possible Roman use of Hellenistic models in financial policy in Nicolet, 1963.

63 Dittenberger, *Sylloge Inscriptionum Graecarum*³ (1915), no. 193.

64 The importance of military command as a model for the Greek conception of government is stressed by both Aymard (1953) and Caster (1937); on the relation between economic and military 'stratagems' see Vidal-Naquet, 1965, p. 137.

65 Gernet, 1910b; see also Gernet, 1909a. Gernet seems to have been the only man to see that the question of 'economic policy' so much debated by primitivists and modernists demanded an analysis of the Greek conception of the State and its economic role.

66 I am not suggesting that structural differentiation and economic individualism are universally necessary preconditions for the development of a 'modern' economy, but only that these concepts, developed in and for the evolution of modern western capitalism (cf. Gershenkron, 1965), are also useful for the understanding of some features of the economic history of the ancient world.

7 Homo politicus and homo economicus: war and trade in the economy of archaic and classical Greece

1 M. Weber, 1921, p. 756 (1956, p. 613; 1958, pp. 212–13).

2 The evidence is collected in Lencman, 1966, but the importance of slavery in the eighth century is here in my opinion underrated.

3 Gernet (1937b) argues that Solon's sumptuary law restricting the amount of wealth which could be transferred on marriage referred only to the trousseau (the term used is *phernē*), and not to the dowry (*proix*). All our data on the *proix* come from classical times when it was paid in cash. The fact that the groom's family had to put up a piece of land as security for the repayment of the dowry in case of divorce might be taken to suggest that land dowries had preceded cash payments; but Germain (1968) considers the *apotimēma* (security) in the case of dowry to be modelled on the land security demanded from those who leased orphans' estates.

4 There are interesting contrasts as well as similarities here with the relationship between kinship and property among the Merina of Madagascar, as Maurice Bloch has pointed out to me (see Bloch, 1975). A slightly different and perhaps over-ingenious explanation of the term *chērōstai* is given by Kamps, 1947.

5   Since Solon liberated many poor Athenians from various forms of slavery
    and dependence, his use of the term *thētes* may have been a programmatic
    declaration that henceforth Athenian citizens would work for others only
    on a contractual basis, rather than a reflection of the frequency of different
    types of labour relation at the time of his reforms. We hear of free women
    working as hired harvesters later (Demosthenes 57.45); for a fuller analysis
    of the place of wage labour in classical Athens see above, chapter 6.

6   Before 508/7 B.C. in Athens a boy became a citizen when he entered his
    phratry at sixteen (Labarbe, 1953; 1957, pp. 61–77). Kleisthenes' reforms
    in 508/7 left the age of entry to the phratry unchanged but transferred the
    responsibility for controlling entry to the citizen body to the demes, which
    admitted new members at the age of eighteen, with a further two-year period
    before full rights could be exercised. The implications of this postponement
    of entry into adulthood have, as far as I know, never been discussed. It
    may perhaps be a sign that pressure on peasant households was less acute
    than it had been in earlier times.

7   Full legal capacity was acquired, after Kleisthenes, at the age of twenty,
    but the rights obviously had a limited significance for those young men who
    had as yet no property of their own.

8   Further discussion in Bravo, 1977. Bravo and I disagree somewhat on the
    interpretation of the data on early trade, but I have learnt much from his
    article and our subsequent correspondence.

9   The point of this passage and of *Odyssey* 5.249 ff. is not to contrast long-
    ships with roundships, but large vessels with small ones.

10 Biremes with about 100 oars were in use by the middle of the sixth century;
    they are portrayed on Exekias' meticulously painted *dinos* Villa Giulia
    50599 (Morrison and Williams, 1968, plate 14c–d). The name *pentēkontoros*,
    'fifty-oared ship', apparently continued to be used for these vessels, which
    had double the power of the original pentekontors, perhaps because the
    same ships were used with only a single bank of oarsmen for cruising. Very
    probably biremes of this size had been in use since the end of the eighth
    century. A. B. Lloyd (1975) argues that the Greeks had had triremes since
    the seventh century, and Williams and Fisher (1973) interpret the purple
    stripe along the upper hull of the two-masted warship on a Late Corinthian
    crater-fragment as the outrigger (*parexeiresion*) of a trireme. But neither of
    these two arguments is conclusive. Thucydides' statement that until the
    Persian wars most Greek fleets were of pentekontors (1.14.3) must be
    accepted. My suggestion that the terms *pentēkontoros* and *triakontoros*
    could be used of biremes with 100 and 60 oars is perhaps supported by
    Herodotus' calculation of the (average?) complement of the smaller vessels
    in the Persian fleet – triakontors, pentekontors, *kerkouroi*, and horse-
    transports – as 80 men (Herodotus 7.97 and 184).

11 Solon's list of the types of association whose rules, if not contrary to Attic
    law, were to be regarded as legally binding on their members includes
    groups formed for expeditions seeking booty or trade (*Digest* 47.22.4,
    Ruschenbusch, 1966, Fr. 76a).

12 See Finley, 1968b for the argument that there was no formal restriction on
    the sale of land in archaic Greece, and n. 3 above on dowry.

13 Herodotus (1.163) records that the Phocaeans used pentekontors for long-
    distance trade in the western Mediterranean in the sixth century. Since he
    was used to fifth-century roundships the fact seemed to him worthy of note,
    but we do not have to believe that the Phocaeans were exceptional in this
    respect.

14   Plutarch, *Kimon* 9; Jacoby, *F.G.H.*, 392 F. 13. On pay and booty see Pritchett, 1971; on the date of the episode, Jacoby, 1947, p. 2.

15   The peculiar character of fifth-century Athens is well analysed by Lanza and Vegetti (1975), although the role of war and tribute in the economy deserves in my opinion even greater stress than they accord to it.

16   I have not tried at all in this article to deal with changes in the economy of Sparta and her Peloponnesian allies in the fifth century, a problem which obviously calls for study.

9 'Transcendence' and intellectual roles: the ancient Greek case

*This paper presents some of the results of a programme of research supported by the Social Science Research Council, carried out in association with Professor A. Momigliano, on transformations in ancient political and religious organization, concepts, and values. It also draws on an earlier study of the Greek intellectuals prepared at the Center for Hellenic Studies, Washington, D.C., in 1972 and delivered as part of my Nef lectures at the University of Chicago in that year. I should like to take this opportunity to express my gratitude for this support and hospitality and my thanks to all those who have helped me by their comments on lectures and seminar papers related to this topic. I am particularly grateful to Professor E. Shils for calling to my attention the question of the relation between intellectuals and authority.

1   Durkheim, 1898. F. Znaniecki's concept of the 'man of knowledge' is rather broader; his analysis (Znaniecki, 1940) remains the fundamental treatment of the problem on a comparative basis.

2   'Transcendence' in primitive and illiterate societies is not inconceivable or even unknown, but transcendental visions are likely to die with their creators or become transformed and assimilated by transmission.

3   This point has been made with especial emphasis recently by Basil Bernstein (1971 ff.). In stratified societies the experience of social structure can vary radically between one stratum and another. On Bernstein's work see n. 26 below.

4   I do not wish to imply that the existence of functionally specialized intellectual organizations excludes 'transcendence' either in the Hellenistic period or in later ages, but the question is too complex to pursue here.

5   Cf. Detienne, 1965. The *oikos* and the land remain, except in Sparta, outside the geometry of the city's institutions, a potent but seldom mentioned residual category, private and therefore ignored until tragedy began to concern itself with the heroic *oikos*.

6   Cf. below, n. 55. It is in the late fifth and the fourth centuries that historians and political philosophers become fascinated by the concept of caste; superficially adapted to the greater glory of Sparta, this interest may well have been generated at a profounder level by consciousness of the increasing importance of occupational categories in large cities such as Athens, Miletus, and Syracuse. A more detailed comparison of Greek and Indian reactions to increased occupational differentiation (for India, cf. Thapar, 1975) would be profitable.

7   On the invocation of the Muses in Homer see Harriott, 1969. The inspiration of the Muses is a guarantee of originality; the poet who learns his song from them is *autodidaktos* (*Odyssey* 22.347–8).

8   The difference between performance in an *oikos* and formal competition has perhaps not been sufficiently considered by Homerists. Some of the remarks

of A. B. Lord on oral dictated poetry (1953, especially pp. 132–3) would apply equally to the competition set-piece.

9 Hesiod, *Works and Days* 342–75, 695–723. Nevertheless, family ties and friendship are chief among the few good things left to the Iron race, which they will lose when Aidōs and Nemesis leave mankind (*ibid.*, 179–201).

10 I believe it is useful to distinguish the situation of the poet with a stake in the village, the poet who lives by travelling from one patron and/or competition to another, and the poet who settles in a single noble *oikos,* but it is quite possible that the same man might pass through all these situations in the course of his career. No doubt poor Perses hoped, when Hesiod won his prize at Chalkis, that he would make poetry his livelihood and leave the farm to his brother.

11 I refer here to structure at its crudest and most obvious level; the question whether Hesiod's digressions from his main structural framework are due to incompetence or a further, more sophisticated level of organization must be left aside. But I agree with Detienne (1963) and Benardete (1967) that the rhythm of work in the farmer's year is for Hesiod a model of Justice.

12 See Fränkel, 1962, pp. 112 ff., on Hesiod's use of genealogy as a mode of reasoning; Fränkel aptly compares Hesiod and Linnaeus.

13 The patterns of association and opposition latent in the *Odyssey* are beautifully analysed by Vidal-Naquet (1970a). On Hesiod, see Vernant, 1960. In my opinion the suggestion of a future sixth race should not be taken as intrinsic to the structure of the myth, because it is essential that the question of the justice of the Iron race should not be prejudged.

14 These occur again in Hesiod, frag. 321 (Merkelbach and West, 1967), 'work for young men, counsel for the middle-aged, prayer for the old'; in the three choruses of a Spartan folk-song, no. 870 in *Poetae Melici Graeci* (Page, 1962); and in Pindar, *Nemean* 3.72–4, and frag. 189 (Bowra, 1947).

15 I owe this point to Jensen, 1966, although I cannot accept all the conclusions she draws from it.

16 See however M. I. Henderson, 1957. Although the story of Archilochos' encounter with the Muses may not go back beyond the fifth century, the contrast between Hesiod's Muses, who teach the poet songs, and those of Archilochos, who give him a lyre, aptly symbolizes the change in orientation between epic and lyric.

17 Lasserre and Bonnard, 1958, frags 17, 224 (note however the metaphorical use of *skytalē* in Pindar, *Olympian* 6.91); see Lasserre, 1962. On the introduction of writing see also Sealey, 1957.

18 Kranz, 1961. A considerable proportion of the other first-person statements in the lyric poets concerns poetry and the poet's role, not his 'personal experience' in the modern sense; on these see Maehler, 1963. The current tendency among scholars is to react against the notion of the lyric poet as individualist (cf. most recently Russo, 1974, 1975); but without a clearer definition of the concept of individualism as applied to poetry, the debate is not likely to be very profitable.

19 On choral lyric see Webster, 1970 and Lefkowitz, 1963; on Archilochos Dover, 1963.

20 Maier, 1970; Bacchylides, frag. 14 (Snell, 1958). Bowra (1938) discusses Xenophanes' claim that his own *sophia* was worth more than victory in the games: I wonder whether such paradoxical claims were not a convention of the symposium, cf. Theognis 699–718, Xenophon, *Symposium* 4.33–44, and the remarks on boasting at symposia in Trumpf, 1958.

21 The change presumably lay partly in technique and partly in the conditions of the poet's life. Before the introduction of writing, since the poet could not hope for a widespread fame unless he travelled in person, those with a secure and prestigious position in their own society would have little incentive to develop their talents.

22 Maier, 1970; Gladigow, 1965. Cf. Detienne, 1962 for a study of the effects of the development of philosophy on conceptions of the poet's wisdom and the interpretation of poetic texts.

23 It is in the late sixth century that the formal competition in poetry (proto-tragedy and dithyramb), which detaches the poet both from the social contexts of the city and from his patron, again becomes important. At the same time Dionysus, a god who 'possesses' his worshippers, tends to replace Apollo as the god of poetry; the mask is interposed between speaker and audience; as prose develops into an alternative medium of public com-munication, poetry takes on more and more the separateness of ritual. On the problems of patronage and payment see Gentile, 1965.

24 Thrasybulus was tyrant in Miletus at the time of the war against Alyattes of Lydia (Herodotus 1.17–22), which preceded Alyattes' campaign against the Medes on the Halys ended by the eclipse of 585 B.C. with which Thales was associated (Herodotus 1.73–4). The tyrants Thoas and Damasenor should probably be dated after Thrasybulus, and their fall was followed by civil war (Plutarch, *Quaestiones Graecae* 32). Herodotus 5.29 speaks of two generations of *stasis* before Miletus rose to take the lead in Ionia at the end of the sixth century.

25 See Vlastos, 1947; Vernant, 1962 and 1963. Even in the political sphere, however, the concept of equality acquired a sharper focus from the emergence of tyranny.

26 Cf. Beattie, 1968 (criticizing R. Needham's representation of Nyoro thought in the form of a Pythagorean table of opposites); and the emphasis in the work of Louis Gernet on the multiple associations and plasticity of mythical images. I am not here criticizing G. E. R. Lloyd's masterly analysis of the development from polarity and analogy to more complex forms of argument in Greek philosophy (Lloyd, 1966), but his conception of 'mythical thought', and a certain degree of over-emphasis on the continuity between myth and rational argument. I think it may be valid to apply the distinction made by Bernstein (1971 ff.) between restricted and elaborated speech codes to the difference in syntax between mythical narrative and 'scientific' discourse. Elaborated codes, in Bernstein's definition, enable their users to convey and receive information in situations where role-definitions and shared con-ventions provide few clues to the speaker's intentions, which consequently have to be made explicit verbally by the use of a rich, well differentiated vocabulary and a complex syntax. Restricted codes are used where shared social experience enables speakers to anticipate one another's intentions, where the verbal communication is only a part of a total message trans-mitted by social context, nuances of tone and demeanour, gestures, etc., and consequently can function with a much more limited lexicon and range of syntactical alternatives. In myth, as in a restricted code, symbols (mythemes) are multivalent and the relation between them is not made explicit in the narrative, but supplied by the social experience of the audi-ence. The concepts of scientific discourse, on the other hand, are more precisely defined and are related to one another by the explicit use of analogical models and taxonomic frameworks or by the use of 'syntactical'

concepts such as causation, equality and inequality, similarity and opposition, etc. (Ideology, as an intermediate form, has an explicit syntax but a vocabulary of symbols which derive their force from the undefined associations that cluster round them, even though the range of these associations narrows as the audience widens?) If this is a valid approach, the early Greek philosophers were not merely making explicit the 'informal logic implicit in primitive or archaic thought' (Lloyd, 1966, p. 6), but were trying to make propositions that were self-evident because of their linguistic form, rather than depending on confirmatory information embedded in the context of communication. (Douglas (1973) denies that there is an absolute distinction here [cf. also recent discussions of indexicality in, for example, Cicourel, 1973; R. Turner, 1974]; but the relative distinction is surely still of considerable importance.) 'Making explicit' means changing from a multiplex to a single-channel mode of communication; the beginning of the change is already visible in Hesiod. Of course the process is gradual, but the implications are revolutionary. (Cf. further chapter 10 below.)

27   Popper, 1963. The political model for philosophical discussion may be the council, or meeting of a college of magistrates, rather than the assembly.

28   Three hundred is the smallest figure given in the sources for the size of the Pythagorean ruling party in Croton; Justin 20.4.14, Iamblichos, *Vita Pythagorica* 254, both of which may derive from (Burkert, 1972, pp. 104–5); Diogenes Laertius 8.3. Note the panic in Athens when Diokleides claimed to have seen as many as three hundred men meeting to carry out the mutilation of the Hermae (Andocides 1. 36 ff., Thucydides 6.27, 60).

29   Burkert, 1972; note also the remarks of Detienne in *Filosofia e Scienze*, 1966, pp. 149–56. Joly (1956) traces the justification of the *bios theōrētikos* as being higher than the political life back to fifth-century Pythagorean circles.

30   References to Diels and Kranz, 1951–2, no. 22. On the rejection of discussion by philosophers of the Heraclitean type, see Plato, *Theaetetus* 179e–180c. Empedokles, too, according to a testimony which may derive from his contemporary Xanthos of Lydia, refused an offer of kingship (Diogenes Laertius 8.63; see Momigliano, 1971, pp. 30 ff.).

31   Gernet, 1945; it was this article which originally stimulated my interest in the problems of role-definition faced by the Greek intellectuals.

32   Cf. the fragments of Gorgias' *On Non-Being* (Diels and Kranz, 1951–2, no. 82, B 3) and *Encomium of Helen* (*ibid.*, B 11), and Plato, *Protagoras* 342a–343b, the defence of the paradox that the Spartans are the leading philosophers of Greece. Cf. also de Romilly, 1956 on Thucydides' use of paired antithetical speeches.

33   Similar reasons presumably underlie the appearance of the Persian wars alongside mythical themes in early tragedy (Phrynichos, Aeschylus' *Persae*) and in art (Pausanias 1.15, the Athenian *Stoa Poikilē*; Jeffery (1965) persuasively suggests that the battle of Oinoe was mythical and not contemporary).

34   For the roots of this attitude in Ionian philosophy see Momigliano, 1931.

35   E. G. Turner, 1951.

36   History differed from political discourse primarily in its temporal viewpoint (Vidal-Naquet, 1960), rather than in its range of subject-matter.

37   Thucydides 6.28–9; the account shows the hesitations felt about trying to bring Alcibiades to trial.

38   I leave aside the question whether the law was passed before the Persian wars; the new evidence published by Keaney and Raubitschek (1972) is not

decisive, since it may well derive from the preoccupations of the late fifth century.

39 Kratinos, frag. 71 Kock; cf. 241, Aspasia as tyrant. Attacks on politicians in comedy are not attested before the age of Pericles, but too little of earlier comedy is preserved for any judgment of its contents to be possible.

40 Friis Johansen, 1970; Garvie, 1969, is sceptical.

41 Sifakis, 1971, pp. 60 ff., suggests that this was an innovation to be dated in Aristophanes' generation or not much earlier. According to Pollux (4.111, ed. Bethe), Euripides sometimes imitated the practice, and so did Sophocles occasionally in his later plays.

42 See Kaimio, 1970.

43 Cf. de Romilly, 1968, pp. 12 ff., 59 ff.

44 The difference between Hesiod and Aeschylus is that Hesiod tries to influence the unjust *basileis* by foretelling that retribution will fall on their *class* in the future, whereas Aeschylus tries to teach the abstract lesson that justice begets injustice by using as a *model* myths that portray retribution falling on *individuals*. The question whether it is just that sons should suffer for the sins of fathers is secondary, overshadowed by the conception of an impersonal, equilibrium-seeking process. But, needless to say, in representing the forces involved in the process of retribution, Aeschylus drew on traditional religious beliefs, anxieties, and imagery alien to the rationalism of the philosophers (Wehrli, 1931).

45 Knox, 1964 [cf. also Knox, 1972]. (There may of course be more than one heroic character in a play.) Erving Goffman's definition of 'action' and its phases and significance (Goffman, 1967, pp. 149–270, 'Where the action is') provides a brilliant analysis of the role of heroic individualism in our own culture, which also throws light on many aspects of Greek tragedy – especially what Sophocles himself called the 'piquant and artificial' element in the earlier of his preserved tragedies (Plutarch, *Moralia* 79 B). The focus in the *Philoctetes* on the effects of lying in social relationships is a new departure; earlier the lie was merely a useful dramatic device.

46 Parry, 1969, 1972.

47 H. North (1966) has some good remarks on the tension between appreciation of *sophrosyne* and of the heroic virtues in Sophocles. Creon's patriotic, short-sighted rationalism is of course Sophocles' most overt criticism of the assumptions of contemporary politics; Creon is also Sophocles' least sympathetic 'hero'. On Euripides see Di Benedetto, 1971.

48 On the relation between rejection of the constrictions of social status and ascetic discipline of bodily appetites, see Douglas, 1970 and Dumont, 1966.

49 Xenophon, *Apologia Socratis* 4–5, *Memorabilia* 4.8.5, says that the *daimonion* inhibited Socrates from composing a defence speech, whereas Plato (*Apology* 41d) says that he received no 'sign' at all about the affair of his trial; both sources agree that he concluded that the time had come for him to die. The *daimonion* prevented him from making an active career in politics 'because a resolute defender of justice could not have survived long in office in Athens' (Plato, *Apology* 31c–32e, cf. *Republic* 496c–e). The reasoning seems to be mainly Plato's; Socrates' *daimonion* did not give reasons for its promptings. It represented an inexplicable feeling of compulsion; sometimes, if Xenophon is right in saying that its warnings could concern Socrates' friends' conduct as well as his own, no more than a 'hunch' (cf. Plato, *Euthydemus* 272e). But this inexplicability is the counterpart of Socrates' determination to think everything out himself, searching his own mind and refusing to accept an opinion untested (Havelock, 1972): the

residue of motivation which, on introspection, proved impossible to rationalize.

50 Athens had, since Solon, a written law code, but very little in the way of executive staff responsible for enforcing it; it was the citizen's duty to 'come to the help of the laws' by prosecuting offenders. There is here a fundamental difference between ancient Athens and modern societies in the relation of the individual to the state.

51 See, for example, Webster, 1967, index, s.v. 'Marriage debates'.

52 Firth, 1956; Firth, Forge, and Hubert, 1969; D. M. Schneider, 1968; Southall, 1961, pp. 31–45. Bernstein's contrast between personal and positional control systems is relevant here.

53 Di Benedetto, 1971, chapter 14; Dugas, 1894; Chase, 1930; Dirlmeier, 1931.

54 Note also the development in the late fifth and fourth centuries of a type of comedy in which myths used in tragedy were presented in modern dress (Webster, 1953).

55 One feels that Euripides has two audiences in mind: the young intelligentsia, who will pick up all his clever allusions, and the rest. At the basis of the formation of common-interest associations lies the assumption that a man is defined by his occupation, education, and interests rather than by ascribed status; the occupational role becomes part of his permanent make-up instead of being assumed only in the appropriate context. The frequent appearance in Middle Comedy of soldiers, philosophers, doctors, prostitutes, parasites, and cooks reflects this new way of perceiving urban society. (All are suitable subjects for comedy because of discrepancies between their pretensions and their actual situation.) An association between occupations and character-types taken to this level of detail could hardly be acceptable to philosophers; Theophrastus' *Characters* seems to respond to a need for a new synthesis by turning from the social experience of the *agora* to that of the neighbourhood or small group. New Comedy also shows a more abstract conception of character; the play on occupational types of Middle Comedy is given a new twist in the theme of the virtuous *hetaira*, whose character is at odds with her situation.

56 See Smith, 1974.

57 It is Plato's conception of the needs of philosophers, rather than the needs of men in general, which determines the form of the ideal society. It is only when Greek philosophers give up the ambition to remodel society and exert a controlling influence in politics that they develop ethical theories which apply to all men, and *paideia* becomes the means of inculcating virtuous habits in the individual (Aristotle), rather than the mechanism by which the institutions and norms of society are reproduced (Plato, Xenophon).

58 I do not wish to become involved here with the question of 'shamanism' in archaic Greece (on which see most recently Burkert, 1972); it may be present as a sporadic phenomenon, but not as an institutionalized role.

59 The oracles of Zeus at Dodona were transmitted through the sounds made by birds and trees (Parke, 1967).

60 Ziehen, 1930; Rudhardt, 1958, s.v. 'mantique'; Jacoby, 1949, s.v. 'manteis', 'exegetai'. The relation between the notions of priest, mantis, and exegete needs further study. *Manteis* and *chrēsmologoi* ('oracle-mongers') did claim to have special expertise in interpreting oracles, but they had to carry their point by plausibility rather than authority.

61 Like Bernstein's 'elaborated codes'; cf. n. 26 above.

10 Evolution and history: approaches to the study of structural differentiation

*This paper presents some of the results of a research project on 'transformations in ancient political and religious concepts, organization, and values' carried out in conjunction with Professor A. Momigliano, with support from the S.S.R.C. I should like to express here my gratitude to both.

1 For a different treatment, focused on the control of potential conflicts between group interests rather than the individual's role-management, see Smith, 1974, pp. 191–2, 260–2.

2 In complex modern societies most interaction settings are supported in one way or another by a complex infrastructure of corporate units even if these units exercise only marginal control over the norms of some settings. But this is much less true of archaic societies.

3 I have to thank Professor Louis Dumont for stimulating me to look at Athenian institutions from this point of view.

4 Theophrastus' Superstitious Man, *Characters* 16, attests this view clearly for the late fourth century. In the fifth century Thucydides 7.69.2 emphasizes religion in a speech made to a demoralized army and consisting entirely of appeals to personal attachments: family pride, safety of wives and children – old-fashioned feelings, he says, such as men are not ashamed to call on in emergencies. I do not think it is entirely Thucydides' historiographic designs which make him present pre-battle speeches in more hopeful circumstances as largely concerned with strategic and tactical factors (e.g. 2. 89). But the subject needs further investigation.

5 This analysis owes much to Vernant's paper 'La Lutte de classe' (1965b). Following a recent discussion with Joel Kahn, I would stress that the Athenian classification of roles and activities as 'economic' or 'political' was based on their experience of society as made up of a variety of social settings with markedly different norms, which obscured for them the connections between these settings. The relationship between political decisions and the level of activity in the market was only partially perceived, and understanding of the interrelations of tribute, military activity, the movements of money and labour, trade and production was hampered by the fact that the most important part of the discussion was carried on in the idiom of politics. It is the concrete social experience which gave the ideology its chance of success.

6 Mystery cults were spreading rapidly already in the sixth century. Both the generally anomic state of Greek society in this period of transition between traditional aristocratic control and the development of formal political organization, and the tendency of tyrants to favour a somewhat impersonal, spectacular type of religious festival may have had an influence here.

7 Sophocles, the least political of the dramatic poets in his plays, is the only one known to have held a major political office; his contemporary, Ion of Chios, tells a story implying that neither he nor Pericles took his election as general very seriously (Jacoby, *F.G.H.*, 392 F.6).

8 Bernstein's work is explicitly based on Durkheim's contrast between the mechanical solidarity of simple societies and the organic solidarity of complex ones. It is also principally concerned with the functioning of speech codes as mechanisms of social control. This aspect of Bernstein's work is not my concern here.

Bibliography

ADAMESTEANU, D. (1973), 'Le suddivisioni di terra nel Metapontino', in Finley, 1973b, pp. 49–61.

ADAMS, R. MCC. (1965), *Land behind Baghdad*, Chicago University Press.

ADAMS, R. MCC. (1966a), *The Evolution of Urban Society: Early Mesopotamia and Pre-Hispanic Mexico*, Aldine, Chicago.

ADAMS, R. MCC. (1966b), 'Trend and tradition in Near Eastern archaeology', in *Archaeology: Horizons Old and New, Proceedings of the American Philosophical Society*, 110, 2, pp. 105–10.

ADAMS, W. Y. (1966), 'Post-Pharaonic Nubia III. Postscript: philosophy, archaeology and history in Nubia', *Journal of Egyptian Archaeology*, 52, pp. 156–62.

ADLER, FRANZ (1957), 'Marxist philosophy and sociology of knowledge', in Becker and Boskoff, 1957, pp. 396–423.

AHRWEILER, H. (1965), 'L'Histoire et la géographie de la région de Smyrne entre les deux occupations Turques, 1081–1317', *Travaux et mémoires*, 1, pp. 1–204.

ALFÖLDI, A. (1965), *Early Rome and the Latins*, University of Michigan Press, Ann Arbor.

ANDLER, CHARLES (1932), *Vie de Lucien Herr*, Rieder, Paris.

ANDREWES, A. (1961), 'Phratries in Homer', *Hermes*, 89, pp. 129–40.

ANDREYEV, V. N. (1967), 'Attičeskoe o obščestvennoe zemlevladenie V–III vv. do n.e.', *Vestnik Drevnej Istorii*, 1967, 2, pp. 47–76.

ANTONI, CARLO (1940), *Dallo storicismo alla sociologia*, Sansoni, Florence (trans. as *From History to Sociology*, Merlin Press, London, 1962).

ANTONIADIS-BIBICOU, H. (1965), 'Villages désertés en Grèce', in *Villages désertés et histoire économique, XIe–XVIIIe siècle*, SEVPEN, Paris, pp. 343–417.

ARGYLE, W. J. (1966), *The Fon of Dahomey: a History and Ethnography of the Old Kingdom*, Clarendon Press, Oxford.

ASHERI, D. (1966), *Distribuzioni di terra nell'antica Grecia, Memorie dell' Accademia delle Scienze di Torino*, classe di Scienze Morali, Storiche e Filologiche, series 4, 10.

ATHENS CENTER OF EKISTICS (1970–3), *Ancient Greek Cities*, 1–20.

AUSTIN, M. (1970), *Greece and Egypt in the Archaic Age*, Cambridge University Press.

AUSTIN, M., and VIDAL-NAQUET, P. (1972), *Économies et sociétés en Grèce ancienne*, Colin, Paris (collection U2).

AYMARD, A. (1943), 'Hiérarchie du travail et autarchie individuelle', *Revue d' histoire de la philosophie*, 11, pp. 124–46 (reprinted in Aymard, 1968, pp. 316–33).

AYMARD, A. (1948), 'L'Idée du travail dans la Grèce archaïque', *Journal de psychologie normale et pathologique*, 41, pp. 29–50.

AYMARD, A. (1953), 'Esprit militaire et administration hellénistique', *Revue des études anciennes*, 55, pp. 132–45 (reprinted in Aymard, 1968, pp. 461–73).

AYMARD, A. (1968), *Études d'histoire ancienne*, Presses Universitaires de France, Paris.

BADIAN, E. (1958), *Foreign Clientelae*, Clarendon Press, Oxford.

BADIAN, E. (1968), *Roman Imperialism in the Late Republic*, 2nd ed., Blackwell, Oxford.

BAILEY, D. M. (1962), 'Lamps from Tharros in the British Museum', *Annual of the British School of Archaeology at Athens*, 57, pp. 35–45.

BAILEY, C.-J. N. (1972), 'The integration of linguistic theory: internal reconstruction and the comparative method in descriptive analysis', in Stockwell and Macaulay, 1972, pp. 22–31.

BALANDIER, G. (1961), 'Phénomènes sociaux totaux et dynamique sociale', *Cahiers internationaux de sociologie*, 30, pp. 23–34.

BALAZS, E. (1960), 'The birth of capitalism in China', *Journal of the Economic and Social History of the Orient*, 3, pp. 196–216 (reprinted in E. Balazs, *Chinese Civilization and Bureaucracy*, Yale University Press, New Haven, 1964, pp. 34–54).

BALDWIN, JOHN W. (1959), *The Medieval Theories of the Just Price, Transactions of the American Philosophical Society*, 49, 4.

BANTON, M., ed. (1965), *The Relevance of Models for Social Anthropology*, ASA Monograph 1, Tavistock, London.

BARIĆ, L. (1964), 'Some aspects of credit, saving and investment in a "non-monetary" economy', in Firth and Yamey, 1964, pp. 35–52.

BARTH, FREDRIK (1966), *Models of Social Organization*, Royal Anthropological Institute, London.

BARTH, FREDRIK (1967), 'On the study of social change', *American Anthropologist*, 69, pp. 661–9.

BASS, G. (1967), *Cape Gelidonya: a Bronze Age Shipwreck, Transactions of the American Philosophical Society*, new series, 57, 8.

BAUER, P. T. (1954), *West African Trade*, Cambridge University Press.

BEATTIE, JOHN (1968), 'Aspects of Nyoro symbolism', *Africa*, 38, pp. 413–42.

BEAZLEY, J. D. (1945), 'The Brygos Tomb', *American Journal of Archaeology*, 49, pp. 153–8.

BEAZLEY, J. D. (1963), *Attic Red-Figure Vase-Painters*, 2nd ed., Clarendon Press, Oxford.

BECKER, HOWARD, and BARNES, HARRY E. (1952), *Social Thought from Lore to Science*, 2nd ed., Harren Press, Washington.

BECKER, HOWARD, and BOSKOFF, ALVIN, eds (1957), *Modern Sociological Theory in Continuity and Change*, Dryden Press, New York.

BELLAH, ROBERT (1973), *Émile Durkheim on Morality and Society*, Chicago University Press.

BELOCH, K. J. (1912–27), *Griechische Geschichte*, 2nd ed., J. Trübner, Strasburg, and de Gruyter, Berlin.

BELSHAW, C. S. (1965), *Traditional Exchange and Modern Markets*, Prentice-Hall, Englewood Cliffs, N.J.

BELSHAW, C. S. (1967), *Under the Ivi Tree*, Routledge & Kegan Paul, London.

BENARDETE, S. (1967), 'Hesiod's *Works and Days*: a first reading', *Agon*, 1, pp. 150–74.

BENET, FRANCISCO (1957), 'Explosive markets: the Berber highlands', in Polanyi, 1957a, pp. 188–217.

BENET, FRANCISCO (1961), 'Weekly suqs and city markets: the transition from rural suq economy to market economy', in C.A.O. van Nieuwenhuijze (ed.), *Research for Development in the Mediterranean Basin: a Proposal*, Mouton, Paris/Hague, pp. 86–97.

BENGTSON, H. (1953) 'Die ptolemäische Staatsverwaltung im Rahmen der hellen-istischen Administration', *Museum Helveticum*, 10, pp. 161–77.

BENOÎT, F. (1965), *Recherches sur l'hellénisation du Midi de la Gaule*, Ophrys, Aix-en-Provence.

BENVENISTE, E. (1951), 'Don et échange dans la vocabulaire indo-européenne', *L'Année sociologique 1948-9*, pp. 7–20 (reprinted in E. Benveniste, *Problèmes de linguistique générale*, Gallimard, Paris, 1966, pp. 315–26).

BENVENISTE, E. (1969), *Le Vocabulaire des institutions indo-européennes*, Éditions de Minuit, Paris.

BERCIU, D. (1966a), 'Problèmes actuels de la civilisation de La Tène chez les Géto-Daces', *Latomus*, 25, pp. 414–25.

BERCIU, D. (1966b), 'Les Celtes et la civilisation de La Tène chez les Géto-Daces', *Institute of Archaeology, London, Bulletin*, 6, pp. 75–94.

BERGQUIST, B. (1967), *The Archaic Greek Temenos. A Study of Structure and Func-tion*, Swedish Institute in Athens, Lund.

BERNSTEIN, BASIL (1971 ff.), *Class, Codes and Control*, vols I–III, Routledge & Kegan Paul, London.

BERNSTEIN, BASIL (1971b), 'On the classification and framing of educational knowledge', in M. F. D. Young (ed.), *Knowledge and Control*, Collier-Macmillan, London (reprinted in Bernstein, 1973, pp. 227–56).

BERNSTEIN, BASIL (1973), *Class, Codes and Control*, vol. I, revised ed., Paladin, St Albans.

BERQUE, JACQUES (1936), *Les Pactes pastoraux, contribution à l'étude des contrats nord-africains*, La Typo-Litho and J. Carbonel, Algiers (non vidi).

BERQUE, JACQUES (1937), 'Sur un coin de terre marocain: seigneur terrien et paysans', *Annales d'histoire économique et sociale*, 9, pp. 227–35.

BERQUE, JACQUES (1955), *Structures sociales du Haut-Atlas*, Presses Universitaires de France, Paris.

BERQUE, JACQUES (1956), '125 ans de sociologie maghrébine', *Annales. Économies, sociétés, civilisations*, 11, pp. 296–324.

BERR, HENRI (1911), *La Synthèse en histoire*, La Renaissance du Livre, Paris (revised ed., Michel, Paris, 1953).

BIESANTZ, H. (1965), *Die Thessalischen Grabreliefs*, von Zabern, Mainz.

BILABEL, F., ed. (1926), *Sammelbuch griechischer Urkunden aus Aegypten*, vol. III, part 1, de Gruyter, Berlin.

BINFORD, L. R. (1972), *An Archaeological Perspective*, Seminar Press, New York.

BINGEN, J. (1975), 'Le Milieu urbain dans la chōra égyptienne à l'époque ptolémaïque', *Proceedings of the XIVth International Congress of Papyrologists (Oxford 1974)*, Egypt Exploration Society, London, pp. 367–73.

BLOCH, MARC (1925), review of Halbwachs, 1925, *Revue de synthèse historique*, 40, pp. 73–83.

BLOCH, MAURICE (1975), 'Property and the end of affinity', in M. Bloch (ed.), *Marxist Analyses and Social Anthropology*, Malaby Press, London, pp. 203–28.

BOARDMAN, J. M. (1956), 'Delphinion in Chios', *Annual of the British School of Archaeology in Athens*, 51, pp. 41–54.

BOARDMAN, J. M. (1959), 'Excavations at Pindakas in Chios', *Annual of the British School of Archaeology in Athens*, 53–4 (1958–9), pp. 295–309.

BOARDMAN, J. M. (1964), *The Greeks Overseas*, Penguin, Harmondsworth (revised ed., 1973).

BOARDMAN, J. M., and HAYES, JOHN (1966), *Excavations at Tocra 1963–1965: the Archaic Deposits*, vol. I, British School of Archaeology at Athens and Thames & Hudson, London.

BODEI GIGLIONI, G. (1970), *Xenophontis De Vectigalibus (introduzione, testo critico, traduzione)*, La Nuova Italia, Florence.

BODEI GIGLIONI, G. (1974), *Lavori pubblici e occupazione nell'antichità classica*, Pátron, Milan.

BOGAERT, R. (1966), *Les Origines antiques de la banque de dépôt*, Sijthoff, Leiden.

BOGAERT, R. (1968), *Banques et banquiers dans les cités grecques*, Sijthoff, Leiden.

BOHANNAN, P. (1955), 'Some principles of exchange and investment among the Tiv', *American Anthropologist*, 57, pp. 60–9.

BOHANNAN, P. (1959), 'The impact of money on an African subsistence economy', *Journal of Economic History*, 19, pp. 491–503 (reprinted in Dalton, 1967, pp. 123–35).

BOHANNAN, P., and DALTON, G., eds (1962), *Markets in Africa*, Northwestern University Press, Evanston.

BOHANNAN, P., and DALTON, G. (1965), 'Karl Polanyi 1886–1964', *American Anthropologist*, 67, pp. 1508–11.

BOLTE, F. (1929), 'Sparta (Topographie)', Pauly-Wissowa, *Realencyclopädie der classischen Altertumswissenschaft*, vol. III A 2, coll. 1350–73.

BON, A. (1930), 'Les Ruines antiques dans l'île de Thasos et en particulier les tours helléniques', *Bulletin de correspondance hellénique*, 54, pp. 147–94.

BOUGLÉ, CÉLESTIN (1922), *Leçons de sociologie sur l'évolution des valeurs*, Colin, Paris.

BOUGLÉ, CÉLESTIN (1936), 'La Méthodologie de François Simiand', *Annales sociologiques*, series A, 2, pp. 5–28.

BOULANGER, ANDRÉ (1923), *Aélius Aristide et la sophistique dans la province d'Asie au IIe siècle de notre ère*, de Boccard, Paris.

BOULANGER, ANDRÉ (1925), *Orphée, rapport de l'Orphisme et du Christianisme*, Rieder, Paris.

BOWRA, C. M. (1938), 'Xenophanes and the Olympic Games', *American Journal of Philology*, 59, pp. 257–79 (reprinted in C. M. Bowra, *Problems of Greek Poetry*, Clarendon Press, Oxford, 1953, pp. 15–37).

BOWRA, C. M., ed. (1947), *Pindar* (Oxford Classical Texts).

BRADFORD, J. (1949), 'Buried landscapes in Southern Italy', *Antiquity*, 23, pp. 58–72.

BRADFORD, J. (1956), 'Fieldwork on aerial discoveries in Attica and Rhodes', *Antiquaries' Journal*, 36, pp. 172–80.

BRADFORD, J. (1957), *Ancient Landscapes*, Bell, London.

BRAKE, JÜRGEN (1935), *Wirtschaft und Charakter in der antiken Bildung*, Schulte-Bulmke, Frankfurt a. M.

BRAVO, BENEDETTO (1970), introduction to Vernant, 1970.

BRAVO, BENEDETTO (1974), 'Une Lettre sur plomb de Beresan: colonisation et modes de contact dans le Pont', *Dialogues d'histoire ancienne*, 1, pp. 111–87.

BRAVO, BENEDETTO (1977), 'Le commerce maritime et la noblesse dans la Grèce archaïque', *Dialogues d'histoire ancienne*, 3 (in press).

BRELICH, A. (1969), *Paides e Parthenoi*, vol. I, Ateneo, Rome.

BROWN, P. R. L. (1971), 'The rise and function of the Holy Man', *Journal of Roman Studies*, 61, pp. 80–101.

BROWN, P. R. L. (1975), 'Society and the supernatural: a medieval change', *Daedalus*, 104, 2, pp. 133–51.

BRUNT, P. (1965), 'The Equites in the late Republic', *2e Conférence internationale d'histoire économique, Aix 1962*, I. *Trade and Politics in the Ancient World*, Mouton, Paris/Hague, pp. 117–49.

BRUNT, P. (1966a), 'The Roman mob', *Past and Present*, 35, pp. 3–27.

BRUNT, P. (1966b), 'Athenian settlements abroad in the fifth century B.C.',

Ancient Society and Institutions, Studies presented to Victor Ehrenberg, Blackwell, Oxford, pp. 71–92.

BUCHANAN, J. (1962), *Theōrika: a Study of Monetary Distributions to the Athenian Citizenry during the Vth and IVth Centuries*, Augustin, Locust Valley, N.Y. (revised ed., 1976).

BÜCHER, KARL (1893), *Die Entstehung der Volkswirtschaft*, Laupp, Tübingen.

BÜCHER, KARL (1901), 'Zur griechische Wirtschaftsgeschichte', *Festgabe für A. Schäffle*, Laupp, Tübingen, pp. 193–254.

BURFORD, ALISON (1969), *The Greek Temple-builders at Epidauros: a Social and Economic Study of Building in the Asklepian Sanctuary during the 4th and Early 3rd Centuries*, Liverpool University Press.

BURGER, A. SZ. (1966), 'The late Roman cemetery at Ságvár', *Acta Archaeologica Academiae Scientiarum Hungaricae*, 18, pp. 99–234.

BURKERT, W. (1972), *Lore and Science in early Pythagoreanism*, Harvard University Press, Cambridge, Mass. (revised version of *Weisheit und Wissenschaft*, Nürnberg, 1962).

BUTZER, KARL W. (1976), *Early Hydraulic Civilization in Egypt: a Study in Cultural Ecology*, Chicago University Press.

CAHEN, MAURICE (1921), *Études sur le vocabulaire religieux scandinave: La Libation*, Champion, Paris.

CANCIAN, FRANK (1966), 'Maximization as norm, strategy and theory: a comment on pragmatic statements in economic anthropology', *American Anthropologist*, 68, pp. 465–70.

CARCOPINO, J. (1965), 'Livres offerts', *Comptes rendus de l'Académie des Inscriptions et Belles-Lettres*, pp. 61–2.

CARDASCIA, G. (1951), *Les Archives des Murashû, une famille d'hommes d'affaires babyloniens à l'époque perse (455–403 av. J.-C.)*, Imprimerie Nationale, Paris.

CARNEY, T. F. (1962), 'The administrative revolution in Rome of the 1st century B.C.', *Proceedings of the African Classical Associations*, 5, pp. 31–42.

CARRINGTON, R. C. (1931), 'Studies in the Campanian *villae rusticae*', *Journal of Roman Studies*, 21, pp. 110–30.

CASSIN, ELENA (1955), 'Symboles de cession immobilière dans l'ancien droit mesopotamien', *L'Année sociologique*, 1952, pp. 107–61.

CASSON, LIONEL (1971), *Ships and Seamanship in the Ancient World*, Princeton University Press.

CASTAGNOLI, F. (1959), 'Dedica arcaica lavinate a Castore e Polluce', *Studi e materiali di storia delle religioni*, 30, pp. 109–17.

CASTAGNOLI, F. (1961), 'Contributi della fotografia aerea agli studi di topografia antica in Italia', in *Atti del 7° Congresso Internazionale di Archeologia Classica, 1958*, vol. I, 'L'Erma' di Bretschneider, Rome, pp. 41–5.

CASTAGNOLI, F. (1962), 'Sulla tipologia degli altari di Lavinio', *Bullettino della commissione archeologica comunale di Roma*, 77 (1959–60), pp. 145–72.

CASTER, MARCEL (1937), 'L'"Économique" de Xénophon', in *Mélanges Desrousseaux*, Hachette, Paris, pp. 49–57.

CATLING, H. W. (1962), 'Patterns of settlement in Bronze Age Cyprus', *Opuscula Atheniensia*, 4, pp. 129–69.

CHADWICK, N. K. (1942), *Poetry and Prophecy*, Cambridge University Press.

CHANTRAINE, P. (1960), 'Encore "authentes"', *Aphierōma stē mnēmē tou M. Triantaphyllidē*, Salonika, pp. 89–93.

CHANTRAINE, P. (1968 ff.), *Dictionnaire étymologique de la langue grecque*, vols I ff., Klincksieck, Paris.

CHAPMAN, A. (1957), 'Port of trade enclaves in Aztec and Maya civilizations', in Polanyi, 1957a, pp. 114–53.

CHASE, ALSTON HURD (1930), 'Quomodo amicitiam tractaverint tragici Graeci quaeritur', *Harvard Studies in Classical Philology*, 41, pp. 186–9.

CHEVALLIER, R. (1957), *Bibliographie des applications archéologiques de la photographie aérienne, Bulletin d'archéologie marocaine*, 2, supplément (also Fondazione Lerici, Milan).

CHEVALLIER, R. (1958), 'Pour une interprétation archéologique de la couverture aérienne grecque: note sur les centuriations', *Bulletin de correspondance hellénique*, 82, pp. 635–6.

CHEVALLIER, R. (1961), 'Les Perspectives françaises de la photographie aérienne archéologique', in *Atti del 7° Congresso Internazionale di Archeologia Classica 1958*, vol. I, 'L'Erma' di Bretschneider, Rome, pp. 47–50.

CHEVALLIER, R. (1966), 'Quelques méthodes modernes de prospection archéologique', in *Mélanges d'archéologie et d'histoire offerts à André Piganiol*, vol. I, SEVPEN, Paris, pp. 79–114.

CHEVALLIER, R. (1974), 'Cité et territoire. Solutions romaines aux problèmes de l'organisation de l'espace. Problématique 1948–1973', in H. Temporini (ed.), *Aufstieg und Niedergang der römischen Welt*, vol. II, part 1, de Gruyter, Berlin, pp. 649–788.

CHRIST, KARL (1967), *Antike Numismatik*, Wissenschaftliche Buchgesellschaft, Darmstadt.

Chronique des fouilles, published annually in *Bulletin de correspondance hellénique*.

CICOUREL, A. (1973), *Cognitive Sociology*, Penguin, Harmondsworth.

Città e il suo territorio, La, (1968), *VII Convegno di Studi sulla Magna Grecia 1967*, L'Arte Tipografica, Naples (actually 1970).

CLAIRMONT, C. (1955), 'Greek pottery from the Near East, I', *Berytus*, 11, pp. 55–141.

CLAIRMONT, C. (1956–8), 'Greek pottery from the Near East, II. Black vases', *Berytus*, 12, pp. 1–34.

CLARK, J. M. (1948), *Alternative to Serfdom*, Blackwell, Oxford.

CLOCHÉ, P. (1941), 'La Démocratie athénienne et les possédants aux Ve et IVe siècles avant J.-C.', *Revue historique*, 192, pp. 1–45, 193–235.

CODERE, H. (1950), *Fighting with Property*, Monographs of the American Ethnological Society, 18, New York.

COHEN, EDWARD E. (1973), *Ancient Athenian Maritime Courts*, Princeton University Press.

COHEN, PERCY S. (1967), 'Economic analysis and economic man', in Firth, 1967a, pp. 91–118.

COJA, M. (1962), 'Activitatea meşteşugărească la Histria în sec. VI–I î. e. n.', *Studi şi Cercetàri de Istorie Veche*, 13, pp. 19–46.

COLBY, B. N. (1966), 'Ethnographic semantics: a preliminary survey', *Current Anthropology*, 7, pp. 3–32.

COLLINGWOOD, R. G. (1929), 'Town and country in Roman Britain', *Antiquity*, 3, pp. 261–76.

CONDANARI-MICHLER, S. (1939), 'Bodem, pignus, hypotheke', *Festschrift Paul Koschaker*, vol. III, Böhlau, Weimar, pp. 350–65.

CONRAD, A. H., *et al.* (1967), 'Slavery as an obstacle to economic growth in the United States: a panel discussion', *Journal of Economic History*, 27, pp. 443–59.

COOK, J. M. (1953), 'The cult of Agamemnon at Mycenae', *Geras Antoniou Keramopoullou*, Athens, pp. 112–18.

COOK, J. M. (1959), 'Old Smyrna 1948–51', *Annual of the British School of Archaeology at Athens*, 53–4 (1958–9), pp. 1–34.

COOK, J. M. (1961), 'The problems of classical Ionia', *Proceedings of the Cambridge Philological Society*, 7, pp. 9–18.

COOK, J. M. (1966), *The Sanctuary of Hemithea at Castabos*, Cambridge University Press.

COOK, R. M. (1958), 'Speculation on the origins of coinage', *Historia*, 7, pp. 257–62.

COOK, R. M. (1959), 'Die Bedeutung der bemalten Keramik für den griechischen Handel', *Jahrbuch des deutschen archäologischen Instituts*, 74, pp. 114–23.

COOK, SCOTT (1966), 'The obsolete "anti-market" mentality: a critique of the substantive approach to economics', *American Anthropologist*, 68, pp. 323–45.

COOK, S. F., and HEIZER, R. (1960), *The Application of Quantitative Methods to the Study of Archaeology*, Quadrangle Books, Chicago.

Corinth XII (1952), *The Minor Objects*, ed. G. Davidson, American School of Classical Studies at Athens, Princeton.

CORNFORD, F. M. (1912), *From Religion to Philosophy*, Arnold, London.

CORNFORD, F. M. (1921), 'The unconscious element in literature and philosophy', *Proceedings of the Classical Association*, 1921, reprinted in Cornford, 1950, pp. 1–13.

CORNFORD, F. M. (1935), 'The unwritten philosophy', lecture, published in Cornford, 1950, pp. 28–46.

CORNFORD, F. M. (1950), *The Unwritten Philosophy and Other Essays*, Cambridge University Press.

CORNFORD, F. M. (1952), *Principium Sapientiae*, Cambridge University Press.

COSENTINI, C. (1949–50), *Studi sui liberti*, vols 1–2, Facoltà giuridica, Catania.

COURBIN, P., ed. (1963), *Études archéologiques*, SEVPEN, Paris.

COURTOIS, CH. (1955), *Les Vandales et l'Afrique*, Arts et Métiers Graphiques, Paris.

CROISET, A. (1909), *Les Démocraties antiques*, Flammarion, Paris.

CROSBY, M. (1951), 'The Poros Building', *Hesperia*, 20, pp. 168–87.

CUMONT, F. (1949), *Lux Perpetua*, Geuthner, Paris.

CURTIN, P. (1967), review of Polanyi, 1966, *Economic History Review*, 20, p. 585.

CZARNOWSKI, S. (1919), *Le Culte des héros et ses conditions sociales. Saint Patrick, héros nationale de l'Irelande*, Alcan, Paris.

D'AGOSTINO, B. (1965), review of Vallet and Villard, 1964, *Archeologia Classica*, 17, pp. 159–67.

DALTON, GEORGE (1959), 'Robert Owen and Karl Polanyi as socio-economic critics and reformers of industrial capitalism', Ph.D. thesis, Oregon.

DALTON, GEORGE (1960), 'A note of clarification on economic surplus', *American Anthropologist*, 62, pp. 483–90.

DALTON, GEORGE (1961), 'Economic theory and primitive society', *American Anthropologist*, 63, pp. 1–25.

DALTON, GEORGE (1962), 'Traditional production in primitive African economies', *Quarterly Journal of Economics*, 76, pp. 360–78 (reprinted in Dalton, 1967, pp. 61–80).

DALTON, GEORGE (1963), 'Economic surplus, once again', *American Anthropologist*, 65, pp. 389–94.

DALTON, GEORGE (1964), 'The development of subsistence and peasant economies in Africa', *International Social Science Journal*, 16, pp. 378–89 (Dalton, 1967, pp. 155–68).

DALTON, GEORGE (1965a), 'Primitive money', *American Anthropologist*, 67, pp. 44–65 (Dalton, 1967, pp. 254–81).

DALTON, GEORGE (1965b), 'Primitive, archaic and modern economies: Karl Polanyi's contribution to economic anthropology and comparative economy', *Essays in Economic Anthropology Dedicated to the Memory of Karl Polanyi, Proceedings of the 1965 Spring Meeting of the American Ethnological Society*,

Washington University Press, Seattle, pp. 1–24 (revised version in Polanyi, 1968, pp. ix–liv).

DALTON, GEORGE (1966), ' "Bridewealth" vs. "brideprice" ', *American Anthropologist*, 68, pp. 732–7.

DALTON, GEORGE, ed. (1967), *Tribal and Peasant Economies*, Natural History Press, Garden City, N.Y.

DALTON, GEORGE (1968), 'Introduction', in Polanyi, 1968, pp. ix–liv (revised version of Dalton, 1965b).

DALTON, GEORGE, ed. (1971a), *Economic Development and Social Change*, Natural History Press, Garden City, N.Y.

DALTON, GEORGE, ed. (1971b), *Studies in Economic Anthropology*, American Anthropological Association, Washington, D.C.

DALTON, GEORGE (1971c), *Economic Anthropology and Development*, Basic Books, New York.

DALTON, G., and BOHANNAN, P. (1965), obituary of K. Polanyi, *American Anthropologist*, 67, pp. 1508–11.

DANOV, C. M. (1962), 'Seuthopolis', Pauly-Wissowa, *Realencyclopädie der classischen Altertumswissenschaft, Supplement* IX, coll. 1370–8.

DARMON, J.-P. (1970), 'Un Cours nouveau dans les études grecques', *Critique* (mars), pp. 265–86.

DAVID, MAXIME (1913a), review of Cornford, 1912, *L'Année sociologique*, 12 (1909–12), pp. 41–4.

DAVID, MAXIME (1913b), review of J. Harrison, 1912, *L'Année sociologique*, 12 (1909–12), pp. 254–60.

DAVIES, J. K. (1967), 'Demosthenes on liturgies', *Journal of Hellenic Studies*, 87, pp. 33–40.

DAVIES, J. K. (1968), 'La storia di Atene e il metodo del Münzer', *Rivista storica italiana*, 80, pp. 209–21.

DAVIES, J. K. (1971), *Athenian Propertied Families*, Clarendon Press, Oxford.

DAVY, GEORGES (1922), *La Foi jurée*, Alcan, Paris.

DEAN, EDWIN R. (1962–3), 'Social determinants of price in several African markets', *Economic Development and Cultural Change*, 11, pp. 239–56.

DE FRANCISCIS, A. (1972), *Stato e società in Locri Epizefiri*, Libreria Scientifica Editrice, Naples.

DELORME, J. (1960), *Gymnasion. Étude sur les monuments consacrés à l'éducation en Grèce*, de Boccard, Paris.

DELOUGAZ, P. (1967), 'Choga Mish', *Iran*, 5, pp. 147–9.

DEMBINSKA, MARIA (1963), *Konsumpcja żywnościowa w Polsce średniowiecznej* (English summary: 'Food consumption in mediaeval Poland'), Zakład Narodowy im. Ossolińskich, Wrocław.

DEMOULE-LYOTARD, L. (1971), 'L'Analyse formelle des textes antiques', *Annales. Économies, sociétés, civilisations*, 26, pp. 705–22.

DEMPSEY, B. (1943), *Interest and Usury*, American Council on Public Affairs, Washington D.C.

DERRETT, J. D. M. (1965), 'The Parable of the Talents, and two Logia', *Zeitschrift für neutestamentliche Wissenschaft*, 56, pp. 184–95.

DESAI, M. (1968), 'Some issues in econometric history', *Economic History Review*, series 2, 21, pp. 1–16.

DETIENNE, MARCEL (1962), *Homère, Hésiode et Pythagore*, Latomus, Brussels.

DETIENNE, MARCEL (1963), *Crise agraire et attitude religieuse chez Hésiode*, Latomus, Brussels.

DETIENNE, MARCEL (1964), 'Simonide de Céos ou la sécularisation de la poésie', *Revue des études grecques*, 77, pp. 405–19.

DETIENNE, MARCEL (1965), 'En Grèce archaïque: géométrie, politique et société', *Annales. Économies, sociétés, civilisations*, 20, pp. 425–41.

DETIENNE, MARCEL (1967), *Les Maîtres de vérité dans la Grèce archaïque*, Maspero, Paris.

DETIENNE, MARCEL (1972), *Les Jardins d'Adonis*, Gallimard, Paris (English translation announced, Harvester Press, London).

DETIENNE, MARCEL (1975), 'Les Grecs ne sont pas comme les autres', *Critique* (janvier), 332, pp. 3–24.

DETIENNE, MARCEL, and VERNANT, J.-P. (1969), 'La Métis du renard et du poulpe', *Revue des études grecques*, 82, pp. 291–317.

DETIENNE, MARCEL, and VERNANT, J.-P. (1974), *Les Ruses de l'intelligence. La métis des Grecs*, Flammarion, Paris.

DI BENEDETTO, V. (1971), *Euripide: teatro e società*, Einaudi, Turin.

DI BENEDETTO, V. (1975), 'Atene e Roma: società di consumatori o di classi?' (discussion of Finley, 1973a), *Rinascita*, 14 (4 April), pp. 33–4.

DIECKMANN, JOHANN (1961), 'Max Webers Begriff des "modernen okzidentalen Rationalismus" ', Düsseldorf (Ph. Diss., Cologne).

DIELS, H., and KRANZ, W. (1951–2), *Die Fragmente der Vorsokratiker*, vols I–III, 6th ed., Weidmann, Berlin.

DIMITROV, D. P. (1958), 'Za ykrepenite vili i rezidenčii y Trakite v predrimskata epocha', in *Izsledvanija v fest na Akad. D. Dečev*, Sofia, pp. 683–701 (resumé: 'Sur les villas fortifiés et les residences chez les Thraces à l'époque préromain').

DIMITROV, D. P. (1961), 'Das Entstehen der thrakischen Stadt und die Eigenart ihrer städtebaulichen Gestaltung und Architektur', in *Atti del 7º Congresso Internazionale di Archeologia Classica 1958*, vol. I, 'L'Erma' di Bretschneider, Rome, pp. 379–87.

DIMON, MURIEL, and FRIEDL, ERNESTINE, eds (1976), *Regional Variation in Modern Greece and Cyprus: Toward a Perspective on the Ethnography of Greece*, Annals of the New York Academy of Sciences, 268.

DIRLMEIER, F. (1931), 'Philos und Philia im vorhellenistischen Griechentum', Diss., Munich.

DITTENBERGER, W. (1915), *Sylloge Inscriptionum Graecarum*, 3rd ed., Hirzel, Leipzig.

DOBB, MAURICE (1965), 'The discussion of the twenties on planning and economic growth', *Soviet Studies*, 17, 2, pp. 198–208 (reprinted in M. Dobb, *Papers on Capitalism, Development and Planning*, 1967, Routledge & Kegan Paul, London, pp. 126–39).

DODDS, E. R. (1951), *The Greeks and the Irrational*, University of California Press, Berkeley.

DOHRN, T. (1964), 'Des Romulus' Grundung Roms', *Mitteilungen des deutschen archäologischen Instituts, römische Abteilung*, 71, pp. 1–18.

DOLE, G., and CARNEIRO, R., eds (1960), *Essays in the Science of Culture in Honor of Leslie A. White*, Crowell, New York.

DOUGLAS, MARY (1962), 'Lele economy compared with the Bushong: a study in economic backwardness', in Bohannan and Dalton, 1962, pp. 211–33.

DOUGLAS, MARY (1967), 'Primitive rationing: a study in controlled exchange', in Firth, 1967a, pp. 119–47.

DOUGLAS, MARY (1970), *Natural Symbols*, Barrie & Rockliff, New York.

DOUGLAS, MARY (1973), 'Self evidence', *Proceedings of the Royal Anthropological Institute, 1972*, pp. 27–43 (reprinted in M. Douglas, *Implicit Meanings*, Routledge & Kegan Paul, London, 1976, pp. 276–318).

DOVER, K. J. (1963), 'The poetry of Archilochus', *Entretiens Hardt*, 10, pp. 181–212.

DOVER, K. J. (1968), *Lysias and the Corpus Lysiacum*, University of California Press, Berkeley.

DOVER, K. J. (1975), *Greek Popular Morality in the Time of Plato and Aristotle*, Blackwell, Oxford.

DOWD, DOUGLAS (1956), 'A comparative analysis of economic development in the American West and South', *Journal of Economic History*, 16, pp. 558–74.

DOWD, DOUGLAS (1967), contributions to 'Slavery as an obstacle to economic growth in the U.S.: a panel discussion', *Journal of Economic History*, 27, pp. 518–60.

DRERUP, H. (1969), 'Griechische Baukunst in geometrischer Zeit', *Archaeologia Homerica*, ed. F. Matz and H.-G. Buchholz, II.O, Vandenhoeck & Ruprecht, Göttingen.

DROYSEN, J. G. (1847), 'Die attische Communalverfassung', *Allgemeine Zeitschrift für Geschichte*, 8, pp. 289–337, 385–411.

DUBY, GEORGES (1973), *Origines de l'économie moderne: guerriers et paysans*, Gallimard, Paris.

DUCZYŃSKA, ILONA POLANYI (1963), 'The Hungarian populists', introduction to I. Duczyńska and K. Polanyi (eds), *The Plough and the Pen: Writings from Hungary 1930–1956*, Peter Owen, London.

DUGAS, LUDOVIC (1894), *L'Amitié antique d'après les moeurs populaires et les théories des philosophes*, Alcan, Paris.

DUMÉZIL, GEORGES (1924), *Le Festin d'immortalité*, Geuthner, Paris.

DUMONT, LOUIS (1966), *Homo Hierarchicus*, Gallimard, Paris.

DUNBABIN, T. J. (1948), *The Western Greeks*, Clarendon Press, Oxford.

DUNCAN, G. (1958), 'Sutri', *Papers of the British School at Rome*, 26, pp. 63–134.

DUNCAN-JONES, R. (1963), 'Wealth and munificence in Roman Africa', *Papers of the British School at Rome*, 31, pp. 159–77.

DUPRONT, A. (1965), 'De l'acculturation', *12e Congrès international des sciences historiques, Vienne 1965, Rapports*, vol. I, pp. 7–36.

DUPRONT, A. (1966), *L'Acculturazione*, translated and enlarged version of Dupront, 1965, Einaudi, Turin.

DUPRONT, A., VAN EFFENTERRE, H., *et al.* (1965), 'L'Acculturation', *12e Congrès international des sciences historiques, Vienne 1965, Rapports*, vol. I, pp. 7–102.

DURKHEIM, ÉMILE (1887), 'La Science positive de la morale en Allemagne', *Revue philosophique*, 24, 2, pp. 33–58, 113–42, 275–84 (reprinted in Durkheim, 1975, vol. I, pp. 267–343).

DURKHEIM, ÉMILE (1888), 'Cours de science sociale. Leçon d'ouverture', *Revue internationale de l'enseignement*, 15, pp. 23–48 (É. Durkheim, *La Science sociale et l'action*, Presses Universitaires de France, Paris, 1970, pp. 77–110).

DURKHEIM, ÉMILE (1893), *De la division du travail social*, Alcan, Paris.

DURKHEIM, ÉMILE (1896), *Les Règles de la méthode sociologique*, Alcan, Paris.

DURKHEIM, ÉMILE (1897), *Le Suicide*, Alcan, Paris.

DURKHEIM, ÉMILE (1898), 'L'Individualisme et les intellectuels', *Revue bleue*, series 4, 10, pp. 7–13 (É. Durkheim, *La Science sociale et l'action*, pp. 261–78; English translation in Bellah, 1973, pp. 43–57).

DURKHEIM, ÉMILE (1899), 'Preface', *L'Année sociologique*, 2, 1897–8 (Durkheim, 1969, pp. 135–9).

DURKHEIM, ÉMILE (1901a), 'Deux lois de l'évolution pénale', *L'Année sociologique*, 4, 1899–1900, pp. 65–95 (Durkheim, 1969, pp. 245–73).

DURKHEIM, ÉMILE (1901b), review of A. Fouillée, *La France au point de vue morale*, *L'Année sociologique*, 4, 1899–1900, pp. 443–5 (Durkheim, 1969, pp. 302–3).

DURKHEIM, ÉMILE (1905), review of Glotz, 1904, *L'Année sociologique*, 8, 1903–4, pp. 465–72 (Durkheim, 1969, pp. 509–25).

- DURKHEIM, ÉMILE (1909), 'Sociologie religieuse et théorie de la connaissance', *Revue de métaphysique et de morale*, 17, pp. 733–58 (cf. Durkheim, 1975, vol. I, pp. 184–8).
- DURKHEIM, ÉMILE (1911), 'Jugements de valeur et jugements de réalité', *Revue de métaphysique et de morale*, 19, pp. 437–53 (Durkheim, 1967, pp. 117–41).
- DURKHEIM, ÉMILE (1912), *Les Formes élémentaires de la vie religieuse*, Alcan, Paris.
- DURKHEIM, ÉMILE (1914), *Pragmatisme et sociologie*, lectures; published Vrin, Paris, 1955.
- DURKHEIM, ÉMILE (1920), 'Introduction à la morale', *Revue philosophique*, 89, pp. 79–97 (Durkheim, 1975, vol. II, pp. 313–31).
- DURKHEIM, ÉMILE (1925), *L'Éducation morale*, Alcan, Paris (cited from the translation, *Moral Education*, Free Press, New York, 1961).
- DURKHEIM, ÉMILE (1928), *Le Socialisme*, Alcan, Paris.
- DURKHEIM, ÉMILE (1938), *L'Évolution pédagogique en France*, Alcan, Paris (English translation 1977, Routledge & Kegan Paul, London).
- DURKHEIM, ÉMILE (1950), *Leçons de sociologie: physique des moeurs et du droit*, Presses Universitaires de France, Paris (translated, *Professional Ethics and Civic Morals*, Routledge & Kegan Paul, London, 1957).
- DURKHEIM, ÉMILE (1967), *Sociologie et philosophie*, 3rd ed., Presses Universitaires de France, Paris.
- DURKHEIM, ÉMILE (1969), *Journal sociologique*, PUF, Paris.
- DURKHEIM, ÉMILE (1975), *Textes*, vols I–III, ed. V. Karady, Éditions de Minuit, Paris.
- DURKHEIM, É., and MAUSS, M. (1903), 'De quelques formes primitives de classification', *L'Année sociologique*, 6, 1901–2, pp. 1–72 (reprinted in Mauss, 1969, vol. II, pp. 13–89; translated, *Primitive Classification*, Cohen & West, London, 1963).
- DUVAL, P.-M. (1952), *La Vie quotidienne en Gaule pendant la paix romaine*, Hachette, Paris.
- *Economia e Società* (1973), *Atti del 12º Convegno di studi sulla Magna Grecia 1972, Economia e società nella Magna Grecia*, L'Arte Tipografica, Naples (actually 1975).
- EFFENTERRE, HENRI VAN (1965), ' "Acculturation" et histoire ancienne', *12e Congrès international des sciences historiques, Vienne 1965, Rapports*, vol. I, pp. 37–44.
- EINAUDI, L. (1950), *Greatness and Decline of Planned Economy in the Hellenistic World*, Francke, Bern.
- EINZIG, PAUL (1949), *Primitive Money*, Eyre & Spottiswoode, London.
- EISENSTADT, S. N. (1963), *The Political Systems of Empires*, Free Press, New York.
- EISENSTADT, S. N. (1964), 'Political modernization: some comparative notes', *International Journal of Comparative Sociology*, 5, pp. 3–24.
- EISENSTADT, S. N. (1965), *Essays on Comparative Institutions*, Wiley, New York.
- ELIOT, C. W. J. (1962), *Coastal Demes of Attika. A Study of the policy of Kleisthenes*, Phoenix, Supplement 5, Toronto.
- ENDENBERG, P. J. (1937), *Koinoonia en gemeenschap van zaken bij de Grieken in den klassieken tijd*, H. Paris, Amsterdam (Proefschrift, Utrecht).
- *Entretiens Hardt* (1963), *Archiloque, Entretiens*, 10, Fondation Hardt, Vandoeuvres-Geneva.
- *Entretiens Hardt* (1967), *Les Origines de la république romaine, Entretiens*, 13.
- EPSTEIN, S. (1969), *Capitalism, Primitive and Modern*, Manchester University Press.
- ERB, OTTO (1938), *Wirtschaft und Gesellschaft im Denken der hellenischen Antike*, Ph. Diss., Basel; Geibel, Altenberg (Thuringen). (Also published by Duncker &

Humblot, Berlin, 1939, and in *Schmollers Jahrbuch*, 61, 1937, pp. 663–96, and 62, 1938, pp. 273–305).

FABRICIUS, E. (1935), 'Die Limesanlagen der dreizehnten Streck im allgemeinen', *Der obergermanische-rätische Limes*, A VI, Streck 13, pp. 8–20.

FARIAS, P. F. DE MORAES (1974), 'Silent trade: myth and historical evidence', *History in Africa*, 1, pp. 9–24.

FAUCONNET, PAUL (1920), *La Responsabilité*, Alcan, Paris.

FAUCONNET, PAUL (1927), 'The Durkheim school in France', *Sociological Review*, 19, pp. 15–20.

FAURE, P. (1964), *Fonctions des cavernes crétoises*, de Boccard, Paris.

FEBVRE, LUCIEN (1913), 'Antoine Meillet et l'histoire. La Grèce ancienne à travers sa langue', *Revue de synthèse historique*, 27, pp. 52–65 (reprinted in Febvre, 1953, pp. 158–68).

FEBVRE, LUCIEN (1928), 'Frontière: le mot et la notion', *Revue de synthèse*, 45, pp. 31–44 (reprinted in Febvre, 1962, pp. 11–24).

FEBVRE, LUCIEN (1930), 'Civilisation', in L. Febvre *et al.*, *Civilisation: le mot et l'idée*, La Renaissance du Livre, Paris, pp. 1–55 (Febvre, 1962, pp. 481–528).

FEBVRE, LUCIEN (1953), *Combats pour l'histoire*, Colin, Paris.

FEBVRE, LUCIEN (1962), *Pour une histoire 'à part entière'*, SEVPEN, Paris.

FERGUSON, W. S. (1918), 'The Zulus and the Spartans: a comparison of their military systems', *Harvard African Studies*, 2, pp. 197–234.

FEYEL, M. (1936), 'Nouvelles inscriptions d'Akraiphia', *Bulletin de correspondance hellénique*, 60, pp. 27–36.

Filosofia e scienze (1966), *Atti del 5º Convegno di studi sulla Magna Grecia 1965*, *Filosofia e scienze in Magna Grecia*, L'Arte Tipografica, Naples.

FINLEY, MOSES I. (1952), *Studies in Land and Credit in Ancient Athens 500–200 B.C.: the Horos Inscriptions*, Rutgers University Press, New Brunswick.

FINLEY, MOSES I. (1953), 'Land, debt and the man of property in classical Athens', *Political Science Quarterly*, 68, pp. 249–68.

FINLEY, MOSES I. (1954), *The World of Odysseus*, Viking Press, New York.

FINLEY, MOSES I. (1955), 'Marriage, sale and gift in the Homeric world', *Revue internationale des droits de l'antiquité*, 2, pp. 167–94.

FINLEY, MOSES I. (1957a), 'Homer and Mycenae: property and tenure', *Historia*, 6, pp. 133–59.

FINLEY, MOSES I. (1957b), 'The Mycenaean tablets and economic history', *Economic History Review*, series 2, 10, pp. 128–41.

FINLEY, MOSES I. (1959), 'Was Greek civilization based on slave labour?', *Historia*, 8, pp. 145–64 (reprinted in Finley, 1960b, pp. 53–72).

FINLEY, MOSES I. (1960a), 'The servile statuses of ancient Greece', *Revue internationale des droits de l'antiquité*, 7, pp. 165–89.

FINLEY, MOSES I., ed. (1960b), *Slavery in Classical Antiquity*, Heffer, Cambridge.

FINLEY, MOSES I. (1964), 'Between slavery and freedom', *Comparative Studies in Society and History*, 6, pp. 233–49.

FINLEY, MOSES I. (1965a), 'Technical innovation and economic progress in the ancient world', *Economic History Review*, 18, pp. 29–45.

FINLEY, MOSES I. (1965b), 'La Servitude pour dettes', *Revue historique de droit français et étranger*, 43, pp. 159–84.

FINLEY, MOSES I. (1965c), 'Classical Greece', *2e Conférence internationale d'histoire économique*, I. *Trade and Politics in the Ancient World*, Mouton, Paris/Hague, pp. 11–35.

FINLEY, MOSES I. (1965d), review of A. French, *The Growth of the Athenian Economy*, *Economic Journal*, 75, pp. 849–51.

FINLEY, MOSES I. (1968a), *Aspects of Antiquity*, Chatto & Windus, London.

FINLEY, MOSES I. (1968b), 'The alienability of land in ancient Greece', *Eirene*, 7, pp. 25–32 (Finley, 1975, pp. 153–60).

FINLEY, MOSES I. (1968c), 'Sparta', in Vernant, 1968a, pp. 143–60 (Finley, 1975, pp. 161–77).

FINLEY, MOSES I. (1968d), 'Slavery', *International Encyclopedia of the Social Sciences*, vol. XIV, pp. 307–13.

FINLEY, MOSES I. (1970), 'Aristotle and economic analysis', *Past and Present*, 47, pp. 3–25.

FINLEY, MOSES I. (1971), 'Archaeology and history', *Daedalus*, 100, pp. 168–86 (Finley, 1975, pp. 87–101).

FINLEY, MOSES I. (1973a), *The Ancient Economy*, Chatto & Windus, London.

FINLEY, MOSES I., ed. (1973b), *Problèmes de la terre en Grèce ancienne*, Mouton, Paris/Hague.

FINLEY, MOSES I. (1975), *The Use and Abuse of History*, Chatto & Windus, London.

FINNEGAN, R. (1967), *Limba Stories and Story-telling*, Clarendon Press, Oxford.

FINNEGAN, R. (1970), *African Oral Literature*, Clarendon Press, Oxford.

FIRTH, RAYMOND (1956), *Two Studies of Kinship in London*, Athlone Press, London.

FIRTH, RAYMOND (1961), *History and Tradition in Tikopia*, Polynesian Society, Wellington, N.Z.

FIRTH, RAYMOND (1964), *Essays on Social Organization and Values*, Athlone Press, London.

FIRTH, RAYMOND, ed. (1967a), *Themes in Economic Anthropology*, ASA monograph 6, Tavistock, London.

FIRTH, RAYMOND (1967b), 'Themes in economic anthropology: a general comment', in Firth, 1967a, pp. 1–28.

FIRTH, RAYMOND (1972), 'Methodological issues in economic anthropology', *Man*, 7, pp. 467–75.

FIRTH, RAYMOND, FORGE, ANTONY, and HUBERT, JANE (1969), *Families and their Relatives*, Routledge & Kegan Paul, London.

FIRTH, RAYMOND, and YAMEY, B. S., eds (1964), *Capital, Saving and Credit in Peasant Societies*, Allen & Unwin, London.

FOIRE, LA (1953), *Recueils de la Société Jean Bodin*, 5.

FONDATION THIERS (1911), *Annuaire de la Fondation Thiers*, Paris.

FORKE, A. (1930), review of Granet, 1929, *Orientalistische Literaturzeitung*, 33, pp. 931–5.

Forma Italiae (1967 ff.), de Luca, Rome.

FOSTER, GEORGE M. (1965), 'The peasant society and the idea of limited good', *American Anthropologist*, 67, pp. 293–315.

FOWLER, H. N., ROBINSON, C. A., JR, and BLEGEN, C. W. (1932), 'Corinth and the Corinthia', *Corinth*, vol. I, 1, Harvard University Press, Cambridge, Mass., pp. 18–114.

FRÄNKEL, H. (1962), *Dichtung und Philosophie des frühen Griechentums*, 2nd ed., Beck, Munich.

FRANCOTTE, H. (1910), 'Le Pain à bon marché et le pain gratuit dans les cités grecques', in H. Francotte, *Mélanges de droit public grec*, Champion, Paris, pp. 291–312.

FRANK, TENNEY (1940), *Economic Survey of the Roman Empire*, vol. V, Johns Hopkins University Press, Baltimore.

FRANKENBERG, R. (1967), 'Economic anthropology: one anthropologist's view', in Firth, 1967a, pp. 47–89.

FRAZER, J. G. (1911), *The Golden Bough*, 3rd ed., Macmillan, London.

FREDERIKSEN, M. W. (1966), 'Caesar, Cicero and the problem of debt', *Journal of Roman Studies*, 56, pp. 128–41.

FREEDMAN, MAURICE (1966), *Chinese Lineage and Society. Fukien and Kwangtung*, Athlone Press, London.

FREEDMAN, MAURICE (1975), 'Marcel Granet, sinologue et sociologue', *Critique*, 337, pp. 624–48.

FREL, J. (1966), 'Ateliers et sculpteurs attiques fin Vème–début IVème s.', *Eirene*, 5, pp. 79–98.

FRÉZOULS, E. (1961), 'Les Théâtres antiques de l'orient syrien', *Atti del 7° Congresso Internazionale di Archeologia Classica 1958*, vol. I, 'L'Erma' di Bretschneider, Rome, pp. 339–51.

FRIED, MORTON H., ed. (1959), *Readings in Anthropology*, vol. II, Crowell, New York.

FRIEDL, ERNESTINE (1962), *Vasilika: a Village in Modern Greece*, Holt, Rinehart & Winston, New York.

FRIEDMANN, GEORGES (1946), 'Maurice Halbwachs 1877–1945', *American Journal of Sociology*, 51, pp. 507–19.

FRIIS JOHANSEN, H. (1970), *Aeschylus, the Suppliants*, Munksgaard, Copenhagen.

FROMM, ERICH, ed. (1965), *Socialist Humanism*, Doubleday, Garden City, N.Y.

FUKS, A. (1968), 'Redistribution of land and houses in Syracuse in 356 B.C. and its ideological aspects', *Classical Quarterly*, 18, pp. 207–23.

FURLEY, D. J., and ALLEN, R. E., eds (1970), *Studies in Presocratic Philosophy*, vol. I, Routledge & Kegan Paul, London.

FUSTEL DE COULANGES, NUMA DENIS (1864), *La Cité antique*, Durand, Paris.

GABBA, E. (1972), 'Urbanizzazione e rinnovamenti urbanistici nell'Italia centro-meridionale del 1 sec. a.C.', *Studi classici e orientali*, 21, pp. 73–112.

GAGÉ, J. (1964), *Les Classes sociales dans l'empire romain*, Payot, Paris.

GAJDUKEVIĆ, V. F., ed. (1964), *Ol'vija. Temenos i Agora*, Moscow.

GAJDUKEVIĆ, V. F. (1966), 'Nekotor'ie vopros'i ekonomičeskoi istorii Bospora', *Vestnik Drevnej Istorii*, 1966, 1, pp. 47–64 (summarized in *Bibliotheca Classica Orientalis*, 11, coll. 341–6).

GAJDUKEVIĆ, V. F. (1971), *Das Bosporanische Reich*, 2nd ed., Akademie-Verlag, Berlin.

GARLAN, Y. (1973), 'L'Oeuvre de Polanyi. La place de l'économie dans les sociétés anciennes', *La Pensée*, 171, pp. 118–27.

GARLAN, Y. (1974), *Recherches de poliorcétique grecque*, École française, Athens.

GARVIE, A. F. (1969), *Aeschylus' Supplices, Play and Trilogy*, Cambridge University Press.

GAUTHIER, PH. (1972), *Symbola: les étrangers et la justice dans les cités grecques*, Université de Nancy.

GEARING, F. (1958), 'The structural poses of 18th-century Cherokee villages', *American Anthropologist*, 60, pp. 1148–57.

GEERTZ, C. (1963), *Agricultural Involution*, University of California Press, Berkeley.

GELB, I. (1967), 'Approaches to the study of ancient society', *Journal of the American Oriental Society*, 87, pp. 1–8.

GENOVESE, E. D. (1965), *The Political Economy of Slavery*, Pantheon, New York.

Genti non greche, Le (1972), *Atti del 11° Convegno di studi sulla Magna Grecia, 1971, Le genti non greche della Magna Grecia*, L'Arte Tipografica, Naples (actually 1975).

GENTILE, BRUNO (1965), 'Aspetti del rapporto poeta, committente, uditorio nella lirica corale greca', *Studi urbinati*, 39, pp. 70–88.

GEORGOUDIS, STELLA (1974), 'Quelques problèmes de la transhumance dans la Grèce ancienne', *Revue des études grecques*, 87, pp. 155–85.

GERMAIN, LOUIS R.-F. (1968), 'La Publicité des sûretés foncières dans la Grèce classique et hellénistique. Les inscriptions d'horoi', thesis in law, University of Paris.

GERNET, LOUIS (1909a), 'L'Approvisionnement d'Athènes en blé au Ve et au IVe siècles', in G. Bloch (ed.), *Mélanges d'histoire ancienne*, Alcan, Paris, pp. 269–391.

GERNET, LOUIS (1909b), 'Authentes', *Revue des études grecques*, 22, pp. 13–32 (reprinted in Gernet, 1955a, pp. 28–38).

GERNET, LOUIS (1910a), review of Croiset, 1909, *L'Année sociologique*, 11, 1906–9, pp. 331–4.

GERNET, LOUIS (1910b), review of Riezler, 1907, *L'Année sociologique*, 11, pp. 559–62.

GERNET, LOUIS (1917a), *Platon, Lois livre IX, traduction et commentaire*, Leroux, Paris.

GERNET, LOUIS (1917b), *Recherches sur le développement de la pensée juridique et morale en Grèce (étude sémantique)*, Leroux, Paris.

GERNET, LOUIS (1917c), 'Hypothèses sur le contrat primitif en Grèce', *Revue des études grecques*, 30, pp. 249–93, 363–83.

GERNET, LOUIS (1920), 'La Création du testament', *Revue des études grecques*, 33, pp. 123–68, 249–90 (abbreviated version in Gernet, 1955a, pp. 121–49).

GERNET, LOUIS (1924), 'Sur l'exécution capitale (à propos d'un ouvrage récent)', *Revue des études grecques*, 37, pp. 261–93 (Gernet, 1968, pp. 302–29).

GERNET, LOUIS (1924–6), *Lysias, Discours*, vols I–II, Les Belles Lettres, Paris.

GERNET, LOUIS (1925), review of L. Landsberg, *Wesen und Bedeutung der Platoni-schen Akademie*, *L'Année sociologique*, new series, 1, 1923–4, pp. 498–500.

GERNET, LOUIS (1927), 'La Diamartyrie, procédure archaïque du droit athénien', *Revue historique du droit français et étranger*, series 4, 6, pp. 5–37 (Gernet, 1955a, pp. 83–102).

GERNET, LOUIS (1928), 'Frairies antiques', *Revue des études grecques*, 41, pp. 313–59 (Gernet, 1968, pp. 21–62).

GERNET, LOUIS (1932a) (with A. Boulanger), *Le Génie grec dans la religion*, La Renaissance du Livre, Paris.

GERNET, LOUIS (1932b), 'Fostérage et légende', *Mélanges Glotz*, vol. I, pp. 385–95 (Gernet, 1955a, pp. 19–28).

GERNET, LOUIS (1933), 'La Cité future et le pays des morts', *Revue des études grecques*, 46, pp. 293–310 (Gernet, 1968, pp. 139–53).

GERNET, LOUIS (1934), review of U. von Wilamowitz-Moellendorff, *Der Glaube der Hellenen*, *Revue de philologie*, 60, pp. 191–201.

GERNET, LOUIS (1936a), 'Dolon le loup (à propos d'Homère et du Rhésus d'Euripide)', *Annuaire de l'Institut de Philologie et d'Histoire Orientales et Slaves*, 4 (*Mélanges Franz Cumont*), pp. 189–208 (Gernet, 1968, pp. 154–71).

GERNET, LOUIS (1936b), 'Quelques rapports entre la pénalité et la religion dans la Grèce ancienne', *L'Antiquité classique*, 5, pp. 325–39 (Gernet, 1968, pp. 288–301).

GERNET, LOUIS (1937a), 'Sur la notion du jugement en droit grec', *Archives d'histoire du droit oriental*, 1, pp. 111–44 (Gernet, 1955a, pp. 61–82).

GERNET, LOUIS (1937b), 'Notes de lexicologie juridique', *Annuaire de l'Institut de Philologie et d'Histoire Orientales et Slaves*, 5 (*Mélanges E. Boisacq*), pp. 391–8.

GERNET, LOUIS (1937c), 'Paricidas', *Revue de philologie*, 63, pp. 13–29 (Gernet, 1955a, pp. 38–50).

GERNET, LOUIS (1938a), 'Les Nobles dans la Grèce antique', *Annales d'histoire économique et sociale*, 10, pp. 36–43 (Gernet, 1968, pp. 333–43).

GERNET, LOUIS (1938b), 'Introduction à l'étude du droit grec ancien', *Archives d'histoire du droit oriental*, 2, pp. 261–92.

GERNET, LOUIS (1938c), 'Sur les actions commerciales en droit athénien', *Revue des études grecques*, 51, pp. 1–44 (Gernet, 1955a, pp. 173–200).

GERNET, LOUIS (1939), 'De la modernité des anciens', *Bulletin de l'Association G. Budé*, 63, pp. 3–15.

GERNET, LOUIS (1944), 'Structures sociales et rites d'adolescence dans la Grèce antique', *Revue des études grecques*, 57, pp. 242–8.

GERNET, LOUIS (1945), 'Les Origines de la philosophie', *Bulletin de l'enseignement public du Maroc*, 183 (October–December), pp. 1–12 (Gernet, 1968, pp. 415–30).

GERNET, LOUIS (1948a), 'La Notion mythique de la valeur en Grèce', *Journal de psychologie normale et pathologique*, 41, pp. 415–62 (Gernet, 1968, pp. 93–138).

GERNET, LOUIS (1948b), 'Jeux et droit', *Revue historique de droit français et étranger*, series 4, 25, pp. 177–88 (Gernet, 1955a, pp. 9–18).

GERNET, LOUIS (1948c), 'La Notion de démocratie chez les Grecs', *Revue de la Méditerranée*, 6, pp. 385–93.

GERNET, LOUIS (1950), 'Aspects du droit athénien de l'esclavage', *Archives d'histoire du droit oriental*, 5, pp. 159–87 (Gernet, 1955a, pp. 151–72).

GERNET, LOUIS (1951a), *Platon Lois I–II*, Les Belles Lettres, Paris.

GERNET, LOUIS (1951b), 'Droit et prédroit en Grèce ancienne', *L'Année sociologique*, series 3, 1948–9, pp. 21–119 (Gernet, 1968, pp. 175–260).

GERNET, LOUIS (1951c), 'Le Droit de la vente et la notion du contrat en Grèce d'après M. Pringsheim', *Revue d'histoire de droit français et étranger*, series 4, 29, pp. 560–84 (Gernet, 1955a, pp. 201–24).

GERNET, LOUIS (1953a), 'Dionysos et la religion dionysiaque. Éléments héritiers et traits originaux', *Revue des études grecques*, 66, pp. 377–95 (Gernet, 1968, pp. 63–89).

GERNET, LOUIS (1953b), introduction to Granet, 1953.

GERNET, LOUIS (1953c), 'Sur l'obligation contractuelle dans la vente hellénique', *Revue internationale des droits de l'antiquité*, 2, pp. 229–47 (Gernet, 1955a, pp. 225–36).

GERNET, LOUIS (1953d), 'Mariages de tyrans', *Hommages à Lucien Febvre*, Colin, Paris, pp. 41–53 (Gernet, 1968, pp. 344–59).

GERNET, LOUIS (1954a), *Antiphon, Discours*, Les Belles Lettres, Paris.

GERNET, LOUIS (1954b), 'Histoire des religions et psychologie. Confrontations d'aujourd'hui', *Journal de psychologie normale et pathologique*, 51, pp. 175–87.

GERNET, LOUIS (1954–60), *Démosthène. Plaidoyers civils*, vols I–IV, Les Belles Lettres, Paris.

GERNET, LOUIS (1955a), *Droit et société dans la Grèce ancienne*, Sirey, Paris.

GERNET, LOUIS (1955b), 'Horoi', *Studi in onore di Ugo Enrico Paoli*, Le Monnier, Florence, pp. 345–53 (Gernet, 1968, pp. 360–70).

GERNET, LOUIS (1955c), review of G. Dumézil, *Les Dieux des Indo-Européens*, *L'Année sociologique*, 1952, pp. 434–6.

GERNET, LOUIS (1955d), 'L'Anthropologie dans la religion grecque', *Anthropologie religieuse*, supplement to *Numen* 2 (Brill, Leiden), pp. 49–59 (Gernet, 1968, pp. 9–20).

GERNET, LOUIS (1956a), 'Le Temps dans les formes archaïques du droit', *Journal de psychologie normale et pathologique*, 53, pp. 379–406 (Gernet, 1968, pp. 261–87).

GERNET, LOUIS (1956b), review of A. Aymard and J. Auboyer, *L'Orient et la Grèce. Rome et son empire*, vols I–II, *L'Année sociologique*, 1953–4, pp. 244–7.

GERNET, LOUIS (1956c), review of Finley, 1954, *L'Année sociologique*, 1953–4, pp. 295–7.

GERNET, LOUIS (1956d), 'Choses visibles et choses invisibles', *Revue philosophique*, 146, pp. 79–86 (Gernet, 1968, pp. 405–14).

GERNET, LOUIS (1957a), *Démosthène. Plaidoyers politiques*, vol. II, Les Belles Lettres, Paris.

GERNET, LOUIS (1957b), review of Berque, 1955, *L'Année sociologique*, 1955–6, pp. 328–39.

GERNET, LOUIS (1959), 'Note sur la notion de délit privé en droit grec', *Droits de l'antiquité et sociologie juridique, Mélanges Lévy-Bruhl*, Sirey, Paris, pp. 393–405.

GERNET, LOUIS (1960a), obituary of H. Jeanmaire, *Revue des études grecques*, 73, pp. xxxviii–ix.

GERNET, LOUIS (1960b), review of G. Dumézil, *Aspects de la fonction guerrier chez les Indo-Européens, L'Année sociologique*, 1959, pp. 362–5.

GERNET, LOUIS (1965), 'Thucydide et l'histoire', *Annales. Économies, sociétés, civilisations*, 20, pp. 570–5.

GERNET, LOUIS (1968), *Anthropologie de la Grèce antique*, Maspero, Paris.

GERSHENKRON, A. (1962), *Economic Backwardness in Historical Perspective*, Harvard University Press, Cambridge, Mass.

GERSHENKRON, A. (1965), 'The typology of industrial development as a tool of analysis', *2e Conférence internationale d'histoire économique, Aix-en-Provence 1962*, vol. II, Mouton, Paris/Hague, pp. 487–506 (Gershenkron, 1968, pp. 77–97).

GERSHENKRON, A. (1967), 'The discipline and I', *Journal of Economic History*, 27, pp. 443–59.

GERSHENKRON, A. (1968), *Continuity in History and Other Essays*, Harvard University Press, Cambridge, Mass.

GHIRSHMAN, R. (1967), 'Suse. Campagne de l'hiver 1965–6. Rapport préliminaire', *Arts asiatiques*, 15, pp. 3–28.

GIESEY, R. F. (1960), *The Royal Funeral Ceremony in Renaissance France*, Droz, Geneva.

GIGON, O. (1966), 'Autarkibegrippet i den klassiska grekiska filosofin', *Ajatus* (Helsinki), 28, pp. 39–52.

GJERSTAD, E. (1948), *The Swedish Cyprus Expedition*, vol. IV, part 2, Swedish Cyprus Expedition, Stockholm.

GJERSTAD, E. (1965), 'Cultural history of early Rome', *Acta Archaeologica*, 36, pp. 1–41.

GJERSTAD, E. (1966), *Early Rome*, vol. IV, parts 1–2, Gleerup, Lund.

GJERSTAD, E. (1967), 'Discussions concerning early Rome', *Historia*, 16, pp. 257–78.

GLADIGOW, B. (1965), *Sophia und Kosmos*, Olms, Hildesheim.

GLOTZ, G. (1904), *La Solidarité de la famille dans le droit criminel en Grèce*, Fontemoing, Paris.

GLOTZ, G. (1906), *Études sociales et juridiques*, Hachette, Paris.

GLOTZ, G. (1907), 'Réflexions sur le but et la méthode de l'histoire', *Revue internationale de l'enseignement*, 54, pp. 481–95.

GLOTZ, G. (1928), *La Cité grecque*, La Renaissance du Livre, Paris.

GLOUSKINA, L. M. (1960), 'Sočial'n'ij aspekt eranos-zaïmov v attike IV v. do n.e.', *Vestnik Drevnej Istorii*, 64, 1, pp. 35–45.

GLUCKMAN, MAX, ed. (1962a), *Essays on the Ritual of Social Relations*, Manchester University Press.

GLUCKMAN, MAX (1962b), 'Les Rites de passage', in Gluckman, 1962a, pp. 1–52.

GLUCKMAN, MAX (1965), *The Ideas of Barotse Jurisprudence*, Yale University Press, New Haven.

GODELIER, MAURICE (1965), 'La Notion de "mode de production asiatique" ', *Les Temps modernes*, 228, pp. 2002–27.

GODELIER, MAURICE (1966), *Rationalité et irrationalité en économie*, Maspero, Paris (trans. 1972, New Left Books, London).

GODELIER, MAURICE (1973), *Horizons, trajets marxistes en économie*, Maspero, Paris (trans. 1977, Cambridge University Press).

GODELIER, MAURICE (1974), introduction to French translation of Polanyi, 1957a, Larousse, Paris (also in J. Friedman and M. Rowlands, eds, *Evolution of Social Systems*, Duckworth, London, in press).

GOFFMAN, ERVING (1956), *The Presentation of Self in Everyday Life*, Edinburgh University Press.

GOFFMAN, ERVING (1961), *Asylums*, Doubleday, Garden City, N.Y.

GOFFMAN, ERVING (1967), *Interaction Ritual*, Doubleday, Garden City, N.Y.

GOLDENWEISER, A. (1936), 'Loose ends of theory on the individual, pattern and involution in primitive societies', in *Essays in Anthropology Presented to A. L. Kroeber*, University of California Press, Berkeley, pp. 99–104.

GOMBRICH, E. H. (1955), 'The Renaissance concept of artistic progress and its consequences', *Actes du XVIIe congrès internationale d'histoire de l'art 1952*, Imprimerie Nationale des Pays-Bas, Hague, pp. 291–307 (reprinted in Gombrich, 1966, pp. 1–10).

GOMBRICH, E. H. (1960), *Art and Illusion*, Pantheon, London.

GOMBRICH, E. H. (1966), *Norm and Form*, Phaidon Press, London.

GOMME, A. W. (1938), 'Aristophanes and politics', in A. W. Gomme, *More Essays in Greek History and Literature*, Blackwell, Oxford, 1962, pp. 70–91.

GOODRICH, CARTER (1960), 'Economic history: one field or two?', *Journal of Economic History*, 20, pp. 531–8.

GOODY, JACK (1973), 'Strategies of heirship', *Comparative Studies in Society and History*, 15, pp. 3–20.

GRANET, MARCEL (1919), *Fêtes et chansons de la Chine ancienne*, Leroux, Paris.

GRANET, MARCEL (1922a), *La Religion des Chinois*, Gauthier-Villars, Paris.

GRANET, MARCEL (1922b), 'Le Langage de la douleur d'après le rituel funéraire de la Chine classique', *Journal de psychologie normale et pathologique*, 19, 2, pp. 97–118 (reprinted in Granet, 1953, pp. 221–42).

GRANET, MARCEL (1926), *Danses et légendes de la Chine ancienne*, Alcan, Paris.

GRANET, MARCEL (1929), *La Civilisation chinoise*, La Renaissance du Livre, Paris.

GRANET, MARCEL (1932), *Festivals and Songs of Ancient China* (translation of Granet, 1919), Routledge, London.

GRANET, MARCEL (1933), 'La Droite et la gauche en Chine', *Bulletin de l'Institut Français de Sociologie*, 3, 3, pp. 87–116 (Granet, 1953, pp. 261–78).

GRANET, MARCEL (1934), *La Pensée chinoise*, La Renaissance du Livre, Paris.

GRANET, MARCEL (1939), *Catégories matrimoniales de la Chine ancienne*, Alcan, Paris (*Annales sociologiques*, series B, 1–3).

GRANET, MARCEL (1952), *La Féodalité chinoise*, Instituttet for Sammelignende Kulturforskning, Oslo.

GRANET, MARCEL (1953), *Études sociologiques sur la Chine*, Presses Universitaires de France, Paris.

GRANET, MARCEL (1976), *The Religion of the Chinese People*, translated and edited by Maurice Freedman, Blackwell, Oxford.

GRAY, DOROTHEA (1974), 'Seewesen', *Archaeologia Homerica*, ed. F. Matz and H.-G. Buchholz, I.G., Vandenhoeck & Ruprecht, Göttingen.

Greci e Italici (1962), *1° Convegno di studi sulla Magna Grecia 1961, Greci e Italici nella Magna Grecia*, L'Arte Tipografica, Naples.

GREENHALGH, P. A. L. (1973), *Early Greek Warfare. Horsemen and Chariots in the Homeric and Archaic ages*, Cambridge University Press.

GRIERSON, P. (1961), 'La Fonction de la monnaie en Angleterre aux 7e–8e siècles', in *Moneta e scambi*, 1961.

GRIERSON, P. (1965–6), 'The interpretation of coin finds', *Numismatic Chronicle*, 5, pp. i–xvi, and 6, pp. i–xxi.

GRIERSON, P. J. HAMILTON (1903), *The Silent Trade*, Green, Edinburgh.

GRINSELL, L., RAHTZ, P., and WARHURST, A. (1966), *The Preparation of Archaeological Reports*, John Baker, London.

GSCHNITZER, F. (1955), 'Stammes- und Ortsgemeinden im alten Griechenland', *Wiener Studien*, 68, pp. 120–44 (reprinted in Gschnitzer, 1969, pp. 271–97).

GSCHNITZER, F., ed. (1969), *Zur griechischen Staatskunde*, Wissenschaftliche Buchgesellschaft, Darmstadt.

GURVITCH, G. (1963), *La Vocation actuelle de la sociologie*, Presses Universitaires de France, Paris.

HALBWACHS, MAURICE (1913), *La Classe ouvrière et les niveaux de vie. Recherches sur la hiérarchie des besoins dans les sociétés industrielles contemporaines*, Alcan, Paris.

HALBWACHS, MAURICE (1925), *Les Cadres sociaux de la mémoire*, Alcan, Paris.

HALBWACHS, MAURICE (1926), 'Histoires dynastiques et légendes religieuses en Chine', *Revue d'histoire des religions*, 94, pp. 1–16.

HALBWACHS, MAURICE (1930), *Les Causes du suicide*, Alcan, Paris.

HALBWACHS, MAURICE (1933), *L'Évolution des besoins dans les classes ouvrières*, Alcan, Paris.

HALBWACHS, MAURICE (1938), *Morphologie sociale*, Alcan, Paris (translated as *Population and Society*, Free Press, Chicago, 1960).

HALBWACHS, MAURICE (1950), *La Mémoire collective*, Presses Universitaires de France, Paris.

HALBWACHS, MAURICE (1972), *Classes sociales et morphologie*, ed. V. Karady, Éditions de Minuit, Paris.

HANDS, A. R. (1968), *Charities and Social Aid in Greece and Rome*, Thames & Hudson, London.

HARRIOTT, R. M. (1969), *Poetry and Criticism before Plato*, Methuen, London.

HARRIS, MARVIN (1959), 'The economy has no surplus?', *American Anthropologist*, 61, pp. 185–99.

HARRIS, W. (1965), 'The Via Cassia and the Via Traiana Nova between Bolsena and Chiusi', *Papers of the British School at Rome*, 33, pp. 113–33.

HARRISON, A. R. W. (1968), *The Law of Athens, I. The Family and Property*, Clarendon Press, Oxford.

HARRISON, JANE (1912), *Themis*, Cambridge University Press.

HARRISON, JANE (1921), *Epilegomena to the Study of Greek Religion*, Cambridge University Press.

HASEBROEK, J. (1923), 'Die Betriebsformen des griechischen Handels im 4. Jh.', *Hermes*, 58, pp. 393–425.

HASEBROEK, J. (1928), *Staat und Handel im alten Griechenland*, Mohr, Tübingen (trans. as *Trade and Politics in ancient Greece*, Bell, London, 1933).

HASEBROEK, J. (1931), *Griechische Wirtschafts- und Gesellschaftsgeschichte*, Mohr, Tübingen.

HATT, J.-J. (1959), 'Problèmes d'archéologie agraire', *Bulletin de la Faculté des Lettres de Strasbourg*, 37, pp. 341–56.

HATT, J.-J. (1966), *Histoire de la Gaule romaine*, Payot, Paris.

HAVELOCK, E. (1972), 'The Socratic self as it is parodied in Aristophanes' "Clouds" ', *Yale Classical Studies*, 22, pp. 1–18.

HAYWARD, J. E. S. (1958), 'The idea of solidarity in French social and political thought in the 19th and early 20th centuries', Ph.D. thesis, University of London.

HAYWARD, J. E. S. (1960), 'Solidarist syndicalism: Durkheim and Duguit', *Sociological Review*, new series, 8, pp. 17–36, 185–202.

HEICHELHEIM, F. M. (1930), *Wirtschaftliche Schwankungen der Zeit von Alexander bis Augustus*, Fischer, Jena.

HEICHELHEIM, F. M. (1938), *Wirtschaftsgeschichte des Altertums*, vol. I, Sijthoff, Leiden.

HEICHELHEIM, F. M. (1948), *Wirtschaftsgeschichte des Altertums*, vol. II, Sijthoff, Leiden.

HEICHELHEIM, F. M. (1960), review of Polanyi, 1957a, *Journal of the Social and Economic History of the Orient*, 3, pp. 108–10.

HEILBRONER, R. (1962), *The Making of Economic Society*, Prentice-Hall, Englewood Cliffs, N.J.

HEIMANN, E. (1934), 'Sociological preoccupations of economic theory', *Social Research*, 1.

HEIMANN, E. (1947), *Freedom and Order*, Scribner, New York.

HEIMANN, E. (1955), *Vernunftglaube und Religion in der modernen Gesellschaft*, Mohr, Tübingen (trans. as *Reason and Faith in Modern Society*, Wesleyan University Press, Middletown, 1961).

HEIMANN, E. (1963), *Soziale Theorie der Wirtschaftssysteme*, Mohr, Tübingen.

HENDERSON, D. (1970), 'Contextual specificity, discretion and cognitive socialization: with special reference to language', *Sociology*, 4, pp. 311–38.

HENDERSON, M. I. (1957), 'Ancient Greek music', in *New Oxford History of Music*, vol. I, Clarendon Press, Oxford, pp. 336–403.

HERSKOVITS, M. (1938), *Dahomey, an ancient West African Kingdom*, Augustin, New York.

HERTZ, ROBERT (1909), 'La Préeminence de la main droite: étude sur la polarité religieuse', *Revue philosophique*, 68, pp. 553–80 (trans. in Hertz, 1960).

HERTZ, ROBERT (1960), *Death and The Right Hand*, Cohen & West, London.

HILDEBRAND, GEORGE, JR (1946), review of Polanyi, 1944, *American Economic Review*, 36, pp. 398–405.

HODGEN, M. T. (1936), *The Doctrine of Survivals*, Allenson, London.

HOFFNER, H. A., JR (1967), review of E. von Schuler, *Die Kaskäer*, *Journal of the American Oriental Society*, 87, pp. 179–85.

HOLLOWAY, R. ROSS (1966), 'Exploration of the Southeast Stoa', *Hesperia*, 35, pp. 79–85.

Hommage à Louis Gernet (1966), Presses Universitaires de France, Paris.

HONIGSHEIM, PAUL (1960), 'The influence of Durkheim and his school on the study of religion', in Kurt H. Wolff (ed.), *Émile Durkheim 1855–1917*, Ohio State University Press, Columbus, pp. 233–46.

HOOD, M. S. F. (1958), *An Archaeological Survey of the Knossos Area*, British School of Archaeology at Athens, London.

HOOD, M. S. F., HUXLEY, G., and SANDARS, N. (1959), 'A Minoan cemetery on upper Gypsades', *Annual of the British School of Archaeology at Athens*, 53–4, 1958–9, pp. 194–262.

HOPE-SIMPSON, R. (1965), *A Gazetteer and Atlas of Mycenaean Sites*, Institute of Classical Studies, London.

HOPKINS, KEITH (1965), 'Elite mobility in the Roman Empire', *Past and Present*, 32, pp. 12–26.

HOPKINS, KEITH (1967), 'Slavery in classical antiquity', in A. de Reuck and J. Knight (eds), *Caste and Race*, CIBA, London, pp. 166–77.

HOPKINS, KEITH (1968), 'Structural differentiation in Rome 200–31 B.C.: the genesis of an historical bureaucratic society', in I. M. Lewis, 1968, pp. 63–79.

HOPKINS, TERENCE K. (1957), 'Sociology and the substantive view of the economy', in Polanyi, 1957a, pp. 270–306.

HOSELITZ, BERT F. (1960), 'The market matrix', in Moore and Feldman, 1960, pp. 217–37.

HUBERT, HENRI (1909), 'Étude sommaire de la représentation du temps dans la religion et la magie', in Hubert and Mauss, 1909, pp. 189–229.

HUBERT, HENRI, and MAUSS, MARCEL (1909), *Mélanges d'histoire des religions*, Alcan, Paris.

HUGHES, H. STUART (1958), *Consciousness and Society*, Knopf, New York.

HUMPHREYS, S. C. (1972), review of Meyer Fortes, *Kinship and the Social Order*, *Comparative Studies in Society and History*, 14, pp. 126–8.

HUMPHREYS, S. C. (1973), contribution to discussion in *Economia e Società*, 1973, pp. 71–7.

HUMPHREYS, S. C. (1977), review of Gray, 1974, *Classical Philology* (in press).

HUVELIN, P. (1897), *Essai historique sur le droit des marchés et des foires*, Rousseau, Paris.

HUVELIN, P. (1907), 'La Magie et le droit individuel', *L'Année sociologique*, 10, 1905–6, pp. 1–47.

HUXLEY, J. (1954), 'The evolutionary process', in J. Huxley, A. C. Hardy and E. B. Ford (eds), *Evolution as a Process*, Allen & Unwin, London, pp. 1–23.

IGNOTUS, PAUL (1961), 'The Hungary of Michael Polanyi', in *The Logic of Personal Knowledge: Essays Presented to Michael Polanyi on his 70th Birthday*, Free Press, New York, pp. 3–12.

IPSEN, G. (1924), 'Der alte Orient und die Indogermanen', in *Stand und Abgaben der Sprachwissenschaft, Festschrift für Wilhelm Streitberg*, Winter, Heidelberg, pp. 200–37.

ISHWARAN, K. (1966), *Tradition and Economy in Village India*, Routledge & Kegan Paul, London.

JACKSON, A. H. (1970), 'Plundering in war and other depredations in Greek history from 800 B.C. to 146 B.C.', PhD. thesis, Cambridge.

JACOBS, M. (1960), 'Thoughts on methodology for comprehension of an oral literature', in A. F. C. Wallace (ed.), *Man and Cultures. Selected Papers of the Fifth International Congress of Anthropological and Ethnological Sciences (1956)*, University of Pennsylvania, Philadelphia, pp. 123–9.

JACOBY, FELIX (1923–58), *Die Fragmente der griechischen Historiker*, vols I–III (*F.G.H.*), Weidmann, Berlin, and Brill, Leiden.

JACOBY, FELIX (1944a), 'Genesia. A forgotten festival of the dead', *Classical Quarterly*, 38, pp. 65–75 (Jacoby, 1956, pp. 243–59).

JACOBY, FELIX (1944b), 'Patrios nomos: state burial in Athens and the public cemetery in the Kerameikos', *Journal of Hellenic Studies*, 64, pp. 37–66 (Jacoby, 1956, pp. 260–315).

JACOBY, FELIX (1947), 'Some remarks on Ion of Chios', *Classical Quarterly*, 41, pp. 1–17 (Jacoby, 1956, pp. 144–68).

JACOBY, FELIX (1949), *Atthis*, Clarendon Press, Oxford.

JACOBY, FELIX (1956), *Abhandlungen zur griechischen Geschichtsschreibung*, Brill, Leiden.

JACOTA, M. (1966), 'Les Pactes de l'esclave en son propre nom', *Revue internationale des droits de l'antiquité*, 13, pp. 205–30.

JAMES, WILLIAM (1902), *The Varieties of Religious Experience*, Longmans, Green, New York.

JAMESON, M. H., TOPPING, P., FORBES, H. A. and M. H. C., KOSTER, H. A. and J. B., GAVRIELIDES, N., and ASCHENBRENNER, S. E. (1976), 'The Peloponnese: history and archaeology in relation to ethnography', in Dimon and Friedl, 1976, pp. 74–285.

JANNORAY, J. (1955), *Ensérune*, de Boccard, Paris.

JAURÈS, JEAN (1895), 'Esquisse provisoire de l'organisation industrielle', *La Revue socialiste* (reprinted in Jaurès, 1931).

JAURÈS, JEAN (1931), *Oeuvres*, ed. Max Bonnafous, *Études Socialistes I, 1888–97*, Rieder, Paris.

JEANMAIRE, H. (1913), 'La Cryptie lacédémonienne', *Revue des études grecques*, 26, pp. 121–50.

JEANMAIRE, H. (1939), *Couroi et Courètes: essai sur l'éducation spartiate et sur les rites d'adolescence dans l'antiquité hellénique*, Bibliothèque Universitaire, Lille.

JEANMAIRE, H. (1951), *Dionysos, histoire du culte de Bacchos*, Payot, Paris.

JEANMAIRE, H. (1956), 'La Naissance d'Athéna et la royauté magique de Zeus', *Revue archéologique*, 48, pp. 12–39.

JEFFERY, L. H. (1965), 'The Battle of Oenoe in the Stoa Poikilē', *Annual of the British School of Archaeology at Athens*, 60, pp. 41–57.

JENSEN, M. S. (1966), 'Tradition and individuality in Hesiod's *Works and Days*', *Classica et Medievalia*, 27, pp. 1–27.

JOHANNOWSKY, W. (1963), 'Relazione preliminare sugli scavi di Teano', *Bollettino d'arte*, 48, pp. 131–59.

JOHNSON, M. (1966), 'The ounce in eighteenth century West African trade', *Journal of African History*, 7, pp. 197–214.

JOHNSTON, A. W. (1972), 'The rehabilitation of Sostratus', *La parola del passato*, 147, pp. 416–23.

JOHNSTON, A. W. (1974), 'Trademarks on Greek vases', *Greece and Rome*, series 2, 21, pp. 138–52.

JOLY, R. (1956), *Le Thème philosophique des genres de vie dans l'antiquité classique*, Académie Royale de Belgique, *Mémoires*, Classe des lettres et sciences morales et politiques, 51, 3.

JONES, A. H. M. (1940), *The Greek City from Alexander to Justinian*, Clarendon Press, Oxford.

JONES, A. H. M. (1957), *Athenian Democracy*, Blackwell, Oxford.

JONES, G. D. B. (1962–3), 'Capena and the Ager Capenas', *Papers of the British School at Rome*, 30, pp. 116–207, and 31, pp. 100–58.

JONES, J. E., SACKETT, L. H., and ELIOT, C. W. J. (1957), 'To Dema: a survey of the Aigaleos-Parnes wall', *Annual of the British School of Archaeology at Athens*, 52, pp. 152–89.

JONES, J. E., SACKETT, L. H., and GRAHAM, A. J. (1962), 'The Dema house in Attica', *Annual of the British School of Archaeology at Athens*, 57, pp. 75–114.

JONES, J. E., SACKETT, L. H., and GRAHAM, A. J. (1973), 'An Attic country house below the cave of Pan at Vari', *Annual of the British School of Archaeology at Athens*, 68, pp. 355–452.

JORDAN, BORIMIR (1975), *The Athenian Navy in the Classical Period*, University of California Press, Berkeley.

JOY, LEONARD (1967), 'One economist's view of the relationship between economics and anthropology', in Firth, 1967a, pp. 29–46.

KAHRSTEDT, ULRICH (1936), *Untersuchungen zur Magistratur in Athen*, Kohlhammer, Stuttgart.

KAHRSTEDT, ULRICH (1954), *Wirtschaftliche Gesicht Griechenlands in der Kaiserzeit*, Francke, Bern.

KAHRSTEDT, ULRICH (1960), *Wirtschaftliche Lage Grossgriechenlands in der Kaiserzeit*, Steiner, Wiesbaden (*Historia-Einzelschriften*, Heft 4).

KAIMIO, MAARIT (1970), *The Chorus of Greek Drama within the light of the person and number used*, Commentationes Humanarum Litterarum, 46 (Helsinki-Helsingfors).

KAMPS, WERNER (1947), 'Heredes, chērōstai, Hantmahal. Étude comparative sur les origines de l'hérédité', *Archives d'histoire du droit oriental*, 3, pp. 236–97.

KAPLAN, DAVID, *et al.* (1966), comments on Foster, 1965, *American Anthropologist*, 68, pp. 202–10, 1202–25.

KARADY, V. (1968), introduction to Mauss, 1968.

KASER, MAX (1938), 'Die Geschichte der Patronatsgewalt über Freilassene', *Zeitschrift der Savigny-Stiftung* (Rom. Abteilung), 58, pp. 88–135.

KASER, MAX (1951), review of Cosentini, 1949–50, *Zeitschrift der Savigny-Stiftung für Rechtsgeschichte* (Rom. Abteilung), 68 (81), pp. 576–86.

KAUTSKY, K. (1895), *Vorläufer des neueren Sozialismus, I.1. Von Plato bis zu den Wiedertäufern*, Dietz, Stuttgart.

KEANEY, J. J., and RAUBITSCHEK, A. E. (1972), 'A late Byzantine account of ostracism', *American Journal of Philology*, 93, pp. 87–91.

KELTER, ERNST (1935), *Geschichte der obrigkeitliche Preisregelung*, Fischer, Jena.

KIRK, G. S. (1970), *Myth, its Meaning and Function in Ancient and Other Cultures*, University of California Press, Berkeley.

KIRK, G. S. (1974), *The Nature of Greek Myth*, Penguin, Harmondsworth.

KIRSTEN, E. (1956), *Die griechische Polis als historisch-geographisches Problem des Mittelmeerraumes*, Dümmler, Bonn.

KNORRINGA, H. (1926), *Emporos. Data on Trade and Trader in Greek Literature from Homer to Aristotle*, H. J. Paris, Amsterdam.

KNOX, B. M. W. (1964), *The Heroic Temper: Studies in Sophoclean Tragedy*, University of California Press, Berkeley.

KNOX, B. M. W. (1972), 'Aeschylus and the third actor', *American Journal of Philology*, 93, pp. 104–24.

Kokalos (1962), special issue on archaeological evidence for Greek colonization in Sicily.

KONDIS, J. (1958), 'Zum antiken Stadtbauplan von Rhodos', *Mitteilungen des deutschen archäologischen Instituts (Athenische Abteilung)*, 73, pp. 146–58.

KRAAY, C. M. (1964), 'Hoards, small change and the origins of coinage', *Journal of Hellenic Studies*, 84, pp. 76–91.

KRAELING, CARL H., and ADAMS, R. MCC., eds (1960), *City Invincible: an Oriental Institute Symposium*, Chicago University Press.

KRANZ, W. (1961), 'Sphragis: Ichform und Namensiegel als Eingangs- und Schlussmotiv antiker Dichtung', *Rheinisches Museum*, N.F. 104, pp. 3–46.

KRAUS, CLEMENS (1972), *Eretria. Ausgrabungen und Forschungen IV. Das Westtor*, Francke, Bern.

KRIS, E., and KURZ, O. (1934), *Die Legende vom Künstler*, Krystall-Verlag, Vienna.

KUHN, T. S. (1962), *The Structure of Scientific Revolutions*, Chicago University Press.

KUPER, ADAM (1971), 'Council structure and decision-making', in A. I. Richards and Adam Kuper (eds), *Councils in Action*, Cambridge University Press, pp. 13–28.

KURTZ, DONNA, and BOARDMAN, J. M. (1971), *Greek Burial Customs*, Thames & Hudson, London.

LABARBE, J. (1953), 'L'Âge correspondant au sacrifice du *koureion* et les données historiques du sixième discours d'Isée', Académie Royale de Belgique, *Bulletin de la classe des lettres et des sciences morales et politiques*, series 5, 39, pp. 358–94.

LABARBE, J. (1957), *La Loi navale de Thémistocle*, Les Belles Lettres, Paris.

LABOV, W. (1969), *The Logic of Non-standard English*, Georgetown Monographs on *Language and Linguistics*, 22 (excerpts reprinted in P. P. Giglioli (ed.), *Language and Social Context*, Penguin, Harmondsworth, 1972, pp. 179–215).

LABOV, W. (1972), 'The internal evolution of linguistic rules', in Stockwell and Macaulay, 1972, pp. 101–71.

LA CAPRA, DOMINICK (1972), *Émile Durkheim. Sociologist and Philosopher*, Cornell University Press, Ithaca.

LACOUR-GAYET, J. (1945), *Platon et l'économie dirigée*, Imprimerie Union, Paris.

LAMBERT, E. (1906–7), 'Les Changeurs et la monnaie en Palestine du Ier au IIIe siècle de l'ére vulgaire, d'après les textes talmudiques', *Revue des études juives*, 51, pp. 217–44, and 52, pp. 24–42.

LAMBERT, J. (1934), *Les Operae liberti, contribution à l'histoire des droits du patronat*, Dalloz, Paris.

LAMBERT, M. (1963), 'L'Usage de l'argent-métal à Lagash au temps du IIIe dynastie d'Ur', *Revue d'Assyriologie*, 57, pp. 79–92.

LAMMERMANN, K. (1935), 'Von der attischen Urbanität und ihrer Auswirkung in der Sprache', Diss., Göttingen.

LANGLOTZ, E. (1957),'Vom Sinngehalt attischer Vasenbilder', in *Robert Boehringer, ein Freundesgabe*, Mohr, Tübingen, pp. 397–421.

LANZA, DIEGO, and VEGETTI, MARIO (1975), 'L'ideologia della città', *Quaderni di storia* (Bari), 1, 2, pp. 1–37.

LASSERRE, F. (1962), 'La Condition du poète dans la Grèce archaïque', *Études de Lettres* (Faculté des Lettres de l'Université de Lausanne), series 2, 5, pp. 3–28.

LASSERRE, F., and BONNARD, A. (1958), *Archiloque, Fragments*, Les Belles Lettres, Paris.

LATTE, KURT (1947), 'Kollektivbesitz und Staatsschatz in Griechenland', *Nachrichten der Akademie der Wissenschaften in Göttingen*, philologisch-historische Klasse, 1946–7, pp. 64–75 (Latte, 1968, pp. 294–312).

LATTE, KURT (1964), 'Zeitgeschichtliches zu Archilochos', *Hermes*, 92, pp. 385–90 (Latte, 1968, pp. 457–63).

LATTE, KURT (1968), *Kleine Schriften*, Beck, Munich.

LAUFFER, S. (1955), 'Die Bergwerkssklaven von Laureion', *Abhandlungen der Akademie der Wissenschaften in Mainz*, geistes- und sozialwissenschaftliche Klasse, 1955, n. 12, pp. 1101–217.

LAUFFER, S. (1958), 'Die Bedeutung des Standesunterschiedes im klassischen Athen', *Historische Zeitschrift*, 185, pp. 497–514.

LAUM, B. (1914), *Stiftungen in der griechischen und römischen Antike*, Teubner, Leipzig.

LAUM, B. (1924), *Heiliges Geld: eine historische Untersuchung über den sakralen Ursprung des Geldes*, Mohr, Tübingen.

LAUM, B. (1933), *Geschlossene Wirtschaft: soziologische Grundlegung des Autarkieproblems*, Mohr, Tübingen.

LAUM, B. (1951–2), 'Über die soziale Funktion der Münze. Ein Beitrag zur Soziologie des Geldes', *Finanzarchiv*, 13, pp. 120–43.

LAUM, B. (1960), *Schenkende Wirtschaft: nicht marktmässiger Güterverkehr und seine soziale Funktion*, Klostermann, Frankfurt a.M.

LAURENT, HENRI (1932), 'Droits des foires et droits urbains aux 13e et 14e siècles', *Revue historique de droit français et étranger*, series 4, 11, pp. 660–710.

LEACH, E. R. (1959), 'Hydraulic society in Ceylon', *Past and Present*, 15, pp. 2–26.

LEACH, E. R. (1964), *Political Systems of Highland Burma*, 2nd ed., Athlone Press, London.

LEE, D. (1959), 'Codifications of reality, lineal and non-lineal', in D. Lee, *Freedom and Culture*, Prentice-Hall, Englewood Cliffs, N.J.

LEEDS, A. (1961), 'The port of trade in pre-European India as an ecological and evolutionary type', *Proceedings of the 1959 Spring Meeting of the American Ethnographical Society*, pp. 26–48.

LEEMANS, W. F. (1958), review of Polanyi, 1957a, *Jaarbericht Ex Oriente Lux*, 15, pp. 203–4.

LEFKOWITZ, MARY (1963), 'Tō kai egō: the first person in Pindar', *Harvard Studies in Classical Philology*, 67, pp. 177–253.

LEHMANN-HARTLEBEN, K. (1923), *Die antiken Hafenanlagen des Mittelmeeres*, Dieterich, Leipzig.

LEMERLE, P. (1963), 'Rapport complémentaire', *Actes du 12e Congrès international d'études byzantines, Ochride 1961*, Belgrade, vol. I, pp. 275–84.

LENCMAN, J. (1966), *Die Sklaverei im mykenischen und homerischen Griechenland*, Steiner, Wiesbaden (original publication Moscow, 1963).

LEPORE, E. (1968), 'La vita politica e sociale', *Storia di Napoli*, vol. I, Edizioni Scientifiche Italiane, Naples, pp. 140–371.

LEROI-GOURHAN, A. (1963), 'Sur les méthodes de fouilles', in Courbin, 1963, pp. 49–57.

LÉVÊQUE, P., and VIDAL-NAQUET, P. (1964), *Clisthène l'Athénien*, Les Belles Lettres, Paris.

LEVI, DORO (1963), 'Le due primi campagne di scavo a Iasos (1960–1)', *Annuario della Scuola Archeologica di Atene*, 39–40 (new series, 23–4, 1961–2), pp. 505–71.

LEVI, M. A. (1958), 'Paideia e pittura nella società attica del IV. secolo', *Archeologia classica*, 10, pp. 180–2.

LÉVI-STRAUSS, CLAUDE (1949), *Les Structures élémentaires de la parenté*, Presses Universitaires de France, Paris (revised ed., 1967).

LÉVI-STRAUSS, CLAUDE (1956), 'The family', in H. Shapiro (ed.), *Man, Culture and Society*, Oxford University Press, New York, pp. 261–85.

LÉVI-STRAUSS, CLAUDE (1958), *Anthropologie structurale*, Plon, Paris.

LÉVI-STRAUSS, CLAUDE (1960), 'La Structure et la forme. Réflexions sur un ouvrage de Vladimir Propp', *Cahiers de l'institut de science économique appliquée*, 9 (series M, 7), pp. 3–36 (reprinted in Lévi-Strauss, 1973, pp. 139–73).

LÉVI-STRAUSS, CLAUDE (1964–71), *Mythologiques*, vols I–IV, Plon, Paris.

LÉVI-STRAUSS, CLAUDE (1966), 'The future of kinship studies', *Proceedings of the Royal Anthropological Institute 1965*, pp. 13–22.

LÉVI-STRAUSS, CLAUDE (1973), *Anthropologie structurale deux*, Plon, Paris.

LEVITT, KARI (1964), 'Karl Polanyi and *Co-Existence*', *Co-Existence*, 1, pp. 113–21.

LÉVY-BRUHL, H. (1962), obituary of Gernet, *Iura*, 13, pp. 211–13.

LÉVY-BRUHL, H. (1966), 'Louis Gernet historien du droit grec' in *Hommage à Louis Gernet*, pp. 14–18.

LEWIS, D. M. (1973), 'The Athenian Rationes Centesimarum', in Finley, 1973b, pp. 187–212.

LEWIS, I. M., ed. (1968), *History and Social Anthropology*, ASA monograph 7, Tavistock, London.

LICHTHEIM, GEORGE (1970), *Lukács*, Fontana, London.

LIPSIUS, J. H. (1905–15), *Das attische Recht und Rechtsverfahren*, Reisland, Leipzig.

LLOYD, A. B. (1975), 'Were Necho's triremes Phoenician?', *Journal of Hellenic Studies*, 95, pp. 45–61.

LLOYD, G. E. R. (1966), *Polarity and Analogy*, Cambridge University Press.

LOBEL, E., and PAGE, D. L. (1955), *Poetarum Lesbiorum Fragmenta*, Clarendon Press, Oxford.

LÖWE, ADOLF (1935), *Economics and Sociology*, Allen & Unwin, London.

LORD, A. B. (1953), 'Homer's originality: oral dictated texts', *Transactions and Proceedings of the American Philological Association*, 84, pp. 124–34.

LOWIE, R. (1920), *Primitive Society*, Liveright, New York.

LUKÁCS, G. (1923), *Geschichte und Klassenbewusstsein*, Malik, Berlin.

LUKÁCS, G. (1955), 'Meine Weg zu Marx', in *Georg Lukács zum 70. Geburtstag*, Aufbau, Berlin.

LUKES, STEVEN (1972), *Émile Durkheim. His Life and Work*, Harper & Row, New York and Allen Lane, London.

MCCREDIE, J. R. (1966), *Fortified Military Camps in Attica*, American School of Classical Studies at Athens, Princeton (*Hesperia*, Supplement 11).

MCDONALD, WILLIAM A. (1964), 'Overland communications in Greece during L.H. III with special reference to Southwest Peloponnese', *Proceedings of the 3rd International Colloquium for Mycenaean Studies*, 1961, University of Wisconsin Press, Madison, pp. 217–40.

MCDONALD, WILLIAM A. (1966), 'Suggestions on directions and a modest proposal', *Hesperia*, 35, pp. 413–18.

MCDONALD, WILLIAM A., and RAPP, GEORGE R. JR (1972), *The Minnesota Messenia Expedition. Reconstructing a Bronze Age Regional Environment*, University of Minnesota Press, Minneapolis.

MACH, ERNST (1886), *Analyse der Empfindungen und das Verhältnis zum Psychischen*, Fischer, Jena.

MACH, ERNST (1910), *Az érzékletek elemzése c. munkájának 3 elsö fejezete*, Polányi Károly forditásában (translation of parts of Mach, 1886), Budapest.

MADDOLI, G. (1967), 'Responsabilità e sanzione nei "decreta de Hecatompede"', *Museum Helveticum*, 24, pp. 1–11.

MAEHLER, HERWIG (1963), *Die Auffassung des Dichterberufs im frühen Griechenland bis zur Zeit Pindars*, Vandenhoeck & Ruprecht, Göttingen.

MAIER, FRIEDRICH (1970), 'Der Sophos-begriff: zur Bedeutung, Wertung und Rolle des Begriffes von Homer bis Euripides', Diss., Munich; Dissertationsdrückerei Blasaditsch, Augsberg.

MAINE, H. S. (1861), *Ancient Law*, Murray, London.

MAIR, LUCY (1934), 'The growth of economic individualism', in Mair, 1957, pp. 23–31.

MAIR, LUCY (1956), 'Applied anthropology and development policies', Mair, 1957, pp. 9–22.

MAIR, LUCY (1957), *Studies in Applied Anthropology*, Athlone Press, London.

MALINOWSKI, B. (1922), *Argonauts of the Western Pacific*, Routledge, London.

MALINOWSKI, B. (1923), 'Meaning in primitive languages', in C. K. Ogden and I. A. Richards (eds), *The Meaning of Meaning*, Kegan Paul, London, pp. 451–510.

MALINOWSKI, B. (1926), *Crime and Custom in Savage Society*, Kegan Paul, London.

MALINOWSKI, B. (1935), *Coral Gardens and Their Magic*, Allen & Unwin, London.

MALINOWSKI, B. (1944), *A Scientific Theory of Culture*, University of North Carolina, Chapel Hill.

MALLOWAN, M. E. (1965), 'Mechanics of ancient trade in Western Asia', *Iran*, 3, pp. 1–7.

MALLOWAN, M. E. (1966), *Nimrud and its Remains*, Collins, London.

MANGANARO, G. (1965), 'Le iscrizioni delle isole Milesie', *Annuario della Scuola Archeologica di Atene*, 41–2 (new series, 25–6, 1963–4), pp. 293–349.

MANNHEIM, KARL (1934), 'German sociology (1918–33)', *Politica*, 1, pp. 12–33.

MANNHEIM, KARL (1943), *Diagnosis of Our Time: Wartime Essays of a Sociologist*, Kegan Paul, London.

MANNONI, O. (1950), *La Psychologie de la colonisation*, Éditions du Seuil, Paris (trans. as *Prosper and Caliban*, Praeger, New York, 1956).

MANSEL, A. M. (1961), 'Die neuesten Funde und Forschungen in Kleinasien auf dem Gebiet der klassischen Archäologie und deren Probleme', *Atti del 7⁰ Congresso Internazionale di Archeologia Classica 1958*, vol. I, 'L'Erma' di Bretschneider, Rome, pp. 293–308.

MANUEL, FRANK E., ed. (1966a), *Utopias and Utopian Thought*, Houghton Mifflin, Boston.

MANUEL, FRANK E. (1966b), 'Towards a psychological history of Utopias', in Manuel, 1966a, pp. 69–98.

MARTIN, ROLAND (1951), *Recherches sur l'Agora grecque*, de Boccard, Paris.

MARTIN, ROLAND (1956), *L'Urbanisme dans la Grèce antique*, Picard, Paris (revised ed., 1975).

MARTIN, ROLAND (1975), 'Problèmes d'urbanisme dans les cités grecques de Sicile', *Kokalos*, 18–19 (1972–3), pp. 348–65.

Marxism and the Classics (1975), *Arethusa*, 8, 1.

MASSON, EMILIA (1967), *Recherches sur les plus anciens emprunts sémitiques en grec*, Klincksieck, Paris.

MAUNIER, R. (1927), 'Recherches sur les échanges rituels en Afrique du Nord', *L'Année sociologique*, new series, 2 (1924–5), pp. 11–97.

MAUNIER, R. (1932), *Sociologie coloniale*, Domat-Montchrestien, Paris.

MAUSS, MARCEL (1907), review of R. E. Dennett, *At the Back of the Black Man's Mind*, *L'Année sociologique*, 10, 1905–6, pp. 305–11 (reprinted in Mauss, 1969, vol. II, pp. 96–7 and 244–5).

MAUSS, MARCEL (1909), 'La Prière. I. Les origines' (privately distributed, reprinted in Mauss, 1968, pp. 357–477).

MAUSS, MARCEL (1914), 'Les Origines de la notion de monnaie', *L'Anthropologie*, 25, supplément, 'Comptes-rendus des séances', II, 1 (Mauss, 1969, vol. II, pp. 106–20).

MAUSS, MARCEL (1921), 'Une Forme ancienne de contrat chez les Thraces', *Revue des études grecques*, 34, pp. 388–97 (Mauss, 1969, vol. III, pp. 35–43).

MAUSS, MARCEL (1925a), 'Essai sur le don. Forme et raison de l'échange dans les sociétés archaïques', *L'Année sociologique*, new series, 1, 1923–4, pp. 30–186 (Mauss, 1966, pp. 143–279; trans. as *The Gift*, Cohen & West, London, 1954).

MAUSS, MARCEL (1925b), 'In Memoriam. L'oeuvre inédite de Durkheim et de ses collaborateurs', *L'Année sociologique*, new series, 1, pp. 7–29 (Mauss, 1969, vol. III, pp. 473–99).

MAUSS, MARCEL (1927a), 'Divisions et proportions des divisions de la sociologie', *L'Année sociologique*, new series, 2, 1924–5, pp. 98–176 (Mauss, 1969, vol. III, pp. 178–245).

MAUSS, MARCEL (1927b), 'Notices biographiques', *L'Année sociologique*, new series, 2, pp. 3–9 (Mauss, 1969, vol. III, pp. 517–24).

MAUSS, MARCEL (1928), introduction to Durkheim, 1928 (Mauss, 1969, vol. III, pp. 505–9).

MAUSS, MARCEL (1932), 'La Cohésion sociale dans les sociétés polysegmentaires', *Bulletin de l'Institut Français de Sociologie*, 1, pp. 49–68 (Mauss, 1969, vol. III, pp. 11–26).

MAUSS, MARCEL (1933), 'La Sociologie en France depuis 1914', in *La Science française*, vol. I, Larousse, Paris, pp. 36–48 (Mauss, 1969, vol. III, pp. 436–50).

MAUSS, MARCEL (1934), 'Fragment d'un plan de sociologie générale descriptive', *Annales Sociologiques*, Series A, 1, pp. 1–56 (Mauss, 1969, vol. III, pp. 302–54).

MAUSS, MARCEL (1935a), 'Les Techniques du corps', *Journal de psychologie normale et pathologique*, 32, pp. 271–93 (Mauss, 1966, pp. 363–86).

MAUSS, MARCEL (1935b), 'Intervention', *Annales sociologiques*, series C, 1, pp. 72–5 (Mauss, 1969, vol. III, pp. 451–4).

MAUSS, MARCEL (1937), 'In memoriam A. Meillet', *Annales sociologiques*, series E, 2, pp. 1–7 (Mauss, 1969, vol. III, pp. 548–53).

MAUSS, MARCEL (1947), *Manuel d'ethnographie*, Payot, Paris.

 MAUSS, MARCEL (1966), *Sociologie et anthropologie*, 3rd ed., Presses Universitaires de France, Paris.

MAUSS, MARCEL (1968), *Oeuvres*, vol. I, ed. V. Karady, Éditions de Minuit, Paris.

MAUSS, MARCEL (1969), *Oeuvres*, vols II–III, ed. V. Karady, Éditions de Minuit, Paris.

 MAUSS, MARCEL, and BEUCHAT, HENRI (1906), 'Essai sur les variations saisonnières des sociétés eskimos', *L'Année sociologique*, 9, 1904–5, pp. 39–132 (Mauss, 1966, pp. 389–477).

 MAUSS, MARCEL, and HUBERT, HENRI (1899), 'Essai sur la nature et fonction du sacrifice', *L'Année sociologique*, 2, pp. 29–138 (Mauss, 1968, pp. 193–307).

MAXWELL-HYSLOP, K. R. (1966), review of Mallowan, 1966, *Archaeological Journal*, 123, pp. 223–4.

 MEAD, MARGARET, ed. (1937), *Cooperation and Competition Among Primitive Peoples*, McGraw-Hill, New York.

MEATES, G. W. (1966), 'Lullingstone', *Archaeologia Cantiana*, 81, pp. lix–lx.

MEDOW, PAUL (1965), 'The humanistic ideals of the enlightenment and mathematical economics', in Fromm, 1965, pp. 376–87.

MEILLASSOUX, CLAUDE (1960), 'Essai d'interprétation du phénomène économique dans les sociétés traditionelles d'auto-subsistence', *Cahiers d'études africaines*, 1, 4, pp. 38–67.

MEILLASSOUX, CLAUDE (1964), *Anthropologie économique des Gouro du Côte d'Ivoire*, Mouton, Paris/Hague.

MEILLASSOUX, CLAUDE (1966), 'Project for research on African economic systems', *Africa*, 36, pp. 445–6.

 MEILLASSOUX, CLAUDE, ed. (1971), *The Development of Indigenous Trade and Markets in West Africa*, 10th international seminar, Oxford University Press and I.A.I., London.

MEILLASSOUX, CLAUDE, ed. (1975), *L'Esclavage en Afrique précoloniale*, Maspero, Paris.

 MEILLASSOUX, CLAUDE (1976), *Femmes, greniers, capitaux*, Maspero, Paris.

MEILLET, A. (1906), 'Comment les mots changent de sens', *L'Année sociologique*, 9, 1904–5, pp. 1–38 (reprinted in Meillet, 1921, pp. 230–71).

MEILLET, A. (1921), *Linguistique historique et linguistique générale*, vol. I, Champion, Paris.

MEILLET, A. (1927), Obituary of Maurice Cahen, *Annuaire de l'École Pratique des Hautes Études* (IVe section), 1926–7, pp. 3 ff. (Meillet, 1938, pp. 206–11).

MEILLET, A. (1930), 'Michel Bréal et la grammaire comparée au Collège de France', in *Quatrième Centenaire du Collège de France*, Presses Universitaires de France, Paris, pp. 279 ff. (Meillet, 1938, pp. 212–27).

MEILLET, A. (1938), *Linguistique historique et linguistique générale*, vol. II, Klincksieck, Paris.

Mélanges Piganiol (1966), *Mélanges d'archéologie et d'histoire offerts à M. André Piganiol*, vols I–III, ed. R. Chevallier, SEVPEN, Paris.

MELLAART, J. (1967), *Çatal Hüyük*, Thames & Hudson, London.

MELLINK, M. J. (1967), 'Archaeology in Asia Minor', *American Journal of Archaeology*, 71, pp. 155–74.

MERKELBACH, R., and WEST, M. L. (1967), *Fragmenta Hesiodea*, Clarendon Press, Oxford.

Metaponto (in press), *Atti del 13⁰ Convegno di studi sulla Magna Grecia 1973*, L'Arte Tipografica, Naples.

METZGER, H. (1951), *Les Représentations dans la céramique attique du IVe siècle*, de Boccard, Paris.

METZGER, H. (1965), *Recherches sur l'imagerie athénienne*, de Bochard, Paris.

MEULI, K. (1935), 'Scythica', *Hermes*, 70, pp. 136–76.

MEYER, EDUARD (1895), 'Die wirtschaftliche Entwicklung des Altertums', *Jahrbücher für Nationalökonomie und Statistik*, 9 (64) (reprinted in Meyer, 1910, pp. 79–168).

MEYER, EDUARD (1907), *Geschichte des Altertums*, 2nd ed., vol. I, *Einleitung. Elemente der Anthropologie*, Cotta, Stuttgart and Berlin.

MEYER, EDUARD (1910), *Kleine Schriften*, vol. I, Niemeyer, Halle a. S.

MEYER, R. M. (1910), 'Bedeutungssysteme', *Zeitschrift für vergleichende Sprachforschung*, 43, pp. 352–68.

MILLIN, AUBIN-LOUIS (1796), *Introduction à l'étude des monuments antiques*, Magasin Encyclopédique, Paris.

MILLS, C. WRIGHT (1940), 'The language and ideas of ancient China: Marcel Granet's contribution to the sociology of knowledge', in Mills, 1963, pp. 469–520.

MILLS, C. WRIGHT (1963), *Power, Politics and People*, Oxford University Press, New York.

MINTZ, S. W. (1955), 'The Jamaican internal marketing pattern', *Social and Economic Studies*, 4, pp. 95–103.

MINTZ, S. W. (1959), 'Internal market systems as mechanisms of social articulation', *Proceedings of the 1959 Spring Meeting of the American Ethnological Society*, pp. 20–30.

MINTZ, S. W. (1961), 'Pratik: Haitian personal economic relationships', *Proceedings of the 1961 Spring Meeting of the American Ethnological Society*, pp. 54–63.

MINTZ, S. W., and HALL, D. (1960), 'The origins of the internal marketing system in Jamaica', in S. W. Mintz (ed.), *Papers in Caribbean Anthropology*, University Publications in Anthropology, 57, Yale, New Haven.

MOMIGLIANO, A. (1931), 'Il razionalismo di Ecateo di Mileto', *Atene e Roma*, new series, 12, 3, pp. 133–42 (reprinted in Momigliano, 1966, pp. 323–33).

MOMIGLIANO, A. (1934), *Filippo il Macedone*, La Nuova Italia, Florence.

MOMIGLIANO, A. (1944), 'Seapower in Greek thought', *Classical Review*, 58, pp. 1–7 (Momigliano, 1960, pp. 57–68).

MOMIGLIANO, A. (1950), 'Ancient history and the Antiquarian', *Journal of the Warburg and Courtauld Institutes*, 13, pp. 285–315 (Momigliano, 1955, pp. 67–106).

MOMIGLIANO, A. (1955), *Contributo alla storia degli studi classici*, Storia e Letteratura, Rome.

MOMIGLIANO, A. (1960), *Secondo contributo alla storia degli studi classici*, Storia e Letteratura, Rome.

MOMIGLIANO, A. (1963), 'An interim report on the origins of Rome', *Journal of Roman Studies*, 53, pp. 95–121 (Momigliano, 1966, pp. 545–98).

MOMIGLIANO, A. (1964), 'Le conseguenze del rinnovamento della storia dei diritti antichi', *Rivista storica italiana*, 76, pp. 133–49 (Momigliano, 1966, pp. 285–302).

MOMIGLIANO, A. (1966), *Terzo contributo alla storia degli studi classici e del mondo antico*, Storia e Letteratura, Rome.

MOMIGLIANO, A. (1967), 'L'ascesa della plebe nella storia arcaica di Roma', *Rivista storica italiana*, 79, pp. 297–312 (Momigliano, 1969a, pp. 437–54).

MOMIGLIANO, A. (1969a), *Quarto contributo alla storia degli studi classici e del mondo antico*, Storia e Letteratura, Rome.

MOMIGLIANO, A. (1969b), 'The origins of the Roman Republic', in C. Singleton (ed.), *Interpretation. Theory and Practice*, Johns Hopkins University Press, Baltimore, pp. 1–34 (Momigliano, 1975, pp. 293–332).

MOMIGLIANO, A. (1970), 'La Città antica di Fustel de Coulanges', *Rivista storica italiana*, 82, pp. 81–98 (Momigliano, 1975, pp. 159–78).

MOMIGLIANO, A. (1971a), *The Development of Greek Biography*, Harvard University Press, Cambridge, Mass.

MOMIGLIANO, A. (1971b), 'Second thoughts on Greek biography', *Mededelingen der Koninklijke Nederlandse Akademie* (afd. Letterkunde), N.R. 34, pp. 245–57 (Momigliano, 1975, pp. 33–47).

MOMIGLIANO, A. (1973), 'Freedom of speech in antiquity' and 'Impiety in the classical world', *Dictionary of the History of Ideas*, Scribner, New York, pp. 252–63, 564–7.

MOMIGLIANO, A. (1975), *Quinto contributo alla storia degli studi classici e del mondo antico*, Storia e Letteratura, Rome.

Moneta e scambi (1961), *Moneta e scambi nell'Alto Medioevo*, Centro Italiano di Studi sull'Alto Medioevo, Spoleto.

MONTINI, R. U. (1959), 'L'acropoli di Lavinio', *Capitolium*, 34, 8, pp. 14–19.

MOORE, WILBERT E. (1967), 'Economic and professional institutions', in Smelser, 1967, pp. 276–328.

MOORE, WILBERT E. and FELDMAN, ARNOLD, eds (1960), *Labor Commitment and Social Change in Developing Areas*, Social Science Research Council, New York.

MORET, A., and DAVY, G. (1923), *Des clans aux empires*, La Renaissance du Livre, Paris.

MORETTI, MARIO (1962), *Tarquinia: la Tomba della Nave*, Lerici, Milan.

MORGAN, LEWIS H. (1877), *Ancient Society*, Kerr, Chicago.

MORRISON, J. S., and WILLIAMS, R. T. (1968), *Greek Oared Ships, 900–322 B.C.*, Cambridge University Press.

MOSSÉ, C. (1962), *La Fin de la démocratie athénienne*, Presses Universitaires de France, Paris.

MOSSÉ, C. (1972), 'La Vie économique d'Athènes au IVe siècle: crise ou renouveau?', in F. Sartori (ed.), *Praelectiones Patavinae*, 'L'Erma' di Bretschneider, Rome, pp. 135–44.

MUND, VERNON A. (1948), *Open Markets, an Essential of Free Enterprise*, Harper, New York.

MUNN-RANKIN, J. M. (1967), review of Mallowan, 1966, *Antiquity*, 41, pp. 153–4.

MURRAY, GILBERT (1943), Obituary of F. M. Cornford, *Proceedings of the British Academy*, 29, pp. 421–32.

MUSSCHE, H. F., *et al.* (1967 ff.), *Thorikos 1965*, etc., Comité de Fouilles Belges en Grèce, Brussels.

NASH, MANNING (1964), 'The organization of economic life', in Tax, 1964, pp. 171–80.

NASH, MANNING (1965), 'Economic anthropology', *Biennial Review of Anthropology*, pp. 121–38.

NASH, MANNING (1966), *Primitive and Peasant Economic Systems*, Chandler, San Francisco.

NASH, MANNING (1968), review of Firth, 1967a, *Man*, 3, pp. 496–7.

NEALE, WALTER C. (1957), 'Reciprocity and redistribution in the Indian village', in Polanyi, 1957a, pp. 208–36.

NEALE, WALTER C. (1962), *Economic Change in Rural India*, Yale University Press, New Haven.

NEPPI-MODONA, A. (1961), *Gli edifici teatrali greci e romani. Teatri, odei, anfiteatri, circhi*, Olschki, Florence.

NICHOLAS, D. M. (1969), 'Medieval urban origins in northern continental Europe: state of research and some tentative conclusions', *Studies in Medieval and Renaissance History*, 6, pp. 53–114.

NICOLET, C. (1963), 'À Rome pendant la seconde guerre punique: techniques financières et manipulations monétaires', *Annales. Économies, sociétés, civilisations*, 18, pp. 417–36.

NICOLET, C. (1966), *L'Ordre équestre à l'époque républicaine*, de Boccard, Paris.

NILSSON, M. P. (1912), 'Die Grundlagen des spartanischen Lebens', *Klio*, 12, pp. 308–40.

NORTH, DOUGLASS (1965), 'The state of economic history', *American Economic Review*, 55, 2, pp. 86–91.

NORTH, HELEN (1966), *Sophrosyne*, Cornell University Press, Ithaca.

ÖHMAN, S. (1953), 'Theories of the linguistic field', *Word*, 9, pp. 123–34.

OERTEL, F. (1925), 'Anhang', in Pöhlmann, 1925, pp. 511–85.

OGILVIE, R. M. (1965), 'Eretum', *Papers of the British School at Rome*, 33, pp. 70–112.

OPPENHEIM, A. L. (1954), 'The sea-faring merchants of Ur', *Journal of the American Oriental Society*, 74, pp. 6–17.

OPPENHEIM, A. L. (1957), 'A bird's-eye view of Mesopotamian economic history', in Polanyi, 1957a, pp. 27–37.

OPPENHEIM, A. L. (1964), *Ancient Mesopotamia. Portrait of a Dead Civilization*, Chicago University Press.

OPPENHEIM, A. L. (1967), 'A new look at the structure of Mesopotamian society', *Journal of the Economic and Social History of the Orient*, 10, pp. 1–16.

ORMEROD, H. A. (1924), 'Towers in the Greek Islands', *Liverpool Annals of Archaeology and Anthropology*, 11, pp. 31–6 (reprinted in H. A. Ormerod, *Piracy in the Ancient World*, Liverpool University Press and Hodder & Stoughton, London, pp. 41–9).

PAGE, D. L. (1955), *Sappho and Alcaeus*, Clarendon Press, Oxford.

PAGE, D. L. (1962), *Poetae Melici Graeci*, Clarendon Press, Oxford.

PANOFSKY, E. (1964), *Tomb Sculpture*, Thames & Hudson, London.

PAOLI, U. E. (1930), 'Il prestito marittimo nel diritto attico', in U. E. Paoli, *Studi di diritto attico*, Bemporad, Florence, pp. 9–137.

PAOLI, U. E., and BISCARDI, A. (1966), 'Prestito a cambio marittimo (diritto greco)', *Novissimo digesto italiano*, vol. XIII, Utet, Turin, s.v.

PARASKEVAÏDIS, M. (1964), 'To mystērion tōn archaiōn pyrgōn tēs voreiou Chiou kai tōn Kykladōn', *Kathimerini*, 8 October, pp. 9–10.

PARKE, H. W. (1933), *Greek Mercenary Soldiers*, Clarendon Press, Oxford.

PARKE, H. W. (1967), *The Oracles of Zeus*, Blackwell, Oxford.

PARRY, ADAM (1969), 'The language of Thucydides' description of the plague', University of London, Institute of Classical Studies, *Bulletin* 16, pp. 106–17.

PARRY, ADAM (1970), 'Thucydides' use of abstract language', *Yale French Studies*, 45, pp. 3–20.

PARRY, ADAM (1972), 'Thucydides' historical perspective', *Yale Classical Studies*, 22, pp. 47–61.

PARSONS, TALCOTT (1928–9), '"Capitalism" in recent German literature: Sombart and Weber', *Journal of Political Economy*, 36, pp. 641–61, and 37, pp. 31–57.

PARSONS, TALCOTT (1940), 'The motivations of economic activities', *Canadian Journal of Economics and Political Science*, 6, pp. 187–203 (reprinted in Parsons, 1954, pp. 50–68).

PARSONS, TALCOTT (1951), *The Social System*, Free Press, Chicago.

PARSONS, TALCOTT (1954), *Essays in Sociological Theory*, Free Press, Chicago.

Bibliography

PARSONS, TALCOTT (1966), *Societies: Evolutionary and Comparative Perspectives*, Prentice-Hall, Englewood Cliffs, N.J.

PARSONS, TALCOTT, and SMELSER, NEIL J. (1956), *Economy and Society*, Free Press, Chicago.

PAYNE, HUMFREY (1940), *Perachora*, vol. I, Clarendon Press, Oxford.

PEARSON, HARRY W. (1957a), 'The economy has no surplus', in Polanyi, 1957a, pp. 320–41.

PEARSON, HARRY W. (1957b), 'Parsons and Smelser on the economy', in Polanyi, 1957a, pp. 307–19.

PEARSON, KARL (1897), 'Kindred group-marriage', in K. Pearson, *Chances of Death and Other Studies in Evolution*, vol. II, Arnold, London, pp. 92–245.

PEČÍRKA, J. (1966), *The Formula for the Grant of Enktesis in Attic Inscriptions*, Acta Universitatis Carolinae, Philosophica et Historica Monographia 15, Prague.

PEČÍRKA, J. (1967), 'A note on Aristotle's conception of citizenship and the role of foreigners in fourth century Athens', *Eirene*, 6, pp. 23–6.

PEČÍRKA, J. (1970), 'Country estates of the polis of Chersonesos in the Crimea', *Ricerche storiche ed economiche in memoria di Corrado Barbagallo*, vol. I, Edizioni Scientifiche Italiane, Naples, pp. 459–77.

PEČÍRKA, J. (1973), 'Homestead farms in classical and Hellenistic Hellas', in Finley, 1973b, pp. 113–47.

PEČÍRKA, J., and DUFKOVA, M. (1970), 'Excavations of farms and farmhouses in the chora of Chersonesos in the Crimea', *Eirene*, 8, pp. 123–74.

PELLOUTIER, F. (1902), *Histoire des Bourses du Travail*, Schleicher, Paris.

PEMBROKE, S. G. (1967), 'The ancient idea of matriarchy', *Journal of the Warburg and Courtauld Institutes*, 30, pp. 1–35.

PEMBROKE, S. G. (1970), 'Locres et Tarente: le rôle des femmes dans la fondation de deux colonies grecques', *Annales. Économies, sociétés, civilisations*, 25, pp. 1240–70.

PESEZ, J. M. (1967), 'Archéologie slave: villes et campagnes', *Annales. Économies, sociétés, civilisations*, 22, pp. 609–15.

PHILIPPSON, A. (1950–9), *Die griechischen Landschaften*, vols I–IV, Klostermann, Frankfurt.

POCOCK, J. G. A. (1968), 'Time, institutions and action: an essay on traditions and their understanding', in Preston King and B. C. Parekh (eds), *Politics and Experience: Essays Presented to Michael Oakeshott*, Cambridge University Press, pp. 209–37 (reprinted in Pocock, 1971, pp. 233–72).

POCOCK, J. G. A. (1971), *Politics. Language and Time: Essays on Political Thought and History*, Athenaeum, New York.

PÖHLMANN, R. VON (1890), 'Zur Beurteilung George Grotes', *Deutsche Zeitschrift für Geschichtswissenschaft* (reprinted in Pöhlmann, 1895, pp. 315–43).

PÖHLMANN, R. VON (1893), *Geschichte des antiken Kommunismus und Sozialismus*, vol. I, Beck, Munich.

PÖHLMANN, R. VON (1895), *Aus Altertum und Gegenwart*, vol. I, Beck, Munich.

PÖHLMANN, R. VON (1902), 'Die Geschichte der Griechen und das 19. Jahrhundert' (Festrede), in Pöhlmann, 1911, pp. 277–322.

PÖHLMANN, R. VON (1911), *Aus Altertum und Gegenwart*, vol. II, Beck, Munich.

PÖHLMANN, R. VON (1925) *Geschichte der sozialen Frage und des Sozialismus in der antiken Welt*, Beck, Munich.

POLANYI, KARL (1922), 'Sozialistische Rechnungslegung', *Archiv für Sozialwissenschaft*, 49, pp. 377–420.

POLANYI, KARL (1932), 'Wirtschaft v. Demokratie', *Österreichische Volkswirt*, 24 December, pp. 301–3.

POLANYI, KARL (1934a), 'England für Budgetwahrheit', *Österreichische Volkswirt*, 28 April, pp. 669 ff.

POLANYI, KARL (1934b), 'Lancashire im Fegefeuer', *Österreichische Volkswirt*, 2 June, pp. 781 f.

POLANYI, KARL (1934c), 'Lancashire als Menschheitsfrage', *Österreichische Volkswirt*, 23 June, pp. 341 ff.

POLANYI, KARL (1937), *Europe Today*, T.U.C., London.

POLANYI, KARL (1944), *Origins of our Time: the Great Transformation*, Farrar & Rinehart, New York (quoted from 2nd ed., with some additions, Gollancz, London, 1945).

POLANYI, KARL (1947), 'Our obsolete market mentality', *Commentary*, 3, pp. 109–17 (reprinted in Polanyi, 1968, pp. 59–77).

POLANYI, KARL (1953), 'Semantics of general economic history', Columbia University, New York (see Polanyi, 1959).

POLANYI, KARL (1957a), *Trade and Market in the Early Empires: Economies in History and Theory*, ed. K. Polanyi, C. Arensberg, and H. W. Pearson, Free Press, Chicago.

POLANYI, KARL (1957b), 'The semantics of money uses', *Explorations* (ed. M. McLuhan), 7 (Polanyi, 1968, pp. 175–203).

POLANYI, KARL (1958), *Towards a New West* (unpublished).

POLANYI, KARL (1959), 'Anthropology and economic theory', in M. Fried (ed.), *Readings in Anthropology*, vol. II, Crowell, New York, pp. 161–84 (revised version of Polanyi, 1953).

POLANYI, KARL (1960), 'On the comparative treatment of economic institutions in antiquity, with illustrations from Athens, Mycenae and Alalakh', in Kraeling and Adams, 1960, pp. 329–50 (Polanyi, 1968, pp. 306–34).

POLANYI, KARL (1962), 'Il pensiero sovietico in transizione', *Nuova Presenza*, 5 (Milan), pp. 39–45.

POLANYI, KARL (1963), 'Ports of trade in early societies', *Journal of Economic History*, 23, pp. 30–45 (Polanyi, 1968, pp. 238–60).

POLANYI, KARL (1964), 'Sortings and "ounce trade" in the West African slave trade', *Journal of African History*, 5, pp. 381–93 (Polanyi, 1968, pp. 261–79).

POLANYI, KARL (1966), *Dahomey and the Slave Trade: an Analysis of an Archaic Economy* (with Abraham Rotstein), University of Washington Press, Seattle.

POLANYI, KARL (1968), *Primitive, Archaic and Modern Economies: Essays of Karl Polanyi*, ed. G. Dalton, Doubleday, Garden City, N.Y.

POLANYI, KARL (1971a), 'Primitive feudalism and the feudalism of decay', in Dalton, 1971a, pp. 141–7.

POLANYI, KARL (1971b), 'Carl Menger's two meanings of "economic"', in Dalton, 1971b, pp. 16–24.

POLANYI, KARL (1974), *La grande trasformazione*, Einaudi, Turin (translation of Polanyi, 1944).

POLANYI, KARL, LEWIS, JOHN D., and KITCHIN, DONALD, eds (1935), *Christianity and the Social Revolution*, Gollancz, London.

POPE-HENNESSY, JOHN (1958), *Italian Renaissance Sculpture*, Phaidon, London.

POPPER, KARL (1945), *The Open Society and its Enemies*, Routledge & Kegan Paul, London.

POPPER, KARL (1963), 'Back to the pre-socratics', in K. Popper, *Conjectures and Refutations*, Routledge & Kegan Paul, London, pp. 136–65 (earlier version, *Proceedings of the Aristotelian Society*, new series, 59, 1958–9).

POSPISIL, L. (1963), *The Kapauku Papuans of West New Guinea*, Holt, Rinehart & Winston, New York.

PRÉAUX, CLAIRE (1954), 'Les Origines des monopoles Lagides', *Chronique d'Égypte*, 29, pp. 302–27.

PRÉAUX, CLAIRE (1961), 'L'Économie Lagide: 1933–1958 ... Points de vue nouveaux', *Proceedings of the IX. International Congress of Papyrology 1958*, Universitetsforlaget, Oslo, pp. 216–32.

PRINGSHEIM, F. (1916), *Die Kauf mit fremden Geld*, Veit, Leipzig.

PRINGSHEIM, F. (1950), *The Greek Law of Sale*, Böhlau, Weimar.

PRITCHETT, W. K. (1971), *Ancient Greek Military Practices*, vol. I, University of California Publications: Classical Studies, 7 (reprinted as Pritchett, *The Greek State at War*, vol. I, University of California, Berkeley, 1974).

PUDDU, R. (1975), 'Istituzioni militari tra medioevo e rinascimento', *Rivista storica italiana*, 87, pp. 749–69.

RADCLIFFE-BROWN, A. R. (1922), *The Andaman Islanders*, Cambridge University Press.

RADCLIFFE-BROWN, A. R. (1935), 'On the concept of function in social science', *American Anthropologist*, 37, pp. 394–402 (reprinted in A. R. Radcliffe-Brown, *Structure and Function in Primitive Society*, Cohen & West, London, 1952, pp. 178–87).

RAMAGE, E. S. (1973), *Urbanitas. Ancient Sophistication and Enlightenment*, University of Cincinnati, Norman, Oklahoma.

RANDOLPH, B. (1687), *The Present State of the Islands in the Archipelago ...*, Venn, Oxford.

Rayonnement des civilisations, Le (1965), *8e Congrès international d'archéologie classique 1963, Le Rayonnement des civilisations grecque et romaine sur les cultures périphériques*, de Boccard, Paris.

REDFIELD, JAMES (1975), *Nature and Culture in the Iliad: the Tragedy of Hector*, Chicago University Press.

REDFIELD, ROBERT (1956), *Peasant Society and Culture*, Chicago University Press.

REDMAN, CHARLES L., ed. (1973), *Research Theory in Current Archaeology*, Wiley-Interscience, New York.

RENFREW, COLIN (1972), *The Emergence of Civilisation: the Cyclades and the Aegean in the 3rd Millennium B.C.*, Methuen, London.

REVERE, ROBERT B. (1957), 'No man's coast: ports of trade in the eastern Mediterranean', in Polanyi, 1957a, pp. 38–63.

RIBBECK, O. (1888), 'Agroikos, eine ethologische Studie', *Abhandlungen der königliche Sächsischen Gesellschaft der Wissenschaften* (philologisch-historische Klasse), 10, pp. 1–68.

RICHMOND, I. A. (1943), 'Appreciation of R. G. Collingwood as an archaeologist', *Proceedings of the British Academy*, 29, pp. 476–85.

RIDGWAY, DAVID (1973), 'The first Western Greeks: Campanian coasts and southern Etruria', in C. F. C. and S. C. Hawkes (eds), *Greeks, Celts and Romans: Studies in Venture and Resistance*, Dent, London, pp. 5–38.

RIEZLER, K. (1907), *Über Finanzen und Monopole im alten Griechenland*, Puttkammer & Mühlbrecht, Berlin.

RIIS, P. J. (1962), 'L'Activité de la mission danoise sur la côte phénicienne en 1960', *Annales archéologiques de Syrie*, 11–12 (1961–2), pp. 133–44.

ROBBINS, LIONEL (1935), *An Essay on the Nature and Significance of Economic Science*, Macmillan, London.

ROBERT, LOUIS (1965a), *Villes d'Asie Mineure*, 2nd ed., de Boccard, Paris.

ROBERT, LOUIS (1965b), 'Rapport sur les travaux de l'École française d'Athènes en 1964', *Comptes rendus de l'Académie des Inscriptions et Belles-Lettres*, pp. 313–28.

ROBERT, LOUIS (1966), 'Inscriptions d'Aphrodisias I', *L'Antiquité classique*, 35, pp. 377–423.

ROBERT, LOUIS, and ROBERT, JEANNE (1954), *La Carie*, vol. II, Maisonneuve, Paris.

ROBINSON, D. M. (1946), *Olynthus XII. Domestic and Public Architecture*, Johns Hopkins University Press, Baltimore.

RODINSON, MAXIME (1966), *Islam et Capitalisme*, Éditions du Seuil, Paris.

ROMILLY, JACQUELINE DE (1956), *Histoire et raison chez Thucydide*, Les Belles Lettres, Paris.

ROMILLY, JACQUELINE DE (1968), *Time in Greek Tragedy*, Cornell University Press, Ithaca.

ROOVER, R. DE (1951), 'Monopoly theory prior to Adam Smith: a revision', *Quarterly Journal of Economics*, 65, pp. 492–524.

ROSTOVTZEFF, M. (1933), review of Hasebroek, 1931, *Zeitschrift für die gesamte Staatswissenschaft*, 92, pp. 333–9.

ROSTOVTZEFF, M. (1936), 'The Hellenistic world and its economic development', *American Historical Review*, 41, 1935–6, pp. 231–52.

ROSTOVTZEFF, M. (1941), *Social and Economic History of the Hellenistic World*, Clarendon Press, Oxford.

ROUSSEL, DENIS (1976), *Tribu et cité. Étude sur les groupes sociaux dans les cités grecques aux époques archaïque et classique*, Les Belles Lettres, Paris.

RUDHARDT, J. (1958), *Notions fondamentales de la pensée religieuse et actes constitutifs du culte de la Grèce classique*, Droz, Geneva.

RUGGINI, LELLIA CRACCO (1961), *Economia e società nell' 'Italia Annonaria'*, Giuffré, Milan.

RUGGINI, LELLIA CRACCO (1968), 'Esperienze economiche e sociali nel mondo romano', in *Nuove questioni di storia antica*, Marzorati, Milan, pp. 685–813.

RUSCHENBUSCH, EBERHARD (1966), *Solōnos Nomoi*, Steiner, Wiesbaden (*Historia-Einzelschriften*, Heft 9).

RUSSO, JOSEPH (1974), 'The inner man in Archilochus and the Odyssey', *Greek, Roman and Byzantine Studies*, 15, pp. 139–52.

RUSSO, JOSEPH (1975), 'Reading the Greek lyric poets (monodists)', *Arion*, new series, 1, 4 (1973–4), pp. 707–30.

SACHS, I. (1966), 'La Notion de surplus et son application aux économies primitives', *L'Homme*, 6, 3, pp. 5–18.

SAGGS, H. W. (1962), *The Greatness that was Babylon*, Hawthorn Books, New York.

SAHLINS, MARSHALL (1960), 'Political power and the economy in primitive society', in Dole and Carneiro, 1960, pp. 390–415.

SAHLINS, MARSHALL (1965a), 'On the sociology of primitive exchange', in Banton, 1965, pp. 139–236 (reprinted in Sahlins, 1972, pp. 185–275).

SAHLINS, MARSHALL (1965b), 'Exchange-value and the diplomacy of primitive trade', *Proceedings of the 1956 Spring Meeting of the American Ethnological Society*, pp. 95–129 (revised version in Sahlins, 1972, pp. 277–314).

SAHLINS, MARSHALL (1968), *Tribesmen*, Prentice-Hall, Englewood Cliffs, N.J.

SAHLINS, MARSHALL (1972), *Stone Age Economics*, Aldine, Chicago.

SAINTE CROIX, G. E. M. DE (1960), review of Polanyi, 1957a, *Economic History Review*, 12, p. 510.

SALIN, E. (1923), 'Der "Sozialismus" in Hellas', *Bilder und Studien aus drei Jahrtausenden, Eberhard Gothein ... Festgabe*, Duncker & Humblot, Munich, pp. 17–59.

SALIN, E. (1944), *Geschichte der Volkswirtschaftslehre*, 3rd ed., Francke, Bern.

SALSANO, ALFREDO (1974), introduction to Polanyi, 1974.

'Schedario topografico' (1966–7), 'Schedario topografico dell'archeologia dell' Agro Fiorentino', *Studi etruschi*, 34, pp. 277–86, and 35, pp. 267–83.

SCHEFOLD, K. (1966), 'Die Grabungen in Eretria im Herbst 1964 und 1965', *Antike Kunst*, 9, pp. 106–24.

SCHLUMBERGER, D. (1953), *L'Argent grec dans l'empire Achéménide*, Klincksieck, Paris.

SCHMIEDT, G. (1957), 'Applicazioni della fotografia aerea in ricerche estensive di topografia in Sicilia', *Kokalos*, 3, pp. 18–30.

SCHMIEDT, G. (1961), 'Metodi dell'impiego e dell'utilizzazione della fotografia aerea nella ricerca archeologica', in *Atti del 7º Congresso Internazionale di Archeologia Classica 1958*, vol. I, 'L'Erma' di Bretschneider, Rome, pp. 9–39.

SCHMIEDT, G. (1966), 'Contribution de la photo-interprétation à la reconstruction de la situation géographico-topographique des établissements antiques disparus en Italie', *Mélanges Piganiol*, vol. I, pp. 155–94.

SCHNEIDER, D. M. (1968), *American Kinship, a Cultural Account*, Prentice-Hall, Englewood Cliffs, N.J.

SCHNEIDER, H. (1974), *Economic Man: the Anthropology of Economics*, Free Press, New York.

SCHROEDER, R. V., S. J. (1974), *Ancient Greece from the Air*, Thames & Hudson, London.

SCHULHOF, E., and HUVELIN, P. (1907), 'Fouilles de Délos (1905): inscriptions. Loi reglant la vente du bois et du charbon à Délos, *Bulletin de correspondance hellénique*, 31, pp. 46–93.

SCHURTZ, H. (1902), *Altersklassen und Männerbünde*, Reimer, Berlin.

SCHWEITZER, B. (1925), 'Der bildende Künstler und der Begriff des Künstlerischen in der Antike', *Neue Heidelberger Jahrbücher*, 25, pp. 26–132 (reprinted in B. Schweitzer, *Zur Kunst der Antike. Ausgewählte Schriften*, Krystall-Verlag, Vienna, 1963, pp. 11–104).

SEAGER, ROBIN (1966), 'Lysias and the corn-dealers', *Historia*, 15, pp. 172–84.

SEALEY, R. (1957), 'From Phemius to Ion', *Revue des études grecques*, 70, pp. 312–51.

SESTON, W. (1967a), 'Des *Portes* de Thugga à la *Constitution* de Carthage', *Revue historique*, 237, pp. 277–94.

SESTON, W. (1967b), 'Remarques sur les institutions politiques et sociales de Carthage', *Comptes rendus de l'Académie des Inscriptions et Belles-Lettres*, pp. 218–33.

SETON WATSON, R. (1911), *Corruption and Reform in Hungary*, Constable, London.

SHKLAR, JUDITH (1966), 'The political theory of Utopia: from melancholy to nostalgia', in Manuel, 1966a, pp. 101–15.

SIEVERS, ALLEN M. (1949), *Has Market Capitalism Collapsed? A Criticism of Karl Polanyi's New Economics*, Columbia University Press, New York.

SIFAKIS, G. M. (1971), *Parabasis and Animal Choruses*, Athlone Press, London.

SIMIAND, F. (1903), review of Sombart, 1902, *L'Année sociologique*, 6, 1901–2, pp. 464–83.

SIMIAND, F. (1910), review of Gernet, 1909a, *L'Année sociologique*, 11, 1906–9, p. 563.

SIMIAND, F. (1934), 'La Monnaie réalité sociale', *Annales sociologiques*, series D, I, pp. 1–58 (discussion by Mauss and others, pp. 59–86).

SINHA, D. P. (1968), *Culture Change in an Inter-tribal Market*, Asia Publishing House, London.

SKINNER, G. W. (1964–5), 'Marketing and social structure in rural China', *Journal of Asian Studies*, 24, pp. 3–43, 195–228, 363–99.

SLAVIA, L. (1960), 'Osnovn'ie etap'i izyčenija Ol'vii', *Zapiski Odesskogo Archeologičeskogo Obšestva*, 1 (34), pp. 47–9 (summarized in *Bibliotheca Classica Orientalis*, 11, 1966, coll. 156–60).

SMELSER, NEIL J. (1959a), *Social Change in the Industrial Revolution*, Chicago University Press.

SMELSER, NEIL J. (1959b), 'A comparative view of exchange systems', *Economic Development and Cultural Change*, 7, pp. 173–82.

SMELSER, NEIL J. (1963), *The Sociology of Economic Life*, Prentice-Hall, Englewood Cliffs, N.J.

SMELSER, NEIL J., ed. (1967), *Sociology: an Introduction*, Wiley, New York.

SMITH, M. G. (1954), 'Slavery and emancipation in two societies', *Social and Economic Studies*, 3, pp. 239–90 (reprinted in Smith, 1965, pp. 116–61).

SMITH, M. G. (1956), 'On segmentary lineage systems', *Journal of the Royal Anthropological Institute*, 86, 2, pp. 39–80 (Smith, 1974, pp. 13–70).

SMITH, M. G. (1960), *Government in Zazzau*, Oxford University Press, London.

SMITH, M. G. (1962a), *West Indian Family Structure*, University of Washington Press, Seattle.

SMITH, M. G. (1962b), 'History and social anthropology', *Journal of the Royal Anthropological Institute*, 92, pp. 73–85.

SMITH, M. G. (1965), *The Plural Society in the British West Indies*, University of California Press, Berkeley.

SMITH, M. G. (1974), *Corporations and Society*, Duckworth, London.

SNELL, B., ed. (1958), *Bacchylidis Carmina cum fragmentis*, Teubner, Leipzig (6th ed.).

SNODGRASS, A. M. (1971), *The Dark Age of Greece*, Edinburgh University Press.

SOLOMON, M. R. (1948), 'The structure of the market in underdeveloped economies', *Quarterly Journal of Economics*, 62, pp. 519–41.

SOMBART, W. (1902), *Der moderne Kapitalismus*, vol. I, Duncker & Humblot, Leipzig.

SOMBART, W. (1925), *Die Ordnungen des Wirtschaftslebens*, Springer, Berlin.

SOMMERFELT, A. (1938), *La Langue et la société. Caractères sociaux d'une langue de type archaïque* (Arunta), Ascheboug, Oslo.

SOROKIN, P. A. (1941), *The Crisis of Our Age: the Social and Cultural Outlook*, Dutton, New York.

SOROKIN, P. A. (1948), *The Reconstruction of Humanity*, Beacon Press, Boston.

SOROKIN, P. A. (1963), *A Long Journey*, College & University Press, New Haven, Conn.

SOUTHALL, AIDAN, ed. (1961), *Social Change in Modern Africa*, Oxford University Press, London.

SPARKES, B. (1962), 'The Greek kitchen', *Journal of Hellenic Studies*, 82, pp. 121–37.

STARR, CHESTER G. (1955), 'The myth of the Minoan Thalassocracy', *Historia*, 3, pp. 283–91.

STARR, CHESTER G. (1961), *The Origins of Greek Civilization*, Knopf, New York.

STEINER, FRANZ (1954), 'Notes on comparative economics', *British Journal of Sociology*, 5, pp. 118–29.

STIESDAL, H. (1962), 'Three deserted medieval villages in the Roman campagna', *Analecta Romana Instituti Danici*, 2, pp. 63–100.

STILLWELL, R. (1932), 'The North Building', *Corinth*, 1, 1, pp. 212–28.

STOCKWELL, R. P., and MACAULAY, R. K. S., eds (1972), *Linguistic Change and Generative Theory. Essays from the UCLA Conference on Historical Linguistics ...*, University of Indiana, Bloomington.

SURÁNYI-UNGER, THEO (1930), 'The social sciences as disciplines. Austria and Hungary', *Encyclopedia of the Social Sciences*, vol. I, pp. 269–73.

SURET-CANALE, J. (1967), 'Structuralisme et anthropologie économique', *Structuralisme et Marxisme, La Pensée*, 135, pp. 94–106.

SUSINI, G. (1966), *Il Lapicida Romano*, Arti Grafiche Tamari, Bologna.

SZLECHTER, E. (1947), *Le Contrat de société en Babylonie, en Grèce et à Rome*, Sirey, Paris.

TARAGNA NOVO, S. (1968), *Economia ed etica nell'Economico di Senofonte*, Giappichelli, Turin.

TARDE, G. (1890), *Les Lois de l'imitation*, Alcan, Paris.

TARDE, G. (1893), *Les Transformations du droit*, Alcan, Paris.

* TARDITS, C., and TARDITS, C. (1962), 'Traditional market economy in south Dahomey', in Bohannan and Dalton, 1962, pp. 89–102.

TAX, SOL, ed. (1964), *Horizons of Anthropology*, Aldine, Chicago.

TCHALENKO, G. (1953), *Villages antiques de la Syrie du Nord*, Geuthner, Paris.

THAPAR, R. (1975), 'Ethics, religion and social protest in the first millennium B.C. in Northern India', in *Wisdom, Revelation and Doubt*, special issue of *Daedalus*, Cambridge, Mass. (1975), pp. 119–32.

THOMPSON, HOMER (1966), 'Classical lands', in *Archaeology: Horizons Old and New, Proceedings of the American Philosophical Society*, 110, 2, pp. 100–4.

THOMSON, GEORGE (1941), *Aeschylus and Athens*, Lawrence & Wishart, London.

THOMSON, GEORGE (1949), *The Prehistoric Aegean* vol. I, Lawrence & Wishart,, London.

THORNDIKE, E. L. (1905), 'Measurement of twins', *Journal of Philosophy, Psychology and Scientific Method*, 2, pp. 547–53.

THORNER, DANIEL (1964), 'L'Économie paysanne, concept pour l'histoire économique', *Annales. Économies, sociétés, civilisations*, 19, pp. 417–32.

THURNWALD, R. (1932), *Economics in Primitive Communities*, Oxford University Press, London.

TIMPANARO, S. (1963), 'A proposito del parallelismo tra lingua e diritto', *Belfagor*, 18, pp. 1–14.

TÖMÖRY, MÁRTA (1960), *Új vizeken járók. A Galilei Kör története*, Budapest.

TÖNNIES, F. (1887), *Gemeinschaft und Gesellschaft*, Reisland, Leipzig (trans. as *Community and Association*, Routledge & Kegan Paul, London, 1955).

TOPPING, P. (1966), 'A Frankish estate near the bay of Navarino', *Hesperia*, 35, pp. 427–36.

TOYNBEE, A. J. (1965), *Hannibal's Legacy*, Oxford University Press, London.

TRAILL, JOHN S. (1975), *The Political Organization of Attica. A Study of the Demes, Trittyes and Phylai and Their Representation in the Athenian Council, Hesperia*, Supplement 14, American School of Classical Studies at Athens, Princeton.

TRAVLOS, J. (1960), *Poleodomikē exelixis tōn Athēnōn*, Constantinidis & Michala, Athens.

TREGGIARI, S. (1969), *Roman Freedmen during the Late Republic*, Clarendon Press, Oxford.

TRIGGER, BRUCE G. (1965), *History and Settlement in Lower Nubia*, Yale University Press, New Haven, Conn.

TRITSCH, F. (1929), 'Die Stadtbildungen des Altertums und die griechische Polis', *Klio*, 22, pp. 1–83.

TRUMPF, JÜRGEN (1958), 'Studien zur griechischen Lyrik', Diss., Cologne.

TURNER, E. G. (1951), *Athenian Books in the Fifth and Fourth Centuries B.C.*, inaugural lecture, University College London.

TURNER, ROY, ed. (1974), *Ethnomethodology*, Penguin, Harmondsworth.

TURNER, V. W. (1968), *The Drums of Affliction*, Clarendon Press, Oxford.

TURNER, V. W. (1969), *The Ritual Process*, Aldine, Chicago.

TWITCHETT, DENIS (1966), 'The T'ang market system', *Asia Major*, 12, pp. 202–48.

TWITCHETT, DENIS (1968), 'Merchant, trade and government in late T'ang', *Asia Major*, 14, pp. 63–95.

UCHENDU, VICTOR (1967), 'Some principles of haggling in peasant markets', *Economic Development and Cultural Change*, 16, pp. 37–50.

UCKO, P. J., TRINGHAM, RUTH, and DIMBLEBY, G. W., eds (1972), *Man, Settlement and Urbanism*, Duckworth, London.

UDOVITCH, A. L. (1962), 'At the origins of the western *Commenda*. Islam, Israel, Byzantium', *Speculum*, 37, pp. 198–207.

UGGERI, G. (1969), '*Kleroi* arcaici e bonifica classica nella chora di Metaponto', *La parola del passato*, 24, pp. 51–71.

ULLMANN, S. (1951), *The Principles of Semantics*, Blackwell, Oxford.

USHER, P. A. (1944), review of Polanyi, 1944, *Political Science Quarterly*, 59, pp. 630–1.

VALIANI, LEO (1966), *La dissoluzione dell'Austria Ungheria*, Il Saggiatore, Milan.

VALLENSI, L., *et al.* (1974), 'Pour une histoire anthropologique: la notion de réciprocité', *Annales. Économies, sociétés, civilisations*, 29, pp. 1309–80.

VALLET, G. (1968), 'La Cité et son territoire dans les colonies grecques d'occident', in *La Città e il suo territorio* (1968), pp. 67–142.

VALLET, G. (1973), 'Espace privé et espace public dans une cité coloniale d'occident: Mégara Hyblaea', in Finley, 1973b, pp. 83–94.

VALLET, G. (1975), 'Les Fouilles de Mégara Hyblaea', *Kokalos*, 18–19 (1972–3), pp. 468–75.

VALLET, G., and VILLARD, F. (1961), 'Céramique et histoire grecque', *Revue historique*, 225, pp. 295–318.

VALLET, G., and VILLARD, F. (1964), *Mégara Hyblaea*, vol. II, *La Céramique archaïque*, de Boccard, Paris.

VALLET, G., and VILLARD, F. (1967), *Mégara Hyblaea*, vol. IV, de Boccard, Paris.

VALLET, G., and VILLARD, F. (1969), 'Mégara Hyblaea IX: les problèmes de l'agora et de la cité archaïque', *Mélanges de l'École Française de Rome*, 81, pp. 7–35.

VANDERPOOL, E. (1965), 'The location of the Attic deme Erchia', *Bulletin de correspondance hellénique*, 89, pp. 21–6.

VANDERPOOL, E., and WALLACE, W. P. (1964), 'The sixth-century laws from Eretria', *Hesperia*, 33, pp. 381–91.

VENTURI, FRANCO (1966), 'Jaurès historien', in F. Venturi, *Historiens du XXe siècle*, Droz, Geneva, pp. 5–70 (original publication in F. Venturi, *Jean Jaurès e altri storici della Rivoluzione francese*, Einaudi, Turin, 1948).

VERNANT, J.-P. (1955), 'Travail et nature dans la Grèce ancienne', *Journal de psychologie normale et pathologique*, 52, pp. 1–29 (reprinted in Vernant, 1965a, pp. 197–217).

VERNANT, J.-P. (1957), 'Remarques sur les formes et les limites de la pensée technique chez les Grecs', *Revue d'histoire des sciences*, 10, pp. 205–25 (Vernant, 1965a, pp. 227–47).

VERNANT, J.-P. (1960), 'Le Mythe hésiodique des races, essai d'analyse structurale', *Revue de l'histoire des religions*, 157, pp. 21–54 (Vernant, 1965a, pp. 19–47).

VERNANT, J.-P. (1962), *Les Origines de la pensée grecque*, Presses Universitaires de France, Paris.

VERNANT, J.-P. (1963), 'Géométrie et astronomie sphérique dans la première cosmologie grecque', *La Pensée*, 109, pp. 82–92 (Vernant, 1965a, pp. 145–58).

VERNANT, J.-P. (1965a), *Mythe et pensée chez les Grecs: études de psychologie historique*, Maspero, Paris.

VERNANT, J.-P. (1965b), 'Remarques sur la lutte de classe dans la Grèce ancienne', *Eirene*, 4, pp. 5–19 (Vernant, 1974, pp. 11–29; trans. in *Critique of Anthropology*, 7, 1976, pp. 67–81).

VERNANT, J.-P., ed. (1968a), *Problèmes de la guerre en Grèce ancienne*, Mouton, Paris/Hague.

VERNANT, J.-P. (1968b), introduction to Gernet, 1968.

VERNANT, J.-P. (1970), *Mito e pensiero presso i Greci*, Einaudi, Turin (translation of Vernant, 1965a).

VERNANT, J.-P. (1972), 'Ébauches de la volonté dans la tragédie grecque', in *Psychologie comparative et art, Hommage à I. Meyerson*, Presses Universitaires de France, Paris, pp. 277–306 (reprinted in Vernant and Vidal-Naquet, 1972, pp. 41–74).

VERNANT, J.-P. (1974), *Mythe et société en Grèce ancienne*, Maspero, Paris.

VERNANT, J.-P., and VIDAL-NAQUET, P. (1972), *Mythe et tragédie en Grèce ancienne*, Maspero, Paris.

VETTERS, H. (1966), 'Die Terrassenhäuser – Das Gebäude südwestlich des Forums', *Carinthia I*, 156, pp. 297–405.

VIDAL-NAQUET, P. (1960), 'Temps des dieux et temps des hommes', *Revue de l'histoire des religions*, 157, pp. 55–80.

VIDAL-NAQUET, P. (1964a), 'Athènes et l'Atlantide', *Revue des études grecques*, 77, pp. 420–44.

VIDAL-NAQUET, P. (1964b), 'Histoire et idéologie: Karl Wittfogel et le concept de "mode de production asiatique",' *Annales. Économies, sociétés, civilisations*, 19, pp. 531–49 (adapted from introduction to the French translation of Wittfogel, 1957).

VIDAL-NAQUET, P. (1965), 'Économie et société dans la Grèce ancienne: l'oeuvre de Moses I. Finley', *Archives européennes de sociologie*, 6, pp. 111–48.

VIDAL-NAQUET, P. (1967), *Le Bordereau d'ensemencement dans l'Égypte ptolémaïque*, Fondation Égyptologique, Brussels.

VIDAL-NAQUET, P. (1968a), 'The Black Hunter and the origins of the Athenian ephebeia', *Proceedings of the Cambridge Philological Society*, 14, pp. 49–64 (French text in *Annales. Économies, sociétés, civilisations*, 23, 1968, pp. 947–64).

VIDAL-NAQUET, P. (1968b), 'Fonction de la monnaie dans la Grèce archaïque', *Annales. Économies, sociétés, civilisations*, 23, 1968, pp. 206–8.

VIDAL-NAQUET, P. (1970a), 'Valeurs reiigieuses et mythiques de la terre et du sacrifice dans l'Odyssée', *Annales. Économies, sociétés, civilisations*, 25, pp. 1278–97 (reprinted in Vernant and Vidal-Naquet, 1972, pp. 269–92).

VIDAL-NAQUET, P. (1970b), 'Grèce. Une civilisation de la parole politique', *Encyclopaedia Universalis* (Paris), vol. VII.

Vie di Magna Grecia (1963), *Atti del 2⁰ Convegno di studi sulla Magna Grecia 1962*, L'Arte Tipografica, Naples.

VILAR, PIERRE (1965), 'Pour une meiileure compréhension entre économistes et historiens', *Revue historique*, 233, pp. 293–312.

VILLARD, F. (1960), *La Céramique grecque de Marseille*, de Boccard, Paris.

VLASTOS, G. (1947), 'Equality and justice in early Greek cosmologies', *Classical Philology*, 42, pp. 156–78 (reprinted in Furley and Allen, 1970, pp. 56–91).

WALLWORK, ERNEST (1972), *Durkheim. Morality and Milieu*, Harvard University Press, Cambridge, Mass.

WARD-PERKINS, J. B. (1955), 'Notes on Southern Etruria and the Ager Veientanus', *Papers of the British School at Rome*, 23, pp. 44–69.

WARD-PERKINS, J. B. (1961), *Veii. The Historical Topography of the Ancient City*, *Papers of the British School at Rome*, 29.

WARD-PERKINS, J. B. (1964), *Landscape and History in Central Italy*, Clarendon Press, Oxford (Myres Lecture).

WARD-PERKINS, J. B. (1972), 'Central authority and patterns of rural settlement', in Ucko, Tringham, and Dimbleby, 1972, pp. 867–82.

WARD-PERKINS, J. B., VON BLANKENHAGEN, P., and COTTON, M. A. (1965), 'Two Roman villas at Francolise, prov. Caserta. Interim report on excavations, 1962–4', *Papers of the British School at Rome*, 33, pp. 55–69.

WARD-PERKINS, J. B., and FREDERIKSEN, M. (1957), 'The ancient road system of the central and northern Ager Faliscus', *Papers of the British School at Rome*, 25, pp. 67–197.

WARE, JAMES R. (1934), review of Granet, 1932, *Journal of the American Oriental Society*, 54, pp. 100–3.

WARREN, P. M. (1972), *Myrtos: an Early Bronze Age Settlement in Crete*, British School of Archaeology at Athens, and Thames & Hudson, London.

WĄSOWICZ, A. (1966), 'À l'époque grecque: le peuplement des côtes de la mer noire et de la Gaule méridionale', *Annales. Économies, sociétés, civilisations*, 21, pp. 553–72.

WĄSOWICZ, A. (1969), 'La Campagne et les villes du littoral septentrionale du Pont-Euxin (nouveaux témoignages archéologiques)', *Dacia*, new series, 13, pp. 73–100.

WĄSOWICZ, A. (1975), *Olbia Pontique et son territoire*, Les Belles Lettres, Paris.

WEAVER, P. R. C. (1967), 'Social mobility in the early Roman empire: the evidence of the Imperial freedmen and slaves', *Past and Present*, 37, pp. 3–20.

WEBER, HEINZ-OTTO (1967), 'Die Bedeutung und Bewertung der Pleonexie', Ph. Diss., Bonn.

WEBER, MAX (1904–5), 'Die protestantische Ethik und der Geist des Kapitalismus', *Archiv für Sozialwissenschaft und Sozialpolitik*, 20–1 (trans. as *The Protestant Ethic and the Spirit of Capitalism*, Allen & Unwin, London, 1930).

WEBER, MAX (1916), 'Die Wirtschaftsethik der Weltreligionen. Religionssozio-logische Skizzen. Der Konfuzianismus', *Archiv für Sozialwissenschaft*, 41, pp. 1–87 (trans. as *The Religion of China*, Free Press, Chicago, 1951).

WEBER, MAX (1921), 'Die Stadt', *Archiv für Sozialwissenschaft*, 47, pp. 621–772 (reprinted in Weber, 1922).

WEBER, MAX (1922), *Wirtschaft und Gesellschaft*, Mohr, Tübingen.

WEBER, MAX (1923), *Wirtschaftsgeschichte*, Duncker & Humblot, Munich/ Leipzig (trans. as *General Economic History*, Allen & Unwin, London, 1923).

WEBER, MAX (1956), 4th revised edition of Weber (1922), Mohr, Tübingen. (Trans. as *Economy and Society*, Bedminster Press, New York, 1968; quotation from partial translation, *The Theory of Social and Economic Organization*, 1964 ed., Free Press, New York.)

WEBER, MAX (1958), *The City*, Free Press, Chicago (translation of Weber, 1921).

WEBSTER, T. B. L. (1953), *Studies in Later Greek Comedy*, Manchester University Press.

WEBSTER, T. B. L. (1967), *The Tragedies of Euripides*, Methuen, London.

WEBSTER, T. B. L. (1970), *The Greek Chorus*, Methuen, London.

WEBSTER, T. B. L. (1972), *Potter and Patron in Classical Athens*, Methuen, London.

WEHRLI, F. (1931), *Lathe Biōsas*, Teubner, Leipzig.

WEINREICH, U., LABOV, W., and HERZOG, M. I. (1968), 'Empirical foundations for a theory of language change', in W. P. Lehmann and Y. Malkiel (eds), *Directions for Historical Linguistics*, University of Texas Press, Austin and London, pp. 95–188.

WELLES, C. B. (1949), 'The Ptolemaic administration in Egypt', *Journal of Juristic Papyrology*, 3, pp. 21–47.

WELSKOPF, E. CH. (1960), 'Einige Bemerkungen zur Lage der Sklaven und des Demos in Athen zur Zeit des dekeleisch-ionischen Kriegs', *Acta Antiqua Academiae Scientiarum Hungaricae*, 8, pp. 295–307.

WEST, M. L. (1971–2), *Iambi et Elegi Graeci*, vols I–II, Clarendon Press, Oxford.

WESTSTRATE, C. (1963), *Types of Economy*, University of Canterbury, Christ Church.

WETTER, E. (1962), 'Studies and strolls in southern Etruria', in *Etruscan Culture, Land and People*, Columbia University Press, New York, and Allhem, Malmö, pp. 163–276.

WHEATLEY, P. (1969), *City as Symbol*, inaugural lecture, University College London.

WILAMOWITZ-MOELLENDORFF, U. VON (1880), *Aus Kydathen*, Weidmann, Berlin.

WILCKEN, U. (1925), 'Punt-Fahren in der Ptolemäer-Zeit', *Zeitschrift für ägyptische Sprache und Altertumskunde*, 60, pp. 86–102.

WILL, ÉDOUARD (1954a), 'Trois quarts de siècle de recherches sur l'économie grecque antique', *Annales, Économies, sociétés, civilisations*, 9, pp. 7–22.

WILL, ÉDOUARD (1954b), 'De l'aspect éthique des origines grecques de la monnaie', *Revue historique*, 212, pp. 209–31.

WILL, ÉDOUARD (1955), 'Réflexions et hypothèses sur les origines du monnayage', *Revue numismatique*, series 5, 17, pp. 5–23.

WILL, ÉDOUARD (1958), 'Archéologie et histoire économique', in *Études d'archéologie classique*, vol. I (1955–6), de Boccard, Paris, pp. 149–66.

WILL, ÉDOUARD (1966), *Histoire politique du monde hellénistique*, Faculté des Lettres, Nancy.

WILL, ÉDOUARD (1972), *Le Monde grec et l'orient*, vol. I, *Le Ve siècle*, Presses Universitaires de France, Paris.

WILLETTS, R. F. (1967), *The Law Code of Gortyn*, de Gruyter, Berlin.

WILLIAMS, C. K., and FISHER, JOAN E. (1973), 'Corinth 1972: the Forum area', *Hesperia*, 42, pp. 1–32.

WILSON, A. J. N. (1966), *Emigration from Italy in the Republican Age of Rome*, Manchester University Press.

WINTER, F. E. (1966), 'Military architecture in the Termessos region', *American Journal of Archaeology*, 70, pp. 127–37.

'Wisdom, revelation and doubt' (1975), 'Wisdom, revelation and doubt. Perspectives on the first millennium B.C.', *Daedalus*, 104, 2.

WISEMAN, J. (1967), 'Excavations at Corinth, the Gymnasium area, 1965', *Hesperia*, 36, pp. 13–41.

WITTFOGEL, K. (1957), *Oriental Despotism*, Yale University Press, New Haven, Conn.

WOLFF, H.-J. (1944), 'Marriage law and family organization in ancient Athens. A study on the interrelation of public and private law in the Greek city', *Traditio*, 2, pp. 43–95.

WOOD, A. C. (1935), *The History of the Levant Company*, Oxford University Press, London.

WOOLLEY, L. (1938), 'Excavations at Al Mina, Sueidia, I. The archaeological report', *Journal of Hellenic Studies*, 58, pp. 1–30.

YAMEY, B. S. (1964), 'The study of peasant economic systems: some concluding comments and questions', in Firth and Yamey, 1964, pp. 376–86.

YOUNG, J. H. (1956a), 'Studies in South Attica: country estates at Sounion', *Hesperia*, 25, pp. 122–46.

YOUNG, J. H. (1956b), 'Greek roads in South Attica', *Antiquity*, 30, pp. 94–7.

YOUNG, R. S. (1951a), 'Sepulturae intra urbem', *Hesperia*, 20, pp. 67–134.

YOUNG, R. S. (1951b), 'An industrial district of ancient Athens', *Hesperia*, 20, pp. 135–288.

ZACCAGNINI, C. (1973), *Lo scambio dei doni nel vicino oriente durante i secoli XV–XIII*, Centro per le Antichità e la Storia dell'Arte del Vicino Oriente, Rome.

ZAWADSKI, T. (1960–1), 'L'Agriculture de la Grèce antique', *Archeologia* (Wrocław), 11, pp. 104–27, and 12, pp. 19–47.

ZEISEL, H. (1968), 'Karl Polanyi', *International Encyclopedia of the Social Sciences*, vol. XII, pp. 172–4.

ZIEBARTH, E. (1896), *Das griechische Vereinswesen*, Hirzel, Leipzig.

ZIEBARTH, E. (1929), *Beiträge zur Geschichte des Seeraubs und Seehandels im alten Griechentum*, Friederichsen, Hamburg.

ZIEHEN, L. (1930), 'Mantis', Pauly-Wissowa, *Realencyclopädie*, vol. XIV, coll. 1345–55.

ZNANIECKI, F. (1940), *The Social Role of the Man of Knowledge*, Columbia University Press, New York.

Index

Routledge Social Science Series

Routledge & Kegan Paul   London, Henley and Boston

39 Store Street, London WC1E 7DD
Broadway House, Newtown Road, Henley-on-Thames,
Oxon RG9 1EN
9 Park Street, Boston, Mass. 02108

Contents

*Authors wishing to submit manuscripts for any series in
this catalogue should send them to the Social Science Editor,
Routledge & Kegan Paul Ltd, 39 Store Street,
London WC1E 7DD*

● *Books so marked are available in paperback*
All books are in Metric Demy 8vo format (216 × 138mm approx.)

International Library of Sociology

General Editor John Rex

GENERAL SOCIOLOGY

Barnsley, J. H. The Social Reality of Ethics. *464 pp.*
Belshaw, Cyril. The Conditions of Social Performance. *An Exploratory Theory. 144 pp.*
Brown, Robert. Explanation in Social Science. *208 pp.*
● Rules and Laws in Sociology. *192 pp.*
Bruford, W. H. Chekhov and His Russia. *A Sociological Study. 244 pp.*
Cain, Maureen E. Society and the Policeman's Role. *326 pp.*
●**Fletcher, Colin.** Beneath the Surface. *An Account of Three Styles of Sociological Research. 221 pp.*
Gibson, Quentin. The Logic of Social Enquiry. *240 pp.*
Glucksmann, M. Structuralist Analysis in Contemporary Social Thought. *212 pp.*
Gurvitch, Georges. Sociology of Law. *Preface by Roscoe Pound. 264 pp.*
Hodge, H. A. Wilhelm Dilthey. *An Introduction. 184 pp.*
Homans, George C. Sentiments and Activities. *336 pp.*
Johnson, Harry M. Sociology: *a Systematic Introduction. Foreword by ∙ Robert K. Merton. 710 pp.*
●**Keat, Russell,** and **Urry, John.** Social Theory as Science. *278 pp.*
Mannheim, Karl. Essays on Sociology and Social Psychology. *Edited by Paul Keckskemeti. With Editorial Note by Adolph Lowe. 344 pp.*
Systematic Sociology: *An Introduction to the Study of Society. Edited by J. S. Erös and Professor W. A. C. Stewart. 220 pp.*
Martindale, Don. The Nature and Types of Sociological Theory. *292 pp.*
●**Maus, Heinz.** A Short History of Sociology. *234 pp.*
Mey, Harald. Field-Theory. *A Study of its Application in the Social Sciences. 352 pp.*
Myrdal, Gunnar. Value in Social Theory: *A Collection of Essays on Methodology. Edited by Paul Streeten. 332 pp.*
Ogburn, William F., and **Nimkoff, Meyer F.** A Handbook of Sociology. *Preface by Karl Mannheim. 656 pp. 46 figures. 35 tables.*
Parsons, Talcott, and **Smelser, Neil J.** Economy and Society: *A Study in the Integration of Economic and Social Theory. 362 pp.*
Podgórecki, Adam. Practical Social Sciences. *About 200 pp.*
●**Rex, John.** Key Problems of Sociological Theory. *220 pp.*
Sociology and the Demystification of the Modern World. *282 pp.*
●**Rex, John** (Ed.) Approaches to Sociology. *Contributions by Peter Abell, Frank Bechhofer, Basil Bernstein, Ronald Fletcher, David Frisby, Miriam Glucksmann, Peter Lassman, Herminio Martins, John Rex, Roland Robertson, John Westergaard and Jock Young. 302 pp.*
Rigby, A. Alternative Realities. *352 pp.*
Roche, M. Phenomenology, Language and the Social Sciences. *374 pp.*

Sahay, A. Sociological Analysis. *220 pp.*

Simirenko, Alex (Ed.) Soviet Sociology. *Historical Antecedents and Current Appraisals. Introduction by Alex Simirenko. 376 pp.*

Strasser, Hermann. The Normative Structure of Sociology. *Conservative and Emancipatory Themes in Social Thought. About 340 pp.*

Urry, John. Reference Groups and the Theory of Revolution. *244 pp.*

Weinberg, E. Development of Sociology in the Soviet Union. *173 pp.*

FOREIGN CLASSICS OF SOCIOLOGY

⬤**Durkheim, Emile.** Suicide. *A Study in Sociology. Edited and with an Introduction by George Simpson. 404 pp.*

⬤**Gerth, H. H.,** and **Mills, C. Wright.** From Max Weber: *Essays in Sociology. 502 pp.*

⬤**Tönnies, Ferdinand.** Community and Association. (*Gemeinschaft und Gesellschaft.*) *Translated and Supplemented by Charles P. Loomis. Foreword by Pitirim A. Sorokin. 334 pp.*

SOCIAL STRUCTURE

Andreski, Stanislav. Military Organization and Society. *Foreword by Professor A. R. Radcliffe-Brown. 226 pp. 1 folder.*

Carlton, Eric. Ideology and Social Order. *Preface by Professor Philip Abrahams. About 320 pp.*

Coontz, Sydney H. Population Theories and the Economic Interpretation. *202 pp.*

Coser, Lewis. The Functions of Social Conflict. *204 pp.*

Dickie-Clark, H. F. Marginal Situation: *A Sociological Study of a Coloured Group. 240 pp. 11 tables.*

Glaser, Barney, and **Strauss, Anselm L.** Status Passage. *A Formal Theory. 208 pp.*

Glass, D. V. (Ed.) Social Mobility in Britain. *Contributions by J. Berent, T. Bottomore, R. C. Chambers, J. Floud, D. V. Glass, J. R. Hall, H. T. Himmelweit, R. K. Kelsall, F. M. Martin, C. A. Moser, R. Mukherjee, and W. Ziegel. 420 pp.*

Johnstone, Frederick A. Class, Race and Gold. *A Study of Class Relations and Racial Discrimination in South Africa. 312 pp.*

Jones, Garth N. Planned Organizational Change: *An Exploratory Study Using an Empirical Approach. 268 pp.*

Kelsall, R. K. Higher Civil Servants in Britain: *From 1870 to the Present Day. 268 pp. 31 tables.*

König, René. The Community. *232 pp. Illustrated.*

⬤**Lawton, Denis.** Social Class, Language and Education. *192 pp.*

McLeish, John. The Theory of Social Change: *Four Views Considered. 128 pp.*

Marsh, David C. The Changing Social Structure of England and Wales, 1871-1961. *288 pp.*

Menzies, Ken. Talcott Parsons and the Social Image of Man. *About 208 pp.*

●**Mouzelis, Nicos.** Organization and Bureaucracy. *An Analysis of Modern Theories. 240 pp.*

Mulkay, M. J. Functionalism, Exchange and Theoretical Strategy. *272 pp.*

Ossowski, Stanislaw. Class Structure in the Social Consciousness. *210 pp.*

●**Podgórecki, Adam.** Law and Society. *302 pp.*

Renner, Karl. Institutions of Private Law and Their Social Functions. *Edited, with an Introduction and Notes, by O. Kahn-Freud. Translated by Agnes Schwarzschild. 316 pp.*

SOCIOLOGY AND POLITICS

Acton, T. A. Gypsy Politics and Social Change. *316 pp.*

Clegg, Stuart. Power, Rule and Domination. *A Critical and Empirical Understanding of Power in Sociological Theory and Organisational Life. About 300 pp.*

Hechter, Michael. Internal Colonialism. *The Celtic Fringe in British National Development, 1536–1966. 361 pp.*

Hertz, Frederick. Nationality in History and Politics: *A Psychology and Sociology of National Sentiment and Nationalism. 432 pp.*

Kornhauser, William. The Politics of Mass Society. *272 pp. 20 tables.*

●**Kroes, R.** Soldiers and Students. *A Study of Right- and Left-wing Students. 174 pp.*

Laidler, Harry W. History of Socialism. *Social-Economic Movements: An Historical and Comparative Survey of Socialism, Communism, Co-operation, Utopianism; and other Systems of Reform and Reconstruction. 992 pp.*

Lasswell, H. D. Analysis of Political Behaviour. *324 pp.*

Martin, David A. Pacifism: *an Historical and Sociological Study. 262 pp.*

Martin, Roderick. Sociology of Power. *About 272 pp.*

Myrdal, Gunnar. The Political Element in the Development of Economic Theory. *Translated from the German by Paul Streeten. 282 pp.*

Wilson, H. T. The American Ideology. *Science, Technology and Organization of Modes of Rationality. About 280 pp.*

Wootton, Graham. Workers, Unions and the State. *188 pp.*

CRIMINOLOGY

Ancel, Marc. Social Defence: *A Modern Approach to Criminal Problems. Foreword by Leon Radzinowicz. 240 pp.*

Cain, Maureen E. Society and the Policeman's Role. *326 pp.*

Cloward, Richard A., and Ohlin, Lloyd E. Delinquency and Opportunity: *A Theory of Delinquent Gangs. 248 pp.*

Downes, David M. The Delinquent Solution. *A Study in Subcultural Theory. 296 pp.*

Dunlop, A. B., and McCabe, S. Young Men in Detention Centres. *192 pp.*

Friedlander, Kate. The Psycho-Analytical Approach to Juvenile Delinquency: *Theory, Case Studies, Treatment. 320 pp.*

Glueck, Sheldon, and Eleanor. Family Environment and Delinquency. *With the statistical assistance of Rose W. Kneznek. 340 pp.*

Lopez-Rey, Manuel. Crime. *An Analytical Appraisal. 288 pp.*

Mannheim, Hermann. Comparative Criminology: *a Text Book. Two volumes. 442 pp. and 380 pp.*

Morris, Terence. The Criminal Area: *A Study in Social Ecology. Foreword by Hermann Mannheim. 232 pp. 25 tables. 4 maps.*

Rock, Paul. Making People Pay. *338 pp.*

● **Taylor, Ian, Walton, Paul,** and **Young, Jock.** The New Criminology. *For a Social Theory of Deviance. 325 pp.*

● **Taylor, Ian, Walton, Paul,** and **Young, Jock** (Eds). Critical Criminology. *268 pp.*

SOCIAL PSYCHOLOGY

Bagley, Christopher. The Social Psychology of the Epileptic Child. *320 pp.*

Barbu, Zevedei. Problems of Historical Psychology. *248 pp.*

Blackburn, Julian. Psychology and the Social Pattern. *184 pp.*

● **Brittan, Arthur.** Meanings and Situations. *224 pp.*

Carroll, J. Break-Out from the Crystal Palace. *200 pp.*

● **Fleming, C. M.** Adolescence: Its Social Psychology. *With an Introduction to recent findings from the fields of Anthropology, Physiology, Medicine, Psychometrics and Sociometry. 288 pp.*

● The Social Psychology of Education: *An Introduction and Guide to Its Study. 136 pp.*

● **Homans, George C.** The Human Group. *Foreword by Bernard DeVoto. Introduction by Robert K. Merton. 526 pp.*

● Social Behaviour: *its Elementary Forms. 416 pp.*

● **Klein, Josephine.** The Study of Groups. *226 pp. 31 figures. 5 tables.*

Linton, Ralph. The Cultural Background of Personality. *132 pp.*

● **Mayo, Elton.** The Social Problems of an Industrial Civilization. *With an appendix on the Political Problem. 180 pp.*

Ottaway, A. K. C. Learning Through Group Experience. *176 pp.*

Plummer, Ken. Sexual Stigma. *An Interactionist Account. 254 pp.*

● **Rose, Arnold M.** (Ed.) Human Behaviour and Social Processes: *an Interactionist Approach. Contributions by Arnold M. Rose, Ralph H. Turner, Anselm Strauss, Everett C. Hughes, E. Franklin Frazier, Howard S. Becker, et al. 696 pp.*

Smelser, Neil J. Theory of Collective Behaviour. *448 pp.*

Stephenson, Geoffrey M. The Development of Conscience. *128 pp.*

Young, Kimball. Handbook of Social Psychology. *658 pp. 16 figures. 10 tables.*

SOCIOLOGY OF THE FAMILY

Banks, J. A. Prosperity and Parenthood: *A Study of Family Planning among The Victorian Middle Classes. 262 pp.*

Bell, Colin R. Middle Class Families: *Social and Geographical Mobility. 224 pp.*

Burton, Lindy. Vulnerable Children. *272 pp.*

Gavron, Hannah. The Captive Wife: *Conflicts of Household Mothers. 190 pp.*

George, Victor, and **Wilding, Paul.** Motherless Families. *248 pp.*

Klein, Josephine. Samples from English Cultures.
1. Three Preliminary Studies and Aspects of Adult Life in England. *447 pp.*
2. Child-Rearing Practices and Index. *247 pp.*

Klein, Viola. The Feminine Character. *History of an Ideology. 244 pp.*

McWhinnie, Alexina M. Adopted Children. *How They Grow Up. 304 pp.*

● **Morgan, D. H. J.** Social Theory and the Family. *About 320 pp.*

● **Myrdal, Alva,** and **Klein, Viola.** Women's Two Roles: *Home and Work. 238 pp. 27 tables.*

Parsons, Talcott, and **Bales, Robert F.** Family: Socialization and Inter-action Process. *In collaboration with James Olds, Morris Zelditch and Philip E. Slater. 456 pp. 50 figures and tables.*

SOCIAL SERVICES

Bastide, Roger. The Sociology of Mental Disorder. *Translated from the French by Jean McNeil. 260 pp.*

Carlebach, Julius. Caring For Children in Trouble. *266 pp.*

George, Victor. Foster Care. *Theory and Practice. 234 pp.*
Social Security: *Beveridge and After. 258 pp.*

George, V., and **Wilding, P.** Motherless Families. *248 pp.*

● **Goetschius, George W.** Working with Community Groups. *256 pp.*

Goetschius, George W., and **Tash, Joan.** Working with Unattached Youth. *416 pp.*

Hall, M. P., and **Howes, I. V.** The Church in Social Work. *A Study of Moral Welfare Work undertaken by the Church of England. 320 pp.*

Heywood, Jean S. Children in Care: *the Development of the Service for the Deprived Child. 264 pp.*

Hoenig, J., and **Hamilton, Marian W.** The De-Segregation of the Mentally Ill. *284 pp.*

Jones, Kathleen. Mental Health and Social Policy, 1845-1959. *264 pp.*

King, Roy D., Raynes, Norma V., and **Tizard, Jack.** Patterns of Residential Care. *356 pp.*

Leigh, John. Young People and Leisure. *256 pp.*

● **Mays, John.** (Ed.) Penelope Hall's Social Services of England and Wales. *About 324 pp.*

Morris, Mary. Voluntary Work and the Welfare State. *300 pp.*

Nokes, P. L. The Professional Task in Welfare Practice. *152 pp.*

Timms, Noel. Psychiatric Social Work in Great Britain (1939-1962). *280 pp.*

● Social Casework: *Principles and Practice. 256 pp.*

Young, A. F. Social Services in British Industry. *272 pp.*

SOCIOLOGY OF EDUCATION

Banks, Olive. Parity and Prestige in English Secondary Education: a Study in Educational Sociology. *272 pp.*

Bentwich, Joseph. Education in Israel. *224 pp. 8 pp. plates.*

●**Blyth, W. A. L.** English Primary Education. *A Sociological Description.*
1. Schools. *232 pp.*
2. Background. *168 pp.*

Collier, K. G. The Social Purposes of Education: *Personal and Social Values in Education. 268 pp.*

Dale, R. R., and **Griffith, S.** Down Stream: *Failure in the Grammar School. 108 pp.*

Evans, K. M. Sociometry and Education. *158 pp.*

●**Ford, Julienne.** Social Class and the Comprehensive School. *192 pp.*

Foster, P. J. Education and Social Change in Ghana. *336 pp. 3 maps.*

Fraser, W. R. Education and Society in Modern France. *150 pp.*

Grace, Gerald R. Role Conflict and the Teacher. *150 pp.*

Hans, Nicholas. New Trends in Education in the Eighteenth Century. *278 pp. 19 tables.*

● Comparative Education: *A Study of Educational Factors and Traditions. 360 pp.*

●**Hargreaves, David.** Interpersonal Relations and Education. *432 pp.*

● Social Relations in a Secondary School. *240 pp.*

Holmes, Brian. Problems in Education. *A Comparative Approach. 336 pp.*

King, Ronald. Values and Involvement in a Grammar School. *164 pp.*

School Organization and Pupil Involvement. *A Study of Secondary Schools.*

●**Mannheim, Karl,** and **Stewart, W. A. C.** An Introduction to the Sociology of Education. *206 pp.*

Morris, Raymond N. The Sixth Form and College Entrance. *231 pp.*

●**Musgrove, F.** Youth and the Social Order. *176 pp.*

●**Ottaway, A. K. C.** Education and Society: An Introduction to the Sociology of Education. *With an Introduction by W. O. Lester Smith. 212 pp.*

Peers, Robert. Adult Education: *A Comparative Study. 398 pp.*

Pritchard, D. G. Education and the Handicapped: *1760 to 1960. 258 pp.*

Stratta, Erica. The Education of Borstal Boys. *A Study of their Educational Experiences prior to, and during, Borstal Training. 256 pp.*

Taylor, P. H., Reid, W. A., and **Holley, B. J.** The English Sixth Form. *A Case Study in Curriculum Research. 200 pp.*

SOCIOLOGY OF CULTURE

Eppel, E. M., and **M.** Adolescents and Morality: *A Study of some Moral Values and Dilemmas of Working Adolescents in the Context of a changing Climate of Opinion. Foreword by W. J. H. Sprott. 268 pp. 39 tables.*

●**Fromm, Erich.** The Fear of Freedom. *286 pp.*

● The Sane Society. *400 pp.*

Mannheim, Karl. Essays on the Sociology of Culture. *Edited by Ernst Mannheim in co-operation with Paul Kecskemeti. Editorial Note by Adolph Lowe. 280 pp.*
Weber, Alfred. Farewell to European History: *or The Conquest of Nihilism. Translated from the German by R. F. C. Hull. 224 pp.*

SOCIOLOGY OF RELIGION

Argyle, Michael and **Beit-Hailahmi, Benjamin.** The Social Psychology of Religion. *About 256 pp.*
Glasner, Peter E. The Sociology of Secularisation. *A Critique of a Concept. About 180 pp.*
Nelson, G. K. Spiritualism and Society. *313 pp.*
Stark, Werner. The Sociology of Religion. *A Study of Christendom.*
  Volume I. *Established Religion. 248 pp.*
  Volume II. *Sectarian Religion. 368 pp.*
  Volume III. *The Universal Church. 464 pp.*
  Volume IV. *Types of Religious Man. 352 pp.*
  Volume V. *Types of Religious Culture. 464 pp.*
Turner, B. S. Weber and Islam. *216 pp.*
Watt, W. Montgomery. Islam and the Integration of Society. *320 pp.*

SOCIOLOGY OF ART AND LITERATURE

Jarvie, Ian C. Towards a Sociology of the Cinema. *A Comparative Essay on the Structure and Functioning of a Major Entertainment Industry. 405 pp.*
Rust, Frances S. Dance in Society. *An Analysis of the Relationships between the Social Dance and Society in England from the Middle Ages to the Present Day. 256 pp. 8 pp. of plates.*
Schücking, L. L. The Sociology of Literary Taste. *112 pp.*
Wolff, Janet. Hermeneutic Philosophy and the Sociology of Art. *150 pp.*

SOCIOLOGY OF KNOWLEDGE

Diesing, P. Patterns of Discovery in the Social Sciences. *262 pp.*
● **Douglas, J. D.** (Ed.) Understanding Everyday Life. *370 pp.*
● **Hamilton, P.** Knowledge and Social Structure. *174 pp.*
Jarvie, I. C. Concepts and Society. *232 pp.*
Mannheim, Karl. Essays on the Sociology of Knowledge. *Edited by Paul Kecskemeti. Editorial Note by Adolph Lowe. 353 pp.*
Remmling, Gunter W. The Sociology of Karl Mannheim. *With a Bibliographical Guide to the Sociology of Knowledge, Ideological Analysis, and Social Planning. 255 pp.*

Remmling, Gunter W. (Ed.) Towards the Sociology of Knowledge. *Origin and Development of a Sociological Thought Style. 463 pp.*

Stark, Werner. The Sociology of Knowledge: *An Essay in Aid of a Deeper Understanding of the History of Ideas. 384 pp.*

URBAN SOCIOLOGY

Ashworth, William. The Genesis of Modern British Town Planning: *A Study in Economic and Social History of the Nineteenth and Twentieth Centuries. 288 pp.*

Cullingworth, J. B. Housing Needs and Planning Policy: *A Restatement of the Problems of Housing Need and 'Overspill' in England and Wales. 232 pp. 44 tables. 8 maps.*

Dickinson, Robert E. City and Region: *A Geographical Interpretation 608 pp. 125 figures.*

The West European City: *A Geographical Interpretation. 600 pp. 129 maps. 29 plates.*

● The City Region in Western Europe. *320 pp. Maps.*

Humphreys, Alexander J. New Dubliners: *Urbanization and the Irish Family. Foreword by George C. Homans. 304 pp.*

Jackson, Brian. Working Class Community: *Some General Notions raised by a Series of Studies in Northern England. 192 pp.*

Jennings, Hilda. Societies in the Making: *a Study of Development and Redevelopment within a County Borough. Foreword by D. A. Clark. 286 pp.*

●**Mann, P. H.** An Approach to Urban Sociology. *240 pp.*

Morris, R. N., and **Mogey, J.** The Sociology of Housing. *Studies at Berinsfield. 232 pp. 4 pp. plates.*

Rosser, C., and **Harris, C.** The Family and Social Change. *A Study of Family and Kinship in a South Wales Town. 352 pp. 8 maps.*

●**Stacey, Margaret, Batsone, Eric, Bell, Colin,** and **Thurcott, Anne.** Power, Persistence and Change. *A Second Study of Banbury. 196 pp.*

RURAL SOCIOLOGY

Haswell, M. R. The Economics of Development in Village India. *120 pp.*

Littlejohn, James. Westrigg: *the Sociology of a Cheviot Parish. 172 pp. 5 figures.*

Mayer, Adrian C. Peasants in the Pacific. *A Study of Fiji Indian Rural Society. 248 pp. 20 plates.*

Williams, W. M. The Sociology of an English Village: *Gosforth. 272 pp. 12 figures. 13 tables.*

SOCIOLOGY OF INDUSTRY AND DISTRIBUTION

Anderson, Nels. Work and Leisure. *280 pp.*

●**Blau, Peter M.**, and **Scott, W. Richard**. Formal Organizations: *a Comparative approach. Introduction and Additional Bibliography by J. H. Smith. 326 pp.*

Dunkerley, David. The Foreman. *Aspects of Task and Structure. 192 pp.*

Eldridge, J. E. T. Industrial Disputes. *Essays in the Sociology of Industrial Relations. 288 pp.*

Hetzler, Stanley. Applied Measures for Promoting Technological Growth. *352 pp.*
Technological Growth and Social Change. *Achieving Modernization. 269 pp.*

Hollowell, Peter G. The Lorry Driver. *272 pp.*

●**Oxaal, I.**, **Barnett, T.**, and **Booth, D.** (Eds). Beyond the Sociology of Development. *Economy and Society in Latin America and Africa. 295 pp.*

Smelser, Neil J. Social Change in the Industrial Revolution: *An Application of Theory to the Lancashire Cotton Industry, 1770–1840. 468 pp. 12 figures. 14 tables.*

ANTHROPOLOGY

Ammar, Hamed. Growing up in an Egyptian Village: *Silwa, Province of Aswan. 336 pp.*

Brandel-Syrier, Mia. Reeftown Elite. *A Study of Social Mobility in a Modern African Community on the Reef. 376 pp.*

Dickie-Clark, H. F. The Marginal Situation. *A Sociological Study of a Coloured Group. 236 pp.*

Dube, S. C. Indian Village. *Foreword by Morris Edward Opler. 276 pp. 4 plates.*
India's Changing Villages: *Human Factors in Community Development. 260 pp. 8 plates. 1 map.*

Firth, Raymond. Malay Fishermen. *Their Peasant Economy. 420 pp. 17 pp. plates.*

Gulliver, P. H. Social Control in an African Society: a Study of the Arusha, Agricultural Masai of Northern Tanganyika. *320 pp. 8 plates. 10 figures.*
Family Herds. *288 pp.*

Ishwaran, K. Tradition and Economy in Village India: *An Interactionist Approach.*
Foreword by Conrad Arensburg. 176 pp.

Jarvie, Ian C. The Revolution in Anthropology. *268 pp.*

Little, Kenneth L. Mende of Sierra Leone. *308 pp. and folder.*
Negroes in Britain. *With a New Introduction and Contemporary Study by Leonard Bloom. 320 pp.*

Lowie, Robert H. Social Organization. *494 pp.*

Mayer, A. C. Peasants in the Pacific. *A Study of Fiji Indian Rural Society. 248 pp.*

Meer, Fatima. Race and Suicide in South Africa. *325 pp.*

Smith, Raymond T. The Negro Family in British Guiana: *Family Structure and Social Status in the Villages. With a Foreword by Meyer Fortes. 314 pp. 8 plates. 1 figure. 4 maps.*

Smooha, Sammy. Israel: Pluralism and Conflict. *About 320 pp.*

SOCIOLOGY AND PHILOSOPHY

Barnsley, John H. The Social Reality of Ethics. *A Comparative Analysis of Moral Codes. 448 pp.*

Diesing, Paul. Patterns of Discovery in the Social Sciences. *362 pp.*

●**Douglas, Jack D.** (Ed.) Understanding Everyday Life. *Toward the Reconstruction of Sociological Knowledge. Contributions by Alan F. Blum. Aaron W. Cicourel, Norman K. Denzin, Jack D. Douglas, John Heeren, Peter McHugh, Peter K. Manning, Melvin Power, Matthew Speier, Roy Turner, D. Lawrence Wieder, Thomas P. Wilson and Don H. Zimmerman. 370 pp.*

Gorman, Robert A. The Dual Vision. *Alfred Schutz and the Myth of Phenomenological Social Science. About 300 pp.*

Jarvie, Ian C. Concepts and Society. *216 pp.*

●**Pelz, Werner.** The Scope of Understanding in Sociology. *Towards a more radical reorientation in the social humanistic sciences. 283 pp.*

Roche, Maurice. Phenomenology, Language and the Social Sciences. *371 pp.*

Sahay, Arun. Sociological Analysis. *212 pp.*

Sklair, Leslie. The Sociology of Progress. *320 pp.*

Slater, P. Origin and Significance of the Frankfurt School. *A Marxist Perspective. About 192 pp.*

Smart, Barry. Sociology, Phenomenology and Marxian Analysis. *A Critical Discussion of the Theory and Practice of a Science of Society. 220 pp.*

International Library of Anthropology

General Editor Adam Kuper

Ahmed, A. S. Millenium and Charisma Among Pathans. *A Critical Essay in Social Anthropology. 192 pp.*

Brown, Paula. The Chimbu. *A Study of Change in the New Guinea Highlands. 151 pp.*

Gudeman, Stephen. Relationships, Residence and the Individual. *A Rural Panamanian Community. 288 pp. 11 Plates, 5 Figures, 2 Maps, 10 Tables.*

Hamnett, Ian. Chieftainship and Legitimacy. *An Anthropological Study of Executive Law in Lesotho. 163 pp.*

Hanson, F. Allan. Meaning in Culture. *127 pp.*

Lloyd, P. C. Power and Independence. *Urban Africans' Perception of Social Inequality. 264 pp.*

Pettigrew, Joyce. Robber Noblemen. *A Study of the Political System of the Sikh Jats. 284 pp.*

Street, Brian V. The Savage in Literature. *Representations of 'Primitive' Society in English Fiction, 1858–1920. 207 pp.*

Van Den Berghe, Pierre L. Power and Privilege at an African University. *278 pp.*

International Library of Social Policy

General Editor Kathleen Jones

Bayley, M. Mental Handicap and Community Care. *426 pp.*

Bottoms, A. E., and **McClean, J. D.** Defendants in the Criminal Process. *284 pp.*

Butler, J. R. Family Doctors and Public Policy. *208 pp.*

Davies, Martin. Prisoners of Society. *Attitudes and Aftercare. 204 pp.*

Gittus, Elizabeth. Flats, Families and the Under-Fives. *285 pp.*

Holman, Robert. Trading in Children. *A Study of Private Fostering. 355 pp.*

Jones, Howard, and **Cornes, Paul.** Open Prisons. *About 248 pp.*

Jones, Kathleen. History of the Mental Health Service. *428 pp.*

Jones, Kathleen, with **Brown, John, Cunningham, W. J., Roberts, Julian,** and **Williams, Peter.** Opening the Door. *A Study of New Policies for the Mentally Handicapped. 278 pp.*

Karn, Valerie. Retiring to the Seaside. *About 280 pp. 2 maps. Numerous tables.*

Thomas, J. E. The English Prison Officer since 1850: *A Study in Conflict. 258 pp.*

Walton, R. G. Women in Social Work. *303 pp.*

Woodward, J. To Do the Sick No Harm. *A Study of the British Voluntary Hospital System to 1875. 221 pp.*

International Library of Welfare and Philosophy

General Editors Noel Timms and David Watson

● **Plant, Raymond.** Community and Ideology. *104 pp.*

● **McDermott, F. E.** (Ed.) Self-Determination in Social Work. *A Collection of Essays on Self-determination and Related Concepts by Philosophers and Social Work Theorists. Contributors: F. P. Biestek, S. Bernstein, A. Keith-Lucas, D. Sayer, H. H. Perelman, C. Whittington, R. F. Stalley, F. E. McDermott, I. Berlin, H. J. McCloskey, H. L. A. Hart, J. Wilson, A. I. Melden, S. I. Benn. 254 pp.*

Ragg, Nicholas M. People Not Cases. *A Philosophical Approach to Social Work. About 250 pp.*

● **Timms, Noel,** and **Watson, David** (Eds). Talking About Welfare. *Readings in Philosophy and Social Policy. Contributors: T. H. Marshall, R. B. Brandt, G. H. von Wright, K. Nielsen, M. Cranston, R. M. Titmuss, R. S. Downie, E. Telfer, D. Donnison, J. Benson, P. Leonard, A. Keith-Lucas, D. Walsh, I. T. Ramsey. 320 pp.*

Primary Socialization, Language and Education

General Editor Basil Bernstein

Adlam, Diana S., *with the assistance of Geoffrey Turner and Lesley Lineker.* Code in Context. *About 272 pp.*

Bernstein, Basil. Class, Codes and Control. *3 volumes.*
    1. *Theoretical Studies Towards a Sociology of Language. 254 pp.*
    2. *Applied Studies Towards a Sociology of Language. 377 pp.*
●   3. *Towards a Theory of Educatiomal Transmission. 167 pp.*

Brandis, W., and **Bernstein, B.** Selection and Control. *176 pp.*

Brandis, Walter, and **Henderson, Dorothy.** Social Class, Language and Communication. *288 pp.*

Cook-Gumperz, Jenny. Social Control and Socialization. *A Study of Class Differences in the Language of Maternal Control. 290 pp.*

● **Gahagan, D. M.,** and **G. A.** Talk Reform. *Exploration in Language for Infant School Children. 160 pp.*

Hawkins, P. R. Social Class, the Nominal Group and Verbal Strategies. *About 220 pp.*

Robinson, W. P., and **Rackstraw, Susan D. A.** A Question of Answers. *2 volumes. 192 pp. and 180 pp.*

Turner, Geoffrey J., and **Mohan, Bernard A.** A Linguistic Description and Computer Programme for Children's Speech. *208 pp.*

Reports of the Institute of Community Studies

● **Cartwright, Ann.** Parents and Family Planning Services. *306 pp.*
    Patients and their Doctors. *A Study of General Practice. 304 pp.*

Dench, Geoff. Maltese in London. *A Case-study in the Erosion of Ethnic Consciousness. 302 pp.*

● **Jackson, Brian.** Streaming: *an Education System in Miniature. 168 pp.*

Jackson, Brian, and **Marsden, Dennis.** Education and the Working Class: *Some General Themes raised by a Study of 88 Working-class Children in a Northern Industrial City. 268 pp. 2 folders.*

Marris, Peter. The Experience of Higher Education. *232 pp. 27 tables.*
    Loss and Change. *192 pp.*

Marris, Peter, and **Rein, Martin.** Dilemmas of Social Reform. *Poverty and Community Action in the United States. 256 pp.*

Marris, Peter, and Somerset, Anthony. African Businessmen. *A Study of Entrepreneurship and Development in Kenya. 256 pp.*

Mills, Richard. Young Outsiders: *a Study in Alternative Communities. 216 pp.*

Runciman, W. G. Relative Deprivation and Social Justice. *A Study of Attitudes to Social Inequality in Twentieth-Century England. 352 pp.*

Willmott, Peter. Adolescent Boys in East London. *230 pp.*

Willmott, Peter, and Young, Michael. Family and Class in a London Suburb. *202 pp. 47 tables.*

Young, Michael. Innovation and Research in Education. *192 pp.*

●Young, Michael, and McGeeney, Patrick. Learning Begins at Home. *A Study of a Junior School and its Parents. 128 pp.*

Young, Michael, and Willmott, Peter. Family and Kinship in East London. *Foreword by Richard M. Titmuss. 252 pp. 39 tables.*
    The Symmetrical Family. *410 pp.*

Reports of the Institute for Social Studies in Medical Care

Cartwright, Ann, Hockey, Lisbeth, and Anderson, John L. Life Before Death. *310 pp.*

Dunnell, Karen, and Cartwright, Ann. Medicine Takers, Prescribers and Hoarders. *190 pp.*

Medicine, Illness and Society

General Editor W. M. Williams

Robinson, David. The Process of Becoming Ill. *142 pp.*

Stacey, Margaret, *et al.* Hospitals, Children and Their Families. *The Report of a Pilot Study. 202 pp.*

Stimson, G. V., and Webb, B. Going to See the Doctor. *The Consultation Process in General Practice. 155 pp.*

Monographs in Social Theory

General Editor Arthur Brittan

●Barnes, B. Scientific Knowledge and Sociological Theory. *192 pp.*

Bauman, Zygmunt. Culture as Praxis. *204 pp.*

●Dixon, Keith. Sociological Theory. *Pretence and Possibility. 142 pp.*

Meltzer, B. N., Petras, J. W., and Reynolds, L. T. Symbolic Interactionism. *Genesis, Varieties and Criticisms. 144 pp.*

●Smith, Anthony D. The Concept of Social Change. *A Critique of the Functionalist Theory of Social Change. 208 pp.*

Routledge Social Science Journals

The British Journal of Sociology. *Editor – Angus Stewart; Associate Editor – Leslie Sklair. Vol. 1, No. 1 – March 1950 and Quarterly. Roy. 8vo. All back issues available. An international journal publishing original papers in the field of sociology and related areas.*
Community Work. *Edited by David Jones and Marjorie Mayo. 1973. Published annually.*
Economy and Society. *Vol. 1, No. 1. February 1972 and Quarterly. Metric Roy. 8vo. A journal for all social scientists covering sociology, philosophy, anthropology, economics and history. All back numbers available.*
Religion. Journal of Religion and Religions. *Chairman of Editorial Board, Ninian Smart. Vol. 1, No. 1, Spring 1971. A journal with an inter-disciplinary approach to the study of the phenomena of religion. All back numbers available.*
Year Book of Social Policy in Britain, The. *Edited by Kathleen Jones. 1971. Published annually.*

Social and Psychological Aspects of Medical Practice

Editor Trevor Silverstone

Lader, Malcolm. Psychophysiology of Mental Illness. *280 pp.*
● **Silverstone, Trevor,** and **Turner, Paul.** Drug Treatment in Psychiatry. *232 pp.*

Printed in Great Britain by
Lowe & Brydone Printers Limited, Thetford, Norfolk